RESEARCH ETHICS IN APPLIED ECONOMICS

Emphasizing the new challenges posed by the data science revolution, digital media, and changing norms, *Research Ethics in Applied Economics* examines the ethical issues faced by quantitative social scientists at each stage of the research process.

The first section of the book considers project development, including issues of project management, selection bias in asking research questions, and political incentives in the development and funding of research ideas. The second section addresses data collection and analysis, discussing concerns about participant rights, data falsification, data management, specification search, *p*-hacking, and replicability. The final section focuses on sharing results with academic audiences and beyond, with an emphasis on self-plagiarism, social media, and the importance of achieving policy impact. The discussion and related recommendations highlight emergent issues in research ethics.

Featuring perspectives from experienced researchers on how they address ethical issues, this book provides practical guidance to both students and experienced practitioners seeking to navigate ethical issues in their applied economics research.

Anna Josephson is an Assistant Professor of Agricultural and Resource Economics at the University of Arizona, USA.

Jeffrey D. Michler is an Associate Professor of Agricultural and Resource Economics at the University of Arizona, USA.

"Josephson and Michler tackle the critical issue of integrating ethics and transparency into empirical research, detailing a set of practical tools and approaches. As data and processing capacity makes empirical analyses widely accessible, this book is a must-read for every social scientist doing quantitative research."

Kathy Baylis, *Professor and Vice Chair of*
Graduate Programs, Department of
Geography, University of California,
Santa Barbara

"In a book that is as broad as it is deep, Josephson and Michler set the standard for what constitutes ethical research in applied economics."

Marc F. Bellemare, *Distinguished McKnight University*
Professor, Department of Applied Economics, University
of Minnesota, Author of Doing Economics:
What You Should Have Learned in Grad
School—But Didn't

"Josephson and Michler have written the textbook applied economics needed on research ethics, transparency, and data collection methods. Engaging and highlighting the latest advances, this book is a must-read for economics graduate students as well as all scholars who want to do social science research the right way."

Edward Miguel, *Oxfam Professor in Environmental and*
Resource Economics, Department of Economics,
University of California, Berkeley; Faculty Director
of the Center for Effective Global Action;
Co-author of Transparent and Reproducible
Social Science Research

RESEARCH ETHICS IN APPLIED ECONOMICS

A Practical Guide

Anna Josephson and Jeffrey D. Michler

Routledge
Taylor & Francis Group

LONDON AND NEW YORK

Designed cover image: HRAUN / Getty Images ©

First published 2024
by Routledge
4 Park Square, Milton Park, Abingdon, Oxon OX14 4RN

and by Routledge
605 Third Avenue, New York, NY 10158

Routledge is an imprint of the Taylor & Francis Group, an informa business

© 2024 Anna Josephson and Jeffrey D. Michler

British Library Cataloguing-in-Publication Data
A catalogue record for this book is available from the British Library

Library of Congress Cataloging-in-Publication Data
Names: Josephson, Anna, author. | Michler, Jeffrey D., author.
Title: Research ethics in applied economics : a practical guide /
    Anna Josephson and Jeffrey D. Michler.
Description: Abingdon, Oxon ; New York, NY : Routledge, 2024. |
    Includes bibliographical references and index.
Identifiers: LCCN 2023007645 | ISBN 9780367457433 (hardback) |
    ISBN 9780367457419 (paperback) | ISBN 9781003025061 (ebook)
Subjects: LCSH: Economics—Moral and ethical aspects. |
    Economics—Study and teaching.
Classification: LCC HB72 .J677 2024 | DDC 174/.4—dc23/eng/20230307
LC record available at https://lccn.loc.gov/2023007645

ISBN: 978-0-367-45743-3 (hbk)
ISBN: 978-0-367-45741-9 (pbk)
ISBN: 978-1-003-02506-1 (ebk)

DOI: 10.4324/9781003025061

Typeset in Times New Roman
by Apex Covantage, LLC

FIGURES

TABLES

PERSPECTIVES

CONTRIBUTORS

Jeffrey R. Bloem
Research Fellow
IFPRI

Heath Henderson
Associate Professor
Drake University

Ani Katchova
Professor & Farm Income
Enhancement Chair
Ohio State University

Jason Kerwin
Assistant Professor
University of Minnesota

Ricardo Labarta
Program Leader SPIA

Hazel Malapit
Senior Research Coordinator
IFPRI

Maria Marshall
Professor & James and Lois
Ackerman Chair
Purdue University

William A. Masters
Professor
Tufts University

Hope C. Michelson
Associate Professor
University of Illinois

David Ortega
Associate Professor
Michigan State University

Agnes Quisumbing
Senior Research Fellow
IFPRI

Melinda Smale
Professor
Michigan State University

Ian Schmutte
Associate Professor
University of Georgia

Lars Vilhuber
Senior Research Associate
Cornell University

Seong Yun
Assistant Professor
Mississippi State University

PART I

Introduction

1

RESEARCH ETHICS FOR THE APPLIED ECONOMIST

1.1 Introduction

We were both still graduate students when we attended one of our first academic conferences, the annual meeting of the Agricultural and Applied Economics Association (AAEA), held in Minneapolis in July 2014. That year, the keynote address was given by Brian Wansink, John S. Dyson Endowed Chair in the Dyson School of Applied Economics at Cornell University, Director of the Cornell Food and Brand Lab, Co-Director of the Cornell Center for Behavioral Economics in Child Nutrition Programs, and Co-Founder of the Smarter Lunchrooms Movement. Wansink was the author of a best-selling book, had given a TED Talk, and was a frequent commentator on national broadcast news and in print media. He was known for his research on consumer behavior and the ways that people's environments influence their behavior beyond the neoclassical rational-actor model. His research was at the nexus of economics, psychology, marketing, and public policy, integrating innovations from each field to create new insights into why people do what they do. As we were applied economists just starting our own research, Wansink had a career one could aspire to.

A few years later, in November 2016, Wansink posted to his blog something that, in his conception, was designed to promote the hard work of an unpaid PhD student. The post "The Grad Student Who Never Said No" discussed how he had given data from a failed study (conducted at an all-you-can-eat Italian buffet) to the PhD student and the ways in which she worked to "make hay while the sun shines." Wansink highlighted her devotion and hard work in the post:

> Every day she came back with puzzling new results, and every day we would scratch our heads, ask "Why," and come up with another way to reanalyze the data with yet another set of plausible hypotheses. Eventually we started discovering solutions that held up regardless of how we pressure-tested them.

DOI: 10.4324/9781003025061-2

Wansink concluded the post by congratulating the student for her hard work and for getting five papers published during her time at his lab. "Most of us will never remember what we read or posted on Twitter or Facebook yesterday. In the meantime, this [student]'s resume will always have the five papers."[1]

However, what people took away from this blog post was not the hard work of the student but rather the *method* of that work. Wansink discussed how he and the student reanalyzed his "failed study" with "null results" until they began "discovering solutions that held up." The post inadvertently shed light on Wansink's method of work, seemingly based on finding something – anything – significant, rather than a hypothesis-driven test of theory. A group of PhD students and early- career researchers, including Tim van der Zee, Jordan Anaya, and Nicholas Brown, began to try to replicate the four papers that Wansink and his various co-authors had published from that single "failed study." The group quickly uncovered numerous errors and statistical anomalies.

The discovery of issues in the Italian buffet study triggered a crowdsourced reanalysis of nearly all of Wansink's published papers. As more and more issues came to light, Cornell University opened an investigation, and media outlets, which formerly provided favorable coverage for Wansink's "discoveries," began to cover the rapid unraveling of his research. Many of Wansink's emails to those in his lab further revealed his unethical approach to statistical analysis. He told one student to "work hard, squeeze some blood out of this rock" and another to try to find results that would "go virally big time" (Lee, 2018). For one study, in which the results were significant at $p = 0.06$, Wansink wrote, "It seems to me it should be lower. Do you want to take a look at it and see what you think. If you can get the data, and it needs some tweaking, it would be good to get that one value below .05" (Lee, 2018). Kristin Sainani, a professor at Stanford, described Wansink's methods as "*p*-hacking on steroids" (Lee, 2018).

A series of corrections and retractions followed. In total, 40 papers with Wansink as a co-author were corrected or retracted. In September 2018, Cornell concluded its investigation, finding that "Wansink committed academic misconduct in his research and scholarship, including misreporting of research data, problematic statistical techniques, failure to properly document and preserve research results, and inappropriate authorship" (Kotlikoff, 2018). With the threat of being fired, Wansink tendered his resignation.

And the unpaid PhD student? All five of her papers with Wansink have been either corrected or retracted – the opposite of Wansink's prediction that she would "always have the five papers" as a reward for her hard work.

1.2 Motivation

It was the revelations about Brian Wansink's research practices that first led us to consider the role ethics play in applied economic research – our own and the field as a whole. Ethical considerations are ever present in how we conduct ourselves and our research in the profession. Ethics are present when interacting with colleagues at conferences or students in a classroom. They are present when we search for new research questions and when we collect, manage, and analyze data to answer those questions. Ethics play a role in how we present and publish our research to other economists, policymakers, journalists, and the public. But, despite all the ways in which ethical concerns continually confront the researcher in applied economics, discussions of ethics in the profession have typically been relegated to one of two arenas.

The first arena is that of ethical obligations, or the lack thereof, that economists should adhere to when publishing research that impacts policy. The discussion in this arena tends to focus on the ethics of using economic models, such as efficient markets, or economic tools, such as marginal analysis, to investigate actions by real humans. The criticism is often twofold: (1) models are gross simplifications based on implausible assumptions that cannot capture the richness of human interactions, and (2) the focus on monetary outcomes, particularly the primacy of efficiency, reduces decision-making to a mercenary endeavor. The rebuttal to these criticisms is often the claim that economics is merely a positive science, not a normative one. Economists simply use models and modes of analysis to describe the world; it is up to those in other disciplines or in politics to decide how to use the information. Work in the arena of ethics in economics include DeMartino (2011), Rodrik (2015), Wight (2015), and DeMartino and McCloskey (2016).

The second arena is the set of rules and duties that institutions, primarily institutional review boards (IRBs), impose on economists and other social scientists who engage in human subjects research. The discussion in this arena tends to focus on the ethics of applying rules and regulations, developed in response to ethical violations in the medical sciences, to social science researchers. Here also the criticism is twofold: (1) the rules and regulations governing medical research are a poor match for the ethical issues faced by social scientists working with research participants, particularly in developing countries, and (2) institutions like IRBs are often more focused on legal compliance than actual ethical behavior. Rebuttals emphasize the need for efficiency in process and claim that universal standards simply form a basis or starting point for ethical review, not a final judgment. Works in the arena of institutional ethical review include Beauchamp (2005), Schrag (2010), Holland (2016), Kara (2018), and Schroeder et al. (2019).

Beyond these two arenas, ethics in economics has generally been ignored. Most economics programs teach research methods as part of the curriculum, but few touch on ethics beyond cursory admonitions against fraud or falsification or research findings (Josephson and Michler, 2018). The purpose of this book is to fill that gap by examining ethical considerations that arise throughout the research process, from initial idea to the (hopefully) long legacy of one's published research. We believe that research and ethics are intrinsically linked: doing rigorous research requires doing ethical research and vice versa. Ethics is not just a subtopic to be touched upon in a seminar on research methods. Rather, ethical considerations are present in and throughout every stage of research and we should be thinking of them and addressing them throughout the research life cycle.

That research, or science as a broad field of inquiry, is intrinsically linked to ethics is not a new idea. It originates with Aristotle, regarded as the father of science and a father of ethics. Aristotle scrutinized the natural world and, in doing so, was perhaps the first to formalize the importance of empirical measurement and research through the application of the scientific method. To many, applying the scientific method to their research may be rote, but its importance makes it worth repeating. We observe something – a phenomenon, an experience, an occurrence – in the real world, develop a theory about why that thing might be happening, and then generate a hypothesis and testable predictions that link our theory to the original observed thing. Upon this foundation, we actually set about testing those predictions, through collecting data, making observations, and undertaking structured investigations. The outcomes of this labor will be some answer or deeper understanding of the thing we observed or, at the very least, an answer to our developed hypothesis.

This, however, is an ideal. In the real world (where we live and work and research), science does not necessarily proceed in this way. Importantly, the process of scientific investigation is intersected throughout with the standards and norms of ethics. This book focuses specifically on these intersections and how we, as researchers, can practice and undertake ethical research in the process of scientific investigation.

When people talk about research ethics they frequently focus on oaths or codes of conduct that codify established norms into a set of rules or duties. But conducting ethical research involves more than just adherence to a code of conduct. It involves the outcomes and consequences of one's decision-making during the research process. It also requires coming to believe or embody the norms and virtues one should aspire to. As Merton (1947) writes, norms are "binding, not only because they are procedurally efficient, but because they are believed to be right and good. They are moral as well as technical prescriptions." Understanding the various existing approaches to ethics, and how they can complement each other, is an important place to start any work on research ethics. For, as DeMartino and McCloskey (2016) observe, ethics is not a set of rules and restrictions, "it is a conversation rather than a constraint, a dance rather than a pose."

1.3 What Is Ethics?

The definition, study, and reflection on ethics or morals is its own field of philosophic inquiry. Any time someone in one discipline tries to integrate research and insights from a different discipline, it can be challenging to parse the language and modes of thought. In this section we try to open up the language of ethics and provide a nonspecialist introduction to the broad categories and concepts of normative ethics. As in economics, ethics distinguishes between normative (prescriptive) and positive (descriptive). Normative ethics is about how people ought to or should make ethical decisions. Positive ethics is about how people actually make ethical decisions (Wight, 2015).

A brief review of seminal works in modern ethics reveals that definitions of ethics are not in short supply. But, for the purpose of a book on research ethics, a broad and practical definition works well:

> Ethics is the study of one's proper interactions with others: It is the analysis of right and wrong.
>
> *(Wight, 2015)*

Some ethicists and philosophers draw a distinction between ethics, which derives from the Greek, relating to a person's character, and morals, which derives from the Latin, relating to choice or rules (McCloskey, 2006). In this book, we use *morals* and *ethics* as closely aligned synonyms, although we will mostly refer to ethics as that is the more common usage when discussing right and wrong in research.

Most books and papers on research ethics divide ethical approaches into one of three broad categories. These are outcome-based or consequentialism, duty- and rule-based or non-consequentialism, and virtue- or character-based. As with any typology, not every ethical approach fits within one of these three categories. And there is often fierce disagreement among ethicists regarding which famous philosopher belongs to which camp. (Was Adam Smith a utilitarian or a virtue ethicist?) In reviewing these broad categories of ethical thought, we are not advocating for the superiority of one over another. In fact, as we discuss at the conclusion of this section, we take a pluralist approach, which is reflected in the content of this book. We see these three approaches to ethics as complements to one another, not substitutes for one another.

1.3.1 Outcome-Based Ethics

Outcome-based ethics relies on consequentialist theories of ethics. Consequentialism, also known as teleological ethics, from the Greek for "end," is so called because it maintains that what determines if an act is ethical is the consequences, outcomes, or end of the act. The character of the actor and the intent of the act do not matter, only the outcome of the action. Thus, an arsonist who burns down an apartment building under construction could have committed a morally good act, if the building contractor had used shoddy materials that would have led to the collapse of the structure and the death of individuals once families moved in.

A prominent early proponent of consequentialism was the British Enlightenment philosopher Jeremy Bentham. Bentham viewed the rightness or wrongness of an action in relation to the amount of pleasure or pain it caused. In his *Introduction to the Principles of Morals and Legislation*, Bentham (1780) wrote: "Nature has placed mankind under the guidance of two sovereign masters, *pain* and *pleasure*.

It is for them alone to point out what we ought to do, as well as to determine what we shall do." The ethical individual was to consider how an action would affect all others and weigh the potential pleasure and pain caused equally with their own. This idea of radical equality led Bentham to be one of the earliest and most vocal abolitionists in Britain (Wight, 2015). For Bentham, the purpose of government was to maximize the overall welfare of the populace, regardless of gender or race, and thus, laws were to be judged as good or bad to the extent that they minimized pain and maximized pleasure.

The immediate problem with a consequentialist approach to ethics should be obvious to an economist: How does one measure an individual's pleasure and pain and then compare it across people? The problem was solved, at least theoretically, by John Stuart Mill who developed the principles of utility and made utilitarianism the best known form of consequentialism (Israel, 2015). Mill (1863) formulated the Greatest Happiness Principle, which states that actions should focus on maximizing the net happiness of society, measured in terms of both the quantity and quality of happiness. This allows for a distinction between the duration of pleasure/pain and the intensity or magnitude of pleasure/pain. This helps avoid unfortunate outcomes of utilitarianism, such as potentially justifying the perpetual torture of one person if it brings a minuscule amount of pleasure to a large number of people.

To anyone who is familiar with microeconomics, consumer theory, and welfare economics, the critiques of the application of utility theory in a consequentialist approach to ethics will come as no surprise. The most trenchant critique is that while utility allows for a theory on how to measure and aggregate happiness, it yields little practical advice on how an individual, policymaker, or government should judge different actions, policies, and laws. Even if one could measure happiness in a way that allowed for comparison across individuals, it is not at all obvious that the aggregate maximization problem would be tractable without the sort of strong assumptions used in consumer theory (e.g., separability, continuity, homogeneity).

1.3.2 Duty- and Rule-Based Ethics

Duty- and rule-based ethics is non-consequentialist, meaning it is not concerned with the outcome or end result of an action. Rather, nonconsequentialism, also known as deontological ethics, from the Greek for "duty," is so called because it maintains that what determines if an act is ethical is whether it conforms to some "proper" characteristic. The character of the actor and the outcome of the action do not matter, only the intent of the act. An arsonist who burns down an apartment building under construction has committed an immoral act because destruction of property is wrong, even if burning down the building averts the eventual collapse of the structure and the death of individuals, once families move in.

One dominant version of the non-consequentialist approach to ethics was developed by the German philosopher Immanuel Kant. Kant argued that human reason provided a means for discerning moral law, an Enlightenment version of the rules or duties present in religious systems of belief, such as the Torah, the Bible, and the Koran (Wight, 2015). In Kant's (1785) *Groundwork of the Metaphysics of Morals*, he formulates what is known as the categorical imperative: "act only according to that maxim whereby you can at the same time will that it should become a universal law." The categorical imperative asks us to imagine a world in which everyone acted as "I" act. This differs in three important ways from the Golden Rule, "do unto others as you would have them do unto you" (Israel, 2015; Wight, 2015). First, the categorical imperative is broader than the Golden Rule in that it asks one to consider a world in which everyone did the same thing to all others, not just to you. Second, the categorical imperative starts from a rational principle while the Golden Rule bases its morality on a tit-for-tat strategy. Third, the categorical imperative provides guidance on how one should treat oneself, while the Golden Rule is silent on this point. As Israel (2015) points out, the categorical imperative suggests that one has a moral duty to not commit suicide, because if this became a universal law it would extinguish humanity. One cannot draw conclusions about the morality of suicide from the Golden Rule.

The challenge of a non-consequentialist approach to ethics has always been, who decides what the moral rules are that humans are duty-bound to fulfill? For Christians, this would be the Bible and its various interpretations by Orthodox, Catholic, or Protestant theologians. For Muslims, this would be the Koran and its various interpretations by Sunni and Shiite imams. For Jews, this would be the Torah and the various Talmudic traditions. For Kant, moral rules could be discerned by reason. These and other traditions create overlapping but contradictory understandings of what is moral. Modern ethics and political philosophy has been dominated by thinkers such as John Rawls (1971), Robert Nozick (1974), T.M. Scanlon (2000), and Derek Parfit (2013). While most, if not all, of these philosophers would reject the non-consequentialist label, they all have worked to formulate a source or definition for the rules one should follow.

Critics of a non-consequentialist approach to ethics frequently focus on the challenge of determining the where and what of the moral rules. Related to the uncertainty regarding what moral rules to follow is: what does one do when duties conflict? If "do not lie" is a moral rule, then what does one do when one promises confidentiality to an acquaintance only to learn that the acquaintance has committed a crime and one is asked to identify the acquaintance in a police lineup? For Kant, moral rules are unchangeable and absolute, but he does not provide a way through conflicting situations. One may consider such hypotheticals as pedantic or nitpicking but a theory of absolutes, such as Kant's, demands to be judged by its own rules. If the system cannot provide clear answers for all situations, then its foundation may not be as strong as it claims.

1.3.3 Virtue- or Character-Based Ethics

Virtue- or character-based ethics is also non-consequentialist but differs from deontological ethics in that it is not concerned about one's duty or following rules like the categorical imperative. Rather, virtue ethics is concerned with having an excellent character that does the right thing, despite obstacles or personal costs. What matters is the character of the actor, not the outcome of the action or the intent of the act. An arsonist who desires to burns down an apartment building under construction is immoral because they lack excellence in character, even if they fail to burn down the building or if their failure alerted building inspectors to the imminent collapse of the structure, averting the death of individuals once families move in.

Virtue ethics has a long tradition in both Western and Eastern thought. The Chinese philosopher Confucius extolled the value of virtues like benevolence and righteousness and the Buddha taught that suffering is overcome through the cultivation of virtues that free one from desire (Wight, 2015). In the Western tradition, virtue ethics begin with Aristotle, who in the *Nicomachean Ethics* asks, "[W]hat kind of person should we want to be?" and "[W]hat sorts of lives should we try to pursue?" (Aristotle, 2019). For Aristotle, virtue was not something one was born with but something that one was taught or one learned through observed behavior over a lifetime. The goal of life was *eudaimonia*, or human flourishing, which was achieved through the cultivation of the four cardinal virtues: temperance, courage, prudence, and justice. This is a positivist approach, in Greek *cataphatic* and in Latin the *via positiva*. This approach is mirrored by the teachings of the Buddha, which focuses on the Four Nobel Truths, or a path of expiation (emptying). This can be seen as a negativist approach, in Greek *apophatic* and in Latin *via negativa*.

Virtue ethics dominated Western thought until Kant. This was mainly because of the writings of Augustine of Hippo and Thomas Aquinas that wedded virtue ethics to the Western Christian tradition. However, with the Enlightenment, virtue ethics fell out of favor, as it was perceived to lack a rational basis for the definition of ethics. In the twentieth century, virtue ethics has seen a resurgence with books by the philosophers Philippa Foot (1973) and Alasdair MacIntyre (1984). Adherence to virtue ethics is common among critics of IRBs and other institutions that govern research ethics using a rules-based approach. These critics point to anecdotal evidence that when vulnerable populations are asked to participate in studies, the group's relationship with the researcher – their personal beliefs in the virtue or character of the researcher – is much more salient than the promised rule-based protection of IRBs (Israel, 2015). Research ethicists like Henry Beecher (1966) and Bruce Macfarlane (2009) have argued for the cultivation of Aristotelian-type virtues by researchers, such as courage, respectfulness, resoluteness, sincerity, humility, and reflexivity. They also argue that a rule-based approach to research ethics has caused harm to vulnerable populations.

As with all approaches to ethics, virtue- or character-based ethics has its critics. The most common criticism is that virtue ethicists cannot agree on what character is, let alone the set of virtues one should cultivate in order to achieve excellence of character. As Wight (2015) points out, virtue ethics has a troubling history, with many proponents ascribing to explicitly racial or gendered views of the world. Maybe the most infamous virtue ethicist was Thomas Carlyle, who first called economics a "dismal science" because economists like John Stuart Mill argued for abolition of slavery and equality before the law, regardless of race. For Carlyle, Africans inherently lacked virtue, and thus, their enslavement was a good thing because it created an opportunity for Africans to learn virtues from their enslavers.

1.3.4 Ethical Pluralism

In ethics, as in economics, hard lines can be drawn between schools or branches of thought. Kant disagreed with Aristotle's approach to ethics and Bentham disagreed with Kant. Mill fiercely disagreed with Carlyle. More recently Nozick's (1974) work is a direct response to that of Rawls (1971). That is not to say that ethicists are always disputatious, but it frequently can appear that this is the case, if adherence to one ethical framework means one must reject all other frameworks.

As applied economists who seek to apply ethics to research, we, personally, are pluralists when it comes to different schools of ethical thought. We consider these three approaches to ethics described earlier as complements to one another and not substitutes for one another. In Wight's (2015) phrase, they "do not so much *compete* with each other as *complete* each other." Figure 1.1 lays out a vision of ethical pluralism, in which the multiple ethical frameworks help explain the behavior and choices of economic actors in the real world. Ethical pluralism builds on ideas laid

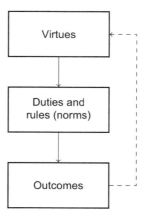

FIGURE 1.1 Ethical Pluralism

Note: Virtues are needed for carrying out duties or adhering to norms. Adhering to norms creates a well-functioning environment that leads to good outcomes. Good outcomes spur moral development that feeds back into virtues. Adapted, with permission, from Wight (2014).

out by Adam Smith (1759) in *The Theory of Moral Sentiments*. Smith believed that emotions and feelings, like the special sympathy one feels towards one's children, were the source of the moral sentiments that form our set of virtues. These individual moral sentiments are then aggregated in a community to form institutions that define the norms of acceptable behavior or establish the rules of the community. The moral duties or ethical norms established by these institutions direct people's actions so as to produce good outcomes. For Smith, these good outcomes, such as greater trust in trade, reduce transaction costs and lead to greater wealth. Increased wealth allows for more leisure for developing virtuous habits and more investment in education to learn virtue (Smith, 1759). Thus, good outcomes create a positive feedback loop: a virtuous cycle.

A pluralistic approach to ethics is particularly applicable when thinking about research ethics. A priori, as applied researchers, we might be inclined to take an outcome-based approach. Economists engage in a "marketplace of ideas" in which they sell their research to other economists, to policymakers, and to the public. As Paul Samuelson is quoted as saying, payment to economists for the research that they sell comes in "the only coin worth having – our own applause" (Coase, 1994). To the extent that economists, like other agents in our economic models, are motivated by self-interest, they will produce ethical and rigorous research as long as the benefits outweigh the costs. However, as Wight (2015) notes, there are many reasons to believe that the market for economic research is not one of perfect competition. Asymmetric information exists. The researcher knows much more about the details of the research, and the decisions made throughout the research process, than those consuming the research. Additionally, the prestige that accrues to publications in what are considered the Top Five journals in economics creates a moral hazard problem.[2] Researchers have much to gain from a hit paper published in a top journal and little to lose, given the low probability of the discovery of fraud. Systematic efforts to replicate published research would raise the probability of uncovering fraud. But replication remains a public good, and as such, it is underprovisioned in the absense of an explicit incentive structure to reward replicators (Christensen et al., 2019).

Given that the marketplace of ideas lacks the competitive structure to strongly incentivize ethical research, the field has generally relied on institutions to define a moral code or establish duties and norms to govern behavior. University of Chicago professor Frank Knight, whose students included future Nobel laureates Milton Friedman, George Stigler, and James Buchanan, wrote:

> Now scientific inquiry has, and rests upon, a moral code, or in sheer fact a "religion"; and it is supremely important that scientists recognize this fact . . . The basic tenet of scientific research – truth or objectivity – is essentially a moral principle, in opposition to any form of self-interest.
>
> *(Knight, 1947)*

For Knight, the benefits to be gained in the market were insufficient to ensure rigorous and ethical research. What was necessary was for researchers to adhere to a moral code, as if to a religion, that placed the objective search for truth above the achievement of outcomes, like the applause from one's peers. In the next section, we discuss four of these norms that make up a moral code of scientists.

It is important to note that these institutional norms were, historically, unwritten or not codified into a code of conduct, as they are in medicine, law, psychology, or other disciplines that license practitioners. This has left, and continues to leave, institutions in the economics profession with little power to police or enforce adherence to a well-defined set of rules. In recent years, this has begun to change, with professional associations, including the American Economic Association (AEA) and the Agricultural and Applied Economics Association (AAEA), establishing written codes of conduct (AEA, 2018; AAEA, 2019). This extends to the journals published by these associations, which have begun to adopt written codes regarding conflicts of interest (COIs), prespecification of experimental designs, and data and code availability (AEA, 2012, 2020; AJAE, nd).

Claiming that there are moral codes or institutional norms that govern behavior leaves an open question regarding the source of the content of these codes or how these institutions were formed. How institutions form is a question long studied by economists, such as Nobel laureate Douglass North and likely future laureate Daron Acemoglu. For Aristotle, the source was *eudaimonia*; for Aquinas, it was the Incarnation of God in human form; for Adam Smith, it was the moral sentiments an individual learned by being sympathetic. Regardless of the source, throughout history, society, both broadly and narrowly defined, has governed itself by agreeing on a set of institutions to enforce moral codes that reflect a set of virtues or ethics closely held by individuals within that society. Frequently, power violates these moral codes and usurps these institutions, but the fundamental process of community formation remains.

Adherence to just one ethical framework or another can lead researchers to make very different choices when faced with the same ethical consideration. If a researcher follows the norms of modern best practices in econometric analysis but finds the results to be morally repugnant, is it ethical for the researcher to abandon the research and file it in their desk drawer? Or does the researcher owe it to the scientific community to publish the results, regardless of how its findings are exploited by politicians? One's answer will depend on if one adheres to a consequentialist or non-consequentialist approach to ethics. As Israel (2015) points out, that different ethical frameworks lead to different choices is a chronic problem for anyone trying to make ethical decisions while conducting research. Hence, our reliance throughout this book on the pragmatic approach of ethical pluralism.

What does ethical pluralism look like for the applied economist engaged in research? As Wight (2015) writes, "A *virtuous* scientist has the motive and the self-control to adhere to *duties* of honesty to others in the community, which will produce beneficial *outcomes* for that community and the wider society." Throughout this book, we focus on the norms or duties, and the outcomes, of ethical considerations that arise when conducting applied economic or any quantitative social science researchers. Ultimately, in the conclusion of this book, we circle around returning to the idea of virtue ethics and present four virtues that we have personally found essential in conducting ethical research.

1.4 What Is Ethical Research?

Much of the discussion of ethical research in science focuses on interactions with research participants, including human participants and animal subjects. There are certainly ethical concerns when interacting with research participants (which we discuss in Chapters 4 and 5), but this is by no means the only place where ethical issues arise in research.

Our obligations as scientists go far beyond simply complying with IRB requirements for working with research participants. They include obligations to the individuals among and communities within which a researcher exists, which includes research participants, as well as our own academic or research coterie and society at large. As Israel (2015) writes:

Ethical behaviour helps protect individuals, communities and environments, and offers the potential to increase the sum of good in the world. As social scientists trying to make the world a better place we should avoid [or at least minimize] doing long-term, systematic harm to those individuals, communities and environments. . . . By caring about ethics and by acting on that concern we promote the integrity of research.

To fulfill these obligations, we draw on a set of norms for researchers and scientists discussed in Christensen et al. (2019) but originally put forward by Robert K. Merton (1947) in his article "A Note on Science and Democracy."

Merton, a sociologist, views scientists as embedded within a community defined by social structures. These social structures are manifested in what Merton calls an ethos of science – its characteristic spirit or nature. What is valuable about this ethos is that it incentivizes individual behavior, through rewards for adherence and punishments for violation by the community. Individuals internalize these norms by buying into the ethos and making it their own. Merton (1947) writes:

The ethos of science is that affectively toned complex of values and norms which is held to be binding on the [person] of science. The norms are expressed in the form of prescriptions, proscriptions and permissions. These are legitimized in terms of institutional values. These imperatives, transmitted by precept and example and reenforced by sanctions, are in varying degrees internalized by the scientist, thus fashioning [their] 'scientific conscience.'

Most graduate programs in applied economics, economics, or other quantitative social sciences do not provide any formal training on research ethics or on the ethos of science. Rather, students tend to pick up the ethos, and other ideas about what is and is not ethical conduct in research, by learning from others or learning from doing. But not every student has or had ethically conscious advisors who taught or modeled ethical research practices. In fact, as Christensen et al. (2019) write, "negative lessons can be passed along this way as well."

In defining the ethos or characteristic spirit of science, Merton (1947) starts by stating the institutional goal of the scientific community: "the extension of certified knowledge." What Merton means by certified knowledge is knowledge that is logically consistent and empirically confirmed. Logically, consistency requires a set of theories to explain empirical observations and then make testable predictions from that theory. Empirical confirmation requires a set of techniques that can consistently observe, measure, and validate empirical evidence and reject or fail to reject the predictions of theory. The core values of the ethos of science that have come to be called "Mertonian norms" have a methodologic rationale in that they help researchers achieve the institutional goal of the scientific community. But, Merton (1947) argues, these norms "are binding, not because they are procedurally efficient, but because they are believed right and good." One could find a different set of norms that might be more efficient in guiding researchers to achieving their goal, but Merton's norms are not just methodologically rational; they are also ethically or morally right.

Merton's norms or duties are (1) universalism, (2) communality, (3) disinterestedness, and (4) organized skepticism. Conducting one's research in line with these norms brings researchers and scientists closer toward ensuring the work is rigorous, ethical, and done with integrity.

1.4.1 Universalism

The first norm is the concept of universalism; or the principle that the acceptance (or rejection) of claims does not depend on the attributes and traits of researchers themselves (Merton, 1947). Universalism is the idea that the process of research is inherently impersonal. In an econometric sense, the researcher's identity is orthogonal or exogenous to the discovery. Regardless of who is doing the research, the laws, theories, and principles of science do not vary or change. And, by extension, the laws, theories, and principles of science are sound, regardless of who may have discovered them.

Universalism suggests a sort of egalitarianism, in which science cannot be corrupted by power. It envisions science to be a space in which anyone with training and opportunity can advance science (Christensen et al., 2019). Scholarly contributions come from achievement in making those contributions, rather than one's social origins. The natural extension of these two definitions of universalism is that by taking all achievements and findings, regardless of who discovered them, science is able to advance more quickly. Science not only benefits from the diverse backgrounds, perspectives, and history of researchers, but simply having many hands in the fields can also make light work.

An example of the triumph of universalism is the story of Srinivasa Ramanujan, an Indian mathematician. Almost completely without formal training, Ramanujan did most of his research alone (Kanigel, 1991). Only in 1913, when he began a correspondence with University of Cambridge professor and mathematician G.H. Hardy (1940), was his genius fully appreciated, at least by the Western world. Hardy wrote that Ramanujan's work "defeated me completely; I had never seen anything in the least like them before." Ramanujan moved to England in 1914, where he spent five years, earning a Bachelor of Arts by Research, as well as being elected to the London Mathematical Society, a fellow of the Royal Society, and a fellow of Trinity College. He completed no further degrees, but during his life, Ramanujan compiled nearly 4,000 results, opening new areas of work and inspiring scores of future research and pathways of investigation. Unfortunately, Ramanujan passed away at the age of 32, from (likely treatable) amoebiasis, which resulted from untreated amoebic dysentery (Young, 1994). Even in these mere three decades, he contributed enormously to the advancement of mathematics and science at large.[3] A journal exists in his name, dedicated to advancements on his works. His contributions to science are enormous and demonstrate – almost ideally – the norm of universalism.

However, even a passing familiarity with Ramanujan's life shows how precarious universalism can be as an operating norm within the scientific community. Universalism exists as much as an ideal as a practiced value. Throughout history, there are numerous cases of individuals or types of people excluded from science or with their contributions to science entirely overlooked. The world is fortunate that G.H. Hardy adhered to universalism as a norm, providing space and an arena for Ramanujan to do his best work. But not everyone holds as strongly to universalism. Consider the life of Rosalind Franklin, a chemist and X-ray crystallographer whose work was integral to the discovery of DNA – but whose contribution was not credited when Francis Crick and James Watson published this discovery (Maddox, 2003). One need not look into the distant past to discover examples of the lack of universalism. Presently, one need look no further for evidence of this than citation counts: scholars of color and women scholars are less frequently cited. They are also more likely to have their findings attributed to their white male colleagues (Kwon, 2022).

Although many of us may hold to universalism in science, we continue to fall short of equity in opportunity. We have a long way to go, but can only achieve ethical research by continuing to work toward universalism and promoting the norm within our own work, citations, and practice.

1.4.2 Communality

The next norm is communality, which Merton (1947) actually termed "communism," or the idea that scientific progress involves the entire community of researchers through a process of open exchange and discussion. Merton (1947) argues that true advancements in science are (1) the product of social collaboration and (2) the scientific achievements are "assigned to the community." The motivation behind the first component of communality is the idea that science is inherently collaborative, an idea we discuss in Chapter 3. The second component of communality is that the "property rights" to a discovery are claimed by the entire scientific community, not an individual researcher. The only "property right" an individual researcher may claim is the recognition and esteem of their peers for the discovery, Samuelson's "con of the realm."

The sharing of information is inherent to the advancement and improvement of science. After all, publication of one's findings is usually the final step in a research project. Because of this, most scientists and researchers probably believe, reflexively, that they practice and value communality. Yet, as we discuss in Chapters 6 and 7, few actually promote what could be considered "radical" communality, through adherence to the principles of open science, including the sharing of all data and code for their work. Sharing data and code with the related paper is necessary for true communality, as this openness allows others to review those findings and build on that work. If one does not share their work with the scientific community, then time and money may be wasted reproducing existing work or investigating uninteresting, unimportant, or already-studied areas. Sharing one's work encourages the widespread improvement of science, by allowing the field to advance step by step, building on others' work and experiences.

A shining example of communality is the golden age of theoretical and experimental physics that occurred between the end of World War I and the start of World War II (Rhodes, 1986). In 1919, Ernest Rutherford first split the atom, allowing researchers the first opportunity to study its nucleus. Over the next 23 years, a constellation of theorists and empiricists worked in international collaboration (and in competition) to theorize about the properties and powers of the atom and build machines to test those theories. In 1929, American Ernest Lawrence designed and built the cyclotron, the first particle accelerator, necessary for observing the nucleus of an atom. In 1932, British James Chadwick, discovered the neutron, a previously unknown subatomic particle. In 1933, Hungarian Leo Szilard first theorized the possibility of a nuclear chain reaction. In 1938, Germans Lise Meitner and Otto Frisch were able to artificially start the process of nuclear fission. And in 1942, Italian Enrico Fermi built the first self-sustaining nuclear chain reaction, the first nuclear reactor, under the stands of the football stadium at the University of Chicago. As each discovery occurred, the physicists would write up a brief letter to the journals *Nature* or *Science*, sharing their discoveries. These letters were often written up the same night as the discovery and mailed the next day. After publication, other researchers would immediately begin to replicate the experiment or re-prove the theory, jump-starting the race to the next major advancement. In a case extreme only for its incredible speed, on the morning of 13 September 1933 Leo Szilard read an article in *The Times of London* quoting Rutherford's description of

Chadwick's discovery of the neutron. That same day Szilard conceived of the idea of a self-sustaining nuclear chain reaction (Rhodes, 1986). The openness in sharing of these discoveries, although not the international collaborative nature of them, ended abruptly with the start of World War II and the creation of the Manhattan Project to build the atomic bomb.

While researchers continue to advocate for communality and push for open science, the research landscape today looks very different than it did in the 1920s and 1930s. Today, most research universities have campus offices whose sole purpose is to patent new discoveries and then sell those patents or spin them off into potentially lucrative start-ups. Academic researchers have learned that retaining property rights to their ideas can be much more profitable than publishing their findings in a journal. Nowhere is this shift against communality more prominent than in the pull of Silicon Valley (Christensen et al., 2019). Consider the case of Elizabeth Holmes and her company Theranos (Carreyrou, 2018). Holmes left a promising academic career while an undergraduate student at Stanford University to pursue the privatization and monetization of her idea for a new way to do blood tests. Over the life of her company, she was able to attract numerous academics who traded the ability to publish their research for higher salaries. Even among Silicon Valley start-ups, Theranos was extremely secretive. In fact, it was an article by John Ioannidis in the *Journal of the American Medical Association*, noting that no peer-reviewed papers had been published by Theranos scientists, that, in part, lead to John Carreyrou's (2018) of fraud at Theranos.

While communality may no longer be a norm universally held by researchers, there are those pushing back against the commodification of science. These include movements to promote open-access publication, open-source software and engineering, and open science. A leader in this cause is the Center for Open Science (COS), which works to create incentives for researchers to commit themselves to make the process, content, and outcomes of research more open and accessible (COS, nd).

1.4.3 Disinterestedness

The third norm is the concept of disinterestedness; or the idea that the work of scientists is and should be remain uncorrupted by self-interested motivations (Merton, 1947). Disinterestedness should not be confused with a lack of passion or a concern for humanity. Most researchers got involved in their field because of a passion for knowledge or a keen interest in helping improve the world through scientific discovery. These altruistic motivating factors are important for spurring on rigorous research. What disinterestedness entails is that a researcher must report findings simply as they are, even if this goes against general wisdom, one's own beliefs, or self-interest in some other way.

Disinterestedness is easily connected to the value of universalism: anyone can contribute to science and contributions can be of any sort, as long as they are founded within ethical and disciplined work. And, like universalism, disinterestedness can be difficult to maintain, given that researchers are human beings and – despite our best efforts – personal considerations and emotions often enter the research process. There are multitudes of situations in which one's personal, professional, moral, or religious tenants or convictions might intersect with one's research. After all, we tend to select topics to investigate which are interesting and close to us. It can be personally challenging when the outcome of one's research does not comport with one's closely held prior beliefs about what the outcome *should* be. In Chapter 2 we discuss the challenge of being too interested or too close to a research topic. And in Chapter 3 we discuss how researchers can use pre-analysis plans and hypothesis registries to pre-commit themselves to releasing results regardless of findings.

Examples of disinterestedness can be hard to come by, as the norm typically applies during the research process. But in 2021, evolutionary biologist Ken Thompson, a fellow at Stanford University, exemplified disinterestedness when he called for the retraction of one of his own papers (Enserink, 2021). As an undergraduate, Thompson had been the lead author on a paper with Steven Newmaster, a distinguished professor at the University of Guelph, who had generated over Canadian $7 million in funding. Thompson's paper compared two different ways of identifying plant species: traditional morphological distinction or extracting DNA and using barcodes. The paper was published in *Biodiversity and Conservation* (Thompson and Newmaster, 2014). Despite the journal's replication policy, the data used in the paper (which was Newmaster's) were never made public. After pressing for publication of the data, they were finally posted in 2020. However, when Thompson reexamined the data, he discovered he could no longer replicate the results in his paper and that the data appeared to be a slightly altered version of publicly available data from a different lab. As Enserink (2021) recounts, Thompson contacted the University of Guelph, pressing for an investigation of the paper. The university began an "initial inquiry," but nothing came of it. Thompson also asked the editor of *Biodiversity and Conservation* to retract the paper, but he was told that the journal would only issue a retraction if Guelph concluded that there was misconduct. Unfortunately, a spokesperson at Guelph stated that "details and outcomes of specific allegations are confidential." Eventually Thompson went public and spoke with reporters, leading to the editor of *Biodiversity and Conservation* granting the requested retraction. The retraction note states that Newmaster "has not responded to any correspondence from the Editor or publisher about this retraction" (Thompson and Newmaster, 2021).

A spirit of disinterestedness is difficult to maintain. After having made a few contributes to a specific area, it can be hard not to want all of one's work to confirm what has come before, particularly what one's self may have contributed before. An investigation in *Science* recently alleged just such a failure in disinterestedness by a leading researcher in Alzheimer's disease, which may have affected the entire field of research on the disease for decades (Piller, 2022). Sylvain Lesné, a researcher at the University of Minnesota, was the lead author on a paper published in *Nature* that purported to discover a connection between memory loss and a previously unknown protein, amyloid beta star 56 ($A\beta^*56$) (Lesné et al., 2006). The amyloid hypothesis of Alzheimer's holds that buildup of $A\beta$ proteins in brain tissue inhibit healthy functioning, causing the disease. Lesné et al. (2006) are the first to show that a specific type of $A\beta$, when injected into mice, causes memory impairment. The paper, which is the fifth-most-cited paper in basic Alzheimer's research since 2006, has led to a tenure track faculty position for Lesné, an R01 grant from the National Institutes of Health (NIH), and numerous other publications on $A\beta^*56$, with Lesné as either the lead author or a senior author. As Piller (2022) reports, several researchers, operating independently, have called into question 10 of Lesné's papers, identifying tampering and duplication of images purporting to show the presence of $A\beta^*56$. Almost no other lab, outside of Lesné's, has ever published a paper that detects $A\beta^*56$, and at least two papers have been published about failure to detect $A\beta^*56$ when it was supposed to be present (Piller, 2022). It now appears that Lesné, having made a name for himself in a paper claiming a link between $A\beta^*56$ and memory loss, has engaged in research misconduct in order to maintain his original claim and advance his career (Piller, 2022).

For science to be accepted and held to be true, it is essential for researchers to be disinterested. Even if one's findings do not align with expectations, it is important to disseminate the work for the wider community. As Christensen et al. (2019) write: "for social science to be credible, researchers must be committed to making results public regardless of their perceived implications. Otherwise, those who would dismiss social science findings as ideologically biased have a point." To protect science and ensure it is not perceived as slanted or biased, we must value and promote disinterestedness.

1.4.4 Organized Skepticism

The last norm is organized skepticism, or the idea that one must suspend judgment until all the facts are in (Merton, 1947). That is, one should not believe everything one hears or reads and should not simply take things at face value. There are more idioms that one could use to describe organized skepticism, but they all coalesce around the idea that one should question results with a detached scrutiny. To some extent, this is inherently a part of science: we complete proofs; we test and retest theories; we replicate and reproduce experiments. We do not just take someone at their word that something is. Part of science is testing to ensure that it really is.

Organized skepticism, and the value of questioning in general, is inherent to the process of science – and even more important to the process of ethical science. Skepticism involves not only questioning the work of others but preparing for one's own work to be questioned. In Chapter 5, we discuss preparing replication packages to allow for one's work to be examined and replicated by other researchers. Merton

(1947), however, extends organized skepticism beyond just the close examination of how research was conducted. He writes that in our role as investigators, we should be skeptical of *all* things. In particular, we should not restrict ourselves to topics that are socially acceptable, trendy, or promoted by those in power. As Christensen et al. (2019) simply state, "the ideal is to critically examine everything."

An example of organized skepticism is the long history of Fermat's Last Theorem. Pierre de Fermat was a French mathematician who contributed to several fields in mathematics, most prominently number theory. In the margin of his copy of *Arithmetica* by the Greek mathematician Diophantus, Fermat wrote:

> It is impossible to separate a cube into two cubes, or a fourth power into two fourth powers, or in general, any power higher than the second, into two like powers. I have discovered a truly marvelous proof of this, which this margin is too narrow to contain.
>
> *(Singh, 1997)*

Essentially, the equation $a^n + b^n = c^n$ has no solution when $n > 2$. The conjecture was published in 1670 by Fermat's son (Singh, 1997). For 350 years mathematicians remained skeptical that Fermat had indeed proven his theorem, and, as hundreds of claimed proofs were shown to be false, the search for a proof became one of the great unsolved math problems in history. Finally, in 1993, Andrew Wiles claimed to have successfully completed a proof, presenting his findings at a conference. While many assumed Wiles's proof was likely correct, it was not blindly accepted as such (Singh, 1997). In fact, as mathematicians examined the proof, a flaw was found, requiring Wiles and a former student, Richard Taylor, to spend more than a year trying to repair the proof. Finally, in 1995, *Annals of Mathematics* dedicated an entire issue to the original Wiles proof and the Taylor–Wiles repair (Wiles, 1995; Taylor and Wiles, 1995).

While skepticism may seem like second nature to research-minded individuals, it is all too easy to be lulled into naive acceptance of the dominant paradigm in one's field of study. A classic example of this is what Stephen Jay Gould and Richard Lewontin call the Panglossian paradigm (Gould and Lewontin, 1979). Dr. Pangloss is a character in Voltaire's comic novel *Candide* who, when confronted with anything pleasant or unpleasant, claims "things cannot be other than they are" (Voltaire, 1759). In discussing the Lisbon earthquake of 1755, which killed 50,000 people, Dr. Pangloss says, "[A]ll is for the best, for there is a volcano at Lisbon, it could not be anywhere else. For it is impossible for things not to be where they are, because everything is for the best" (Voltaire, 1759). Gould and Lewontin (1979) use Dr. Pangloss to criticize a school of thought in evolutionary biology that assumes every trait of every plant and animal must be an efficient adaptation, optimally designed by natural selection. Adherence to this school of thought, Gould and Lewontin (1979) claim, is characterized by "a lack of suspicion that a different kind of explanation might be required." Some adherents of this school, as quoted by Gould and Lewontin (1979), write that the results of their study are consistent with their prior theory, "as we presume any careful study would [be]." Gould and Lewontin (1979) point out that a theory that cannot fail in careful study is not a particularly useful theory. In a particularly piquant metaphor, Gould and Lewontin (1979) claim that many in evolutionary biology have mistaken the spandrels of San Marco Cathedral in Venice as existing for the purpose of containing painted images of the Christian faith as opposed to existing as the architecturally necessary feature of round domes supported by square base. Spandrels exist as a necessary by-product of the architectural design, and once they exist, they are put to use. In economic terms, those that Gould and Lewontin (1979) criticize have reversed the causality, thinking that if spandrels are painted they must exist for that purpose. Dr. Pangloss and his followers fail to exert sufficient skepticism, accepting that "everything is made for the best purpose" (Voltaire, 1759).

Organized skepticism should be an integral part of the research process. It requires proof and verification of that proof before a fact is accepted as such. It requires challenging the status quo, which involves challenging positions of power, and that can be difficult for those not protected by institutional guards, like tenure at universities. Any time power is involved, there are ethical issues at stake. Ensuring that others can practice and undertake challenges to the status quo is integral to the exercise of ethics in applied economics, both for ensuring the value of organized skepticism and for encouraging adoption of the virtues of universalism, communality, and disinterestedness.

1.5 The Role of Ethics in Economics

Good research should be ethical. And ethical research should adhere to the four Mertonian Norms discussed earlier. However, just because we as individuals may hold to these norms, that does not mean that other researchers will. Making economics an ethical science is a collective action problem. An individual may hold their research to high ethical standards, but another individual may, in the interests of career advancement, forgo these norms, refraining from sharing their data and code and falsifying their results in order to place papers in better journals. If the economics community fails to identify and punish the unethical researcher – that is, fails to exert the norms of science on the members of the community – then the incentives for other researchers to conduct ethical research are diminished. This could result in a low-level equilibrium, where unethical individuals and their research dominate the field.

Ethical failures in economics are well documented (Ferguson, 2010b; DeMartino, 2011; Wight, 2015; DeMartino and McCloskey, 2016; Searing and Searing, 2016b; Christensen et al., 2019; Lee, 2018). And we discuss many of these failures throughout this book. Yet, it is difficult to know just how pervasive unethical research is in economics because (1) it is difficult to determine the probability of getting caught and so determine the overall rate of unethical conduct (Becker, 1968) and (2) it is difficult to distinguish between unethical research and sloppy research (Ioannidis, 2005). One way to, at least tangentially, determine how pervasive research misconduct is, is to ask researchers directly about their beliefs and practices in terms of their own behavior and their perceptions regarding the behavior of others.

Anderson et al. (2007) report on the results of a survey they conducted of U.S.-based researchers and Mertonian norms. The survey of 3,247 researchers is based on a representative sample of researchers who have received funding by the the NIH. The sample is split into early career researchers and mid-career researchers, the later defined as those who had received R01 funding for their lab. The survey collected information about the four Mertonian norms plus four counter-norms: particularism (counter to universalism), secrecy (counter to communality), self-interestedness (counter to disinterestedness), and organized dogmatism (counter to organized skepticism).[4] Table 1.1 presents definitions of these counter-norms along with the already-discussed norms.

In the survey, Anderson et al. (2007) asked respondents to rate their support of each norm and each counter-norm in terms of (1) their own subscription, (2) enactment, and (3) perception of other's typical behavior. For subscription,

TABLE 1.1 Mertonian Norms and Counter-Norms

Norm	*Counter-Norm*
Universalism Researchers evaluate research solely on its merits, contexualized by commonly accepted standards in the field.	**Particularism** Researchers assess new knowledge, in the context of the reputation and past productivity of the individual or research group who generated the knowledge.
Communality Researchers share findings with colleagues.	**Secrecy** Researchers protect their newest findings to ensure priority in its dissemination.
Disinterestedness Researchers are driven by the desire for knowledge and discovery and are not solely motivated by opportunities for personal gain.	**Self-Interestedness** Researchers compete with others for funding and recognition.
Organized Skepticism Researchers consider all evidence, hypotheses, theories, and innovations, even those that challenge or are counter to their own work.	**Organized Dogmatism** Researchers invest only in promoting their own most important findings, theories, or innovations.

Note: Table reproduces information from a similar table in Anderson et al. (2007).

respondents were asked "for each item [norm or counter-norm], please indicated the extent to which you personally feel it *should* represent behavior of scientists." For enactment, respondents were asked "please indicate the extent to which it represents *your own* behavior." And for the assessment of others, respondents were asked "please indicated the extent to which you feel that it *actually does* represent *the typical behavior of scientists.*" Respondents could choose "to a great extent" (2), "to some extent" (1), or "very little or not at all" (0). Anderson et al. (2007) sum up the scores for all the norms and than compare them to the same individual's sum of scores for the counter-norms.

Figure 1.2 summarizes the main results in Anderson et al. (2007), with findings divided by if the respondent was early or mid-career. The figure shows the percentage of respondents whose norm scores are higher than, equal to, or lower than their counter-norm scores. The top two bars compare early- and mid-career researchers and their own subscription to the Mertonian norms. About 90 percent of researchers, regardless of career stage, claim that the norms *should* represent researcher behavior, with 70 percent rating norms and counter-norms equally and only 1–2 percent rating counter-norms higher than norms. We begin to see a divergence between early- and mid-career researchers when they are asked about the role norms play in their own behavior. For early-career researchers, 60 percent enact the norms more than the counter-norms while close to 70 percent of mid-career researchers claim to enact the norms. Fewer early career researchers (27 percent) rate the norms and counter-norms equally

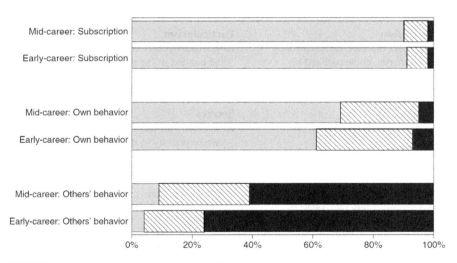

FIGURE 1.2 Perceptions of Behavior by Researchers

Note: Percentage of respondents with higher norm scores than counter-norm (norm > counter-norm) are represented with light gray dots. Percentage of respondents with norm scores equal to counter-norm (norm = counter-norm) are represented with striped lines. Percentage of respondents with lower norm scores than counter-norm (norm < counter-norm) are represented with solid black. The figure comes from Anderson et al. (2007).

in their own behavior compared to mid-career researchers (32 percent). Similar differences exist for those who rate their own behavior as more counter-normative than normative (5 percent for early career compared to 7 percent for mid-career).

The largest differences, what Anderson et al. (2007) term dissonance, occurs when each group is asked about the behavior of others. Nearly 80 percent of early-career researchers believe that counter-norms dominate norms for other researchers, and only 4 percent view the research of others as being dominantly normative. This compares to a (slightly but significantly) rosier outlook for mid-career researchers, where only 60 percent think that counter-norms dominate the behavior of others. Anderson et al. (2007) interpret these results as reflecting a distrust of other researchers, manifesting in dissonance between the beliefs and behavior of respondents. Nearly all researchers subscribe to the norms, but given that a majority think other researchers are behaving unethically, their own behavior is more unethical than their beliefs would dictate. This hints at a low-level equilibrium where individuals believe that everyone else is behaving badly and so they must act similarly. That the dissonance is greatest among early-career researchers, still trying to make a name for themselves, provides further evidence of this collective action problem.

Anderson et al. (2007) are focused primarily on researchers in health science, but, as Christensen et al. (2019) write, there is little reason to think these trends do not also reflect the state of research ethics in economics, sociology, political science, or other quantitative social sciences. Competing interests between researchers over tenure, promotion, publication, funding, and so on create incentives to engage in scientific misconduct, particularly if one believes that others have not internalized an agreed-on set of scientific norms. Addressing these competing interests is not simply a mechanism design problem, where one tries to align incentives in a way that is both acceptable and efficient. This is because the conflicts between researchers create externalities that affect others in the research community as well as the myriad other communities of people that contribute to and are impacted by economic research.

This complex web of interactions – much more complex than can be represented by a tractable mechanism design problem – is why we agree with Peterson and Davis (1999), who argue that "there is an unavoidable link between ethics and economic analysis." When our research is based on data that represent people and when our results are designed to influence decision-making and policy, applied economists must, of necessity, be concerned with, in the words of the philosopher T.M. Scanlon (2000) "what we owe each other."

In particular, as applied economic researchers we have an obligation to

- our fellow researchers, both our colleagues and students and associates who work for us;
- our research participants, whether or not we personally collected data from them;

- our students, for those engaged in teaching, training, and education;
- the broader scientific community, to which our research aspires to add true, new knowledge;
- society as a whole, to which our research aspires to affect and influence.

In Chapter 2, we discuss in more detail what a researcher owes to each of these communities. For now it is sufficient to say that, regardless of what type or mode of ethics one adheres to and regardless of what individual or which community one is interacting with, there are basic actions that define the role of ethics in economics. These actions are protect others, minimize harm, and increase good; assure trust; ensure the integrity of work; and satisfy institutional, professional, and industry standards and guidance (Israel, 2015). What these actions look like when faced with a specific ethical issue or dilemma is context dependent. Providing a practical guide to ethically navigating these various contexts is the purpose of this book.

1.6 Guide to This Book: The Research Life Cycle

Ethics is rarely if ever incorporated into teaching or learning about how to do research. It is typically a chapter or a week in a research methods course, and often the focus is on IRB. We have designed this book to discuss ethics at all stages of the research process. To facilitate this, we have structured the book to follow a stylized "life cycle" of a research idea, with each chapter representing a new stage or phase in the process. Figure 1.3 visualizes this life cycle, which we originally developed in Michler et al. (2021).

We divide the life cycle into three stages, which begins with (1) an initial idea, including idea and project development (Chapters 2 and 3); moves into (2) data collection, management, and analysis (Chapters 4, 5, and 6); and finally concludes with (3) publication and dissemination efforts both inside and beyond the academy (Chapters 7 and 8). The life cycle presented is, of course, a stylized rendering of the research process, and any given research project need not map exactly to this structure.

The life cycle of research begins with the germ of an idea. The researcher seeks to develop this germ into actionable research by formulating an appropriate research design. Applied economists select topics to research for a variety of reasons, affected by the economist's interests and incentives. In these early stages of research, it is essential for us to clearly define and delineate our responsibilities as researchers to our research communities, both local and global. Another important component of the early stages of research, which ultimately affects which research ideas grow and which ones fail to flourish, occurs when researchers seek external funding for their ideas. Ideas attract or fail to attract funding for a number of reasons. But, the ability to attract funding often determines what research questions become actual research projects.

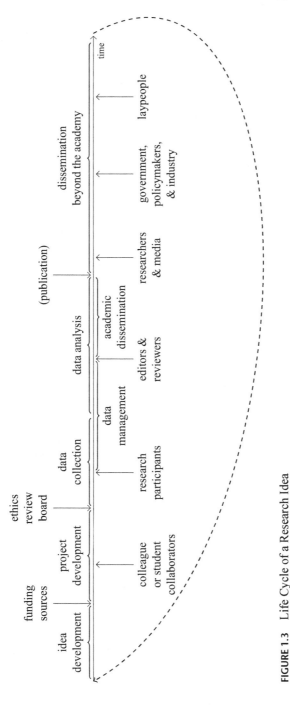

FIGURE 1.3 Life Cycle of a Research Idea

Note: Image represents a stylized life cycle of a research idea. Braces represent stages in the life cycle and correspond to the chapters in this book. The arrows represent individuals, communities, or institutions that a researcher interacts with at each stage of the life cycle. Adapted from Michler et al. (2021).

Once a research idea has been developed into a project and any necessary funding has been secured, the next stage in the life cycle is the assembling of the research team and detailed planning of the research design. In recent years, applied economists have begun using pre-analysis plans to help guide research design and help ensure ethical, transparent, and reproducible research (Janzen and Michler, 2021). As Angrist and Pischke (2009) suggest, steps taken at this initial stage narrow the range of questions that can be addressed later.

Having finalized the project elements, the researcher begins to interact with research participants. Though there are innumerable types of research participants, due to the breadth of research in the field of applied economics, the process and procedures of these interactions are governed by IRBs. Many view IRB policies as burdensome, a poor fit for much of social science research, and more focused on compliance than the actual ethics of the research (Schrag, 2010; Van Den Hoonaard and Hamilton, 2016; Josephson and Smale, 2021). But the harms that can come to research participants may not be trivial, even within the social science. Because of the potential harm, IRBs are distinctive in the research life cycle as they serve as *ex ante* gatekeepers, providing a license to conduct each research project one at a time instead of a blanket license to an individual researcher.

The next two stages in the life cycle of a research idea (data management and data analysis) frequently overlap with the penultimate stage, dissemination to the academy. Data management is a process that begins with data collection and extends far beyond publication. This is because IRBs typically require maintenance of data for at least six years and the preservation of participant privacy and data confidentiality in perpetuity. In terms of data analysis, initial results are typically presented at conferences, seminars, and workshops where feedback is sought to improve the analysis. During this stage of the life cycle, researchers interact with colleagues at academic events and begin the process of publication. These activities are governed by explicit rules (IRB requirements), codes of conduct (journal or association policies), and implicit expectations in terms of how one analyzes data (Lybbert and Buccola, 2021). Codes of conduct stipulate behavior at institutional and association sponsored events and are more concerned with the ethics of interpersonal interactions than with the ethics of research (AEA, 2018; AAEA, 2019). Additionally, publication policies now define a variety of criteria that must be met for research to be deemed ethical and thus acceptable for publication.

The last stage of the life cycle of a research idea is the impact it has on researchers and media, government, policymakers, industry, and, finally, the public. Generally, this impact begins during the process of dissemination with fellow researchers and the scientific community. In recent years, the media has played an increasingly important role in disseminating research, amplifying findings and influencing policy that results from research work. Administrators at universities and other institutions have taken notice and begun rewarding researchers who gain fame by appealing directly to the media and policymakers.

It may be the case that the push at research institutions for "impact" beyond scientific contributions is changing how and what research is done.

Within this life cycle, the researcher is required to, at several stages, verify their adherence to explicit ethical criteria. Without IRB approval or signed COI statements, research is likely to end prematurely. However, there are many other stages in the research life cycle that are not governed by explicit ethical criteria, although implicit norms within the field exert influence on the researcher. Potentially the most critical stage in the life cycle is the initial one, where ideas are formed and research is designed. Many of the considerations and pitfalls of ethical behavior that a researcher faces during the life cycle arise at this earliest of stages. Throughout this book, we use this life cycle of research as a framework to delve into the components of the life cycle in depth.

1.7   Conclusion

Throughout this book, we present a variety of ethical issues and considerations that arise at every stage of the life cycle of a research idea. Some issues, like human subjects research or p-hacking, are well documented and discussed extensively in the existing literature. But many issues, such as idea generation or working with the media, are less discussed, at least in the formal academic literature. In many places, we provide our personal opinions on what constitutes the ethically correct action. In these cases, we are guided by our approach to ethical pluralism and our adherence to Mertonian norms. That said, we do not claim to have the solutions to all the issues raised in this book, nor do we claim to be arbiters of ethical behavior in the profession. We present issues, solutions, and ideas, hoping to serve as a guide for economists struggling with how to conduct their own ethical research. In reading this book, it is useful to remember that ethics is ongoing in any project, changing throughout the course of research and requiring continuous reexamination and recommitment.

In addressing research ethics, we cover a wide range of issues, but our coverage is far from exhaustive. In particular, we do not discuss ethical issues surrounding workplace or classroom behavior, taking as given that legal, institutional, and professional codes of conduct are definitive in their rejection of discriminatory and harassing behavior (although these codes are far from frequently, fairly, effectively, or equitably enforced). We also do not discuss the ethics of economic models or whether economics is or should be a normative science. We leave that discussion to the numerous books that already exist on the subject.

Notes

1 Wansink's blog has since been deleted. It exists, at this time, only in the Internet Archives: https://web.archive.org/web/20170312041524/http:/www.brianwansink.com/phdadvice/the-grad-student-who-never-said-no.
2 The Top Five economics journals, informally measured in terms of prestige, citations, and perceived rigor are the *American Economic Review*, *Econometrica*, the *Journal of*

Political Economy, the *Quarterly Journal of Economics*, and the *Review of Economic Studies*.

3 A favorite contribution of ours is the Hardy–Ramanujan number 1729. The story goes that Hardy was visiting Ramanujan at the hospital. Hardy remarked that his taxicab number (1729) seemed a rather "dull one" and that he hoped it was "not an unfavorable omen." Ramanujan replied that in fact, 1729 as a very interesting number: "it is the smallest number expressible as the sum of two cubes in two different ways." The two different ways are $1729 = 1^3 + 12^3 = 9^3 + 10^3$. This has given rise to the idea of the "taxicab number," of which only six are known.

4 Anderson et al. (2007) add to their survey two additional norms (with counter-norms): governance (administration) and quality (quantity). Christensen et al. (2019) discuss these in more detail.

PART II
Developing Research

2

IDEA DEVELOPMENT

2.1   Introduction

At the 2003 annual meeting of the American Economic Association (AEA), association president and recent Nobel laureate Robert Lucas delivered the presidential address. He opened his address by stating:

> Macroeconomics was born as a distinct field in the 1940's, as a part of the intellectual response to the Great Depression. The term then referred to the body of knowledge and expertise that we hoped would prevent the recurrence of that economic disaster. My thesis in this lecture is that macroeconomics in this original sense has succeeded: Its central problem of depression prevention has been solved, for all practical purposes, and has in fact been solved for many decades.
>
> *(Lucas, 2003)*

After reviewing the theory that led him to his claim, Lucas (2003) conclude that "the potential gains from improved stabilization policies are . . . perhaps two orders of magnitude smaller than the potential benefits of available 'supplyside' fiscal reforms."

Lucas was not alone in his view that fiscal reforms, such as reduced taxes, smaller budgets, and less regulation, were the way forward in macroeconomic policy. In fact, new classical economics, as opposed to Keynesian economics, dominated the field of macroeconomics, with proponents including Milton Friedman, Robert C. Merton,[1] Myron Scholes, Robert Mundell, Finn Keyland, Edward Prescott, and Eugene Fama all winning Nobel Prizes. As Lucas wrote as early as 1980, "one cannot find good, under-forty economists who identify themselves or their work as

DOI: 10.4324/9781003025061-4

'Keysian.' . . . At research seminars, people don't take Keynesian theorizing seriously anymore; the audience starts to whisper and giggle to one another" (Lucas, 2013).

And yet, just four years after Lucas declared victory over prolonged recessions and proclaimed the superiority of fiscal, supply-side reform, the U.S. and most high-income countries experienced the greatest economic downturn since the Great Depression. How could the best and brightest of the profession and their decades of award-winninng research have missed the coming economic collapse?

At a very basic level, new classical economic thought was caught in a paradigm shift, like that outlined in Thomas Kuhn's (1962) *The Structure of Scientific Revolutions.* The dominate paradigm in macroeconomic theory became incommensurable with experience in the real world. As Krugman (2009) writes, "economists, as a group, mistook beauty, clad in impressive-looking mathematics, for truth." New classical economic theory is built on two key hypotheses. The first hypothesis is the efficient market hypothesis formulated by Eugene Fama. The hypothesis states that financial markets always price things (e.g., assets, stocks, bonds, risk) correctly, taking into account all possible information (Fama, 1970). Building a model on the efficient market hypothesis means that financial markets always work and that there is no possibility for speculative bubbles. The second hypothesis is the rational expectations hypothesis, developed by John Muth (1961) for a market with a single good and adapted to macroeconomic theory by Robert Lucas (2013). The hypothesis simply states that everyone knows how the market works and makes accurate predictions about prices every time. Building a macroeconomic model on the rational expectations hypothesis means there is no place for mistakes in the market, including no place for mis-priced goods, credit crunches, or other sorts of errors.

Modeling the macroeconomy using these assumptions means that the model, by design, excludes the possibility of booms and busts and, by extension, the need for a regulatory framework to provide stabilization policies or guardrails. There is no point in asking, "[W]hat if . . . there was a housing bubble . . . a credit crunch . . . a liquidity crisis?" because these questions make no sense within the terms of the model. There is also no point in developing policies to protect against eventualities that the model says are actually impossibilities. Complicating the issue of paradigmatic incommensurability is the fact that many proponents of new classical economics had many real or perceived conflicts of interest, from the political (Krugman, 2009) to the financial (Cassidy, 2010).

The story of macroeconomic hubris in the latter part of the 20th and early part of the 21st centuries is told elsewhere (see Cassidy, 2010, and McLean and Nocera, 2010). And the hubris is not unique to new classical economics: a similar fate befell Keynesian theorists in the 1970s. Nor is it unique to macroeconomics as a field or economics as a profession. Our interest in this chapter is not the hubris of one specific set of theories or ideas. Rather, it is the different ways in which beliefs, incentives, and funding can distort or ossify a research agenda.

We begin this chapter by asking if an idea itself is ethical, reflecting on the way a researchers' own beliefs, preferences, and implicit biases influence what ideas they may have. This can occur through a lack of identity with or lived experience in a research context. But it can also occur through too close of a connection to that context, creating blind spots or conflicts of interest. Next, we ask if a research idea is answerable and discuss how asking only the easily answerable questions can create bias in the body of scientific evidence. Finally, we ask if a research idea is fundable and assess the ways in which the availability of funding can induce innovation in research.

When it comes to developing new ideas, researchers can become path dependent, always traveling in one direction and only looking one way. This path dependency can affect the research topics we pursue and the research questions we ask. And, ultimately, the choices made by researchers and funders about what questions to pursue affects the direction of institutional and policy change. When everyone is looking for *A*, they might find it. Without a similar search to find *B*, all evidence will point to *A* (Michler et al., 2021).

2.2 Responsibility of the Researcher to the Community

What is the purpose of the research? To gain new knowledge about humans? To allocate resources more efficiently? To better understand how the world works? To satisfy our own curiosity? To keep us employed? To help others? To do good? As researchers, we would probably answer at least a qualified "yes" to the preceding questions. But the community that we live in, and the public and privates agencies that fund our research, are likely to answer "yes" to a circumscribed set of the previously mentioned questions. They might even have their own answers to the question of what is the purpose of our research.

As researchers, we have a responsibility to our community to engage in ethical research. Our community can be variously defined as society at large, research participants, and our own academic or research coterie. To ensure our research is ethically done, at a minimum, we owe it to our community to be honest, accurate, and understandable in the reporting of our findings. We would argue that our responsibility also extends to ensuring that our research does no harm to our community: a modified Hippocratic Oath. But, while being honest, accurate, and understandable are actions we as researchers have control over, how can we ensure our research does no harm? Is a "do no harm" criteria too stringent for applied economists as, *a priori*, we do not know the outcomes of our research our how our results will be used by others? We cannot know if our research will satisfy a consequentialist approach to ethics.

Given that we do not know the outcomes of our research or how our findings can or will be used, there is the possibility that our research might actively do harm. One can think of the retracted Wakefield et al. (1998) study linking autism to the measles, mumps, and rubella vaccine. While Wakefield et al. was the product of misconduct, one need not have engaged in research misconduct to imagine producing research that causes harm. Doleac and Mukherjee (2022) study the moral hazard of providing access to naloxone, a lifesaving drug that can be administered during an opioid overdose to rapidly reverse or reduce its effects. They find that while greater access to naloxone reduced mortality of those who overdose, it is also associated with increased use of opioids, resulting in no change in the overall number of deaths.[2] Furthermore, because greater naloxone access is associated with an increase in the number of opioid users, it is also associated with an increase in theft. Municipalities and states might read Doleac and Mukherjee (2022) and decide to reduce access to naloxone, directly contributing to the deaths of specific individuals who would, absent the research, have lived in a community where an overdose could have been reversed and their lives saved.

Distinguishing between the knowledge created by Doleac and Mukherjee (2022) and the use that others might might make of that knowledge is common among ethicists and philosophers. The distinction identified is between an entity or action that might be *intrinsically* good and an entity or action that might be *instrumentally* good (Oliver, 2010). In economic models, relaxing constraints allows agents to achieve greater optimality and therefore, we (Anna and Jeff) believe that more knowledge in almost any domain of inquiry is *intrinsically* good. The knowledge expressed in Le Chatelier's principle, which describes the effect of a change in chemical equilibria, is intrinsically good. This knowledge was then used by Fritz Haber to create an instrumental good: the Haber–Bosch process of fixing atmospheric nitrogen to create chemical fertilizer, which contributed to increased agricultural yields and reduced global hunger (Smil, 2000). However, Haber also used Le Chatelier's principle to produce an instrumental bad: chlorine gas. Haber oversaw the deployment of chlorine gas by the Germans at the Second Battle of Ypres in World War I (Hoffman, 2010). That the same knowledge was used for both an instrumental good and an instrumental bad does not affect Le Chatelier's principle as an intrinsic good.

As researchers, does our responsibility to the community extend beyond simply producing knowledge (an intrinsic good)? As long as our intention is to produce knowledge, is that sufficient to fulfill our moral obligation? Can we safely ignore ethical consequentialism? Or do we owe our community more? While we believe that producing new knowledge is an intrinsic good, as economists we spend a lot of our time thinking about efficiency, costs and benefits, and opportunity costs. Is research that is never put to a practical use as "good" as research that improves the quality of life in our community? As applied economists, the goal of our research should be to have a practical or policy relevant impact. Furthermore, when much of our research is supported by public funds, either to our salaries at public universities or through state and federal grants, there is a strong moral justification for producing research that will have an impact on the community that supported our work.

However, as a researcher starting out on a research project, it is difficult to determine the type and magnitude of impact that our research will have. There is work that we have published on COVID-19 that we were confident would have a large and positive impact on policymaking. But other research we thought would be put to practical use has never rated more than a couple of dozen reads and a handful of citations and, as far as we can tell, has never had a meaningful impact on anyone beyond ourselves. As research outcomes and impacts are unknown at the initial stages of a research idea, we believe that a "do no harm" criteria for conducting ethical research is too stringent. Rather, researchers should enter projects with an intention to "do no harm," engaging in research with the intention that their work will have positive, practical, and meaningful impact on the community: a prospective consequentialism.

Moving from a community broadly defined, we can think of specific communities with which the applied economist, or any researcher, engages and hence has a responsibility to. The first is the public, specifically those outside of the academic community. Both of us work at a Land Grant institution, as do many agricultural and applied economists. As such, we are state employees, with our salaries paid, in part, by state tax dollars. Even if one does not work at a state-funded institution, most research grants come from federal or local government institutions, meaning that research is funded by tax dollars. As researchers spending public funds, we owe it to these donors to spend their money wisely. We are responsible to the public to engage in research that will provide a solid return on investment. This is one of the main justifications for the Land Grant system and part of the reason why Land Grant institutions have cooperative extension programs.[3] We discuss the responsibility of the researcher regarding funding later in this chapter.

Beyond being stewards of public funds, we as researchers have a responsibility to communicate research findings to those impacted by the research. Those impacted may not be the same as those who funded the research or those who participated in the research. Consider, for example, the findings from an economic lab experiment conducted with undergraduates at a private university which have implications for anti-trust policy. How researchers can fulfill their responsibility to communicating research findings to the public is the subject of Chapter 8.

A second group to whom researchers have responsibility is the community of research participants. Typically, this community overlaps with the general public, but given that members of the community of research participants actually engaged in the research, they are owed additional considerations. First and foremost, there are a number of institutional ethical obligations involved in engaging in human subjects research. We discuss this at length in Chapters 4 and 5. But, even beyond the strictures of institutional, or ethics, review boards (IRBs), researchers have ethical commitments to those who consent to participate in our work. As development economists, we too often see research conducted in low-income countries and among marginalized people groups with zero follow-up once the data collection is complete. While IRBs typically require research results to be shared with participants, this is rarely done beyond posting a research paper in some online public access space. Farmers in rural Zambia who participated in a randomized control trial (RCT) are unlikely to see a research paper based on their data. It requires time, energy, and skill to distill complex regression results into a style that can be understood by non-experts. Furthermore, it takes funds to return to research sites and communicate findings. We ourselves have not been effective at ensuring that this post-study debriefing is supported by our grants, though we are working to improve.

The final group that researchers have responsibility to is the academic community. Oliver (2010) writes that we "exist within a network of ethical obligations to other members of the academic community." As discussed in Chapter 1, ethical research is grounded in open science and adheres to Mertonian norms. But one should avoid dogmatism in terms of research methods, appreciating that for many research questions, there are multiple valid approaches to answering the question.[4] Beyond these broad or general ethical norms, there are numerous specific and special ethical issues regarding fellow researchers. These include issues of power dynamics, authorship, and the intellectual property of ideas (Chapter 3); issues of transparency in data cleaning and analyses (Chapters 5 and 6); and conflict-of-interest issues in publishing (Chapter 7).

All these ideas and issues, as they relate to the various communities with which a researcher engages, are discussed in more detail where they enter into the research life cycle. Throughout, remember that ethical issues are implicit in our responsibilities to our communities, even when an explicit ethical element or requirement is absent.

2.3 Asking Ethical Research Questions

In popular lore, inspiration comes in the form of a lightning bolt striking or a light bulb turning on: a "eureka" moment. From Archimedes to Sherlock Holmes, people are suddenly struck by some deep insight while sitting in the bath or playing the violin. However, these classic tropes of inspiration from literature and film are in fact examples of inspired solutions to an existing question. The source of initial ideas or research questions are often more mundane. Archimedes's eureka moment was his solution to a question he had been charged with by King Hiero II of Syracuse to answer. Sherlock Holmes did not come up with his own cases but was hired by someone with a mystery to solve. Researchers frequently come up with research questions by identifying gaps in the existing literature, observing the world around them, or by pondering deep unknowns. But, as Bellemare (2022a) writes, "often 'research' questions are answered because someone outside the research community (e.g. government, firm, NGO [nongovernmental organization]) has an interest in knowing the answer to a question and is willing to fund it." In our experience as applied economists, our research ideas are equally likely to come as jobs offered by a third party looking for an answer as they are from our own powers of observation.

Once one has an initial idea, the kernel of a research question, the first thing to do is ask, "Is this idea ethical?" This question differs from the questions that IRBs will ask about research. It also differs from many of the questions and issues we will raise throughout this book, which are often focused on doing research ethically. But it is essential during the nascency of an idea to pause and reflect on the ethics implicit in the idea itself.

This is work that is often done independently without institutional oversight. As we discuss in Chapter 4, IRBs are primarily focused on the ethics of the process used to answer a research question – not the ethics of the question itself. There are studies based on research questions that have obtained IRB approval that are ethically dubious, at best, and downright unethical, at worst. Concerns about the ethics of a study or research question first entered economics with the adoption of RCTs as a research design. Prior to that, most applied economics work was observational and did not involved experimenting or intervening in people's lives. An early ethically dubious but IRB approved RCT was a study of bribery in India (Bertrand et al., 2007). The authors randomized incentives for participants to obtain a driver's license. A pure control group received no additional incentives, a "lesson group" got free driving lessons, and a "bonus group" got cash if they obtained their license quickly. The implicit purpose of the inclusion of "quickly" was to encourage participants in the bonus group to bribe officials in order to obtain a license. The RCT confirmed something that was not really in doubt: corruption and bribery are common features in the bureaucracies of India, as well as in other countries. The consequences of encouraging unsafe drivers to obtain licenses illegally is never explored in Bertrand et al. (2007). However, as Barrett and Carter (2010) and Ravallion (2020) detail, the outcome of this experiment was to put innocent nonparticipants, as well as the participants, at risk by adding unsafe drivers to the road. That this RCT was irresponsible and unethical did not stop the paper being published in a Top Five economics journal, the *Quarterly Journal of Economics*.

Studies like Bertrand et al. (2007), which have a strong potential to do harm to participants as well as others, are outliers in economic research. Instead, much of the controversy around the use of RCTs by economists was whether it was ethical to provide beneficial treatment to some and withhold it from others (Banerjee, 2005; Bardhan, 2005; Basu, 2005; Mookherjee, 2005).[5] Classic cases involved the random distribution of deworming medication (Miguel and Kremer, 2004), malarial bed nets (Cohen and Dupas, 2010), and eyeglasses (Glewwe et al., 2016). Critics of these studies argue that it was unethical to withhold cheap, effective, lifesaving technology and medicine in order to study a behavioral or economic question.

The ethical concerns with the questions being asked in these studies center on the issue of equipoise. In medical science, clinical equipoise means that there is uncertainty within the medical community regarding whether or not the treatment is effective (Freedman, 1987). Physician and anthropologist Paul Farmer wrote that RCTs "can only be carried out ethically if the intervention being assessed is in equipoise"

(Farmer, 2013). Critics of RCTs (e.g., Ravallion, 2014; McCloskey, 2019b; Abramowicz and Szafarz, 2020) seize on the previously mentioned studies as examples of unethical research questions because the treatments being studied were not in equipoise. Obviously, deworming medication kills parasitic worms, insecticide treated bed nets reduce the probability of getting malaria, and eyeglasses improve sight.

But, as McKenzie (2013) points out, the principle of clinical equipoise does not take into account the relative costs and benefits of the treatment. McKenzie writes:

> We don't live in a world of no budget constraints, and so the standard of clinical equipoise needs to be more along the lines of doubts over whether this use of funds makes people better off relative to any other possible use of funds in the country, or for international organizations, the world.
>
> (McKenzie, 2013)

While simple efficacy studies of deworming medication, malaria bed nets, and eyeglasses would be ethically unjustified by the principle of clinical equipoise, the studies by Miguel and Kremer (2004), Cohen and Dupas (2010), and Glewwe et al. (2016) are not efficacy studies. Rather, they are studies about the cost-effectiveness of deworming medication on educational attainment, the relative merits of free bed nets versus charging a nominal fee, and the cost-effectiveness of providing free eyeglasses on educational attainment. By McKenzie's principle of social science equipoise, these studies all seem to be ethical.

Most economists have come to judge, willingly or begrudgingly, the randomization of things like deworming medication, malaria bed nets, and eyeglasses by the principle of social science equipoise. Such studies are viewed as ethical if (1) the study does more then test efficacy, (2) the economic or behavioral research question is important enough to warrant even a temporary withholding of the treatment, and (3) control populations will be granted access to the treatment once the experiment is over.

There are studies which may satisfy the principle of social science equipoise, get approved by IRBs, and still raise ethical concerns and generate controversy among economists and other social scientists. Two recent examples are studies by Bryan et al. (2021) in the Philippines and by Coville et al. (2020) in Kenya. In their study titled "Randomizing Religion," Bryan et al. (2021) conduct an experimental evaluation of an Evangelical Christian proselytization program combined with a health and livelihood education program. Households were randomized into a group that received only an Evangelical Christian values training curriculum, a group that received only the health and livelihood curriculum, a group that received both, and a pure control. The authors find that six months after the end of training, the Evangelical-values-only group had higher religiosity, higher income, and lower perceived relative economic status. At 30 months, the Evangelical-values-only group no longer has higher religiosity, income was now only marginally higher, and they no longer perceived themselves as having a lower relative economic status. By comparison, at six months those in the health-and-livelihood group had experienced no change in religiosity, income, or perceived relative economic status, relative to the control. But at 30 months, the health-and-livelihood group had higher income and higher perceived relative economic status. Bryan et al. (2021) interpret the combination of results as suggesting that the religious training altered religiosity and instilled "grit" and conclude that "this churchbased program may represent a method of increasing non-cognitive skills and reducing poverty among adults in developing countries." But one could also interpret these results as suggesting that the Evangelical values education encouraged participants to see themselves as embattled or marginalized, despite a higher income. This perception decreased as the effects of the religious training faded with time. In the end, the health-and-livelihood group had higher income with none of the negative – and demonstrably false – self-perception. Neither of these alternative, negative, and equally plausible interpretations of the evidence nor the ethical implications of Evangelical proselytization in Catholic communities is explored in the paper. It is not difficult to imagine a Catholic Christian (which neither of us are) viewing the economic results and ethical implications of Bryan et al. (2021) very differently from their Evangelical co-religionist.

Another recent problematic paper that passed the IRB and satisfies McKenzie's (2013) criterion for social science equipoise is by Coville et al. (2020). The authors use an RCT to study ways to encourage landowner payment of water utility in Nairobi's slums. In one treatment arm, utility employees met face-to-face to encourage building tenants to complain to or to shame their landlords into paying the landlord's unpaid water utility bills. In the second treatment the utility threatened to shut off water to the property, effectively punishing the tenants for the landlord's failure to pay. This study satisfies social science equipoise because it tests the relative efficacy or cost-effectiveness of two different behavioral interventions. And, according to Coville et al. (2020), the water utility had a written, although lightly enforced, policy of water shutoff, which they were looking to scale up. Thus, at the end of the experiment, control groups would likely be "granted access" to the shutoff treatment. Despite this, there are clear ethical issues with designing a study that seeks to offload the costs of contract enforcement from the utility to the tenants. That tenants bear the costs of forcing landlords to adhere to their contracts with the water utility is exactly what Coville et al. (2020) found. While the shutoff treatment had no impact on access to water or quality of service, it had negative welfare effects on tenants. In order to finally satisfy their outstanding commitments to the water utility, landlords increased the number of tenants in the buildings and charged tenants higher rents.

These studies obtained approval from IRBs, but the question being asked, at heart, begs an ethical consideration deeper than the mandated ethical review or even the principle of social science equipoise. To proactively address this issue, Asiedu et al. (2021) call for a structured ethical appendix to social science research papers. Such an appendix would address what the authors call policy equipoise, the role the researcher played in research design, potential harm to both participants and nonparticipants, conflicts of interest, intellectual freedom, how researchers planned to provide feedback to participants, and potential future misuses of research findings. Table 2.1 provides more detail on each of these ethical topics.

TABLE 2.1 Elements of A Structured Ethical Appendix

Topic	Questions
Policy Equipoise & Scarcity	Is there policy equipoise? If not (1) was there scarcity and (2) do all ex ante identifiable participants have equal moral or legal claims to the scarce programs?
Research Roles with Respect to Implementation	Did the researchers have direct decision-making power over how to implement the program? If yes, what was the disclosure to participants and informed consent process? If no, that is, implementation was separate, explain the separation.
Potential Harms to Participants or Nonparticipants	Does the intervention, policy, or product being studied pose potential harm to participants or nonparticipants? Are participants or likely affected nonparticipants particularly vulnerable? Are participants' access to future services or policies changed because of participation? If the answer is yes to any of these, what is being done to mitigate such risks?
Potential Harm from Data Collection or Research Protocols	Are data collection and/or research procedures adherent to privacy, confidentiality, risk management, and informed consent protocols with regard to human subjects? Are they respectful of community norms? Are there potential harms to research staff?
Financial & Reputational Conflicts of Interest	Do any of the researchers have financial conflicts of interest with regard to the results of the research? Do any of the researchers have potential reputational conflicts of interest?
Intellectual Freedom	Were there any contractual limitations on the ability of the researchers to report the results of the study? If so, what were those restrictions, and who were they from?
Feedback to Participants or Communities	Is there a plan for providing feedback on research results to participants or communities? If yes, what is the plan? If not, why not?
Foreseeable Misuse of Research Results	Is there a foreseeable and plausible risk that the results of the research will be misused and/or deliberately misinterpreted by interested parties to the detriment of other interested parties?

Note: Table represents ideas put forward in Asiedu et al. (2021).

While applied economists are only just beginning to discuss the merits of ethical appendices, and no journal currently requires them, we also believe that they are eminently valuable.

In the remainder of this chapter and throughout this book, we discuss the importance of the specific topics that Asiedu et al. (2021) argue should make up a structured ethical appendix. While a structured appendix would not see the light of day until publication (discussed in Chapter 7), as Kara (2018) notes, "ethical work begins as soon as you think of a possible research question." Thus, from the moment one begins to formulate a research question, one should be thinking about how one's research question, research design, and research activity are ethical.

The issues of equipoise, potential harm done to participants and nonparticipants, and potential misuses of research findings ideas raise two important considerations. First one should reflect on the context of one's research. This amounts to asking the question, "Am I too far from or too close to the research context?" If one is too far, then one risks conducting bad research which perpetuates long-standing colonial issues of Euro-Western researchers and theft from indigenous communities. Too close and one is open to the criticism that one's personal priorities and perspectives bias one's work. Second one should reflect on intellectual property regulations, in particular around the property of ideas. This amounts to asking, "Is this idea really mine?" and considering both the chain of inspiration for getting that idea and who else may be able to claim its origin.

2.3.1   Context Considerations

The political scientist and anthropologist James Scott (1998) writes, "all environments are intractably local." Understanding the general environment and specifics of the local context are imperative for researchers conducting applied economic research. As Karlan and Appel (2016) discuss in their book about field experiments gone awry, understanding the research setting and being aware of partner challenges are important precursors to successful applied work. Local context is also important for asking ethical research questions. In fact, the majority of books on research ethics that we have read focus on how to conduct ethically responsible research in context, that is, outside the researcher's "own" context.[6] Understanding the local economic and policy environment is important for ensuring policy equipoise. Being aware of indigenous (non-Euro-Western) perspectives and ways of knowing is important for ensuring no harm comes to research participants and nonparticipants.[7] Appreciating the social context that, in part, defines interpersonal relationships is important for ensuring no harm arises in the data collection process. Investing in relationships with local collaborators and research participants helps ensure that feedback on research results is provided to the community.

While understanding the local context has long been important in applied economics research, in recent years there is a rising recognition that familiarity with the local environment may not be sufficient for ensuring that one is asking ethical research questions. Motivating factors in this reassessment of context considerations include the Rhodes Must Fall movement in South Africa to remove vestiges of the colonial and apartheid system of discrimination, and the Black Lives Matter movement after the murder of Trayvon Martin by George Zimmerman and the murder of George Floyd by Minneapolis police officer Derek Chauvin. As Edward Said (1979) points out in *Orientalism*, knowledge itself is used as a tool of colonial exploitation. The continued production of knowledge by Euro-Western researchers, using indigenous research participants as an input, the coding of that knowledge in academic and technical jargon, and the storing of that knowledge in gated journals can be seen as an extension of colonialism. For Euro-Western researchers, being deeply familiar with the local context may no longer exclude one from criticism that one's work is neocolonial. After all, arch-colonialists from Warren Hastings, first governor-general of India, to Cecil Rhodes, prime minister of the Cape Colony, lived most of their lives in and were deeply familiar with the local context of the peoples and places they were exploiting.

In broad, political terms, this recognition can be framed both with respect to representation and decolonization. Representation involves the explicit inclusion of researchers who identify with the race, ethnicity, gender, or orientation of the group being studied. Decolonization involves not just encouraging diversity and inclusion on a research team but also creating space for discussion and reflection on the historical legacy of colonialism in one's research. Universities, granting agencies, professional associations, and other research-oriented institutions are beginning to appreciate the importance of having representatives of indigenous communities involved in research about those communities. This goes beyond just having local contacts provide some context and input into the data collection process. Rather, it involves training, supporting, and including indigenous researchers in all stages of the research process from idea conception to results dissemination. Many granting agencies now explicitly include participation from local or indigenous researchers as part of their scoring criteria. Some of this move toward local representation is simply performative. Both Hedt-Gauthier et al. (2019) and Naritomi et al. (2020) provide suggestive evidence of the exclusion of indigenous researchers from final author lists for papers study indigenous communities, suggesting that, in career terms, these researchers are omitted when it matters most. Ultimately, science is stronger when it grows from a diverse set of experiences and perspectives. Representation from local or indigenous communities in research about those communities will help ensure one is doing both good research and ethical research.

Recognizing the importance of representation in formulating ethical research questions, there also exists a tension in research with respect to remaining aloof, disinterested, or outside the context of one's population of study. The Mertonian norm of disinterestedness has been used in the past as an exclusionary tool to argue that people from a community cannot maintain objectivity when studying their community. We reject that argument for the discriminatory trope that it is: we have never seen anyone raise doubts about the ability of a white man who grew up on a farm to objectively study the economics of agricultural production. The norm of disinterestedness does not imply that one cannot objectively study a population with which one shares identity. Rather, disinterestedness is a norm that places truth-telling above personal gain or self-interest. Thus, when one closely identifies with one's population of study, disinterestedness involves disclosing that fact as a way to strengthen the integrity of the study and author(s).

Disclosing real or perceived conflicts of interest (COIs) are traditionally limited to financial or material relationships. But, as Ioannidis and Trepanowski (2018) argue, COIs go beyond the monetary and can exist anytime one has formed allegiances, preferences, or opinions about a topic of study. They present the case of a hypothetical nutritionist on the Atkin's diet whose research demonstrates that the nutritionist's dietary choices are in fact beneficial. In this example, the nutritionist has a personal conflict of interest and should disclose their dietary habits. Ioannidis and Trepanowski (2018) write that "as a general rule, if an author's living example could be reasonably expected to influence how some readers perceive an article, disclosure should be encouraged." The concern is that how we identify ourselves, our tastes, preferences, and strongly held beliefs, and what we identify with, our politics, advocacy, and activism, might influence the type of research questions we ask and the results that we find, meaning that this potential bias is disclosure-worthy information.

In interrogating one's initial idea to determine if the question itself is ethical, it is important to ask, "Am I too far from or too close to the research context?" Too far, and one runs the risk of perpetuating long-standing colonial archetypes regarding how Euro-Western researchers extract or steal knowledge from indigenous communities. Too close, and one is open to the criticism that one's personal priorities and perspectives are biasing the work. Asking ethical research questions involves ensuring inclusion of and representation from those in the community of study as well as disclosing both financial and nonfinancial interests throughout the research process.

PERSPECTIVE 2.1   CONFIRMATION BIAS BY HEATH HENDERSON

Applied economics is a messy business. The social world is complex, data are error-prone, and the results of our analyses are frequently ambiguous. While economists often aspire to be value-neutral, the messiness of economic research leaves ample room for subjectivity and bias, whether through our choice of research questions, our manipulation and analysis of the data, or the interpretation of our results. One especially important form of bias is confirmation bias, which refers to the human tendency to seek out and interpret evidence as confirmation of one's existing beliefs.

The Baby's First Years study is a vivid recent example of confirmation bias (Troller-Renfree et al., 2022). In the study, a group of researchers sought to examine the effect of income poverty on infant brain activity by randomly assigning roughly 1,000 new mothers into one of two groups: a group receiving a large monthly cash transfer ($333 per month) and a group receiving a modest monthly cash transfer ($20 per month). The mothers began receiving the cash right after the birth of their child, and then the researchers followed up with them after one year. At the follow-up, the researchers used electroencephalography (EEG) to measure the "power" of the infants' brain activity across several different frequency bands.

The researchers found that the infants in the group receiving large cash transfers saw increased power in the alpha, beta, and gamma frequency bands, which had previously been linked to better language, cognitive, and socio-emotional outcomes. As their preferred analyses showed that these effects were statistically different from zero, the authors concluded that "the weight of the evidence supports the conclusion that monthly unconditional cash transfers given to mothers in our study affect brain activity in their infants" (Troller-Renfree et al., 2022). The study was published in the *Proceedings of the National Academy of Sciences* and also received considerable media attention, with features in the *New York Times*, *Forbes, Vox,* and the *Los Angeles Times,* among others.

There was just one problem: as the study gained attention, several people took a closer look at the results and found that the conclusions were not well supported by the data (Ritchie, 2022). Perhaps most importantly, their main results were remarkably fragile and often lost significance when they adjusted for some important statistical issues (e.g., multiple hypothesis testing and differences between the two groups due to attrition). Furthermore, several people challenged the authors' claim that brain activity was linked to better developmental outcomes, as that claim was not directly tested in the study and instead based on limited previous research. The results were seemingly overstated, and several media outlets responded to the criticisms by either updating their articles on the study or removing them altogether.

There are several possible reasons why the researchers, either consciously or unconsciously, misrepresented their findings. One possibility is that it is difficult to get null findings published in scholarly journals and that the authors were motivated to publish their paper. Another possibility is that they were worried that they would not get further funding for their research if they did not show interesting results. Finally, it is possible that the authors wanted the findings to be true simply because they wanted to provide a compelling justification for policies to support women and children. Whatever the reason, the researchers had motivation to believe that cash transfers have beneficial effects and they appeared to interpret the evidence as a confirmation of that belief.

How can applied researchers avoid falling victim to such confirmation bias? One simple strategy is to honestly consider the possibility of unfavorable results, especially null results, at the earliest stages of the research process. This should entail answering several questions: Can I accept a null result? If not, what other question could I pursue where I would be more impartial? If so, what would a null study look like in my case? Can I learn anything from a null result that might be illuminating to my research topic and worthy of publication? These questions are only a starting point and should ideally be accompanied by other strategies for mitigating confirmation, such as building diverse research teams, using pre-registered research plans, or soliciting outside feedback prior to publication.

2.3.2 Intellectual Property

In addition to considering if there are issues of context or COIs involved in one's research question, one should also assess the intellectual history and ownership of the idea itself. Ideas are the lifeblood of research and are at the heart of innovation, both inside and outside the academy. Researchers, entrepreneurs, and corporations all jealously guard their ideas because coming up with new, interesting, answerable, or marketable ideas is a challenge. It takes time to refine an idea into an answerable research question and then develop that idea into something that is marketable. And, while it is common to think of ideas as the intellectual property (IP) of their creator, IP law in fact governs how other people can use ideas that are embedded in physical form, not the idea itself (Boldrin and Levin, 2005). This combination of the high value for ideas but a lack of legal protection for them creates an environment in which individuals have an incentive to steal ideas from others.

However, what constitutes idea theft is not straightforward. Ideas themselves may have intrinsic value but, to borrow from Karl Marx (1867), they have no use value or exchange value until they are copied into some physical or tradeable form. It is the copies of the idea in the form of books, software, hardware, and so on that has use value, exchange value, and are governed by copyright or patent law (Boldrin and Levin, 2005). So what, then, does it mean to steal an idea from someone else if that idea has not yet been copied into some physical form? If such theft is not ruled out by IP law, is it considered plagiarism? In a survey of 117 editors of economics journals, Enders and Hoover (2004) found that 48 percent do no consider the unattributed use of an idea to be plagiarism, while 36 percent consider it "likely" plagiarism. Only 17 percent of editors surveyed responded that they consider the unattributed use of an idea to be "definitely" plagiarism. Some editors justified their perspective that idea theft was not really theft or plagiarism by arguing that it can be difficult to attribute an idea to a single person or the theft to a single deliberate, malicious act. As one editor stated, "an author may hear an idea and later develop papers without knowing where the idea came from." This idea can alternatively be expressed in the quote from Wilson Izner that Enders and Hoover (2004) use as the epigraph to their paper: "When you steal from one author, it's plagiarism; if you steal from many, it's research." Or, as Vogel (2013) asks, "[I]s the use of someone else's ideas theft or just streamlined knowledge transfer and exchange?"

Although solid evidence on the prevalence of idea theft is difficult to come by, the issue is raised with alarming frequency on internet forums and blogs. The fear of having one's ideas stolen appears particularly common among graduate students and early-career researchers. In the case of students, such theft may have lasting consequences on the student's ability to obtain a research position upon graduation – or to graduate at all. This very concept, however, is a depressingly common thread on graduate student discussion boards and in advice columns (e.g., Woolston, 2002; Kelsky, 2014). There is recent evidence that, relative to their male peers, women researchers are more likely to have their ideas stolen or to have credit for their ideas withheld. Using administrative data from the Institute for Research on Innovation and Science at the University of Michigan, Ross et al. (2022) were able to compare the structure of research teams on grants with published articles and patents. They find that women on research teams are significantly less likely to be named as authors on publications or patents than their male team members. Additionally, while women and men are equally likely to be listed as authors on articles with zero citations, women are less likely to be named as authors on articles with more than 25 citations. These gender biases in attribution persist when controlling for field of study, team size, and career position. This amounts to a sort of idea theft from women.

Neither the legal code that governs IP nor the social norms that govern plagiarism in the profession provide much assurance against the theft of one's ideas. In the absence of strong institutions, it is necessary to look to other methods and technologies. Increasingly, blockchain-like tracking helps verify who wrote an idea down first. Researchers can use directories with a storage service that provides versioning or includes a license file in the directory. Yet, these protections are only effective if the profession is in agreement on the extent to which researchers own their ideas even if they are not crystallized yet into a research paper and if researchers are in a position to broadcast the theft. For students, this second condition may prove unreachable. In theory, a university's institutions, including the dean of students and the Office of the Ombudsman, protect students in these situations. However, the power dynamics within a university may limit a student's willingness to report their professor for fear of retaliation and its career consequences.

Potentially, the institutions best situated to disincentivize the theft of ideas through policing and punishment are funding agencies. A funding agency that wittingly or unwittingly provided money to research based on a stolen idea is likely to suffer reputational damage, in addition to its misallocation of monies. Funding agencies protect themselves from such circumstances through their own review and auditing system and the legal code. This includes internal review in the pre-award stage and outside evaluation, as well as periodic reporting in the post-award stage. In the best-case scenario, the funding agency will identify that a researcher is seeking to fund an idea that was stolen from someone else and reject the proposal. In the worst-case scenario, the agency will fund the idea and only later find out that they have been a party to idea theft. This worst-case scenario motivates the screening of research ideas prior to funding and the monitoring of researchers after funds are allocated by the agency.

While Mandal et al. (2012) note that "the responsibility for ensuring that funds and resources are utilized optimally without any misconduct rests on the shoulders of the researchers," some responsibility is also attributable to the researcher's home institution. While rare, it is not unheard of for funding agencies to engage the legal system in the recovery of funds spent on stolen or fraudulent research ideas. Comstock (2013) tells the story Elizabeth Goodwin, a professor at the University of Wisconsin, Madison, who falsified a federal grant proposal in 2006. Goodwin was forced to resign and, in a 2010 settlement, pay $50,000 in restitution to both the U.S. Department of Health and Human Services and the University of Wisconsin. More recently, in 2018, Christian Schunn, a professor at the University of Pittsburgh, agreed to pay the U.S. $132,027 to resolve allegations that he violated the False Claims Act by submitting false documents to the National Science Foundation (NSF) in order to obtain federal grants to fund his research (U.S. Department of Justice, 2018).

However, solely relying on funding institutions to regulate the theft of ideas is not an ideal solution. Under current law, documenting that an agency has been defrauded by funding a stolen research idea is quite difficult. Unless the funder is a federal agency that can pressure the researcher's home institution, there is little hope for recovering misused or mismanaged monies. Schneider (2015) writes that

> the fractions awarded as direct salaries to PIs are either too small or legally hardly accessible for such damage claims. . . . Lab heads rarely keep their funding stashed in a bank account waiting to be raided by the furious grant giver. Instead, the money is already invested and consumed in the institutional research and part of the institutional budget.

Stronger professional norms are needed that distinguish between when using someone else's idea is research and when it is theft. Recent experimental evidence suggests that, as the knowledge economy grows, individuals are more likely to consider stealing ideas as severe, if not more severe, than stealing money (Ellis, 2022). However, it may take a long time for the interpersonal consequences of stealing ideas documented by Ellis (2022) to transform into social norms sufficient to protect researchers from having their research idea stolen.

2.4 Designing Ethical Research

Once a researcher has satisfied themselves that their research question is ethical, the next step in developing a research idea is to begin the process of research design. Decisions made at the earliest stages of the design process can drive the way in which researchers engage with funds and funders, other researchers, students, and research participants. In developing a research design, one frequently starts by defining the aims of the research; for example, the research will provide better understanding of what allows households to adapt to weather shocks, by examining how the adoption of climate smart agricultural practices impact welfare outcomes in the presence of these shocks. Defining research aims will often shed light on other potential ethical issues that will arise as one moves through the research life cycle. As Oliver (2010) writes, "it is never too early to be thinking about ethical issues when planning research!"

While research has never occurred in a vacuum, research today is increasingly available at its earliest stages to interested parties around the world. As Hamermesh (2018) observes:

> One's research can, for better or worse, influence broad public attitudes and/or public policy, and it can affect how businesses and individuals organize their activities and make decisions. Moreover, these effects may be direct or indirect, as our research filters through others' research and through the media.

In a world where research in its various stages of completion can be easily accessed and quickly disseminated, a researcher may have no control over who sees the research, how it is interpreted, or how it is used (Josephson and Michler, 2018). This means that from the beginning of the research process, economists must work to develop both sound and ethical research designs to ensure sound and ethical work, for interpretation and use by whoever might access it in the future. While academics may still rely on the peer review process to render judgment on the quality and competency of a research design, accessibility to preprints, working papers, and conference presentations means that the media and broader public can access and use research that has yet to be peer-reviewed.

The 2022 controversy surrounding Alan Krueger's work for the ride-sharing company Uber illustrates this point. In 2015, Uber hired Krueger to write a paper on the labor market for Uber's "drive-partners" (the company's term for those who drive "for" the company). Krueger was a well-respected and well-liked economist who, if not for his untimely and tragic death by suicide, likely would have shared the 2021 Nobel Prize with his longtime colleague, David Card. The Uber paper, which is a descriptive analysis of an Uber-sponsored survey of drivers, paints a fairly rosy picture of the company's labor practices and pay schedule. In the paper, Krueger discloses that he was paid by Uber for this time. Furthermore, Jonathan Hall, an Uber economist, was a co-author on the paper. The paper was first published as part of the non-peer-reviewed National Bureau of Economic Research (NBER) working paper series and, in part because of obvious methodological issues (Berg and Johnston, 2019), would eventually be published in a mid-tier labor journal, the *ILR Review* (Hall and Krueger, 2018).

From a professional economist's perspective, there is no story here. A corporation hired a prominent academic economist to help improve the quality of the research undertaken by economists on the corporation's payroll. The results were not that interesting, due to limitations in the research design and its publication in a mid-tier journal reflects that. Additionally, Krueger disclosed that he was paid by Uber and that the terms of the agreement granted Krueger "full discretion over the content of the report."

However, the fact that a working version of the paper was included in the NBER, an organization Krueger had been a member of throughout his career, was viewed by the media as an imprimatur of the paper's quality. Even well-known business and finance journalists, like Felix Salmon of Axios, misunderstood (or misunderstand) what an NBER working paper is. Salmon (2022), in his coverage of the controversy, writes of the NBER working paper series that "there is no more prestigious venue in which to publish economic research" – a risable statement to any economist. When the paper came out in the NBER in 2016 it did not matter to Uber's proponents or opponents that the paper had yet to be vetted by the peer-review process.

That early-stage papers can have such an impact on wider society means that it is important to ensure one's research design is both ethical and rigorous. While much of this book focuses on the ethics of research implementation (e.g., data collection, management, analysis), designing ethical research involves its own special considerations. First, it is essential to determine if selection bias is playing a roll in which research questions one asks. This means asking not only, "What are the ethical implications of the research questions I ask?" but also "What are the ethical implications of the research questions I do not ask?" Second, it is crucial to strike the fine balance between the plausibly answerable and the plausibly important. This amounts to asking oneself, "Am I asking easily answerable but unimportant questions, or am I asking hard-to-answer but important questions?"

2.4.1 Induced Innovation; or, Be Careful Where You Look

In an ideal world, we observe a phenomenon, speculate on its causes, develop a hypothesis to test, collect data to test it, write up results, and publish them. But frequently our research is not driven by our dispassionate observation of the world. Rather, as Bellemare (2022a) notes, someone outside of the scientific community, often someone with money, has a question they want answered. As a result, the research questions we ask are not randomly drawn from the set of all possible research questions, but rather, there is some nonrandom inducement to ask certain questions. The corollary is that there is some inducement to *not ask* certain other questions.

This can create selection bias in the scientific record, as some topics or research questions may be overrepresented while others may be underrepresented.

In our paper with William Masters titled "Beyond the IRB: Selection Bias in Applied Economics Research" we show that one can think of selection bias as a form of induced innovation in the scientific record (Michler et al., 2021). Since Hicks (1932), economists have understood how changes in relative prices can induce innovation in technologies that more efficiently use the relatively more expensive input. In an empirical setting, Hayami and Ruttan (1985) show how innovation in agricultural technology is induced by the relatively scarce input, be it labor or land. While the typical story of induced innovation relates to research and development (R&D) responses to price changes, institutional priorities also affect the direction of R&D and, in turn, technical change. As Michler et al. (2021) indicate, there are multiple optimal outcomes at various prices, and so the question becomes, How do we decide which type of technology – or research question, in our case – to pursue?

Figure 2.1 adapts the induced innovation model to research topics in applied economics. The horizontal axis is a community's potential production of public goods and services. These may include classic public goods such as schooling, infrastructure, or defense but also can include goods with substantial positive or negative externalities, such as vaccinations or carbon emissions. The vertical axis is the community's potential output of private goods and services, such as clothing, houses, or other rival and excludable goods. The community's cost of taxing private activity to fund public goods is represented by the slope of the revenue lines, which are equal to the total level of income or the sum of private and public

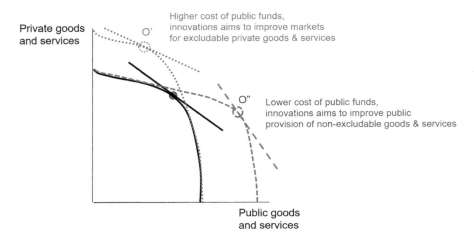

FIGURE 2.1 Induced Innovation of Development

Note: A depiction of different development paths induced by a change in cost of public funds. From Michler et al. (2021).

activity. In public finance, the slope of the revenue line is known as the cost of public funds. As Michler et al. (2021) argue, there may be increasing returns when shifting resources out of one sector into the other, so the production possibilities frontier (PPF) may not be concave everywhere. If the community uses its resources efficiently it will move along its PPF to the highest possible level of income, where the cost of public funds just equals the slope of the PPF.

As the mathematician George E.P. Box writes, "all models are wrong, but some are useful." The model in Figure 2.1 is no exception. A two-dimensional model of public finance abstracts away from many important features of real world public policy and financial decision-making. But the model is useful as a thought experiment. If innovators expect the cost of public funds to be lower than in the past, they will research ways of providing more public goods and services. Conversely, if innovators believe that the cost of public funds will be higher than in the past, they will look to save public funds and improve the market for private goods.

PERSPECTIVE 2.2   IDEA DEVELOPMENT: WHERE DID FIGURE 2.1 OF THIS BOOK COME FROM? BY WILLIAM A. MASTERS

This chapter includes a section on how topic selection in applied economics could be understood using the induced innovation model of incentives for technological change, as illustrated in Figure 2.1. Where did that idea come from, and what ethical issues does it raise?

The induced innovation model illustrated in Figure 2.1 first appeared in Michler et al. (2021) as a way to discuss how incentives for different kinds of discovery help drive the direction of research. This simplest possible version of an induced innovation model shows a production possibilities frontier for social welfare that could expand toward more government provision of public goods and services or toward a larger fraction of all activity in the private sector. Which direction is followed depends in part of the direction of applied economics research, where we might (or might not) find evidence to help policymakers and entrepreneurs expand society's production possibilities frontier in one direction or the other.

In the simple model sketched in Figure 2.1, the evidence discovered by any given research project could lead to expansion in either direction; for example, a project designed to improve and expand private-sector insurance could discover that adverse selection and other market failures are insurmountable, leading governments to step in with public-sector provision. Likewise, a project designed to measure the value of public development of agricultural technology might find that many innovations are in fact marketable, leading to more private funding.

The outcomes of research are not predetermined, but incentives will influence what questions are asked and which discoveries get adopted and scaled up.

The idea shown in Figure 2.1 arose for me in the late 2010s, when real interest rates and the cost of public borrowing had been zero or negative for more than a decade, coinciding with the rapid expansion of academic economics research toward expanded government activity. This was a sharp contrast with my graduate school experience of the 1980s, when real interest rates and the cost of public funds was high, and economists were focused mainly on how to shrink government in favor of the private sector. Economics research about public- versus private-sector activity is often seen as an ideological question of moral judgment, with the pro-government turn after the 2008 recession seen as a rebuke to excessively antigovernment sentiments of the 1980s and 1990s.

My own personal research ethics, as spelled out in a farewell speech to graduate students when I left Purdue in 2010, involves trying to explain differences among people as their responses to different circumstances (Dubner, 2010). The purpose of this is to identify how outcomes could be improved and thereby accelerate progress. Applying that same logic to the direction of economics research, perhaps the rightward turn to less government in the 1980s and 1990s, followed by a leftward turn to more public activity in the 2010s were both explainable, and indeed justifiable, as appropriate responses to different circumstances. Explaining the swing between more libertarian views and support for more collective action could help build a more unified community with greater respect across political divides.

The model shown in Figure 2.1 is a good example of idea development in part because it is such an early-stage hypothesis. Figure 2.1 is just an initial cartoon model, designed to illustrate how the well-established principle of induced innovation might be applied to help explain the political orientation of researchers and governments. How useful this model could be might never be known. The ideas in Figure 2.1 would be tested empirically only if other researchers choose to investigate that which in turn might hinge on whether they share my interest in more unified explanations of choice as a response to incentives. Ethics plays an important role in topic selection, in this case toward understanding political divisions for or against government intervention.

The historical experience in the U.S. is one of cyclical fluctuations between periods of relatively more and less costly public funds. In the 1930s and through much of the middle of the 20th century, public funds were relatively inexpensive. This was reflected in the large number of public goods and services provided during this period, not only through New Deal agencies but through postwar public investment in infrastructure (e.g., interstate highways and damns) and research institutions (e.g., Land Grant Universities and national laboratories). But, starting in

Cartwright (2007), a strong research design requires answering three questions about causes:

1. What do they mean?
2. How do we confirm them?
3. What use can we make of them?

The first question concerns the metaphysics of what is a cause. For applied economists today, causes are typically defined in terms of counterfactual thinking, mathematical models, and DAGs. But there are systems of causal relations beyond those associated with Rubin (1974) and Pearl (2009). They include systems of thinking about causes put forward by Wright (1928), Granger (1969), and Hausman (1998), among others. As Cartwright (2007) argues, these different systems should not be thought of as "alternative, incompatible views about causation." Rather, there is "plurality in causality," meaning the appropriate causal system will depend on the causal relationship being studied. In the same way, RCTs, instrumental variables (IVs), difference-in-difference (DID), and regression discontinuity (RD) are all different tools for confirming causal relationships, the appropriate use of which is context-specific (Murnane and Willett, 2011).

The questions that Angrist and Pischke (2009) define only address the second of Cartwright's questions. We would argue that answering the four questions defined by Angrist and Pischke (2009) facilitates a rigorous research design, but to move from a rigorous design to an ethical research design one must also address Cartwright's third question. The third question involves defining the boundaries for where we can use evidence (external validity). In applied economics, answering the third question is frequently little more than hand-waving and speculation in some section title "conclusions and policy implications." But answering Cartwright's questions one and three provide a warrant for use: they justify why the evidence generated by answering question two is good evidence for the conclusions we want to draw.

Designing research that answers all three of Cartwright's questions can help to ensure that one's research design is both rigorous and ethical. The questions allow a researcher to clarify why the methods used in certain setting are justified and why the evidence generated is useful. As Cartwright (2007) puts it, "metaphysics, methods and use must march hand in hand." Only with all three elements together can we then be confident that we are designing ethical research. Or, at a minimum, research that satisfies policy equipoise.

2.5 Ethically Funding Research

Having established that both the research question and the research design is ethical, the next step in developing a research idea is finding funding to conduct the actual research. Funding is neither a necessary nor a sufficient condition for doing good research. But funding often helps improve upon good research ideas. It allows one to collect primary data or to purchase and combine existing data sets. It allows one to hire students, postdoctoral fellows, or dedicated research scientists to help share the workload. It can allow for faculty to buy out of teaching obligations and focus more of their attention, in the short term, on the research question. It can cover the cost of travel to academic conferences and stakeholder events to disseminate the research findings.

While funding helps pay for research activities, obtaining funding is not costless. One can think of the researcher as a firm in a perfectly competitive market, looking to produce research. In this case, additional funds would relax the budget or capacity constraint of the researcher, allowing them to produce greater amounts of research. A more accurate representation of the researcher in relation to funding their research is a principal–agent model. In a principal–agent framework, the funding agency is the principal looking to fund the researcher, the agent, to produce research that is of value to the principal. In the standard principal–agent problem, it is typical to assume the agent's costs are convex. The implication of this assumption is that the costs of the agent are increasing in effort. As Bellemare (2022a) points out, this means that the researcher needs to balance the certain costs of securing funding with the expected benefits from obtaining that funding. So working to obtain unlimited funding may not be worth the researcher's time.

Using a principal–agent model to frame issues involving research funding also allows us to use the theory of incentives to think more deeply about the competing objectives of funder and researcher (Laffont and Martimort, 2002). Funders are looking to "purchase" a research output. Funders could be agnostic about the specific results of the research, viewing whatever the results say as interesting and a valuable addition to the scientific record. Or funders could want answers to a specific question about the effectiveness of a program, technology, or activity. Or funders could want to buy a specific answer to a specific question. Each of these different funder objectives have different ethical implications for the researcher when considering whether or not to sign a contract with the funder. As Oliver (2010) blithely observes, "a useful general guide here is that the research should be carried out in broadly the same way as it would be conducted if it were not being funded by a sponsor . . . there is no general reason for the intervention of funding to alter the ethical standards of the research." Yet, when funding is a critical input to research and when funders have their own objectives in paying for research, Oliver's general guide may not be particularly useful to address issue surrounding how to ethically fund research.

In thinking more about incentives, and ethical funding of research, it is useful to return to the case of Alan Krueger's work for Uber. In the previous subsection, we focused on the ethics of research design and the need to have both a rigorous and ethical design at the earliest stages of research. We saw how poorly designed research, or research at an early stage, can still be picked up by the news media and interpreted as definitive, or at least peer-reviewed, evidence. Prior to publication, Krueger's paper with Uber economist Jonathan Hall was an NBER working paper, meaning it was not peer-reviewed. But that fact did not percolate into the media coverage of the paper, even coverage by well-respected business and financial journalists. In this subsection, we focus on a different issue in the Krueger/Uber case: the principal–agent relationship between Uber and Krueger and what each party in the relationship owed to each other.

When the paper was included as part of the NBER working paper series in 2016, the title page included a disclosure that Krueger had been paid as a consultant for writing the paper and that he had "full discretion over the content of the report." The leak of the "Uber files" to *The Guardian* newspaper revealed several new pieces of information about the principal–agent relationship between Uber, Krueger, and other economists (Lawrence, 2022). In her reporting, Lawrence (2022) reveals that Krueger's consulting fee for the paper was $100,000. Even for a well-known economics professor at an Ivy League school, the consulting fee was substantial in relation to academic salaries. The size of the consulting fee raises questions about what exactly Uber was buying. For that amount of money, was Uber a disinterested party looking for any and all insights from an economic analysis of their data? Was Uber looking for an answer to a specific question? Or was Uber purchasing a specific answer to a specific question? As the Uber files reveal, the company was looking for results that were "actionable for direct PR to prove Uber's positive economic role" (Lawrence, 2022). These revelations call into question whether the standard financial disclosure for economics papers, which Krueger provided, was sufficient. It further calls into question whether Krueger's statement about him maintaining "full discretion over the content of the report" was true. This raises an important question about disclosures: should researchers disclose the size or magnitude of their financial COI, not just the existence of the interest itself? It would be foolish to claim that size does not matter, in this regard, and so disclosure may be appropriate.

More shocking than the size of Krueger's consulting fee was the revelation that Uber had attempted to deceive or manipulate Krueger, and other economists hired as consultants, by selectively sharing data. As Lawrence (2022) reports, Uber used "techniques common in party political campaigns" to target well-known but potentially sympathetic academics with the goal of using the academic research "as part of a production line of political ammunition that could be fed to politicians and the media." Furthermore, the Uber files reveal that senior company staffers openly discussed how they would maintain control of the data, allowing them to decide what data were actually shared with the consultants. Both of these revelations show an asymmetry in Uber's relationship to its hired agents that the agents were unlikely to have been aware of. Krueger may have been unswayed by the $100,000 consulting fee and he may have actually had "full discretion" of the report. But Uber targeted Krueger because they believed his report, without Uber editorial control, would still be favorable to Uber. And Uber withheld or released data that would help them achieve their business and political goals.[8] When working with funders, be they public, private, or philanthropic, how can applied economists avoid this sort of "economist capture"?

The Krueger/Uber case raises two important issues. First it is necessary to reflect on one's financial COIs. This amounts to asking the question, "Do the standard disclosure forms adequately reflect my financial conflict of interest or do I need to provide greater transparency than is currently standard for the profession?" Second one should assess the degree to which one might be vulnerable to capture by a funder. This amounts to asking the question, "As an agent, am I being sufficiently vigilant to the competing objectives of the principal who hired me to produce research?"

2.5.1   Financial COIs

In his Academy Award–winning documentary *Inside Job*, which investigates the causes of the Great Recession, Charles Ferguson (2010a) shines a spotlight on the many academic economists who had close ties to financial firms. Most prominent among the economists the movie discusses are Larry Summers, Martin Feldstein, and Glenn Hubbard. Each of these academic economists had served in Republican and Democratic administrations, had academic appointments, consulted for or served on the board for large firms in the financial sector, and published academic papers that argued for deregulation of banking and finance:

- Larry Summers was the secretary of the Treasury under Bill Clinton and is a professor at Harvard. In both his government and academic work, Summers argued for the deregulation of the financial sector, including supporting the repeal of the Depression-era Glass-Steagall Act. He has made $20 million from the financial services industry over his career (Ferguson, 2010b).
- Martin Feldstein served as the chair of the Council of Economic Advisors in the Reagan administration and is a professor at Harvard. In his government and academic work, Feldstein argued for the deregulation of financial derivatives. He served on the board of directors for AIG, which paid him more than $6 million (Ferguson, 2010b).
- Glenn Hubbard served as the chair of the Council of Economic Advisors in the George W. Bush administration and is a professor at Columbia. In his government and academic work, Hubbard argued that financial derivatives and securitization increased market stability, per the efficient market hypothesis. He served on the board of directors for Capmark and Metropolitan Life, which paid him more than $250,000 a year (Ferguson, 2010b).

According to Ferguson (2010b), none of these researchers ever "make[s] policy statements contrary to the financial interests of their clients." But Summers, Feldstein, and Hubbard were not (and are not) unique. Carrick-Hagenbarth and Epstein (2012) analyze the statements of 13 academic economists with private financial affiliations. They find that disclosure of these affiliations were infrequent and that only one consistently disclosed their financial COI.

The consulting fees paid to academic economists highlighted by *Inside Job* is only one source of financial COI. The need for public or private monies to fund research arguably presents a larger source of financial COIs than consulting fees from or service on the board for a for-profit corporation. That research is financed by institutions external to the university imposes a substantial constraint on which questions researchers ask and which questions they leave unasked. While one would prefer to think that good research questions will attract funding, incentives exist wherever research is conducted that can lead to financial COIs (Josephson and Michler, 2018). For those at public universities, the reduction of state funding for public education has given rise to academic freelancing for industry. This means that private-sector concerns, beyond simple financial payments to researchers, play a larger role in guiding research decisions of those in the academy than in the past.

In part as a response to the revelation of undisclosed financial conflicts of interest in the wake of the Great Recession, the AEA instituted a policy requiring financial disclosure of authors for papers published in AEA journals (Berrett, 2012). The policy requires authors to disclose any "significant" financial interests that they or their close relatives might possess (AEA, 2012). Significant is defined as financial support of $10,000 or more over the previous three years. The financial support need not come only as money but also covers in-kind support, such as access to data. Importantly, the disclosure policy requires disclosure of consulting fees as well as financial support for the research. So, if instead of accepting a consulting fee, a researcher had the firm use the funds to pay for a research assistant, this would need to be disclosed. Since the move by the AEA, many other professional associations and journals have adopted similar policies. Ten of the 15 journals published by professional associations of agricultural and applied economists require authors to sign disclosure statements (see Table 2.2).

However, those with something relevant to disclose have an incentive to misrepresent their financial payments from and obligations to funding institutions. While the penalties for failing to disclose relevant information are clear at most journals, what is unclear is how journals can verify the accuracy of a disclosure statement. In the last few years, universities have begun to require all faculty to file COI statements every year. But, again, it is not clear how universities can police or verify the accuracy of these statements. At least for COIs in the medical sciences, 90 percent of universities solely rely on the researchers themselves to determine if their relationship with drug and device manufacturers is disclosure worthy (Harris, 2009). The difficulty of verifying if disclosures are complete is one reason why DeMartino (2011) calls for a professional code of conduct for economists. Thompson (2016) goes further, calling for the establishment of independent oversight bodies that could require conflicted researchers to divest of assets or set up blind trusts.

TABLE 2.2 Reported Policies in Agricultural and Applied Economics Journals

Association	Journal	Republication Policy?	IRB Policy?	Disclosure Policy?†
AAAE	African Journal of Agricultural and Resource Economics (AfJARE)	No	Yes	Yes
AAEA	American Journal of Agricultural Economics (AJAE)	Encouraged	Yes	Yes
	Applied Economic Perspectives and Policy (AEPP)	Encouraged	Yes	Yes
	Journal of the Agricultural and Applied Economics Association (JAAEA)	Encouraged	Yes	Yes
	Choices	No	No	Yes
AES	Journal of Agricultural Economics (JAE)	Encouraged	No	No
AARES	Australian Journal of Agricultural and Resource Economics (AJARE)‡	Encouraged	Yes	Yes
AERE	Journal of the Association of Environmental and Resource Economists (JAERE)	Yes	No	Yes
CAES	Canadian Journal of Agricultural Economics (CJAE)	Encouraged	No	No
EAAE	European Review of Agricultural Economics (ERAE)	Yes	Yes	Yes
	Q Open‡	Yes	No	Yes
IAAE	Agricultural Economics (AE)	Encouraged	No	No
IFAMA	International Food and Agribusiness Management Review	No	No	Encouraged
NAREA	Agricultural and Resource Economics Review (ARER)‡	No	No	Yes
SAEA	Journal of Agriculture and Applied Economics (JAAE)‡	Encouraged	No	Yes
WAEA	Journal of Agricultural and Resource Economics (JARE)	Encouraged	Yes	Yes

Note: Data compiled by authors in 2022. Definition of association abbreviations in order of appearance: AAAE - African Association of Agricultural Economists, AAEA - Agricultural and Applied Economics Association, AES - Agricultural Economics Society, AARES - Australian Agricultural and Resource Economics Society, AERE - Association of Environmental and Resource Economics, CAES - Canadian Agricultural Economics Society, EAAE - European Association of Agricultural Economists, IAAE - International Association of Agricultural Economics, IFAMA - International Food and Agribusiness Management Association, NAREA - Northeast Agricultural and Resource Economics Association, SAEA - Southern Agricultural Economics Association, WAEA - Western Agricultural Economics Association. † Includes both disclosure of funding resources and of conflicts of interest. ‡ Journal adheres to guidance from the Committee on Publication Ethics (COPE).

Disclosure of financial COIs in published papers addresses some of the issues associated with financing research because it alerts readers of potential bias in the research. Yet, more can and should be done. Current disclosure statements focus on positions held or financial support received by the researcher and close relatives. Krueger's disclosure on his Uber-funded research satisfied existing norms. But once the size of the consulting fee was made known, journalists and some economists questioned if more transparency should be required (Salmon, 2022). We concur with Zingales (2013), who suggests journals include disclosure of the type of agreement and terms of reference for the research being funded. Additionally, disclosure statements should explicitly ask for relevant personal financial stakes in the research, such as personal or family ownership of a farm when the research concerns the Farm Bill. This broader approach to COIs focuses on relationship disclosure and not just financial disclosure.

2.5.2 Economist Capture

The Nobel Prize winner George Stigler was one of the first economists to develop the theory of regulatory capture. In his paper "The Theory of Economic Regulation," Stigler (1971) writes that "every industry or occupation that has enough political power to utilize the state will seek to control entry. In addition, the regulatory policy will often be so fashioned as to retard the rate of growth of new firms." In the same way that regulators are prone to capture by industry, economists themselves are subject to capture by funding agencies. Zingales (2013) calls this economist capture. Economist capture is related to the financing that an economist receives to conduct research, but it goes beyond simple financial COIs.

The ways in which economists might be captured by those financing research is a function of the type of institution doing the funding. It is useful to delineate the different major sources of funding for economic research: (1) public, (2) private, and (3) philanthropic. In the U.S., public funding for education has been the norm since the Civil War. Similarly, public funding for research has been the norm since the end of World War II. However, over the last several decades, public funding for research and education has been a declining share of overall funding (CRS, 2022). While public funding, particularly federal funding, remains a large source of monies for bench science, engineering, and medical science, only a small fraction of federal dollars goes to social science research. Jones (2021) notes that since 1990, social sciences have received between 1.8 and 2.9 percent of annual U.S. research funds. This is despite social sciences producing between 8.6 and 9.5 percent of all PhDs over that same period. Relative to economics as a whole, federal and state funding still plays an important roll in funding agricultural and applied economic research. This is because agricultural and applied economics departments tend to exist at Land Grant Universities and in colleges of agriculture or life science, which receive substantial funds from the U.S. Department of Agriculture and the National Institute of Food and Agriculture.

The decline in the share of public funding for research is not necessarily due to a decline in the amount of Federal dollars for research, but in the rapid increase in the amount of money from private business and industry as well as from philanthropic foundations. Private businesses provide the largest amount of R&D dollars, representing 73 percent of all research funding as of 2020 (CRS, 2022). By comparison, funding from nonprofit and philanthropic foundations make up only 3.5 percent of total research dollars. Relevant for economists capture is not just the amount of money coming from each source but what stage of the research process each source puts their money. Public and philanthropic sources contribute over 60 percent of funds for basic research while business sources make up 56 percent of funding for applied research and 87 percent of funding for development (see Table 2.3). Where each funding source puts its money tells us about their objectives and where the threat of economist capture lies.

Public funding for research primarily goes to basic and applied research, reflecting the nature of research as a public good with positive externalities. In an ideal world, public funding would perfectly represent some social optimum. Yet public funding may be misallocated due to governance failures in representing public interests. Michler et al. (2021) highlight the variety of sources that may contribute to these failures. Governments may be unable or unwilling to recognize the public good nature of research and its outcomes, and thus may underinvest in research. This may be due to regulatory capture per Stigler (1971), in which individuals in government institutes fund policies and research priorities favorable to a small, industry-oriented portion of the electorate. Or it may be that governments are captured by the current electorate, which discounts the government's mandate to protect the long-lived citizenry (although individual citizens are not themselves long-lived).

Private business or industry funding for research primarily goes to applied research and to development, reflecting the private benefits that accrue to innovations that can be brought to market. If markets were perfectly competitive, and the efficient market hypothesis were true, then private funding would, through the market mechanism, maximize social welfare. Absent perfect competition, however, there is no guarantee that the benefits of private expenditure on R&D will do anything but accrue to the private firm. Firms may have welfare-reducing goals in mind, with research focused on increasing a firm's market share or market power, reducing competition and extracting a greater share of consumer surplus. These goals may result in industry support for academic research creating bias in the scientific record from a quid pro quo or through the censorship of unpopular results.

As Michler et al. (2021) write, in a quid pro quo situation, the researcher, either implicitly or explicitly, forms an agreement with the funder regarding the type of results that the research will generate. Alternatively, firms may sign nondisclosure agreements (NDAs) with multiple researchers working in parallel on the same topic or idea. Without any quid pro quo, the researcher undertakes the research and submits the results to the funder. Because each researcher has waived their right to

TABLE 2.3 U.S. Research and Development Funding by Sector and Character, 2020

Sector	Basic Research		Applied Research		Development		Total	
	Dollars	*Percentage*	*Dollars*	*Percentage*	*Dollars*	*Percentage*	*Dollars*	*Percentage*
Federal Government	43.8	40.6	43.7	31.3	50.3	10.9	137.8	19.5
Non-Federal Government	2.7	2.5	1.7	1.2	0.6	0.1	5.0	0.7
Business	36.2	33.5	78.6	56.3	402.7	87.4	517.5	73.1
Higher Education	14.3	13.3	6.0	4.3	2.2	0.5	22.5	3.2
Nonprofits	10.9	10.1	9.5	6.8	4.7	1.0	25.1	3.5
Total	107.8	100.0	139.5	100.0	460.5	100.0	708.0	100.0

Note: Amounts reported in billions of 2020 dollars. Table reproduced from CRS (2022) with original data from CRS analysis of National Science Foundation, National Patterns of R&D Resources: 2019–20 Data Update, NSF 22–320, Tables 7–9, February 22, 2022.

release results, the firm can suppress results that run contrary to their interests and only promote the results that support their interests.

Similar to public funding for research, philanthropic funding for research primarily goes to basic and applied research, reflecting the public good nature of research and the positive externalities it can create. Assuming the goal of all wealthy donors and philanthropists is maximizing the return to social welfare on their investment, then there would be no concern about economist capture. However, philanthropic funding is often driven by the interests – or whims – of the wealthy donor. Donor interest will in turn affect the types of research questions they are willing to fund, or the types of answers they would like to find. As philanthropic funding continues to play a larger role in financing research, concerns have arisen about the influence donors may exert on research outcomes (NSF, 2016; Mervis, 2017). It is unclear how the personal and political interests of the individuals who finance the Bill and Melinda Gates Foundation, the Chan Zuckerberg Initiative, the Clinton Foundation, the Charles Koch Foundation – or any other philanthropic agency – will induce innovation in research.

As with regulatory capture, economist capture does not imply that the captured individuals are corrupt or engaged in illegal activity. Rather, capture arises naturally from the incentive structure between the regulators and the regulated and between the economic researcher and research funder. It is easy to see in a principal–agent framework that the agent will need to produce for the principal what the principal asked for. But beyond that, if there is competition among agents for scarce funds from the principal, and agents all have the same cost function, then agents will seek ways to cater to the principal to help ensure they obtain the contract. Access to proprietary data, like Uber's, provides a publishing and career advantage for the economist who can convince the firm to give them those data. Cultivating a reputation for treating data sources nicely may provide a researcher with the advantage needed to convince a new firm to let them have the data (Zingales, 2013). When it comes time for firms to make decisions about potentially lucrative consulting opportunities, the economists whose research caters to business interests are likely to be at the top of any hiring list.

Zingales (2013) identifies four forces that lead to economist capture. First is career concerns. These include obtaining consulting gigs or permanent employment outside of academia, catering research papers to journal editors with known pro- or anti-business biases, and catering to senior colleagues on promotion and tenure committees with known research track records that reflect the senior colleague's personal and political views. Second is information needs. These include gaining access to proprietary business or government data and may require quid pro quos or NDAs to obtain access. Third is environmental or social pressures. These include the pressure to belong to, and therefore conform to, certain groups. The more homogeneous Beltway insiders or business elite are, the stronger the pressure to conform becomes. Fourth is relation asymmetries. These include asymmetries in power and influence, with funders who have more money to give to research able to command more fealty from the economists they hire.

As Josephson and Michler (2018) write, research funding, regardless of its source, always presents an opportunity for economist capture. The agendas at government agencies change with the political winds, determining both the budgets for broad research areas and the specific research proposals that will receive funding. As private businesses fund a larger share of research, their private interests play a larger roll in determining what research questions get asked. The rise of a wealthy donor class with billions of dollars to spend on research means that more research activity may be spent on donor pet projects. Currently, applied economists have little guidance in this area. Should one only accept money when given without explicit strings attached? What if these strings are suggested? And then, what organization does not have implicit interests? Producer associations and agribusinesses surely have their own interests, but even research organizations, governments, and philanthropists have their own interests. The applied economics profession needs to reflect more on the ways in which economists can be captured and how to prevent it. As for now, "the most important remedy to reduce capture is awareness by economists that this risk exists" (Zingales, 2013).

2.6 Conclusion

This chapter began with a story about the lack of awareness among macroeconomists that could be laughable if it had not led to such tragic economic outcomes. But their lack of awareness was not unique to the new classical school of economic theory. Rather, all scientific fields have dominant paradigms that blind scientists to emerging paradigm shifts. And all researchers have their own blind spots, implicit biases, and prevailing prejudices that influence their research. In this chapter, we discussed how the characteristics of the researcher and their environment can create ethical issues in the research questions we ask, how we try to answer those questions, and how we fund our research. Without even being aware of it, we can all fall into a path dependency that results in a biased picture of the way the world works.

To try to combat this bias, we focus on how applied economists can ask, design, and fund ethical research. We began by shinning a spotlight on the responsibilities researchers have to their community – responsibilities that are frequently overlooked. With a researcher's responsibilities made explicit, it is easier to frame the discussion of how to ethically develop a research idea. The process of idea development involves being sensitive to the research context, aware of the myriad potential uses one's research can have, and cognizant of the ways in which the need for funding can define our research.

Many of the solutions to the ethical problems we raise in this chapter amount to simply being more aware of the implications and repercussions of decisions made at the earliest stages of research. But we would be remiss if we did not ask the question: what causes this lack of awareness among us as individual researchers, and in the aggregate, as a profession? One contributing factor is the homogeneity within the profession in terms of identity and lived experience. This homogeneity contributes to a form of group think epitomized recently by the myopia of new classical economic theory. The lack of diversity in our profession manifests itself by narrowing our priors and limiting the types of research questions we ask. Too often, economic models have understated the role and impact of discrimination through choices of research topics and modeling assumptions that reflect a limited view of how society functions. In applied economics, a field of study that remains primarily male and white, this presents many of us with the challenge and the opportunity of incorporating the experience and perspectives of underrepresented minorities or marginalized individuals. Both implicit bias and a lack of identity and lived experience have profound consequences not just on representation in our profession but also on the ethics of our research and the efficacy of our work to critique and analyze policy. That said, racism and discrimination are more than research and policy concerns. They are critically important moral concerns that our research can address.

Notes

1 It is worth noting that Robert C. Merton, the Nobel Prize–winning economist, is not the same as Robert K. Merton, the renowed sociologist and originator of the Mertonian norms discussed in Chapter 1.
2 In this way, providing access to Naloxone is similar to seat belt laws. By making people safer in a car crash (i.e., reducing mortality in a crash) people drive more recklessly, causing the number of car crashes to go up and resulting in no change in the overall number of car crash deaths (Peltzman, 1975).
3 Based on evidence in Alston et al. (2011), those of us involved in agricultural research have been good stewards of public funds.
4 The late 2000s was a time of fierce debate, bordering on the doctrinaire, about the value of RCTs relative to other methods. See the symposium published in *Economics and Political Weekly* (Banerjee, 2005; Bardhan, 2005; Basu, 2005; Kanbur, 2005; Mookherjee, 2005), as well as Rodrik (2008) and Deaton (2010).
5 This discussion was reignited with the awarding of the 2019 Nobel prize to Abhijit Banerjee, Esther Duflo, and Michael Kremer for their pioneering work in field experiments. See Abramowicz and Szafarz (2020), Deaton (2020), Pritchett (2020), Ravallion (2020), and the other chapters in that volume.
6 Oliver (2010), Macfarlane (2009), Sieber and Tolich (2006), Israel (2015), Kara (2018), Schroeder et al. (2019), and Barrett et al. (2020) are just a few.
7 We follow Kara (2018) in using the word *indigenous* to mean any person, community, or people group that lives in lands colonized or settled by people from other lands. Given the historic movement of people, this definition is not without its problems. Normans are not indigenous to Britain, nor are Arabs to North Africa. We use *indigenous* in a pragmatic way to distinguish between those who work within their own lived context and environment and those, like us as development economists, who work outside our own lived context and environment.
8 For legal reasons it is important to note that, without access to the full universe of Uber rider–partner data, and the subset of data shared with Krueger for the study, it is impossible for us or anyone else to conclusively demonstrate that Uber's control of the data had a material effect on the results in Hall and Krueger (2018).

3

PROJECT DEVELOPMENT

3.1 Introduction

"All happy families are alike; each unhappy family is unhappy in its own way" (Tolstoy, 1878). The first sentence of Leo Tolstoy's novel *Anna Karenina* works not only as a preview of the story – unhappy families, affairs, and, eventually, death – but also as a handy aphorism. While nowhere near as important as creating or choosing a family, Tolstoy's sentiment can be applied to the development of a research idea or project. As Dean Karlan and Jacob Appel detail in their book *Failing in the Field*, unhappy research projects can fall apart in many different ways. However, just as in *Anna Karenina*, certain themes occur and recur. One of those themes is the importance of building a research team and designing the technical aspects of the project.

Consider a story told in Karlan and Appel (2016) regarding a research project run by Karlan, Alberto Chong, and Martin Valdivia in collaboration with a microfinance institution, Arariwa, in Peru in 2009. The idea was to test the impact of multimedia financial education on Arariwa's clients by randomizing who received the educational training. The training included nine in-person meetings with a loan officer lasting 40 minutes, nine videos on DVD that ran between five to seven minutes, a 25-minute radio broadcast, and written homework assignments to gauge learning. Arariwa made loans to "community banks," which were lending groups of 10 to 30 individuals. The design was a simple A–B test, in which half of 666 community banks were randomized to receive all the training and the other half received placebo information on personal health and self-esteem.

Like many other failed projects in Karlan and Appel (2016), the problems in the Peru microfinance project first arose in the development stage. While the upper

DOI: 10.4324/9781003025061-5

management of Arariwa were keen to collaborate, many of the individual loan officers who would be responsible for actual implementation were not. The educational training had a number of parts, including in-person, DVD, radio, and written components, but Arariwa assured the researchers that they could simultaneously implement all of them effectively. Arariwa was confident that loan officers could borrow TVs and DVD players from clients, that attendance by clients at community bank meetings was strong, that all clients had access to radio, and that loan officers would be enthusiastic about their role as teachers of financial literacy. In reality, none of this was true.

As Karlan and Appel (2016) detail, at community bank meetings, attendance was very low. Some members reported to the researchers that they skipped meetings precisely to avoid the educational training. Even among those who did attend, many arrived late or left early because of other obligations. Less than 1 percent of the groups randomized to the treatment completed the entire nine-part course. Despite Arariwa's assurances, loan officers were not able to borrow TVs and DVD players, meaning that few clients actually saw the video. The median group saw only one video, and more than 40 percent of all groups saw no video at all. While it was true that most clients had radios, some lived in regions without reception while others did not know how to tune the radio to the correct radio station. Additionally, program broadcasts were at off-peak times, when many clients were either working or asleep. In total, less than 7 percent of clients listened to the radio program. Perhaps most important, many loan officers did not want to take on the additional work of teaching financial literacy, something they were not paid extra to do. Loan officers did not prioritize the training, often racing through it or skipping it all together.

Karlan, Chong, and Valdivia had developed the project in close collaboration with the management of Arariwa. But, as Karlan and Appel (2016) admit, neither the researchers nor Arariwa's management worked to get buy-in from the loan officers who would be doing the extra work of implementation. The financial literacy training fit into the long-term goals of Arariwa as a company but was a competing priority for the loan officers, who saw their job as giving new loans and collecting on old loans. The research team also failed to spend adequate time in developing and testing the material and implementation plan. The project occurred prior to the adoption of pre-analysis plans (PAPs) by economists, so it would be unfair to expect the researchers to have developed one. But the researchers failed to pilot the project, collaborate with those who would actually be charged with implementing the program, develop plans to manage attrition, or ensure sufficient power in their study in the face of attrition.

As Karlan and Appel (2016) readily admit, with hindsight there were a number of actions the researchers could have taken at the project development stage to help avert future failure. Working more closely with Arariwa and spending more time on the technical design of the experiment are two obvious actions. In our own experience, projects frequently come to us when they are already well into the planning and design stages. Some even come to us after data collection has been completed, when the original implementer realizes something went wrong as is looking for an applied economist who can work some statistical wizardry to make the analysis "work." As Karlan and Appel (2016) and Tolstoy (1878) observe, each unhappy project or family is unhappy in its own way. But equally true, many of the issues have their root at the project development and family formation stage. If more time had been taken in building a research team and developing a PAP – or if Anna had a longer courtship before marrying Karenin – much unhappiness could be avoided.

In this chapter, we focus on two key ideas: the cultivation of a team and the development of a research plan, specifically through the writing of a PAP. We focus throughout on the tools and practices which are integral in developing an initial idea into an actionable project. We also present a pitfall of discounting: the researcher is laying the groundwork for the future and so may engage in discounting – delaying time inputs now with the intent of simply doing it later. But, as we demonstrate throughout, this leaves researchers prone to more difficulties and ethical quandaries throughout the research process. Investment now can pay off later. It is essential to undertake project development carefully to ensure the research is fruitful, but it is also critical to consider the ethical implications of decision made at this phase, as they can have long-lasting impacts. Similar to the previous chapter, in this chapter, many of the activities and decisions we discuss here occur prior to any institutional review or outside the purview of institutional ethical codes of conduct.[1] The fact that the ethics of project development are not often part of the discussion of research ethics does not mean there are no ethical challenges. Rather, the challenges tend to arise from interpersonal power dynamics, our individual cognitive bias, and what Kennedy (2002) referred to (in a different context) as the temptation to "sin in the basement."

The objective of this chapter is to provide an overview and tools on both team development and the use of PAPs in applied economics work. We demonstrate the values, costs, and complexities of working in teams (an increasingly common practices across scientific fields), as well as the cases of using PAPs in both experimental and nonexperimental work. Throughout this chapter, we emphasize the importance of clarity, communication, and investments in time to make a plan before research begins, with the overall goal of improving research experiences and outcomes for all involved.

3.2 The Rise of Team Research in Economics

Historically, economics, like most sciences, was a solo pursuit. One can picture Galileo Galilei, Blaise Pascal, Adam Smith, and Charles Darwin, toiling alone by candlelight to translate the ideas in their head to paper. Behind this independence, was a technological limitation to collaboration. The time, money, and effort made physical travel difficult – even between places as close as Cambridge and Oxford (today, less than two hours by train). Written correspondence, which was prolific between scientists and thinkers, took substantial time to travel between authors.

Before regularly established postal services, correspondence would have to wait until it could be carried by someone making the trip. Collaboration between scientists was simply a logistical challenge.

One can imagine the controversies that could have been avoided, and the knowledge generated, if scientists in the pre-industrial age had been able to collaborate. Imagine if Isaac Newton had been able to chat with Gottfried Wilhelm Leibniz at a conference, instead of both having to work out, in isolation, the details of differentiation and integration. Or imagine if Pierre de Fermat had been able to share via email the details of his last theorem.

The reduction in travel and communication costs brought on by the industrial revolution is one reason for the increase in team research. The career of Louis Pasteur spans this period of the introduction of rapid transit. Whether historically accurate or not, Pasteur is remembered as one of the last great lone scientists, working most of his career alone in his lab, as represented by Albert Edelfelt's famous portrait of Pasteur. But, by the end of Pasteur's career, in the late 1880s, he was the director of a great collaborative lab: the Pasteur Institute. A few years earlier, in 1876, Thomas Edison established his Menlo Park laboratory. As Edison biographer Edmund Morris (2019) argues, Edison's greatest invention was not anything physical but rather was the creation of team-based research. While in popular memory Edison is the sole inventor of the light bulb, the phonograph, and the motion picture camera, these all came out of the collaborative environment that Edison cultivated at Menlo Park. Edison's team-based success was so great that it would be emulated by governments (e.g., Los Alamos), universities (e.g., Jet Propulsion), and companies (e.g., RAND Corp, DuPont Experiment Station, Xerox Palo Alto Research Center) for the rest of the century. The advent of digital communication technologies for sending data, not just written or voice communication, has only accelerated the pace of collaboration in the sciences (Agrawal and Goldfarb, 2008).

The move away from the lone scientist working in a room of his own toward team research was not invented by Edison, nor was it due solely to changes in technology that allowed for cheaper travel and communication. The simple accumulation of scientific knowledge has resulted in the inability of any one person to stay at the leading edge of more than a subfield in their discipline (Jones, 2008). This need for specialization can be seen in the pioneering work of chemists and physicists during the early 20th century. As Rhodes (1986) demonstrates, the development of atomic theory, with the discovery of radiation, and the splitting of the atom all required expertise in a variety of scientific fields and command of various technical skills. The combination of theoretical and experimental researchers at places like the University of Manchester (Ernest Rutherford, Hans Gieger, and others), the University of Paris (Marie and Pierre Curie and others), and Kaiser Wilhelm Gesellschaft (Walter Bothe, Otto Hahn, and others) was key to such discoveries. Theoreticians worked out the mathematics of the

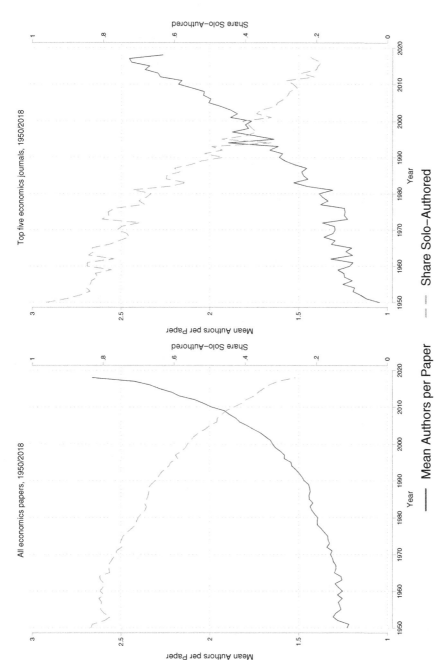

FIGURE 3.1 Rise of Team Size in Economics

Note: Figure displays mean number of authors per paper as well as the share of solo authored papers in all of economics and in the traditional top five journals. Data are from Microsoft Academic Graph (MAG), which indexes 1.7 million papers in economics from 1816–2019. The figure is adapted using data and code from Jones (2021) under CC BY 4.0.

problems while empiricists developed and built the physical devices required to measure and confirm the theory.[2]

While research teams have been the norm in hard sciences for over a century, the move away from independent work in the social sciences only began in the last 40 years. The difference in how research is conducted can be seen in how many people win Nobel Prizes in Chemistry, Physics, and Physiology or Medicine compared with Economics. The average recipients for Nobel Prizes in Chemistry is 1.53 (180 recipients in 117 years). In Physics, an average of 1.85 receive each award (215 recipients in 119 years). In Physiology or Medicine, an average of two people win each award (222 recipients in 111 years). In Economics, however, the average recipients for the Nobel Prize was 1.42 from 1969 through 1999 (44 recipients in 31 years). But, from 2000 through 2020, the average number of recipients of the economics prize is now two (42 recipients in 21 years).

There are a number of different ways to measure the shift from solo research to group research: in terms of patent holders of inventions, intellectual property (IP) owners on software or code, the rise of principal investigator-led economic "labs," the use of non-co-author research assistance, and/or the sourcing of intellectual feedback from outside the formal review process through formal and informal sharing and presentation of the research (Oettl, 2012). We discuss many of these types of collaboration within team research in the next section but here focus on authorship as our measure of team research.

In his paper on the benefits and costs of team research, Jones (2021) documents an increase in multiple authored research papers in economics. Figure 3.1 adapts data and code from Jones (2021) to show the rise in team size in economics. The data for the figure come from the Microsoft Academic Graph (MAG), which indexes 1.7 million papers in economics from 1816 to 2019. The left panel of the figure charts the mean number of authors per paper and the share of solo-authored papers for all economics papers. The right panel presents the same indicators but only for papers published in the so-called Top Five economics journals.

In 1950, the mean number of authors on an economics paper was about 1.25 while papers in the Top Five had even fewer authors, barely more than one. The share of solo-authored papers in economics was over 80 percent, while almost all papers in the Top Five were solo-authored. This began to change in the late 1960s, with the pace accelerating in the 1990s. Despite the greater prevalence of solo-authored papers in the Top Five relative to all economic journals, the change from primarily solo-authored papers to primarily multi-author papers happened quicker in the top five. As of the late 2010s, the share of solo-authored papers in the Top Five was less than those in economics in general.

We can also see how authorship has changed within different fields of economics. The MAG data contain a field for each paper. We map these as close as possible to the *Journal of Economic Literature (JEL)* codes used in economics. Using code from Jones (2021), we then calculate the share of team-authored papers in each field in

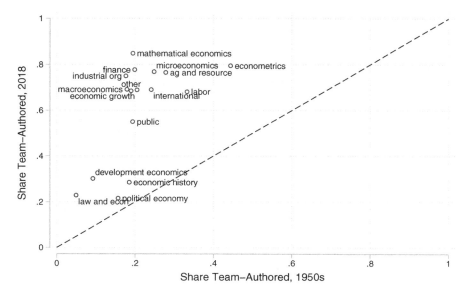

FIGURE 3.2   Team Size in Economic Fields

Note: Figure displays the share of team-authored papers in the 1950s compared to 2018 by field. Data are from Microsoft Academic Graph (MAG), which indexes 1.7 million papers in economics from 1816 to 2019. We sought to match the field codes in MAG as closely as possible to the field codes defined by the Journal of Economic Literature (JEL). The figure is adapted using data and code from Jones (2021) under CC BY 4.0.

the 1950s and plot it against the share of team-authored papers in 2018. Observations above the 45-degree line indicate an increase in the share of team-authored papers.

While team research in economics has lagged behind team research in the hard sciences, data on authorship from the last 70 years shows that is changing. The change is not limited to a set of journals or fields within economics but extends to all of economics and many of the social sciences. In fact, in economics, team-authored papers now generate a bigger impact than solo authored papers, on average (Wuchty et al., 2007). As Jones (2021) notes, the rise in team research appears to be a trend across all disciplines of science. This suggests changing trends, including the reduction in communication costs from technological innovation and the increased need for specialization in knowledge. Regardless of mechanism, team research is more common now than ever before in history, and as such, new researchers should be prepared to learn and collaborate as part of a team.

3.3   Building a Research Team

The process of building and managing a research team, or being a good collaborator within a research team, is not a skill taught in graduate economic programs.

Some students are lucky enough to have research assistantship positions with high productivity professors that have "labs" or research groups that encompass a number of students and other faculty members. But many students (ourselves included) spend their graduate school years either working one-on-one with a single professor or working largely independently, with only minimal guidance from a faculty member. While we very much enjoyed and greatly benefited from the autonomy we had as graduate students, it did mean that we faced a steep learning curve once we became faculty members and began to build our own research group. Some of our learning was from trial and error (with thanks and apologies to our early students who survived this learning process), and much of our learning was from candid discussions with our mentors and senior colleagues.

This section includes a number of things we wish we had known when leaving graduate school. But, what follows is applicable not only to graduate students or to new assistant professors but also to researchers at any stage of their career. In our time working with colleagues of different ages, different genders, different sexual identities, different races, and different nationalities, we have observed a discouraging amount of stasis and rigidity regarding who leads research in the field of applied economics. Those interested in engaging in ethical research will need to grapple with emerging calls from students and faculty favoring identity and lived experience as the most legitimate foundations for research and teaching. For those who engage in international research or those who work with minority or disadvantaged communities, new calls for decolonizing research will need to be heard and taken seriously.

Shifting norms need not be threatening if we as a profession are willing to take them seriously and commit to diversity and inclusion. With that in mind, what follows are considerations when building a successful research team, one that is concerned with producing quality, ethical applied economic research.

3.3.1 *Selecting Peer Collaborators*

As presented in the previous section, the specialization in scientific knowledge and the reduced costs of communication mean that a great deal of work done by economists is now completed in teams. The question then becomes, How to build a team – and then, what sort of team *should* it be? One could form a team of two, in which the team is either a horizontal combination of individuals at a similar place in the profession, or a vertical combination of individuals at different stages. The idea of horizontal and vertical combinations can be easily expanded to a team of more than two. In some cases, teams can be organized along the principle of a "lab," in which there are a number of combinations (graduate students or research assistants) and a limited set of vertical combinations (graduate students with a principal investigator or PI). Each set of combinations has its benefits and costs, in the following.

Outside of the job market paper, one's first publication will almost always be with one's advisor or a more senior colleague. This sort of pairing, a vertical combination of more established (or higher-impact) collaborators with less established (or lower-impact) collaborators, could follow either a "max" or a "min" process. At one extreme, there is a min process in which output is constrained or limited by the abilities of the weakest team member. At the other extreme, there is a max process, in which output is elevated by the abilities of the strongest team member.

If collaboration follows a min process, then there is little incentive for higher-impact individuals to form vertical collaborations, as their output will be diminished by relatively lower-impact colleagues. Nor would there be any value for lower-impact individuals to work with their higher-impact colleagues, as they would not reap any benefits from the collaboration. A min process thus implies that researchers of a similar level should work together. This process is known as positive assortative matching and is the same process described in Becker (1973) in which individuals with similar educational attainment marry each other.

On the other side, if collaboration follows a max process, then individuals would always want to form teams with higher-impact collaborators, a process referred to as negative assortative matching or dis-assortative matching. A max process implies that separating individuals so that each team has one higher-impact researcher would be most efficient for the team on the whole.

Ahmadpoor and Jones (2019) present evidence on whether or not team research follows a min or a max process. To do this, they analyze 24 million research articles written by 13 million individuals from the Web of Science. They find universal evidence for an "averaging down" in terms of the impact of team publications. This result, that collaboration follows a min process with team impact best predicted by the lower-impact members, is true for all fields of research, inclusive of the hard sciences and social sciences. This finding suggests that positive assortative matching is the most efficient way to form research teams, and indeed, Ahmadpoor and Jones (2019) find universal evidence of this.

Based on the evidence, if there is no "averaging up" from collaboration, one can reasonably ask, Why form research teams in the first place? To this, Jones (2021) provides the answer. He shows that a team of two with the same measured publication quality (i.e., not a vertical combination) typically get double the publication impact than the same individual working alone. This suggests that forming horizontal combination collaborations are most useful. Furthermore, this may be even more pronounced, with respect to long-term impact for one's career, for young researchers, who are looking to demonstrate independence from advisors.

The efficient combination of collaborators is its own research topic in economic theory (e.g., Durlauf and Seshardi, 2003). But it provides little insight into what attributes one should look for in those collaborators in order to generate the highest impact or greatest volume of creative output. Schumpeter (1939) views creativity as the combining of existing material in new and fruitful ways. The combination process itself is what generates creative new ideas. Working with a diverse group of people can facilitate this creativity, as collaborators come together bringing the existing material of their own background, experiences, and identities. This combination of diverse perspectives applies not only to diversity in research subject or field of study but also to diversity in ethnic, racial, national, sexual, gender, or religious identities. As discussed in Chapter 2, economic models have understated the role and impact of discrimination through selection bias in research topics that reflect a limited view of how society functions. In economics generally and applied economics specifically, the field remains very male and very white (Hilsenroth et al., 2021). This homogeneity presents a challenge for incorporating the experience and perspectives of underrepresented or marginalized individuals. But it also presents an opportunity, as research teams that contain heterogeneity in their membership's identities may be better positioned to produce high-impact work, compared with research teams that solely embody members who share the same conventional perspective.

The combination of the conventional with the novel, different, or unique is a particularly powerful way to generate creative, high-impact research. Uzzi et al. (2013) study the characteristics of high-impact ideas using a data set of 17.9 million academic papers from the Web of Science. The authors create pairwise combinations of references in each paper's bibliography. They then compare the frequency with which each pair occurs across all citation pairs in that year. Pairs that occur frequently are characterized as conventional while infrequent pairs were characterized as novel. As an example, in Acemoglu et al. (2001) the pairwise combination of citations to a paper in the *Journal of Political Economy* and a paper in the *Quarterly Journal of Economics* would be considered conventional. But the pairwise combination of citations to a paper in the *Journal of the American Statistical Association* and a paper in the *American Historical Review* would be considered novel. Uzzi et al. (2013) find that the most cited ("hit") papers in Web of Science, regardless of the field of study, are those papers with a "high median conventionality" and "high tail novelty." And – important for this section – Uzzi et al. (2013) find that teams, as opposed to solo authors, are most likely to bring forth this creative combination. Hit papers draw on and reference many existing studies within a given field (e.g., many conventional citation pairs). The level of conventionality in hit papers is, in fact, higher than the median level of conventionality within the Web of Science data set. In addition to being highly conventional, hit papers reference many papers not within the field (e.g., many novel citation pairs). Larger or fatter tails in the distribution of citation combinations signify more novel combinations then the typical paper. Papers that combine "high median conventionality" and "high tail novelty" are nearly twice as likely to become a hit than papers that lack this combination.

To further explore these hit papers, Uzzi et al. (2013) then look to see who is best at combining novelty with conventionality to create such a hit.

Papers by solo authors, pairs of authors, or teams (three or more authors) are not significantly different from each other in terms of the level of conventionality. But papers written by pairs of authors and teams are significantly more likely to have "high tail novelty" than solo-authored papers. In fact, team papers are 38 percent more likely to have "high tail novelty" than solo-authored papers. Even among researchers who produce hits when they are the sole author, the same researchers are more likely to produce hits when working as part of a team. Uzzi et al. (2013) conclude that highly cited works are those deeply embedded in existing literature that are also highly novel. While this might sound obvious, the key is that these hit papers bring together a set of unusual combinations.

Summarizing the preceding evidence, teams of researchers are more likely to produce the creative combinations of the conventional and the unique that result in high-impact papers than solo researchers. When forming a research team, one should look to make horizontal combinations of colleagues who are at relatively the same level. This is because collaborations tend to follow a min process, meaning positive assortative matching is most efficient. But, within the uniformity of horizontal combinations, teams should look to find members with diverse experience, skills, expertise, and so on. In fact, AlShebli et al. (2018) show that ethnic diversity among team members is strongly correlated with scientific impact, regardless of scientific discipline. The diversity of perspectives on teams helps generate new insights that contribute to that ideal creative combination of conventional and unique.

Despite all of the benefits of team research, collaboration is not without costs. Jones (2021) defines three challenges that team research poses to both the individual team member and the field of economics as a whole:

1. The difficulty of the community to assess and reward an individual's contribution to team research
2. The existing bias within the community to credit team members based on gender, race, or other characteristics
3. The tendency for positive assortative matching to reinforce closed communities of researchers, limiting access for those not already in the high impact networks

When looking to build a research team, one should not underestimate the difficulty in overcoming any one of these challenges.

The first challenge Jones (2021) outlines is the difficulty in determining what an individual contributes to the team effort. In the academy, grant proposals and manuscripts might be developed as part of a team, but promotion and tenure decisions are made at the individual level. When most economic papers were solo-authored, it was straightforward to determine individual performance. But now that the majority of economic research is done in teams, the community lacks a simple way to assess any one person's contribution. This is because, unlike other fields, economics lacks strong norms regarding authorship order. Frequently, but not always, in economics, author order is lexicographic, based on author last name, making it difficult to assess relative contributions. But it is also common for the non-lexicographic orderings to occur, in which the first author is lead author, making the primary contribution to the paper.

In an attempt to clarify issues of author ordering, the American Economic Association (AEA) website now offers an Author Randomization Tool.[3] The goal of the AEA in offering the tool is to provide more information to the community when author order is not randomized. When neither lexicographic ordering nor relative contribution ordering are dominant, it can be difficult to determine the meaning a hypothetical citations, such as Josephson and Michler (2023). Does Josephson come first because J precedes M in the alphabet? Or does Josephson come first because she contributed more to the work than Michler? If random author ordering were the norm instead of lexicographic, then the meaning of Josephson and Michler (2023) would be clear: Josephson provided a greater contribution to the work than Michler. The symbol ⓡ is used to distinguish between random ordering and relative contribution ordering. Thus, Josephson ⓡ Michler (2023) and Michler ⓡ Josephson (2023) both mean something different from Josephson and Michler (2021) as well as from Michler and Josephson (2023). But, until random author ordering becomes the norm in economics, it remains difficult to tell the meaning of Josephson and Michler (2023). While the random author order is specific to economics as a posed solution, there are different methods employed in other fields. In particular, in the hard sciences, the Contributor Roles Taxonomy or "CRediT model" has become increasingly common. We discuss this taxonomy – and its opportunities for applications in economics – in Chapter 7. In brief, while the CRediT model offers the chance for a better demarcation and identification of work by authors, it still requires self-reporting of this information and so may be subject to bias of the included team members who perceive their own work as tremendously important – whether or not it actually is.

To signal one's strength is to work with a wide variety of researchers so that the community can estimate researcher "fixed effects." By working with different individuals or on teams with varied compositions, the community can see one's performance across a variety of settings. If all of one's publications are high quality, regardless of the set of co-authors, it suggests that *you* may be the stronger link. This author "fixed effect" signal becomes stronger if one has a few solo-authored papers in addition to team-authored papers.

While individuals can work to signal the community about their relative contributions to team research, there is little they can do as individuals to address the second challenge raised by Jones (2021). In the absence of strong signals of researcher quality, the members of the community may consciously or unconsciously rely on characteristics of the individual to make judgments. While providing a strong signal regarding one's quality as a researcher may make conscious bias less likely, it is unlikely to have any affect on implicit or unconscious bias.

Sarsons et al. (2021) provide empirical evidence that these biases do indeed exist in promotion and tenure in economics. They compare tenure decisions for male and female economists based on authorship patterns. Female economists are just as likely to receive tenure as their male counterparts when they mostly publish independently – that is, when they are the sole author on their publications. Additionally, male economists who frequently co-author their research are just as likely to receive tenure as their solo-authoring male colleagues. But female economists who frequently co-author are less likely to receive tenure compared to male co-authoring colleagues as well as female solo-authoring colleagues. Thus, female economists are penalized when they choose to primarily co-author papers – a penalty that male economists do not suffer. Quantifying this, Sarsons et al. (2021) report that one additional coauthored paper is associated with a seven percent increase in the probability of tenure for male economists but only a five percent increase in the probability of tenure for female economists.

The final challenge that Jones (2021) notes is the tendency of positive assortative matching to exacerbate inequality in the allocation of resources by reinforcing existing closed networks of researchers. This "access bias" can involve job placement, funding decisions, and publications. A survey from the AEA on climate in the profession reveals a widespread feeling that a closed network exists among those institutions and individuals at the top of the profession (Allgood et al., 2019). There is the sense that economists at elite institutions only form collaborations with other researchers at elite institutions. They control access to the top journals through editor positions, only publishing those within the network. They then dominate funding competitions by dint of their association with elite institutions and their access to elite publications. They then only hire each other's graduate students, perpetuating the closed network through nepotism. While there is a lack of evidence on the extent of this access bias in economics, there is evidence that across geographic distances collaborations tend to form among those who were previously located at the same elite institutions (Jones et al., 2008; Freeman et al., 2015). It is rare for someone at an elite institution to form a long-distance collaboration with someone at a lower ranked institution. Whether this is simply the result of positive assortative matching or evidence of access bias is unclear.

Summarizing the research on selecting peer collaborators, there are substantial benefits for forming research teams with individuals at a similar stage of one's career. This is because the benefits of positive assortative matching are greater than those from negative assortative matching, with respect to publication impact. That is not to say that publication impact is the only consideration when forming a research team. Most graduate students (and we were no exception) benefit tremendously from working with a senior colleague or mentor. This mentor–mentee relationship provides valuable experience, insight, and expertise beyond the value of any resulting publication. But, we recommend, even during graduate school, to begin to form the horizontal combinations that can grow and expand during the early years of one's career. Given publication lags in economics, it is never too early to start searching for collaborative partnerships.

While horizontal combinations based on career stage tend to be more fruitful than vertical combinations, one should take care not to fall into the trap of forming a research team that is homogeneous in terms of other characteristics. Research partnerships can reflect different training, different expertise, and different lived experience – representing diversity across a number of different parameters. Evidence shows this sort of variety helps in generating high-impact research. It also helps in ensuring we are not blind to the views, considerations, and concerns of others. Diversity and inclusion is not just good and ethical social policy. It makes for good – better – research too.

Finally, while there are many well documented benefits to forming a research team, there are also well documented costs, particularly for women in the profession. Understanding these issues, and proactively working to address them as early in one's career as possible, is essential to changing outcomes for both individuals and, ultimately, the profession. As co-authors, we have a policy of switching authorship order with each paper, so that author order is quasi-randomized for our joint work. With our graduate students, we have clearly defined authorship criteria regarding what qualifies as an authorshipworthy contribution and how we determine author ordering.[4] Careful documentation of and transparency in contributions to research can help alleviate some of the existing bias, although the profession should not perpetually put the burden of proof regarding one's contribution on the vulnerable.

3.3.2   The Role of Graduate Students

Graduate students, even within the subdiscipline of applied economics, come from a diversity of backgrounds and have a diversity of interests. Our PhD cohorts at Purdue University were equally split between domestic and international students. Some students (like Anna) joined the PhD program after going straight through her undergraduate and MSc programs. Other students (like Jeff) took several years off between undergraduate work and the PhD program, working, living abroad, and studying other topics before settling on economics. Students had varied research interests and varied goals in obtaining a PhD. Some students wanted to work in the agriculture industry, some wanted to work for the World Bank or other international organizations, some wanted to work for the government in their country of birth, and some wanted to get a faculty position at a research university.

At our current institution, the University of Arizona, we have a Master of Science (MSc) program but no PhD program. The diversity of background and goals among our MSc students is just as varied as it was among our PhD cohort at Purdue, graduate students. Our students have come from Kenya, Zimbabwe, Bangladesh, California, New Hampshire, and Florida. Some have wanted to work in industry, some in government, and some wanted to go on and earn a PhD, either in applied economics or related fields, like public policy.

But, within all this diversity, graduate students (and undergraduate research assistants) share a common set of duties. These duties include adherence to employment or scholarship contracts, student codes of conduct related to academic integrity, nondiscrimination, and anti-harassment, and a duty to avoid research misconduct. Many forms of research misconduct are covered by university codes of academic integrity, which have strict rules (and correspondingly harsh punishments) about "purposely reporting inaccurate results, copy another's data, pretending someone else's words are yours, or using other unapproved means to get academic credit" (Comstock, 2013). Other forms of research misconduct are governed by the norms of the profession, which are formed around the researcher's responsibility to society at large. These include norms regarding "truth-telling, accuracy of reporting findings, trying to make research understandable, and being honest about both the successes and failings of a research project" (Oliver, 2010).

In addition to one's obligations to the university and society at large, student researchers have ethical obligations to their faculty advisor(s). Similarly, faculty have ethical obligations to their students. Working with graduate students (from the professor's perspective) or working with faculty advisors (from the [under] graduate student's perspective) is challenging because it is a vertical combination and hierarchical power relationships are always open to abuse. The most talked about abuses in the student–faculty relationship are harassment and discrimination (Calarco, 2020). But the student–faculty relationship may suffer from other types of dysfunction (Johnson and Huwe, 2002). A common issue is student overwork and faculty under-mentoring. Students often find themselves overloaded with work as professors try to extract as much productivity from the student as possible. Or, alternatively, the professor has simply forgotten how steep the learning curve can be for students and has expectations that are out of line with the possible. Once something has become rote for a professor, it can be easy to forget how difficult that skill was once to learn – and, as such, expectations rapidly fall out of line with appropriateness for student skill and job. Exacerbating this overwork is under-mentoring. Faculty are generally not rewarded for mentorship in promotion and tenure cases. Rather, rewards accrue to faculty who generate external funding and who publish a large quantity of high-quality papers. With this incentive structure, it is understandable, though not excusable, for faculty to exploit graduate student labor to the detriment of graduate student mentoring.

Setting aside the types of abuse which are illegal or violate university rules regarding interpersonal relations, we focus on responsibilities and obligations where ethical issues are implicit. In our experience, the most difficult conversations we have had as students with our advisors and as professors with our students is the assignment of intellectual property (IP) rights and, by extension, the determination of authorship credit. Due to the power dynamic inherent in student–professor relations, the situation is most frequently one of students believing their professors are making a greater claim to IP rights and co-authorship credit than the professor deserves. In extreme cases, the professor may actually engage in IP theft, taking or adapting a student's idea and publishing it on their own.

Two institutions exist to assist in assigning IP rights and protecting the victims of IP theft. First is the legal code that governs IP, and the second are the social norms that govern professional conduct, as mentioned in Chapter 2. When it comes to protecting ideas, IP law is not particularly effective, as the legal requirements to prove ownership of an idea are onerous. Regarding social norms, their effectiveness in governing IP disputes is debatable. While researchers do not want to get a bad reputation as someone who steals their students' ideas, it may be difficult to define how much of an idea really belongs to someone. If the profession is uncertain about the extent of individual ownership of a research idea, then strong social norms cannot form to protect those who view themselves as victims of IP theft. In student–faculty relationships, where the professor is providing education and guidance on research design and research methods, providing funding, access to resources, and access to data, the professor might view as justified claiming at least partial ownership in a student's ideas. This is particularly true in bench sciences, where discoveries in a lab are often "owned" by the scientist whose lab it is (or by the university in which the lab is situated!).

Even if a faculty member is not trying to steal or deny credit to a student for a research idea, interpersonal conflict around IP ownership can arise. As both students and faculty, we have found the best way to avoid these conflicts is address them before they arise by establishing clear and consistent guidelines for the student–faculty working relationship and clear expectations regarding what constitutes authorship on a paper. As we referenced earlier, the CRediT model provides an opportunity for negotiating this attribution. We ourselves have developed our own criteria, building on the CRediT taxonomy and adapting it to our work as applied economists. While establishing guidelines early in the process may reduce the potential for conflict, it is unlikely to completely eliminate the opportunities for abuse. The faculty mentor will always have power that can be imposed on the graduate student. And even when using a system like CRediT, students may feel obliged to be overly generous with crediting the senior author (Comstock, 2013; Jones, 2021).

Even after the co-authorship issue is resolved, how the profession assigns value to each author's contribution can cause consternation or conflict. This is because in the profession perspectives on who gets credit in faculty–student coauthored papers are mixed. As Ahmadpoor and Jones (2019) show, research tends to follow a min process in which publication impact is most correlated with lower-impact team members – in this case the student. This "averaging down" effect suggests that a professor's publications with a student are likely to be lower impact than if the research was undertaken with a colleague as part of a horizontal combination. However, there is a common perception among graduate students that faculty co-authors are often free riders on student research, with faculty using their position of power to add their name to research where they made little to no contribution. These opposing perceptions are succinctly summarized in Figure 3.3, which presents a screenshot of a thread on

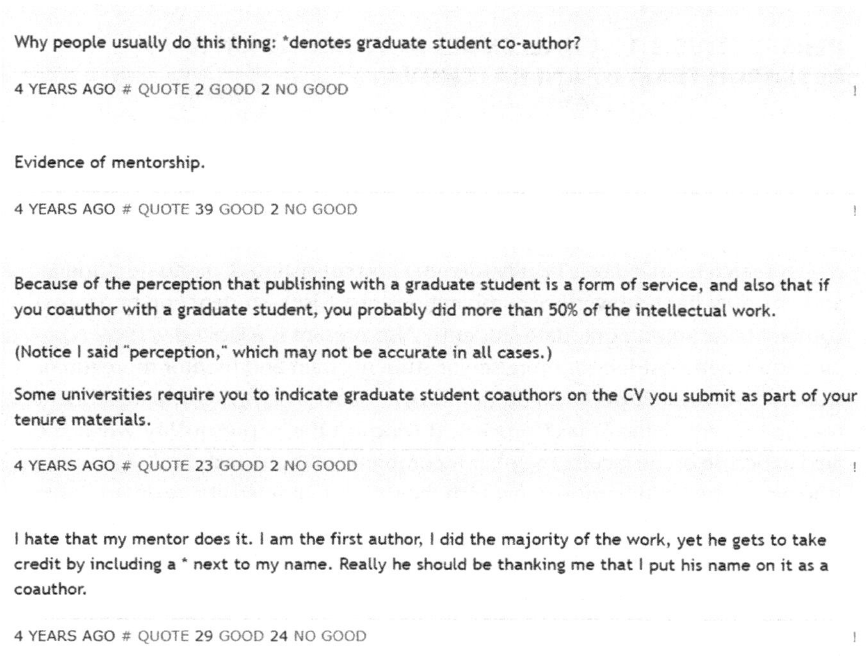

Why people usually do this thing: *denotes graduate student co-author?

4 YEARS AGO # QUOTE 2 GOOD 2 NO GOOD   !

Evidence of mentorship.

4 YEARS AGO # QUOTE 39 GOOD 2 NO GOOD   !

Because of the perception that publishing with a graduate student is a form of service, and also that if you coauthor with a graduate student, you probably did more than 50% of the intellectual work.

(Notice I said "perception," which may not be accurate in all cases.)

Some universities require you to indicate graduate student coauthors on the CV you submit as part of your tenure materials.

4 YEARS AGO # QUOTE 23 GOOD 2 NO GOOD   !

I hate that my mentor does it. I am the first author, I did the majority of the work, yet he gets to take credit by including a * next to my name. Really he should be thanking me that I put his name on it as a coauthor.

4 YEARS AGO # QUOTE 29 GOOD 24 NO GOOD   !

FIGURE 3.3   Perceptions of Graduate Student–Faculty Co-Authors

Note: Screen capture from socjobrumors.com from a thread titled "* denotes graduate student co-author."

the website socjobrumors.com, a sociology-focused offshoot of the economics-focused econjobrumors.com.

The student–faculty relationship in economics traditionally was a one-on-one relationship. The move to team research means that more and more economists are emulating the "lab" structure of bench science. This may be more prevalent in applied economics departments, which are typically in colleges of agriculture and life science, where labs are standard. This means that more and more frequently graduate students exist within an ethical network of obligations to their fellow student collaborators, in addition to the faculty with whom they work. Working in a lab has its own challenges. For faculty, there is the need to generate funds, manage personnel, find students to fill gaps, and replace students when they graduate. It can also be difficult to monitor student work to ensure workflow is efficient and projects stay on time. For student, it can be difficult to find one's place, know lab expectations, understand that work on a project might not lead to authorship, get one-on-one time with the professor, and work with others closely. Again, we highly recommend Calarco (2020) and Bellemare (2022a) for advice on how to manage these interpersonal challenges.

PERSPECTIVE 3.1   CHALLENGES IN WORKING ON A RESEARCH TEAM BY ANI KATCHOVA

While an advisor–student collaboration is prevalent in the applied economics field, a faculty member may have an opportunity to build a research team of graduate students and postdoctoral researchers as part of an endowed program, a grant opportunity, or a research project.

A research team led by a faculty member and consisting of graduate students and postdocs has both vertical combinations of advisor–student and horizontal combinations among graduate students. Also present is a limited vertical combination when postdocs or more senior students train and mentor more junior students. A research paper co-authored by an advisor and a graduate student may follow either the "max" process, driving up the paper quality when the field expertise of the faculty member is combined with the technical skills of the student, or the "min" process, in which the student's limited ability drives down the paper quality, which can sometimes be remedied with additional mentoring. The most successful graduate students tend toward the max process, driving the visibility and success of work by the research team and program.

There is a well-documented shift from solo to team-based research in economics with a rising number of co-authored publications. However, a PhD student still needs to produce a solo-authored paper or a paper co-authored with the advisor that would become part of their dissertation. Therefore, graduate students may not be able to fully benefit from horizontal collaborations with their fellow students on the same research team. Even so, there are benefits for students to be part of a research team. One benefit is when the more senior students train and mentor the more junior students either directly or indirectly (via team meetings and presentations and by providing examples and feedback). Another benefit of a research team is when the paper topics of the team members are closely aligned so that aggregation of knowledge can occur by working on the same data sets, with the same agency, or using the same models and coding. Finally, there are opportunities for horizontal collaboration among graduate students to produce joint outreach reports or closely related outreach reports that become part of a theme. While there are benefits to having closely aligned topics in a research team, the research topics within a research team are most frequently diverse to reflect student interests or grant and research opportunities.

Managing a research team with close horizontal collaborations may also have disadvantages, particularly when an unsatisfactory performance or personal issues of a team member may affect the rest of the team members. The multigenerational aspect of the vertical collaboration may also present challenges when the advisor, who may value autonomy and independent work may need to grow their mentoring and leadership style to provide a working environment and incentives for graduate students who may value teamwork, learning opportunities, frequent feedback and interactions, and strong mentoring.

3.3.3 Working with Nonacademic Collaborators

For those in the academy, working with nonacademic collaborators has its own unique set of ethical and logistical challenges. These challenges arise because the objective function and constraints that an academic researcher and their institution are trying to optimize over is different than the optimization problem for a non-academic researcher and their institution. What qualifies as a successful research outcome may look very different for a researcher at a university, a researcher at a for-profit corporation, and a researcher at a government agency. Additionally, the workplace environment, with its expectations and constraints, defines a different set of parameters for each researcher. Incorporating these individual objective functions, with their constraints, into a team objective function is a daunting task. Yet, as Uzzi et al. (2013), AlShebli et al. (2018), and others have shown, there can be great rewards for building a research team with a diversity of experiences and perspectives.

Potentially the most challenging aspect of academic collaboration with non-academics is the differences in objective function. While all researchers would view a successful project as one that has high impact, how impact is measured differs by institutional setting. In academia, impact is typically measured by the journal in which an article is published and by the number of citations to that article. For a researcher in a for-profit organization, impact is typically measured by the return on investment in the project. For a researcher at a nonprofit, intergovernmental organization (IGO), nongovernmental organization (NGO), or governmental agency, impact is likely measured in terms of "policy changes." A policy change can be measured in a number of ways: a change in statute; an allocation or reallocation of budget; an organizational realignment that expands the power or purvey of an agency or institution; the winning of votes for an initiative or the election of a favored candidate. This differences in objective play an important role in defining the terms of research collaborations and partnerships.

Researcher objectives are endogenous to the institutional environment the researcher finds themself in. As discussed in Chapter 1, when we talk about research ethics we are really talking about a set of norms that we, as a scientific community, would like to see govern individuals and collective action within the community. As Anderson et al. (2007) show, subscription to Mertonian norms is a function of whether a research is in a private, for-profit institution, as opposed to an academic or nonprofit institution. Researchers in for-profit institutions are more likely to subscribe to the counter-norms than researchers in other types of institutions. If research impact is measured by return on investment in for-profit firms, then researchers in those firms have a strong incentive to maintain secrecy, pursue self-interestedness (for the firm), and rely on administration to direct research focus. This is not to suggest that research at for-profit companies is inherently unethical. Rather, collaboration with nonacademic researchers presents a challenge given the differences in objective functions and institutional environment.

In addition to differences in objective functions differences in workplace environment can create challenges for collaborators. Unlike most workplace environments, the academic environment for researchers tends to lack hard deadlines. Yes, classes are offered on a schedule. And there is likely a looming deadline for a grant application. But the research process, uncertain and sprawling, has no real deadline. For those in academic careers, the lack of deadlines is both a benefit and a burden. It allows researchers to explore new ideas, improve on research design, run a few more robustness checks, and proofread the manuscript one last time. Yet the lack of deadlines for submitting any given research product or manuscript to a journal means one can put off completing a project almost indefinitely. In this situation it can be very easy to allow the perfect to be the enemy of the good.

The lack of hard deadlines for much of applied economic research in academia can also create problems when collaborating with nonacademic partners. For those in business or government institutions there are often hard deadlines for delivering results. This could be reports to management about product effectiveness or market analyses that are critical to a release date. Or it could be reports to congressional committees or state agencies regarding economic impact analyses that is required for hearings, budgets, or audits. For academics used to taking their time to perfect a research design or a manuscript, the need to deliver research output on a deadline can create interpersonal and/or intra-team conflict.

Another source of potential conflict when working with nonacademic collaborators is simply the pace of activity. In a meeting we had with the CEO of a weather technology start-up to discuss working together, the difference in business and academic timelines was an immediate hurdle. The company had a very strong social responsibility statement and had funded a 501(c)(3) nonprofit organization to facilitate the use of their technology to improve the prospects for individuals in developing countries. Initially, there was a lot of excitement about the opportunity to conduct rigorous evaluations of the technology to demonstrate its impact in a developing-country setting. However, the CEO was shocked when we discussed the typical duration of a research project from inception to results. This included a month or two for developing the research idea and design for submission as a grant proposal. Then months waiting to hear back if the grant was successful. Then a month or two before the funding was in place. Then a year or two to conduct the randomized control trial (RCT) and write a report. For the CEO, whose company had only existed for a couple years, collaborating in a years long project was a nonstarter. In this case, the pace of academic research and the pace of business for a tech start-up was simply incompatible. The incentives were aligned for a successful collaboration but we could not satisfy the time constraints for both of us simultaneously.

Yet another source of potential conflict in working with nonacademics is the creation of IP. For those who work in a university system, one's research output while on the job is owned by the university. Thus, when collaborating with businesses, it can be challenging to negotiate and navigate ownership of the IP produced from the research. Layered onto the issue of IP is the frequent need for confidentiality or NDAs. Issues of IP and confidentiality are not limited to academic–private business collaborations. For us, these issues have arisen in contract negotiations with IGOs and NGOs. As an example, one issue which arose had to do with the organization's request for confidentiality regarding the terms of the agreement. The issue was that we work at a state university which requires compliance with Arizona's open records law. Thus, any contract would become a public record, and as a result, the university could not treat the contract as a "confidential" document. Furthermore, as state employees our emails and communications are subject to Freedom of Information Act (FOIA) requests. This makes confidentiality a difficult item to negotiate. Another conflict had to do with the assignment of IP and copyright. Luckily for us, the monetary value to the university of the data, code, and publications we as applied economists produce is very small. Still, it has required substantial legal wrangling to get these sort of agreements in place. In our most recent experience, it took eight months from the time that our nonacademic partner organization issued a contract and the final signing by both parties of the negotiated agreement.

All theses issues are only potential sources of conflict. In most cases, through patience, diligence, clear communication, and persistence, we have been able to overcome the issues and establish productive relationships. We have collaborated with individuals in business, at NGOs and IGOs, in the U.S. federal government, and with Cooperative Extension services in governments around the world. These partnerships pose challenges, both interpersonal and institutional. An awareness of these potential sources of conflict, and a commitment to collaborative transparency has allowed us to overcome interpersonal challenges. For institutional hurdles, such as IP and confidentiality, we have found that a clear articulation of what might be called the value proposition, that is, why the potential partnership is of value to the institutions themselves, is key to breaking through institutional inertia.

3.3.4 Working WITH Local Partners

For economists working in a wide variety of contexts, although in particular those working outside the country of their institution, a collaboration with a local partner is an essential part of the research process. A local partner is the person or person on the ground, where the research is occurring. This individual or individuals are often responsible for integral work which must be done in person, in order for research to take place. This might include recruiting enumerators, defining survey locations, organizing logistics, or any number of tasks that are imperative for the execution of a successful research program. Despite the importance of these relationships to research success, local partners are often left out of the discussion regarding idea development and authorship attribution.

As with all collaborations that we have discussed, there are challenges. In fact, working with local partners combines the challenges of collaborating with students and the challenges of collaborating with nonacademics. The relationship between researchers at Western academic institutions and local partners frequently reflect a power dynamic similar to that of advisor and student. And, similar to collaboration with nonacademics, local partners frequently have very different objective functions and constraints from those researchers in academia. For academic researchers, particularly those working in an international development setting, these challenges are frequently used as excuses for not integrating local researchers and institutions into one's research team. The resulting exclusion of local researchers and institutions from much of the research process has not only implications for research but also ethical implications resulting from colonization and representation in the social sciences. We believe that by understanding the challenges inherent in these collaborative relationships and having the difficult conversations about those challenges, we as a profession can do a better job of building strong partnerships with local collaborators.

There are a number of potentially challenges in working with local partners. Consider, first the perhaps most obvious and pernicious challenge: the relationship often contains an asymmetric power dynamic. One party is based at Western institutions, is relatively resource-rich, and frequently engages in international research collaborations. Kweik (2020) calls these researchers "internationalists." Their research may not have an international focus. In fact, their research may be exclusively domestic or very localized.[5] But these internationalists compete internationally for research funding, their research is published in indexed journals, and they have professional recognition. Their research is produced for and consumed by the international market. By contrast, Kweik (2020) defines "local" researchers as those who work in relatively resource-poor institutions, infrequently engage in international collaborations, and, for various reasons, are largely shut out of competing in the international research market. Because of differences in resources and professional prestige, "internationalists" will tend to hold the power in collaborations with "locals."

One place where we see this asymmetric power dynamic reflected is in how frequently local researchers are included as co-authors on final published, peer-reviewed journal articles. Hedt-Gauthier et al. (2019) provide evidence on the marginalization of local researchers in co-authored research from the medical profession. Their work investigates the population of health research papers in PubMed from 2014 to 2016 that focus on a single sub-Saharan African country. This corresponds to 7,100 papers with 43,429 authors. Overall, 54 percent of all authors and 53 percent of first authors on a paper were from the country of the paper's focus. But the share of authors from the country of focus dropped if a paper has an author from an institution in the U.S., Canada, or Europe. When papers had an "internationalist" author from one of these regions, the share of authors from the country of focused dropped to about 45 percent. The drop in representation was most pronounced in the first author position. For papers with an author affiliated with a top U.S. university, only 22 percent had a research from the country of focus in the first author position – compared to 53 percent of papers overall. Over the entire sample, 14 percent of papers had no author from the country of focus.[6]

The evidence from Hedt-Gauthier et al. (2019), while not definitive, is suggestive regarding the systematic exclusion or marginalization of "local" researchers. And we believe the evidence is strong enough to encourage academic research to actively work toward greater inclusion of local partners in the publication of research outputs. A first step is recognizing that we, as individuals and as a profession, have, consciously or unconsciously, failed to build collaborative relationships in which our local partners can participate as co-authors. While recognition is a first step, we also need to undertake tangible actions toward strengthening collaborations with local partners. And this leads us to the second challenge, which is that "local" researchers frequently have different objective functions and operate in different institutional environments than their "internationalist" collaborators.

As discussed in Section 3.3.3, differences in researcher and institutional objectives can create challenges in building successful research teams. The literature on why collaborations fail is too broad to review here, but we can focus on a few themes that influence success, based on research by Porter and Birdi (2018). Drawing on our own experience, we focus on following four questions:

- Who should be involved?
- How to get everyone to work together effectively?
- How to design the process?
- How to keep the process on track?

Answering these questions is useful whenever one forms new collaborative relationships, but we find them particularly useful when engaging with local partners. In asking who should be involved, it is not enough to be open to participation from all potential stakeholders. Many stakeholders who want to participate may lack the capacity to participate. We as "internationalists" need to dedicate resources (including energy, time, funds) to ensuring interested local partners can actively engage in the project. This includes capacity building and knowledge transfer to help bridge the academic–practitioner gap (Parker et al., 2020).

In asking how to get everyone working together, attention needs to be paid to promoting inclusive and diverse perspectives. Naritomi et al. (2020) discusses this in the context of RCTs, which require in-depth knowledge of the local environment and thereby creates opportunities for including different values, norms, and cultures to ensure local participation. In working together efficiently, being sensitive to power imbalances, establishing clear decision and process rules, and being willing to engage in difficult conversations are all important themes for successful collaboration (Porter and Birdi, 2018).

Many of the examples Karlan and Appel (2016) cite involve breakdowns in internationalist–local collaborative relationships at the research design stage before the research is even off the ground. Often these breakdowns are due to an attempt to implement research in an inappropriate setting, a technical design flaw, or a failure to understand the demands placed on local partner organizations. In our experience, establishing a realistic timeline is particularly challenging. As an example, consider economists focused on agricultural development. For these economists, data collection frequently needs to occur during harvest. This can place a tremendous pressure on research timelines, causing breakdowns in collaborative relationships. Sufficient planning and communication to avoid time crunches and the resulting frustrations are crucial to avoiding conflict in relationships with local partners.

These logistical points, however, offer opportunity for improved collaboration. The design phase of research is an ideal time to build engagement and strengthen local ownership of the process by capturing multiple realities and voices (Zaveri, 2020). The data that we as internationalist researchers are interested in may not be the data points that the local researcher, local implementing partner, or the local community are interested in. And so, formulating a research design that can answer questions of interest for all parties is vital to building effective and resilient collaborations. Furthermore, checking in and ensuring that the objectives of all parties are still being served throughout the research process provides an opportunity to keep the relationship on track throughout the research process.

Laying a strong foundation by building an inclusive and engaged research team is only useful if one has a plan for keeping the process on track. After all, a foundation is just that – the ground on which we build our research. To keep the process on track, we believe it is essential to (1) establish clear roles and responsibilities, (2) ensure clear methods for evaluating and measuring outcomes, and (3) articulate clear decision and process rules (Porter and Birdi, 2018). These three item are essential components to establishing effective processes in any organizational environment. But, as research-focused economists, we have begun to adopt a new tool for incorporating these items into not only our collaborative relationships but also into the research design process itself. This tool is a PAP.

PERSPECTIVE 3.2 BUILDING INTERDISCIPLINARY RESEARCH TEAMS BY RICARDO LABARTA

Applied economics has the potential to contribute to multidisciplinary research. It uses economic frameworks to analyze different problems that are identified from other disciplines. Therefore, the use of economic theory and associated economic tools and approaches will require a close interaction with researchers/professionals with different backgrounds and to understand where distinct research questions come from. This is particularly evident in the field of international agricultural development.

Agricultural researchers and development practitioners that are (1) aiming at developing innovations (technological, policy, institutional, etc.) and (2) contributing to meet sustainable development goals (poverty reduction, food/nutrition security, environmental sustainability, etc.) are keen to get insights on whether their work can offer solutions to real-world problems. These professionals are, on one hand, subject to their disciplinary biases and expectations and, on the other hand, are under constant pressure to show positive returns to their project investments in the short term. It is, however, important to keep in mind the uncertainties around developing agricultural innovations and the fact that results are usually feasible and observable only in the long term. Finding the right balance between rigorous applied economic analysis and the short-term needs of these professionals is an important challenge.

There are plenty of opportunities for relevant applied economics research proposed and even funded by agricultural research/development organizations. However, before starting any research project, it is imperative to understand the key objectives that partner organizations are expected to achieve with collaborative work. Being clear from the beginning on the role, contributions, and research questions of mutual interest between the applied economist and the organization members is the core of successful collaborative research. As such, one of the key messages to keep in mind is that the work of the applied economist must be governed by research ethics and scientific rigor. At the same time, it is important to frame collaboration as a learning experience where the objective is not to assess the performance of the agricultural researcher/development practitioner but to offer insights on how to improve their own work. Showing the collaborators the value of economic analysis and the benefits they can obtain can improve the probability of a successful collaboration.

Acknowledging that professionals from different disciplines and backgrounds bring distinct perspectives and often have particular frameworks for analytical work is critical. It is worth investing the time in working with these perspectives and objectives that a research project may have in order to keep the expectations of the economic analysis at the right level. In addition, it is important not to assume that everyone is familiar with the economic concepts and approaches, and the use of simplified language may be necessary. When possible, it would be beneficial to bring to the table applied economists from the partner institution that speak the same language and that could be the main mechanism for clear communication and understanding. Providing the right incentives for these economists (i.e., co-authorship in publications) will facilitate strong integration.

Selecting a team of collaborators to design a relevant applied economics project is challenging. Understanding the sensitivities and different perspectives is the starting point. Having a clear understanding of team responsibilities and recognizing their contributions can make the work successful.

3.4 Developing a Pre-Analysis Plan (PAP)

Developing a research team is just one step on the path of developing a successful research program. Another, still nascent but rapidly expanding, component of project development is formulating a PAP. At its most basic, a PAP is a document that, prior to any analysis taking place, defines how the researcher plans to analyze a set of data while answering a hypothesis or several hypotheses. However, what specifically gets included in a PAP is still somewhat up for debate (Humphreys et al., 2013; Coffman and Niederle, 2015; Olken, 2015; Christensen and Miguel, 2018; Duflo et al., 2020; Janzen and Michler, 2021). There are substantial differences in what might be included, based on the overall thoroughness of the final PAP. Depending on how thorough a PAPA is, and depending on the academic field in which it is used, the plans can be referred to as a statistical analysis plan, a hypothesis registration, or a prespecified research design. Frequently these plans are registered in a repository, where they receive a timestamp that lets future researchers know when the plan was filed and that it was filed prior to data collection or analysis. This timestamp and public availability of the plan are essential components to the role that PAPs can play in conducting ethical research .

Developing a PAP and registering a PAP are often referred to as a single action, with the implication that the two go hand in hand and thus accomplish the same goal. However, the purpose of a PAP and the purpose of a registry of prespecified plans or hypotheses are quite distinct in terms of the ethical issues they are designed to resolve. The development of a PAP are designed to protect against *p*-hacking or other forms of unethical behavior at the data analysis stage while the purpose of the repositories in which PAPs are filed are to solve the so-called file-drawer problem. The file-drawer problem describes a type of publication bias in which studies that do not produce significant results are less likely to be published than those that produce significant results (Rosenthal, 1979). So, while the creation of a PAP and its deposit in a registry can go hand in hand, they are distinct actions working to solve distinct problems. As such, one can develop a PAP and never register it with a repository. Alternatively, one can simply register a list of hypotheses to be tested with a repository, something that many in the economics field would consider inadequate as a PAP. Regardless, simply writing a plan or putting it online is not sufficient to address both problems which PAPs are intended to rectify.

The goal of a PAP is to form a Ulysses pact that binds the researcher to implementing the plan, regardless of what the results might be (Janzen and Michler, 2021). The term *Ulysses pact* comes from the legal profession and refers to a pre-commitment device that binds a person to a specified future commitment or action. The plan will typically define the hypotheses to be tested, the data to be collected or used, how key variables are to be created, the econometric model to be estimated, and a description of any subgroup analysis. The purpose of such a pact is to reduce the researcher's degrees of freedom, by which we mean the inherent flexibility a researcher has in collecting, cleaning, and analyzing data. Absent such a pact, the researcher may be inclined to analyze many versions of the data but only report versions of the data that produce significant results (data dredging), estimate many models but only report the ones that yield the "correct" results (specification search), reanalyze the data, and reestimate the models to arrive at a target result (p-hacking), or Hypothesize After Results are Known (HARKing) by presenting results as arising from *a priori* hypotheses. A Ulysses pact not only allows the researcher to confirm the hypotheses that were preregistered, it also allows the researcher to take advantage of all the statistical power at their disposal. A well-documented PAP can allow researchers to use one-sided tests (instead of the two-sided tests typically used in economics), as well as avoid the loss of power from correcting for the problem of multiple inference.

Because the purpose of the PAP is to bind the researcher to the plan they committed themselves to, that plan must be filed with a reputable third party. In economics, this is frequently with a social science or open science registry.[7] But using one of the repositories is not the only way to credibly commit oneself to the plan. A growing number of journals now accept what they term registered reports. The plan, including motivation and literature review, are submitted to the journal, which then reviews and either accepts or rejects the plan based on the merits of the research idea. We discuss registered reports in more detail in Chapter 7 on research dissemination.

Recall that the use of a repository for registering an analysis plan has a different purpose than the repository itself. The development and filing of a PAP is designed to protect against p-hacking or other forms of unethical behavior at the data analysis stage. The purpose of the repositories themselves are to solve the file drawer problem. In principle, the file drawer problem is similar to the drunkard's search, when only results supporting Conclusion A see the light of day, the evidence appears to point to Conclusion A. But this is only due to an absence of visible light or published evidence on Alternative Conclusion B. The goal of repositories or registries is to document all research undertaken on a given topic. One can conduct meta-analysis using the published evidence and the hypotheses registered in the repository and determine the extent of the file-drawer problem or publication bias (Christensen et al., 2019). In Chapter 7, we present evidence of the extent of publication bias in social science and applied economics and discuss possible solutions to rectify the problem, in addition to the potential of PAPs, which we discuss here.

3.4.1   A Brief History of PAPs and Registries

The registration of statistical analysis plans has been required by law in the U.S. for any drug trials since 1997 (Casey et al., 2012). The primary purpose of the law and the registry creating ClinicalTrials.gov was to counter the strong incentives of drug companies to falsify research on the effectiveness of the drugs they develop. While the law governed drug trials in the U.S., other clinical and medical trials, and drug trials outside of the U.S., did not need registration. This changed in 2004 when the twelve journals belonging to the International Committee of Medical Journal Editors (ICMJE) announced that public trial registration would be a prerequisite for publication in any of the journals (De Angelis et al., 2004). Prior to the change in editorial policy,

ClinicalTrials.gov averaged 1,879 registrations per year. Since the change in policy, the average number of new registrations made each year at ClinicalTrials.gov is 22,088.[8]

The reasoning of the editors for requiring pre-registration was different than the reason the U.S. government required registration. De Angelis et al. (2004) state that the purpose of the new policy is to combat selective reporting, that is, the file drawer problem (Franco et al., 2014). The concern is that researchers and journals are more excited about new results that are large in magnitude and are statistically significant than about small magnitude or nonsignificant findings. Results that simply confirm previous work or are not statistically significant (a null result) are frequently ignored. The result of this publication bias is a distortion of the scientific record. De Angelis et al. (2004) write that "anyone should be able to learn of any trial's existence and its important characteristics." Learning what works and what does not work is essential in science – and without publishing null results, we only see part of the picture in the full scope of scientific progress and investigation.

Most economists first became aware of PAPs in the work of Casey et al. (2012) and Finkelstein et al. (2012), both published in the same year in the *Quarterly Journal of Economics* (Humphreys et al., 2013; Coffman and Niederle, 2015; Olken, 2015; Christensen and Miguel, 2018). Because both of these papers are RCTs, and because researchers at the Abdul Latif Jameel Poverty Action Lab (JPAL) were early proponents of PAPs, economists have almost exclusively focused on using PAPs for experimental work. In fact, the AEA Registry restricts submissions to only experiments.

Somewhat surprisingly then, is the fact that the first use of a PAP in economics, to our knowledge, was for a nonexperimental study. The paper, Neumark (2001), is a study of the the employment effects of a change in federal minimum wage. According to an editorial accompanying the article (Levine, 2001), the idea of a prespecified study came from Alan Krueger. Krueger, according to Levine (2001), suggested the journal *Industrial Relations* publish a series of studies examining the effects of the 1996 and 1997 minimum wage increase. Research in the 1990s on the employment effects of the minimum wage had produced widely varied results, with some papers reporting large positive impacts and others reporting moderate negative impacts. As Neumark (2001) notes in his paper, not only did results vary from study to study, but multiple studies by the same author or authors also tended to find the same results, suggesting the existence of "author effects," in which an author or authors publish results that confirm or are consistent with their previous published research. Table 3.1 summarizes the motivating table in Neumark (2001). There is a wide variety of findings in the literature, from increases in the minimum wage reducing, increasing, or having no effect on employment. What is perhaps most interesting is that papers by David Card and/or Alan Krueger tend to show a small but significant increase in employment with an increase in minimum wage. Conversely, David Neumark and William Wascher tend to find small but significant decreases in employment with an increase in minimum wage.

Krueger's idea was motivated by the timing and size of the minimum wage increases. As these elements are known ahead of time, researchers could submit to the

TABLE 3.1 Elasticities of Employment with Respect to the Minimum Wage in Different Studies

Study	Workers Studied	Elasticities
Card and Krueger (1994)	Fast-food workers in NJ & PA	+
Card (1992b)	Teenagers nationally (1989–90)	0
Card (1992a)	Teenagers nationally (1987–89)	+
Katz and Krueger (1992)	Fast-food workers in TX	+
Neumark and Wascher (1992, 1994)	Young adults aged 16–24 nationally	−
Card et al. (1994)	Teenagers nationally (1973–89)	+
Kim and Taylor (1995)	Retail workers (1988–89)	
Deere et al. (1995)	Teenagers nationally (1985–93)	
Currie and Fallick (1996)	Young adults aged 14–21 nationally	
Neumark and Wascher (1998)	Fast-food workers in NJ & PA	−

Note: Table summarizes content from Neumark (2001).

journal their econometric specifications to be reviewed and approved by the editor and reviewers. These prespecified research designs would be submitted prior to the wage increase and known to the editors and reviewers, meaning the authors would be effectively committed to a Ulysses pact. After the minimum wage increase, the authors would analyze the data following their prespecified design, and the results would be published regardless of what they showed. The precommitment by the authors would restrict the ability to engage in specification search or *p*-hacking to arrive at a given conclusion. The registering of these prespecified research designs with the journal, and the journal's precommitment to publishing the result-blind papers resolved the file-drawer problem. However, in the end, only Neumark followed through with the idea.

To guard against potential author bias, Neumark developed a PAP in which he described his research question, defined the data to be used and the construction of variables, and wrote out the statistical models he would estimate. As described earlier, the timing was opportune and a key component of the plan was that Neumark (2001) would use government data released at the end of May 1997, allowing him to file the plan with journal editors prior to May 1997.

Even with Neumark's advancements in applying PAPs in economics, it would be a decade before the field rediscovered PAPs. The likely candidate for the second use of a PAP in economics is Casey et al. (2012), who filed their plan more than a year before Finkelstein et al. (2012). The primary reason why they developed and filed an analysis plan was that in their study context, an RCT on strengthening institutions, there were multiple ways one could define and measure "success." Casey et al. (2012) study a program called GoBifo Sierra Leone designed to make institutions more democratic and egalitarian. Program funds were spent on a variety of community-building projects (e.g., schools, latrines, roads) as well as training programs. The overall goal of both the physical infrastructure and the training was to increase collective action, make institutions more egalitarian, increase trust, strengthen community groups, and increase participation in local government. In total, the authors define 12 sets of hypotheses: three regarding the physical infrastructure and nine regarding institutional improvement. There are obviously numerous different ways that one could choose to measure each of these nine hypotheses on institution building. To avoid the temptation of HARKing, the authors developed a PAP and specified their main measure of interest: the mean effect for well-defined measures of each of the nine institutional hypotheses.

The authors illustrate the value of their PAP by showing program effects on their prespecified outcome as well as effects if they cherry-picked results. Table 3.2 summarizes the findings of Casey et al. (2012). When estimating the program effect on their prespecified outcome variable, the authors find no statistically significant impact. The GoBifo program was largely ineffectual at improving institutions. But, the authors then consider: what if there had been no PAP to bind their hands? Casey et al. (2012) go on to show that they could have presented two opposite sets of conclusions: one that showed GoBifo strengthening institutions and the other showing GoBifo weakened institutions. Absent the PAP, and a strong commitment to ethical research, the authors could have written the paper to present any finding they wanted.

TABLE 3.2 Research Degrees of Freedom in Measuring Treatment Effects on Institutions

Outcome Variable	Treatment Effect	Standard Error
A. Main institutional effect		
Mean effect for family of hypotheses	0.03	0.02
B. GoBifo "weakened institutions"		
Attended meeting to decide what to do with the tarp	−0.04*	0.02
Everybody had equal say in deciding how to use tarp	−0.11*	0.06
Community used the tarp	−0.08*	0.04
Community can show research team the tarp	−0.12**	0.05
Respondent would like to be member of Village Development Committee	−0.04**	0.02
Respondent voted in local government election	−0.04**	0.02
C. GoBifo "strengthened institutions"		
Community teachers have been trained	0.12*	0.07
Respondent is a member of women's group	0.06***	0.02
Someone took minutes at most recent meeting	0.14**	0.06
Building materials stored in public place	0.25**	0.10
Chiefdom official did not influence use of tarp	0.06**	0.03
Respondent agrees with "Responsible young people can be good leaders"	0.04**	0.02
Correctly able to name the year of next election	0.04**	0.02

Note: Table is adapted from Christensen et al. (2019), originally from Casey et al. (2012). Significance levels with robust standard errors are *$p < 0.10$, **$p < 0.05$, ***$p < 0.01$.

A second reason that Casey et al. (2012) used a PAP was that the researchers were assessing the effectiveness of a development project whose leaders had a vested interest in a positive outcome. This second reason, to reduce any organizational pressure to come up with favorable results, is an important but underappreciated benefit of PAPs. As mentioned in Section 3.3.4, we find the use of PAPs extremely helpful in setting expectations, defining roles, establishing decision rules, and the like when working with local partners as well as nonacademic collaborators. Finkelstein et al. (2012) provide an early example of using a PAP to help define the scope of work and set expectations in regards to collaborations with a government institution. One of our former students, Ann Furbush, further extended this idea and has worked on establishing parameters for PAPs in industry, in particular in consulting, where a client may have a strong and vested interest in a certain outcome – and there may be pressures at the end of a project to deliver that outcome, in the absence of a defined PAP.

Current trends in economics mimic the medical field, as, similar to medical trials, the use of PAPs by economists has been strongly influenced by journal requirements. In January 2018, the editorial policy at journals published by the AEA began to require registration of all RCTs before publication. This policy is mandatory and applies to both lab and field experiments. As with the ICMJE policy change, there was an immediate uptick in registrations on the AEA RCT Registry. Figure 3.4 shows the number of new registrations per quarter and the cumulative number of registrations.

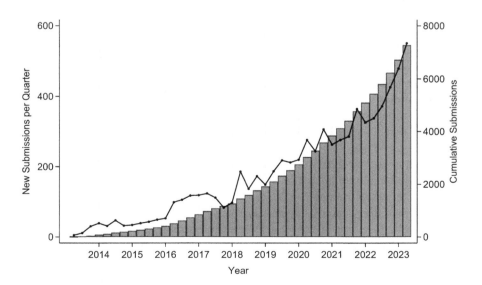

FIGURE 3.4 New and Cumulative Registrations on AEA RCT Registry

Note: Figure displays the number of new registrations per quarter on the AEA RCT Registry along with the cumulative number of registrations. The figure is adapted using code developed by Christensen (2016) under CC BY 4.0.

Looking back, a potential reason why Neumark (2001) is often overlooked is that he developed a PAP for an observational study, not for an experimental one. As noted earlier, the AEA Registry is restricted to experimental studies. Duflo et al. (2020), a team in which several of the authors were responsible for the creation of the AEA registry, state that the registry was designed to be a social science version of ClinicalTrials.gov, with the goal of providing "a list of the universe of randomized control trials (RCTs)." Yet, ClinicalTrials.gov does not restrict registration to experiments. Of the universe of trials registered at ClinicalTrials.gov, 72,801 are observational studies, or about 21 percent of all entries.[9] If the AEA registry seeks to solve the file-drawer problem per De Angelis et al. (2004), then it remains unclear why the registry excludes nonexperimental work.[10]

3.4.2 Contents of PAPs

There is general agreement among researchers among what a basic PAP should contain. The following is adapted from Janzen and Michler (2021):

1. **Data description:** A PAP should adequately describe the process by which data was generated or collected. This includes the source of data, including not only where exactly it comes from (e.g., place and time) but also how it was collected (e.g., survey instruments, administrative data). Information on sampling method should be included. If the study relies on an experiment, information on the randomization method should be detailed enough that a different researcher could confidently replicate the method. Furthermore, information on sample size and power calculations should be included. Much of this information, including power calculation, should be included even if the researcher is collecting new data for an observational study. Ensuring sufficient power to reject nulls is as every bit as important in observational studies as it is in experimental studies (Brown et al., 2019).

2. **Hypotheses testing:** Ideally, researchers would not only list the hypotheses they will test but would also write down a theoretical model, theory of change, or causal diagram that justifies the selected hypotheses. In additional to the causal model, a PAP should include clear definitions of the primary outcome variables as well as any secondary outcomes to be tested. The researcher should also address how multiple inference will be dealt with. There are numerous ways to adjust for either the family-wise error rate (FWER) or the false discovery rate (FDR) and the economics profession has yet to settle on what is the preferred approach. This lack of consensus makes prespecifying which method will be used extremely important. As with power calculation, adjusting for multiple hypotheses testing is frequently discussed as an issue in experiments, but sound inference is just as important in studies based on observational data.

3. **Variable construction:** In economics, there can be considerable leeway in how an outcome of interest is measured. For example, if the hypothesis to be tested is how a new technology impacts welfare, there are enumerable ways to actually measure

welfare. A PAP should precisely define how each outcome variable is constructed, as well as how any control variables will be constructed. The researcher should also outline basic operating principles for how data cleaning will be conducted, such as dropping outliers or winsorizing outliers, correcting for dropouts in a study or attrition, and adjusting for contamination. As with correcting for multiple inference, whenever the researcher has substantial degrees of freedom to choose one method over another, the researcher should prespecify a preferred approach.

4. **Model specification:** A PAP should spell out what statistical methods will be used in the analysis. Ideally, the researcher will write out the exact equations to be estimated. One might even choose to generate fake data, as in Humphreys et al. (2013), to conduct trial runs on different statistical models. In addition to defining the exact estimator, the PAP should list which covariates will be included and how inference will be conducted (e.g., clustering of standard errors, bootstrapping, randomization inference).

5. **Subgroup analysis:** The last key component of a PAP is the explication of any subgroup or heterogeneity analysis. Both in medical trials and in economics, there are numerous ways that the researcher can subdivide the data in order to find heterogeneous effects. By prespecifying what subgroup analysis will be conducted, the researcher is binding themselves and avoiding the temptation to data mine for clever or unusual differences across different populations (Bellemare, 2022a). As with many of the previous points, there is nothing that would limit a researcher from implementing this component of a PAP in a study using nonexperimental data.

Beyond these basic elements, PAPs can be, and often are, much more comprehensive. We ourselves have written PAPs as short as 5 pages and as long as 20. However, Janzen and Michler (2021) and Duflo et al. (2020) both caution against over-specifying, since comprehensive plans can become difficult to execute on. Again, following Janzen and Michler (2021), a more comprehensive PAP would contain one or more of the following elements:

- **Motivation:** Provide motivation and context for the study. This may include literature review.
- **Theoretical model or theory of change:** Include the theoretical model being tested or a causal diagram or theory of change that explains the mechanisms behind the effects being tested.
- **Multiple inference adjustments:** If multiple hypotheses are being tested, address how multiple inference will be dealt with. This may be either a correction for the FWER or the FDR.
- **Data cleaning:** Outline basic operating principles for how decisions will be made during data. This includes elements such as imputing missing values, winsorizing, correcting for attrition, and adjusting for contamination.
- **Power calculations:** Include information on sample size, power calculations, and minimal detectable effect (MDE) size.

- **Exploratory analysis:** Anderson and Magruder (2017) and Fafchamps and Labonne (2017) develop split-sample strategies for conducting exploratory analysis on a subset of the data. After the exploratory research, the PAP can be updated and the prespecified analysis can be carried out on the confirmatory portion of the data. Alternatively, one could generate a data set through simulation, as in Humphreys et al. (2013), and then test models on the simulated data. The PAP would then be updated, and the analysis would be carried out on the actual data to be collected.

3.4.3   Using PAPs

We believe that the reason for ignoring the use of PAPs in economic nonexperimental studies is because the early literature was primarily focused on their precommitment aspect, rather than the file drawer problem. One challenge with writing a PAP for nonexperimental studies is the retrospective nature of many such studies (Olken, 2015). In most cases, the researcher would be writing a plan with the data in hand. This provides an opportunity for a nefarious researcher to write a plan while simultaneously analyzing the data. The concern is that there is limited scope for curtailing the p-hacking that the PAP was supposed to prevent, rendering the PAP no better than the status quo. As a point of contrast, split-sample methods recently proposed by Anderson and Magruder (2017) and Fafchamps and Labonne (2017) require having at least some data in hand at the time of writing the PAP.

Nonetheless, Brodeur et al. (2016) provide evidence that p-hacking is a bigger problem in nonexperimental work than experimental research.[11] This seems to suggest there is value in finding creative ways to credibly document limited data access while writing a PAP, as Neumark (2001) and others have done, to curtail concerns regarding p-hacking in observational studies. Moreover, precommitment is not the only benefit of writing a PAP. If the primary value of a PAP is related to the file drawer problem, then as Olken (2015) writes, "in principle, there is no reason" that a registered PAP cannot be used for an observational study (see Humphreys et al., 2013; Coffman and Niederle, 2015; and Duflo et al., 2020, for variations on this perspective).

Janzen and Michler (2021) promote a pragmatic approach to PAPs that is less restrictive than a comprehensive PAP, and may be more conducive to nonexperimental work than a Ulysses pact. We see three potentially fruitful extensions of pre-analysis into beyond their use in experimental work. First, PAPs can help guide purely observational research. While the use of PAPs in observational studies are common in the medical sciences, they remains exceedingly rare in economics. As of this writing, we are aware of only four PAPs used in observational studies that seek to answer new research questions (i.e., not replications). These are Neumark (2001), Chang et al. (2020a), Michler et al. (2021), Furbush et al. (2021).[12] Common criticisms of PAPs for observational studies is that there is no way for authors to credibly communicate that the plan was filed prior to engaging in the analysis and that observational studies require more exploratory work than experimental studies. Neumark (2001) deals with these two criticisms by filing the PAP with journal editors ahead of the release of government data and by focusing on a simple and well-defined research question. Chang et al. (2020a) use existing data but implement a split sample method to address both criticisms. After collecting the data but prior to looking at it, they split the sample into an exploratory data set that contained a subset of older observations. They used these data for exploratory analysis, filed their PAP on Open Science Foundation, and only then were given access to the full confirmatory data set (Chang et al., 2020b).

Second, PAPs can be used to guide replications. Replications have frequently been put forward as a substitute for PAPs in that they provide the sort of confidence in results meant to be conveyed by PAPs (Coffman and Niederle, 2015; Coffman et al., 2017; Duvendack et al., 2017). However, PAPs can complement and even facilitate replication. Using a plan to guide replication work helps ensure objectivity in the replication process and insulates authors from unhappy researchers. Coffman et al. (2017) argue that one reason replications remain uncommon in economics is that journals are reluctant to publish replications that confirm the initial analysis. This creates an ethical issue in that publication bias incentivizes the replicating researcher to find a way to overturn the findings of the original work. The use of PAPs to restrict researcher degrees of freedom seems tailor made for this purpose. Furthermore, prespecifying the analysis provides a shield against unhappy researchers whose results were subject to scrutiny (Chang, 2020). But the key criticism of PAPs, that they inhibit exploration, is not valid for PAPs used in replication work. As researchers are narrowly focused on replicating existing work, there is little fear that a PAP will hinder valuable scientific discovery. While still uncommon in economics, there is a small group of authors using PAPs to direct their replication work (Chang and Li, 2017; Chang, 2018; Chang and Li, 2018, 2022).

Third, PAPs can be used in graduate student instruction. The vast majority of students in applied economics graduate programs will not employ experimental methods in their master's thesis or PhD dissertation, but there is no reason this should preclude them from the benefits of writing a well-thought-out plan for their intended work. In fact, it is typical for PhD programs in the agricultural and applied economics field to require defense of a prospectus. In practice, the prospectus is rarely prospective in nature: it typically requires presentation of some early results. We propose that a PAP could be presented instead. In presenting a PAP instead, the student would carefully contemplate the empirical strategy in a detailed manner, with both strong theoretical and ethical roots. With this change, the prospectus becomes an opportunity to focus on the empirical approach – without knowing the results so that the student and committee can maintain impartiality – and accommodates an opportunity for feedback on those methods early on in the research process. Then, down the line, the dissertation defense becomes a time for discussing challenges and modifications, research findings, and implications. For programs that do not use prospectuses as part of their PhD programs, it might instead be appropriate to include and require the writing of a PAP in applied graduate-level classes. This could replace the typical research paper, often completed in a student's second year of coursework. With a shift toward including PAPs throughout the graduate student experience, students would be encouraged to spend less time running regressions early in their studies and more time thinking through model specification. As the profession pays increasing attention to methodological rigor, we think this is time well spent.

3.5 Conclusion

The objective of this chapter has been to discuss the essential dynamics and ethical concerns involved with project development, in particular the generation of a team and the use of PAPs in applied economics work.

Throughout this chapter, we have worked to underscore the essential nature of clarity in communication and the value in making investments to plan before work begins on a research project. With the final objective of improving research work – both in terms of quality and its ethical nature – there are important costs and values that must be considered in developing a research plan to ensure its success.

To assist in this planning process, we have focused on two primary ideas: the deliberate development of a team and the generation of a research plan, specifically through the writing of a PAP. Our focus throughout this chapter has been on the specific tools and implementable practices that can be used while in developing an initial idea into an ready-to-go project. The fact that the ethics of project development are not frequently part of the discussion of research ethics does not mean there are no ethical challenges. Rather, the challenges tend to arise from interpersonal power dynamics and from our individual cognitive bias – and thus can be much more difficult to navigate. However, making time investments in mitigating and addressing these ethical conundrums before beginning work on a research project will pay dividends later in the research life cycle.

Notes

1 As a reminder, in this book we focus on research ethics and do not discuss other ethical or moral issues that may arise in interpersonal relationships, such as harassment and discrimination. These are wrong.

2 As an interesting side note, when it came time to develop the theory of implosion and design the lenses required to create an atomic explosion, the scientists at Los Alamos called in John von Neumann, a man whose prodigious mathematical ability astounded the great mathematicians and physicists of his generation (Rhodes, 1986). With Oskar Morgenstern, von Neumann would go on after the war to make substantial contributions in economics to utility theory, general equilibrium theory, and game theory.

3 The tool is available at www.aeaweb.org/journals/policies/random-authororder/generator. The Author Randomization Tool archives the results of the randomization so it can be verified by others.

4 We discuss this policy in more detail in Chapter 7.
5 Kweik (2020) focuses on collaborations between "internationalists" and "locals" exclusively among scientists in Poland.
6 Evidence from the economics profession is not as well documented. However, using Web of Science, Naritomi et al. (2020) calculate that only 10 percent of papers in development economics contain an author from a lower income country.
7 Options include the AEA RCT Registry, which only allows for RCTs; the International Initiative for Impact Evaluations (3ie) Registry for International Development Impact Evaluations, which only allows for impact evaluations in middle or lower income countries; and the Open Science Foundation (OSF), which has no restrictions.
8 This calculation does not take into account a number of other public registries that have been created since 2004. The calculation is based on the number of trials listed in the registry (344,473) as of July 5, 2020. The number of pre-announcement registrations comes from Humphreys et al. (2013).
9 Numbers as of July 5, 2020.
10 Duflo et al. (2020) write that "PAPs for non-experimental research, which tends to be retrospective, are rarely advocated for or used (yet) in practice, presumably because they are neither desirable nor, in most cases, practical." We note that this logic uses the lack of observational PAPs in the AEA Registry, which does not allow them, as evidence that they are undesirable and not practical.
11 We explore this more in Chapters 6 and 7.
12 Monogan III (2013) provides an example from political science of a PAP used to guide a study based on observational data. Similar to Neumark (2001), the data that Monogan III (2013) relies on had a timed release, so the authors could credibly file their PAP prior to ever having access to the data.

PART III
Doing Research

4

DATA COLLECTION

4.1 Introduction

In the mid-1960s, Laud Humphreys, a sociology PhD student at Washington University in St. Louis, could frequently be found loitering around public toilets. This, naturally, could raise questions as to what he was doing. As Humphreys (1970) describes, "any man who remains in a public restroom for more than five minutes is apt to be either a member of the vice squad or someone on the make." But Humphreys was not a member of law enforcement. He was not there to use the bathroom. Nor was he their to participate in "tea-rooming" as homosexual encounters in public toilets were then known. Instead, Humphreys was there to do something nobody as yet suspected. He was there as a researcher, collecting data for his dissertation, which would be published in 1970 as *Tearoom Trade: Impersonal Sex in Public Places* (Humphreys, 1970).

On his data-collecting missions, Humphreys did not reveal his purpose to anyone. Instead, he played the roll of a "watchqueen" or lookout, for those engaged in sex acts. Given that at that time in Missouri, as in much of the U.S., engaging in same-sex intercourse was illegal, the men engaged in the teamroom trade were at considerable risk. Complicating the matter even further, as Humphreys (1970) reports, 54 percent of his subjects identified as heterosexual males, many with a wife and family at home. By playing the watchqueen, Humphreys provided protection for those engaged in sexual activity while also allowing him to observe that activity for his research.

While misrepresenting oneself in order to observe illicit behavior, and then writing up one's notes for publication is ethically questionable, Humphreys went further. After observing men having sex in public toilets, he would go outside and note down the license plate numbers of those who visited the tearoom. He then would hang

DOI: 10.4324/9781003025061-7

around the area and chat with 'friendly policeman' or present himself as a market researcher in order to learn the names and addresses of the men (Humphreys, 1970). About a year after his initial data collection in the tearooms, Humphreys obtained a job as a member of a public health survey team. In disguise, he then tracked down the men at their homes and pretended that the men had been randomly selected for the health survey. Subsequently, Humphreys destroyed the names and addresses of all involved so as to protect their identities and privacy.

Humphreys' methods were controversial at the time, and that controversy has not been resolved (Babbie, 2009). It is likely to remain a subject of debate for long to come . . . but why? Some have argued that Humphreys's methods were necessary in order to conduct his research and receive honest answers. Furthermore, defenders indicate that the participants in Humphreys's work were not harmed by their participation, as they were anonymous in the final work.[1] On the other side, Humphreys obscured his role to the participants in his research, gained information from them without their consent and deceived them about the purpose of his work. Even without further discussion of ethics in data collection, many of those actions are clearly unethical. Such was the outrage among some researchers at the sociology department in Washington University that a number of faculty petitioned the president of the university to rescind Humphreys's degree. Furthermore, a fistfight broke out among faculty members, and about half of the department departed to positions at other universities (Sieber, nd).

In this chapter, we consider cases such as Humphreys's and move beyond the previous two chapters, to discuss what happens after one has formed an idea and developed a project and are moving into the processes of collecting data. To understand the ethical questions around Humphreys's (1970) and similar studies, we discuss the ethical requirements, decisions, and motivations associated with data collection. We begin by differentiating between different types of data collection. We focus on experimental and nonexperimental data, the types of data that economists typically collect, and discuss the ethical issues and considerations relevant for each type of data.

We then turn to institutional review boards (IRBs) which dictate regulations and procedures for most economists who are collecting data. While some research projects, specifically those without human subjects data, may be entirely exempt from these reviews, this chapter still provides a helpful overview of the history of ethical regulation in the U.S. and around the world. We discuss the history of IRB requirements, as well as their motivations and the specific practices in obtaining IRB approval. We present the evolution of these codes from the Hippocratic Oath to the Nuremberg Code to the Belmont Report to the contemporary IRB. We highlight the principles of respect for subjects, beneficence, and justice which motivate these codes and regulations and tie them to the respective practices required to ensure they are upheld, including informed consent, risk–benefit assessment, and recruitment and selection.

The objective of this chapter is to provide an overview of the requirements associated with data collection and a review of the history and motivation of these requirements and provide context for how these requirements may be implemented in various types of data collection.

4.2   Types of Data

To fix terms and ideas, we begin by discussing the various types of data that applied economists may use. Defining and describing these terms are helpful for understanding the associated ethical requirements for collecting data. This section also touches on the fabrication of data. We do not discuss how to collect data, as this is outside of the scope of this book. There are existing good resources for this work, including Duflo et al. (2007) and Barrett et al. (2020), among others.

4.2.1   Experimental Data

Economic experiments study human behavior in a laboratory setting, online, or in the field. These experiments allow researchers to test choices made by individuals under a set of constructed conditions. Lab experiments are often conducted with college students on campus. These experiments are generally designed to test microeconomic theory or some prediction from game theory. They typically pose minimal risk to participants, who sit at computer terminals in a room on campus and play economic games. Lab experiments also come with benefits for participants, who are typically paid based on their performance, which helps ensure incentive compatibility in the experiment. Online experiments are similar to lab experiments, as they pose minimal risk and provide a monetary benefit. The big difference is that the population of study in online experiments tends to be the general population and not just college students.

Field experiments occur outside of a formal lab or online setting, often in developing countries. Researchers interact with participants and frequently conduct long socioeconomic surveys before and after the experiment. Participants are typically from some target population (farmers, women, the ultrapoor) instead of the general population. Risk tends to be minimal, but since the experiment or treatment typically involves some real-world activity risk is likely higher than the games played on a computer in a lab. Additionally, participants may or may not be paid or payment may be in kind. Artifactual or lab-in-the-field experiments are a hybrid of the lab and field experiment. They involve playing the economic games typical of the lab experiment but out in the field, such as playing auction games with food vendors in Kampala. Like lab experiments, artifactual experiments tend to be low risk and involve payment for performance. Regardless of the type of experiment, all are similar in that researchers manipulate a treatment that has been randomly assigned to some participants and not others. The fact that the researcher controls the participants experience is an important component in the ethical review process.

4.2.2 Nonexperimental Data

Nonexperimental data or observational data are any data not collected as part of an explicit experimental protocol. These data are generally drawn from a population that attempts to proxy for or otherwise represent a broader population of interest. Data are generally drawn from interviews with research participants, following a survey instrument or structured questionnaire. Participants are typically paid cash or in kind for their time in responding to the survey enumerators. Primary data, which are collected by the researcher, will undergo an ethical review process similar to that required for experimental data. The big difference between the two types of data is that in nonexperimental data collection the researcher is only "observing" and recording participant actions or responses instead of giving or withholding some treatment. This difference tends to result in a lower degree of scrutiny in ethical review, since there are no issues of fairness in withholding the treatment from some participants, nor is the researcher introducing any potential risk by providing the treatment to others.

4.2.3 Other Data

In addition to collecting their own experimental or nonexperimental data, applied economists frequently use secondary data, which is data that has already been collected. Secondary data may include administrative data, price data, trade data, scanner data, and public use data. One type of data which is increasingly used by applied economists is Global Positioning System (GPS) data, Geographic Information System (GIS) data, and other types of remote sensing and/or location data.

Since secondary data are not collected by the researcher themsevles, use of the data does not require any ethical approvals, as it would already require approvals prior to its collection. That said, there are a number of complications associated with privacy in using secondary data. We discuss these privacy issues in detail in Chapter 5.

4.2.4 Fabrication or Falsification *of Data*

While the focus of this chapter is on how to manage the ethical issues that arise when collecting experimental or nonexperimental data from human participants, we would be remiss if we did not discuss the possibility that some researchers simply fabricate their data. The terms *fabrication* and *falsification* are often used in conjunction with each other. And while both involve manipulation or making up of data or results, their meanings are distinct (Comstock, 2013). The Office of

Research Integrity at the U.S. Department of Health and Human Services (DHHS) provides the following definitions:

- **Fabrication** is the making up of data and the recording or reporting of results based on that data as if the data had actually been collected.
- **Falsification** is the manipulation of research materials, equipment, or processes, or the changing of or omission of data or results so that the results are not accurately represented in the research record.

Since fabrication tends to involve the creation of fake data, we discuss this practice in detail here. Falsification, which tends to involve fake analysis, we leave for discussion in Chapter 6.

Fabrication is a clear, purposeful bad action, well outside ethical research practices and behaviors, as it constitutes fraud to the scientific record. Fabrication is considered research misconduct if (1) the act was committed intentionally, knowingly, or recklessly; (2) it can be proven by a preponderance of evidence; and (3) the action represents a significant departure from accepted practices (Comstock, 2013). In the most serious cases, the fabrication of data in research is a federal crime. The resulting penalties may include being declared ineligible for government grants or losing one's job.

The reason to discuss fraud is not to iterate penalties or to enumerate the reasons why fabrication is wrong but rather to empower researchers to identify fraud in others' studies. The case of Michael LaCour provides an example. In 2014, LaCour and Donald Green published a study titled "When Contact Changes Minds: An Experiment on Transmission of Support for Gay Equality" in *Science*. LaCour was a graduate student at UCLA and Green a professor at Columbia University. Their study presented a remarkable finding: going door to door to persuade people to support same-sex marriage works and works particularly well in cases where the canvasser delivering the persuasive message is themselves gay. Further spillover effects were identified, suggesting that people who lived with those who had spoken to a gay canvasser became more supportive of same-sex marriage. But, as a 2015 retraction of the paper indicated, LaCour fabricated the data (LaCour and Green, 2014).[2]

The fraud was uncovered by two UC Berkeley graduate students, David Broockman and Josh Kalla (Konnikova, 2015). Broockman and Kalla identified that LaCour must have taken a preexisting survey, added some statistical noise, and then passed it off as the findings of a canvassing experiment (Broockman et al., 2015). When suspicions rose, Green contacted LaCour's adviser at UCLA, Lynn Vavreck, who found that the study's raw data could not be traced to the survey platform LaCour claimed to have used. LaCour told Vavreck he had deleted the source files by accident, but the survey platform found no evidence that this happened. Vavreck asked LaCour for contact information for the survey respondents, to verify their participation, but he refused.

Fraud of this sort is often not uncovered. Replications are difficult, as we discuss in Chapter 6. It is primarily due to the coverage of LaCour and Green's paper in the popular press that Broockman and Kalla began digging into it. But, because the probability of being caught committing fraud is low, the incentives to fabricate data can become tempting. In the *New York Times*, the editorial board considered how they were conned by LaCour, concluding that fraud is mostly the result of a deceptive or overly ambitious actor who misbehaves but is enabled ultimately by researchers and collaborators who do not scrutinize the work of their co-authors (Konnikova, 2015).

4.3 Codes and Principles

Ethics codes have long been a part of many professions and are perhaps most closely associated with the medical profession. In this section, we discuss the history of a number of codes and principles, leading to the present day and the relevant codes which dictate the research practices of applied economists.

These codes are useful in the practice of research itself, but beyond that they help to set standards, define common behavior, and raise awareness of potential unethical behaviors that exist. However, it is important to bear in mind that adherence to codes and principles alone does not necessarily mean that ethical behavior is achieved.

4.3.1 Nuremberg Codes

The birth of modern research ethics occurred following World War II. The Allied Nations were horrified at the cruelty and exploitation that prisoners endured at concentration camps. Following the end of the War, an International Military Tribunal was convened in Nuremberg, a former bastion of Nazi power. The first trial involved 24 of the highest ranking Nazi political and military leaders for war crimes, crimes against peace, and crimes against humanity. Subsequent to this first trial, a series of trials were conducted against doctors, judges, and industrialists for complicity in the crimes committed by the Nazi state. The most famous of these subsequent trials was *The United States of America v. Karl Brandt, et al.*, which came to be known as the "Doctors' Trial." In the Doctors' Trial, 23 physicians were tried for crimes against humanity for the experiments they carried out on prisoners of war. Of the 23 defendants, 16 were found guilty (of which 7 received death sentences and 9 received prison sentences ranging from ten years to life). The other seven defendants were acquitted.

As the defendants were medical doctors, there was a perception that beyond the crimes themselves, a greater harm had been perpetrated. Most physicians take the Hippocratic Oath before assuming practice. The Hippocratic Oath is, in part:

I swear to fulfill, to the best of my ability and judgment, this covenant: I will respect the hard-won scientific gains of those physicians in whose steps I walk, and gladly share such knowledge as is mine with those who are to follow. . . . I will remember that I remain a member of society, with special obligations to all my fellow human beings, those sound of mind and body as well as the infirm.

The thrust of the Hippocratic Oath, however, specifies principles of beneficence, nonmaleficence, and the rule of confidentiality in working as a physician and specifically treating patients. The actions of those tried in the Doctors' Trial eroded public faith in science and in medicine. To address this, in addition to rendering verdicts, the court in *U.S. v. Brandt* created the Nuremberg Code, a set of ten ethical principles for human experimentation.

The Nuremberg Code was motivated by hopes of restoring faith in science. There was fear among many scientists that the public revulsion at the experimentation on humans during the War would limit people's willingness to participate in future medical research. The purpose of the Nuremberg Code was to define a set of principles to guide future research and help ensure the atrocities committed by Nazi doctors would never happen again. The ten tenants of the Nuremberg Code are presented in Box 4.1. The Code defines who can participate in medical research: healthy, adult, competent individuals, who are fully informed and able to consent.

BOX 4.1   TENANTS OF THE NUREMBERG CODE

1. The voluntary consent of the human subject is absolutely essential.
2. The experiment should be such as to yield fruitful results for the good of society, un-procurable by other methods or means of study, and not random and unnecessary in nature.
3. The experiment should be so designed and based on the results of animal experimentation and a knowledge of the natural history of the disease or other problem under study that the anticipated results will justify the performance of the experiment.
4. The experiment should be so conducted as to avoid all unnecessary physical and mental suffering and injury.
5. No experiment should be conducted where there is an *a priori* reason to believe that death or disabling injury will occur; except, perhaps, in those experiments where the experimental physicians also serve as subjects.
6. The degree of risk to be taken should never exceed that determined by the humanitarian importance of the problem to be solved by the experiment.

7. Proper preparations should be made and adequate facilities provided to protect the experimental subject against even remote possibilities of injury, disability, or death.

8. The experiment should be conducted only by scientifically qualified persons. The highest degree of skill and care should be required through all stages of the experiment of those who conduct or engage in the experiment.

9. During the course of the experiment the human subject should be at liberty to bring the experiment to an end if he has reached the physical or mental state where continuation of the experiment seems to him to be impossible.

10. During the course of the experiment the scientist in charge must be prepared to terminate the experiment at any stage, if he has probable cause to believe, in the exercise of the good faith, superior skill and careful judgment required of him that a continuation of the experiment is likely to result in injury, disability, or death to the experimental subject.

Taken together, the tenants in the Code emphasize the need to ensure that participant subjects can voluntarily withdraw from experiments, that harm is minimized throughout the experiment, and that efforts are made to maximize both social and scientific benefit through the work.

Of course, the lack of an existing code or any perceived shortcomings of the Hippocratic Oath were not the reason nor justification for the atrocities committed during World War II. As Macfarlane (2009) notes, "the lack of an international code was considered no excuse by the tribunal for treating human beings purely as a means to an end, and without humanity." But the creation of the Code is positioned as a rebirth and new start for modern ethics.

A summary version of the Nuremberg Code was quickly adopted as an explicit requirement of the Geneva Conventions of 1949 and the International Covenant on Civil and Political Rights (ICCPR) in 1966. Specifically, the principle of informed consent asserted that the "inalienable rights of all members of the human family . . . derive from the inherent dignity of the human person" (United Nations, 1996, quoted in Hoffmann, 2020). Of course, the universal acknowledgment of this right and the advancement and refinement of the Nuremberg Code and similar codes in the decades to come did not completely eliminate research misconduct.

4.3.2 Declaration of Helsinki

In the years immediately following the creation of the Nuremberg Code it was viewed by many as a code for barbarian Nazis, not pragmatic and ethically minded doctors in the Allied Nations (Katz, 1996). As with the Hippocratic Oath, the Nuremberg Code was perceived as more of a suggestion than a requirement. As such, 15 years after the Nuremberg Code's creation, the World Medical Association (WMA) convened and created the Declaration of Helsinki. Although it moves beyond the Nuremberg Code in many ways, much of it is still derived from provisions in the Code.

The first Declaration of Helsinki was signed in 1964, although it has evolved significantly over the subsequent decades. The original Declaration includes 12 tenants that require that researchers conform to scientific principles, that their work be guided by principles, and that research be conducted by an expert in the field. The current Declaration includes 37 tenants and was signed at the 64th WMA General Assembly in Fortaleza, Brazil, in 2013 (WMA, nd). This much extended modern version also discusses ethical review boards, use of placebos, and unproven interventions, among a list of other general principles and tenants.

Like many of the codes that precede it, the emphasis of the Declaration maintains the perspective that all ethical responsibilities are with the physician or researcher. However, it underscores that the bad behavior of a physician or researcher cannot and should not be protected by laws within their own countries, which might otherwise excuse them. Israel (2015) states that "the Declaration was positioned as having universal ethical primacy and standing above diverse, culturally specific regulations." This suggests an improvement over previous codes at least in intent and motivation.

But in practice, the Declaration has come to be seen as complicit in the process of global homogenization for its failure to acknowledge differences in culture and context. The Declaration also marks the beginning of the transference of ethical principles in the medical sciences to other disciplines, without attention to the differences that exist between fields. This process, in which the ethical standards from one field or profession are applied to others, is known as "ethical creep" or "ethical imperialism" (Schrag, 2010). Although early versions of the Declaration left interpretations broad, the 2008 Declaration was the first to explicitly encourage all scholars to adopt its principles. This was updated in 2013 to indicate that the Declaration places requirements on "every research study involving human subjects" (WMA, nd).

4.3.3 Belmont Report

Both the Nuremberg Code and the Declaration of Helsinki have Euro-centric origins, which, to some extent, limited their adoption in the U.S. Furthermore, the foundations of both the Code and the Declaration are rooted in medical research and so, despite some ethical creep, there was limited use of the principles outside of the field of medicine.

The U.S. began to frame an ethics code of its own following a series of ethical breeches. Of these, perhaps the most egregious is the case of the "Tuskegee

Syphilis Study." Much of the story of Tuskegee we describe here, comes from the documentation of Tuskegee (nd). At Tuskegee, a study was undertaken by the U.S. Public Health Service (PHS). The PHS was entrusted to monitor and identify trends and develop interventions to treat disease in the country. The PHS began working with the Tuskegee Institute in 1932 to study hundreds of Black men with syphilis from Macon County, Alabama. The intent of this work was to record the natural history of syphilis in Black men and was so titled the "Tuskegee Study of Untreated Syphilis in the Negro Male." PHS researchers simply told the participants that they were to be treated for "bad blood." Six hundred men enrolled in the study, of which 399 had syphilis and served as part of the experimental group, with the remaining 201 as control. Most of the men were poor and were offered medical care and survivors insurance for participating, as well as other incentives, such as meals, rides to the clinic, and treatment for other ailments.

When the study began in 1932, there were no known effective treatments for syphilis. Thus, in the early years of the study, there was no ethical issue with simply observing and monitoring the progress of an incurable disease. While Alexander Fleming had discovered penicillin in 1928 in the U.K., the mold was not used to treat syphilis in the U.S. until 1943 (Tuskegee, nd). Despite discovery of a treatment for the disease, the men enrolled in the Tuskegee Syphilis Study were not treated. There are even reports that PHS prevented the men from participating in government-sponsored rapid test and treatment clinics to eradicate the disease (Reverby, 2000). Peter Buxton, a young social worker for the PHS, learned of the still ongoing study in 1966 (Elliott, 2017). He filed official complaints with the PHS but was overruled because the study was not yet complete. Buxton left the PHS in 1970 but continued to be bothered by the study. In 1972, he met with Edith Lederer and Jean Heller, reporters at the Associated Press and blew the whistle (Heller, 1972). The public outcry that resulted from the article finally put an end to the study.

By the time the four-decade "study" on the effects of untreated syphilis on Black men came to an end, only 74 of the original 600 subjects were still alive (Reverby, 2000). Among the 399 men in the syphilis group, 28 had died of syphilis, and 100 had died of related complications. Furthermore, 40 of the wives of the men with syphilis had been infected, and 19 children had been born with congenital syphilis. A review of the study was undertaken, which ultimately concluded that the study was "ethically unjustified." Some of the reasons for this decision included a lack of respect or concern for the safety of the men involved, a lack of informed consent by the men in fully understanding their participation (they were not even informed of the name of the study), and no opportunity provided to the men to quit the study.

Motivated by the ethical violations of Tuskegee, a congressional mandate charged the National Commission for the Protection of Human Subjects of Biomedical and Behavioral Research with the objective to "identify the ethical principles which should underlie the conduct of biomedical and behavioral research with human subjects and develop guidelines and should be followed in such research."[3] The perceived goal of this work was to bring together and reconcile the protection of individual rights with the pursuit of collective enterprise through research. The outcome of the Commission's work was "The Belmont Report: Ethical Principles and Guidelines for the Protection of Human Subjects of Research, Report of the National Commission for the Protection of Human Subjects of Biomedical and Behavioral Research" or, more simply, the Belmont Report. The Belmont Report was issued in 1978 and published in the Federal Register in 1979.

The Belmont Report provides the guidance and principles for research conducted in the U.S. It details ethical principles and guidelines for research involving human subject and provides a framework to resolve ethical problems associated with human subject research. Importantly, this is the first place that the three core principles that guide IRBs today were defined. These include (1) respect for persons, (2) beneficence, and (3) justice. How these principles are to be applied are also detailed, including (1) informed consent, (2) assessment of risks and benefits, and (3) selection of subjects (see Table 4.1). These principles were designed to be obvious. From Beauchamp (2005):

> Every morally sensitive person believes that a moral way of life requires that we respect persons and take into account their well-being into our actions. *Belmont*'s principles are so woven into the fabric of morality in morally sensitive cultures that no responsible research investigator could conduct research without reference to them.

While the Belmont Report provides the first code to which researchers in the U.S. must adhere, it is not without shortcomings. The first, is that the Report, rather than being treated as a living document with a related agency to oversee it – as recommended by its creators – has by and large been simply treated as law, as is. The Belmont Report was put together with the expectation that an ethical advisory board (EAB) would be permanently housed, as a standing agency, within the DHHS. This agency would serve to provide and update the guidelines and policies of Belmont, as well as to address "apparently irreconcilable" questions. This has not taken place, although "the EAB lingers in ghostly form, as an ignored imperative within 46.204 of the Federal Regulations 45 CFR 46" (Jonsen, 2005). A second shortcoming of the Belmont Report is the persistent trend, as observed in the Nuremberg Code and the Helsinki Declaration, that the requirements designed for medical researchers are then applied to anyone engaged in research with human subjects. These requirements are widely applied to a number of disciplines, often with little accounting for or adjustment to heterogeneity in practices across fields. At base, however, the Belmont Report was designed as a moral framework for research ethics and it has, to a large degree, succeeded in this primary objective (Beauchamp, 2005).

4.4 Regulating Ethics

In this section, we review the role of IRBs in regulating ethics in the U.S., as well as how similar boards use nation-relevant guidance in other countries. We then discuss the specific tenants of ethical research that applies to research in applied economics, and discuss the related practices undertaken to ensure that these tenants hold.

4.4.1 IRBs in the U.S.

IRBs are responsible for ensuring institutional compliance with federal regulations.[4] Here, we review the responsibilities of IRBs as they pertain to applied economists engaged in research involving human subjects. Although regulations vary across countries, Schrag (2010) notes that the regulations in the U.S. set the tone for much of what is adopted by other countries, both Western nations and others across the world.

The guiding principle of IRB practice in the U.S. is known as the Common Rule (Title 45 of the Code of Federal Regulations Part 46 (45 CFR 46)). The Common Rule effectively mandates that all federally funded work, involving human subjects, be reviewed and/or regulated by an IRB. The Common Rule involves a number of prescriptions, structures, and policies for human subjects research, with the primary outcome of ensuring human subjects research funded by federal agencies meets the principles defined in the Belmont Report of respect for persons, beneficence, and justice.

Beyond ensuring appropriate application of the Common Rule, there is process-related heterogeneity within IRBs across institutions U.S. The specific information required by an IRB in a Protocol for Human Subjects Research and the process for approval varies from institution to institution. We encourage readers to visit their own IRB's website to find out more about their specific procedures. Typically, the IRB is an independent review committee made up of faculty that is tasked with ensuring that research complies with the Common Rule. At our home institution, the University of Arizona, this independent committee is supported by the Human Subjects Protection Program (HSPP), an administrative program that provides the infrastructure, documentation, and initial review of documents for the actual IRB.

At our university, submission of a protocol to the IRB follows the procedure outlined in Figure 4.1. A researcher downloads IRB forms and fills them out as is relevant for their proposed study, well in advance of any data collection. For applied economists, these forms typically include the Protocol for Human Subjects Research and the Informed Consent form. Additional supporting documents are often required, such as experiment instructions, recruitment material, or translations of the informed consent form. All these documents are submitted via an electronic "eIRB" system, and an HSPP staff member makes an initial review of the documents for completeness. This initial review frequently results

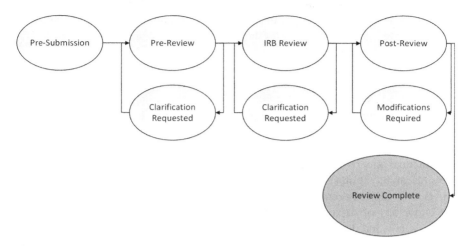

FIGURE 4.1   IRB Process workflow at the University of Arizona

Note: Figure by the authors, based on information from the Human Subjects Protection Program at the University of Arizona. Figure represents the workflow for protocol submission and approval of the Protocol for Human Subjects Research at the University of Arizona.

in a number of requests for revisions to ensure completeness of documents and compliance with federal guidelines. The researcher makes these changes, after which the protocol is submitted to the review board for approval. At this point, the IRB may require modifications of the protocol in order to be in compliance with the Common Rule. Once approval is granted, the researcher can proceed with the study as proposed. After approval, the IRB typically has no role in the research process.

Generally speaking, IRB approval processes are straightforward: obey the rules, get approval for your research before beginning it, and if that is done, then a researcher can call their research ethical. The actual procedures to obtain IRB approval are simplistic.

Rather than a process-focused discussion, we instead focus on the history and motivation for the IRB's role in research and how it intersects with the work of applied economists. As the history of ethical codes from the Nuremberg Code to the present day suggests, much of current ethical practices in the U.S. are rooted in bioethics (Beauchamp, 2005). Even today, much of the focus of any single IRB is on medical trials. This is reflected in the makeup of a board, which is typically dominated by faculty from the health sciences. A frequent criticism of IRBs from those conducting researcher outside of the health sciences is that IRBs are not designed to review economics or social science research (Holland, 2016). As Schrag (2010) writes, "IRBs are never comprised of researchers in a single discipline in the social sciences or humanities and they may not have any members familiar with ethics and methods of the scholars who come before them." Many social science ethicists who study IRBs suggest that the typical makeup of a board, dominated by biomedical researchers, disqualifies the board from reviewing social science work altogether (Lederman, 2016).

Given that IRBs evolved out of ethical violations made in the health sciences, there is a contentious past between IRBs and the social sciences. The most trenchant criticism has come from the fields of history, philosophy, and sociology, with many arguing that IRBs have no jurisdiction on their research as no one on the board has the appropriate expertise to review the work (Schrag, 2010; Adler and Adler, 2016; Marzano, 2016; Kara, 2018). This problem is, to a large degree, a hypothetical one. IRBs do have jurisdiction to review and approve all human subjects research, yet most social science research poses minimal risk to participants and is thus ruled as exempt from full board review. In many institutions, including the University of Arizona, a set of exempt reviewers drawn from the social sciences review and determine if the research is minimal risk.[5] All the research that we have ever conducted which involved new data collection was eventually ruled as exempt. An exemption request still requires completing and submitting all the IRB forms and still can take several months for the exemption request to be approved. Thus, applied economists must still conform to an administrative structure designed for medical trials, even if their research is eventually determined by other social scientists as exempt from full board review. For many applied economists, this arrangement feels like a misalignment of incentives, with the focus on regulatory compliance and not on actual ethical competence (Lederman, 2016; Josephson and Smale, 2021).

The concerns of social scientists about the qualification and jurisdiction of IRBs relate to several other issues regarding ethical review. First and foremost, IRBs are legal institutions rather than moral ones. Their foundation and principles are in line with adhering to federal rules and regulations and, as such, put legal requirements first. This may leave ethical behavior and scientific advancement at the wayside, in an effort to ensure fulfillment of the letter – rather than the spirit – of the law (Israel, 2015; Iphofen, 2016). This adherence to regulation may lead to poor quality and/or unrealistic review. In cases where IRB reviewers are not familiar with the intricacies of field-specific methods, certain practices may raise flags. Problems can arise in cases in which IRB reviewers are unwilling to envision and/or consider new research methods (Dahringer, 2016; Murray, 2016). In these situations, Kara (2018) observes that researchers may try to "game the system" through being "economical with the truth" about methods, recruitment, or other practices instead of being fully transparent about their research practices. As structured, the system encourages simple rule following rather than complex, ethical reflection.

An example from our own work is illustrative. We applied for exempt approval for a survey in which we followed up with households in Bangladesh that had previously been surveyed in 2014 and 2017. The purpose of this survey was to use GPS devices to record the exact location and size of rice plots. Since this location data would be connected to previously collected household survey data, we believed that it required IRB approval because that data contained personally identifiable information (PII). Also, since the current survey work was only collecting the GPS data, we believe the study posed no more than minimal risk and would quickly receive exempt approval. However, IRB exemption was not immediately forthcoming because a number of issues that were raised in the pre-review stage. One such issue was the demand by HSPP staff that we include the following text in our informed consent form for the Bangladeshi households:

> Compensation for participation in a research study is considered taxable income for you. If your compensation for this research study or a combination of research studies is $600 or more in a calendar year (January to December), you will receive an IRS Form 1099 to report on your taxes.

We eventually were able to persuade the HSPP staff that it was highly unlikely that these households would get paid $600 for survey participation over the course of a year. And that it was even less likely that the University of Arizona would mail tax forms to them in Bangladesh. And that, as these households did not live in the U.S., they were not subject to U.S. tax law. But all this caused several weeks of delay at a time when we needed to have the field team out collecting data prior to the harvest of the rice crop. Failure to collect the data before harvest would mean waiting an entire year until the agricultural season came back around. Eventually we made the decision to go ahead and collect the data without exempt approval, using the as-yet-unapproved informed consent forms. When HSPP learned about this, they notified us that we needed to stop collecting data immediately and destroy any data that had already been collected.

Over several days of escalating back-and-forth between the field team in Bangladesh, us, HSPP staff, and IBR administrators, it was eventually decided that our survey work was "not research involving human subjects as defined by DHHS and FDA regulations" and thus did not require IRB approval, exempt or otherwise. The reasoning was that the new GPS information would be matched to personally identifiable information in the 2014 and 2017 surveys collected by our in-country collaborators, which had not been subject to the university's IRB. Therefore, this new data collection effort, even though university faculty were now involved in the project, did not require the university's IRB approval. No matter that the new data collection effort would have required the university's IRB approval if university faculty had been involved in the earlier effort. What mattered was that the university could plausibly argue that it did not have jurisdiction and therefore need not review the project. Since the research would not be reviewed by the university's IRB, we were instructed to stop using the university's informed consent forms to obtain consent from the surveyed households. It was up to us to decide if we wanted to use a different, not-university-approved, consent form or not obtain consent at all. Adler and Adler (2016) relate a similar story regarding research in Africa.

A second issue with IRBs is related to mission creep (White, 2007). Although IRBs are not institutionally unique in their succumbing to mission creep or mission drift, which has been documented in businesses, charities, churches, and political organizations (Greer and Horst, 2014). Adler and Adler (2016) suggest that to sustain themselves IBRs are "entrenching and expanding their mission and reach." Adler and Adler (2016) document a shift in review requirements, where research that was deemed exempt in the mid-2000s now requires expedited review in the mid-2010s, and studies that had previously received expedited review now require full board review. Social science researchers have also documented a tendency for IRBs to become more restrictive in what research they will even approve, with some ethnographic, sociological, and psychological research questions being deemed not researchable by IRB. Adler and Adler (2016) provide examples that range from talking to children about self-harm to work on nonconformist behavior, like sadomasochism. This mission creep serves to earlier exacerbate the belief that IRBs are burdensome regulation divorced from real ethical content.

The main shortcoming of the current IRB system in the U.S. is that researchers tend to go through IRB to receive approval rather than reflect on the ethical content of their research. At its worst, the focus on regulatory compliance gives cover to researchers and institutions to disregard issues involving the ethics of the research question, the ethics of working in different cultures, and the ethics of the existing ethical review system itself. As Kara (2018) notes, simply "doing" IRB is often perceived as "doing" ethics. But ethics is an ongoing process of frequent review and reconsideration. It is not and cannot be simply completed with approval from an IRB. This is particularly true if research changes, adapts, or otherwise shifts during the process.

There are any number of suggestions to improve the process of IRB at U.S. institutions, ranging from the complete abolition of ethical reivew in the social science (Schrag, 2010) to the reduction of mission creep through limited, case-specific review, to moving toward mid-research or post-experiment approval. A suggestion from Glennerster (2017) for field experiments in economics is that approval is not needed until later in the research process. Despite these pushes for reform, it seems unlikely that there will be any meaningful changes, in the short-term, to the IRB process, save for perhaps expansion of their administrative oversight and extension of the review process.

4.4.2 IRBs around the World

There are often significant differences in ethics regulations across countries. We briefly outline some of the similarities and differences in IRB requirements and procedures that exist between the U.S. and other countries around the world.

As outlined in the evolution of codes and principles, discussed in Section 4.3, many of the policies which underlie IRB regulation and practice in the U.S. also underlie those in other Western countries. For universities across high-income countries, IRBs are a common component of the research process at colleges and universities.

Kirigia et al. (2005) contend that "every country, irrespective of its level of economic development, should have in place a functional research ethics review system in order to protect the dignity, integrity and safety of its citizens who participate in research." While these are frequently well developed in Western and high-income countries, few ethics review systems exist in other parts of the world. This is in spite of the massive amount of medical, pharmaceutical, economic, ethnographic, and anthropological research that occurs there. Within low- and middle-income countries, regulations are sparse and somewhat variable. This situation, where high-income countries have strong regulatory procedures for research and low- and middle-income countries do not, has given rise to a concern about "ethics dumping" (Schroeder et al., 2019). Ethics dumping is when research projects that may not be able to obtain informed consent in high-income countries move to low- and middle-income countries, where people may be more willing to consent to participate in research with risky procedures. As ethics dumping has become more of a concern, governments in low- and middle-income countries are establishing policies and ethics review boards to regulate research within their borders. The World Health Organization (WHO, nd) maintains a list of countries that have biomedical or bioethics reviews. Although not surprising, it is more difficult to find a similar list for review boards that govern economic or social science research. While currently the focus of ethical review boards in low- and middle-income countries seems to be on biomedical research, this is likely to change in coming years as review boards in these countries follow a similar trajectory to in the U.S.

Even in countries that lack legislation on the necessity for ethical review, researchers working in these countries may have IRB review through their home institution. As an example, researchers in CGIAR institutions like the International Food Policy Research Institute (IFPRI) or the International Rice Research Institute (IRRI) are required to obtain ethical review by ethics boards at their own institutions. Additionally, not withstanding our earlier story, when local researchers collaborate with academic researchers in places like the U.S., the work typically undergoes ethical review by the IRB at the U.S. institution. There are also IRBs that are not associated with any institution but operate for-profit ethics review boards.[6] Such unaffiliated review boards typically service researchers without access to IRBs. These unaffiliated review boards have become necessary for research in low- and middle-income countries looking to publish research in top academic journals, most of which now require proof of ethical approval prior to publication of research. The requirement of ethical approval of research as a condition for publication obviously creates barriers to entry for those conducting research outside of high-income countries. While local IRBs may rectify some of these concerns, Schroeder et al. (2019) recommend that a global code of ethics or review boards managed by professional associations, such as the American Economic Association (AEA), the Agricultural and Applied Economics Association (AAEA), or International Association of Agricultural Economists (IAAE) could mitigate these issues by providing easier access to the review necessary to satisfy journal requirements.

At present, U.S. codes of ethics based on the Common Rule presently serve as a de facto global code of ethics.

Regardless of location, there needs to be a "deeper understanding of and engagement with how different societies, cultures and peoples understand ethics, research and ethical research" (Israel, 2015). Due to the shortcomings with IRBs regarding economic and social science research, there is room for improvement in their presences and structure around the globe. For those looking to learn more, we refer readers to Israel (2015) for a comprehensive review of the specifics of how IRBs work in the U.S. and around the world.

PERSPECTIVE 4.1   ETHICAL CONSIDERATIONS IN DOING FIELD RESEARCH IN LOW- AND MIDDLE-INCOME COUNTRIES BY AGNES QUISUMBING AND HAZEL MALAPIT

Although social science research is often considered to pose minimal risk to participants, additional ethical considerations come into play when doing field research in low- and middle-income countries, particularly among vulnerable populations.

Both of us are researchers from the Global South (the Philippines) now working in a research institution in the Global North (IFPRI, headquartered in Washington, D.C., though with offices worldwide), part of the CGIAR, a global network of agricultural research centers. Our research has focused on gender and intrahousehold issues and the measurement of women's empowerment. Research on gender issues often involves ethical issues that IRBs do not routinely handle. The CGIAR has adopted system-wide ethics policies that provides general standards for research on human subjects and developed a complementary toolkit on the ethical issues and standards for gender research (CGIAR, nd). A few examples illustrate some of the ethical issues we face in the field.

Foremost is the possibility of putting our respondents at risk when we deal with sensitive topics like intimate partner violence (IPV). Although we routinely hire women interviewers to interview women (and male interviewers to interview men), when interviewing women about this topic, we must also ensure that interviews are conducted privately, with no one able to hear. This is not that easy in the often small and crowded homes in which many of our respondents live; our field teams have often conducted interviews outside our respondents' homes – in gardens, a doorstep, a porch. Beyond that is the ethical obligation to provide help or referral services should a problem be detected. If a respondent is diagnosed with a medical condition or malnutrition, it is relatively easy to make a referral to a health center. But in the case of IPV, social stigma and the lack of trained providers make this issue more difficult.

For this reason, we frequently use questions about attitudes toward IPV from the demographic and health surveys, rather than questions about the respondent's own experience of IPV, which does not carry the same ethical obligation to provide referrals in an environment where there are few trained providers. In other cases, we have explicitly linked up with psychologists or others who are trained to provide counseling and other support.

There are many more ethical issues related to research on vulnerable populations that are discussed in the CGIAR's gender ethics and standards toolkit (Faas et al., 2022), but one that is often neglected is the power imbalance between researchers in the Global North and their collaborators and research subjects in the Global South, and between researchers in the field and respondents. While individual studies can be approved by IRBs, we must recognize that our research should be part of efforts to decolonize development research – to bring to light broader and more informed, local perspectives from planning and inception to execution and dissemination. This means more meaningful collaboration between researchers from the Global North and Global South, respect of host-country institutions (like local IRBs) and ensuring that the ethical acceptability of the research be appropriately assessed against customs and traditions at the study site.

Power imbalances can also manifest themselves during data collection, particularly in highly stratified societies. Interviewers may be more educated than people they interview, especially in poor communities. We have tried to address gender imbalances in power relations by having interviewers of the same sex as the respondent, but this doesn't eliminate all power imbalances due to caste or class.

4.5 Principles and Requirements

Regardless of location in the world or research discipline, the requirements for ethical research are approximately the same: respect for persons, beneficence, and justice. As outlined by Beauchamp (2005), these are derived from the Belmont Report and in turn the Nuremberg Code and Helsinki Declaration. In Belmont, each principle was designed to correspond with a specific guideline or practice that researchers are required to implement when seeking IRB approval. The principles and corresponding practices are presented in Table 4.1.

Of late, privacy for participants and the confidentiality of data in research programs has come to be considered an additional principle. The elevation of privacy and confidentiality to a principle reflects the recent concern within the U.S. regarding how governments, corporations, and scientists use people's data. Historically, however, privacy and confidentiality were considered a practice, with respect for persons, we maintain this organizational structure. In the follow subsections, we discuss each principle in relation to its matching practice.

TABLE 4.1 Principles and Practices

Principle	Practice
respect for subjects	informed consent
	privacy & confidentiality
beneficence	risk–benefit assessment
justice	recruitment & selection

4.5.1 Respect for Persons: Informed Consent

In January 1951, a young mother named Henrietta Lacks visited Johns Hopkins Hospital with complaints of vaginal bleeding. When examined, a large and malignant tumor was found on her cervix. Although Mrs. Lacks received medical treatment, she passed away in October 1951. Before she passed, a sample of her cancer cells were retrieved and given to a tissue lab. While the cells in most tissue samples died after a few days, Mrs. Lacks's cells doubled every 20 to 24 hours. This provided – and continues to provide – tremendous opportunity for medical research. "HeLa" cells, as they would come to be called, have been used to study cancer, test the effects of radiation and poisons, study the human genome, and learn more about how viruses work, and played a role in the development of the polio vaccine.

Despite the tremendous opportunities which HeLa cells provide medical researchers, Mrs. Lacks, a Black woman, was unaware that her cells would be used in such a way. In the 1950s, Johns Hopkins was the only hospital in Baltimore that treated Black patients. Johns Hopkins, like other hospitals at the time, had no formal or required practices for informing or obtaining consent from patients when obtaining tissue samples for research purposes. Nor were there any regulations on the use of these cells in future research.[7] Today, failure to inform Mrs. Lacks that her cells would or could be used for research purposes would violate the principle of respect for persons because the doctors did not seek her informed consent.[8]

The principle of respect for persons is rooted in the need to treat individuals "as autonomous agents [and] that persons with diminished autonomy are entitled to protections" (United States, 1978). For individuals to retain autonomy requires that they have the freedom to decide whether or not to participate in the research. However, freedom to decide is insufficient. True autonomy requires sufficient information to make a decision. Having decided to participate in the research, individuals then must have the freedom to withdraw from participation at any time. This again requires that individuals have sufficient information throughout the research program to continually decide to remain as participants. The Belmont Report succinctly describes that respect for persons allows the participant to engage "voluntarily and with adequate information" (United States, 1978). It goes on to state: for situations in which individuals may have "diminished autonomy" (e.g. children, mentally disabled, prisoners), there are additional protections to ensure that respect for persons is maintained.

**BOX 4.5.1   THE BELMONT REPORT, ON AUTONOMY
AND RESPECT FOR PERSONS**

The autonomous person is an individual capable of deliberation about personal goals, and of acting under the direction of such deliberation. To respect autonomy is to give weight to autonomous persons' considered options and choices, while refraining for obstructing their actions, unless they are clearly detrimental to others. To show lack of respect for an autonomous agent is to repudiate that person's considered judgments, to deny an individual the freedom to act on those considered judgments, or to withhold information necessary to make a considered judgment, when there are no compelling reasons to do so.

The way in which IRBs and researchers uphold the principle of respect for persons is through the practice of obtaining informed consent. Informed consent has two important, related components:

1. That research participants comprehend the nature of the research and their role in that research
2. That research participants agree to participate in the research

Intuitively, this breaks down into the two elements of "informed" and "consent." First, to be informed requires that the researcher share information about the purpose, methods, demands, risks, troubles, and outcomes of the research project and program with the research participant. This includes telling the participant what the study does, why the study is being done, what will happen to individuals if they participate, the length of the study, the number of others participating, what risks and benefits can be expected from the study, if they will be compensated, and what their data will be used for. Individuals must also be able to ask any questions which may arise from this information sharing. Next, consent must be voluntary. When consent is voluntary it is an autonomous act, committed intentionally, with understanding and without influences from coercion or manipulation by others.

Unfortunately, there are cases in which researchers take advantage of weak ethics systems or low information among research participants. Hoffmann (2020) finds that while 65 percent of research participants in Europe and the U.S. knew they were part of an experiment, only 34 percent of research participants in Africa, Asia, and Latin America were similarly aware. Further still, Hoffmann (2020) finds that 78 percent of authors do not discuss informed consent with research participants.

The process for ensuring that participants are informed and participating voluntarily can vary significantly depending on the research context. Regardless of circumstance, there are two procedures that constitute a researcher having obtained informed consent. First, the researcher must obtain a "signed" informed consent form from all research participants to demonstrate that the research participant understands their rights. There are a wide variety of signatures which could be accepted by the IRB. These include a "wet" (written) signature, digital signature, verbal signature, filmed signature, or some other authorized signature. Second, the researcher must always allow a research participant to withdraw or redecide about their consent at any point in the research process. While most think of "at any point" to be in the course of the research program, it also extends to any future date. Research participants always have the freedom to withdrawn their informed consent and have their data removed from the study.

With this formal process in mind, there are contexts in which obtaining consent may not be straightforward. First, there may be difficulties that arise from working in nonliterate or nonwritten communities. These are issues tend to have a straight-forward solution. There are flexible and creative approaches to obtaining consent and alternatives to wet signatures. As Josephson and Smale (2021) report from their survey of development economists, there are a wide variety of ways consent is obtained, including oral, witnessed, and verbal communal consent. While a signed consent form is considered standard, oral consent was the most frequently used method by those surveyed (Josephson and Smale, 2021).

Second, there may be difficulties about from whom or at what level consent should be obtained. In most cases, the individual participating in the research should be the person who provides their consent. In cases where an individual may have diminished autonomy, a parent or guardian may provide consent, even though that person will not be a research participant. The trouble arises when an intervention is applied to an entire area or when cultural contexts may not make it appropriate to obtain consent from the research participant. In the former case, it may ultimately be appropriate to waive informed consent. Glennerster (2017) discusses a study of the effect of billboards encouraging smoking cessation on smoking. In this case it would be impractical to try to obtain consent from everyone the billboards might impact. Rather than seeking consent from all individuals who participate in the study (all who are exposed to the treatment or control billboard), it is more appropriate to obtain informed consent from those individuals who are surveyed about their response to the billboards. Similarly, Hutton et al. (2008) describe cases in which someone cannot opt out of participation, for example, adding chlorine to a community well or erecting streetlights. In many of these cases, it is likely that most IRBs will waive the requirement for obtaining consent for study participants and only require informed consent for survey participants, that is, those who will have their data collected.

In the latter case, cultural context may not make it appropriate to obtain in-formed consent from the research participant. In many cultures and countries the age of consent may differ from that age in the U.S. In the U.S., research involving anyone under 18 requires parental consent, but in other countries, this age may be lower or higher. In some places, it may be deemed inappropriate to obtain consent from an adult woman unless an adult man has first consented. In these cases, the adult woman may not feel free to express autonomy if the adult man has already provided his consent, raising the question of whether she can actually give consent. In some communities, it may be that consent from the community's leaders is considered locally sufficient and that individual consent is unnecessary. It is important to recognize that the understanding of the individual in many cultures differ from the individualism prevalent in the U.S. and other Western countries (Taylor, 1990). These examples demonstrate how the use of individual-based models of consent become problematic when applied to cultures and environments where individual autonomy is not emphasized (Tindana et al., 2006). However, as Josephson and Smale (2021) discuss, differences in conceptions of the self and individual autonomy do not necessarily preclude the ability to make an individual decision. In particular, iterative and collective reflection can encourage an aspect of collective assent while still ultimately permitting an individual decision.

PERSPECTIVE 4.2   DIFFERENT LEVELS OF INFORMED CONSENT BY MELINDA SMALE

In my experience with CGIAR centers from the mid-1980s to 2008, the *modus operandi* for conducting social science research was top-down and pro-science, mirroring the research of the crop improvement programs. Our mission was to work with and through national research organizations. Later, as funding sources and approaches diversified, we undertook research that was "participatory" in the sense that farmer perspectives occupied a central role. Yet, we never questioned farmer willingness to participate. Whether our partners were staff of national research organizations or other nongovernmental organizations, we relied on our "counterparts" (the terminology at that time) to translate language and mediate cultural differences for us in order to obtain tacit, oral consent. It was rare for farmer respondents to refuse an interview with us – given they faced significant power differences. The ideology was that we were there to serve them and they would be pleased to tell us the story of their use of new seed varieties and farming practices. We know, however, that variety introductions and new techniques do not always produce benefits and can produce losses. Because of wide variability in growing conditions, a seed variety may not germinate or may yield poorly for an individual farmer despite its generally good performance in on-station trials or on-farm demonstrations.

I recall fieldwork in which I participated in Pakistan, Malawi, Mexico, Hungary, India, Uganda, Kenya, Mali, Ghana, and Bolivia during that period. Often the research I led was part of a larger project that included surveys led by colleagues in multiple countries with similar methods and the same *modus operandi*. In the field, we had tiered approach to consent. The first tier was research clearance by national, regional, and district officials that involved research clearance with wet signatures. This formal approval process was followed by informal discussions with village leaders whose role it was to represent and protect the interests of the villagers. Typically, we drew our samples from the household lists provided by the village leaders. When working for the CGIAR in those years, when we surveyed households, we were typically interested in detailed data about crop management and production, as well as assets and income of the farm household. We often sought to disaggregate data on plot management, asset ownership, crop harvests, and sales by gender. In this third tier of the consent process, if we intended to conduct any intra-household analysis, we needed consent to interview both husbands and wives as individuals. Obtaining oral consent from both husbands and wives was not always a comfortable process, and consent patterns were not always predictable.

In many of the cultural settings where I worked, male household heads considered it their responsibility to make the consent decision on behalf of their household and to be present for all interviews conducted with household members. In other settings, women made their own decision to be interviewed or not. I was trained to hire both male and female enumerators in most settings. Over the years, many of the areas where we worked were more heavily surveyed by a range of teams funded by various donors and using different approaches. Respondent fatigue became evident – and there was also growing respondent recognition of individual rights.

Barrett et al. (2009) find that CGIAR social scientists were often unaware of IRBs and routinely failed to adhere to current international practices for the ethical protection of human participants in data collection. In December 2018, only 8 of the 15 CGIAR centers required research involving human participants to be cleared by an ethical review board (Josephson and Smale, 2021). By contrast, today's One CGIAR endorses a single all-encompassing ethics framework. A 2019 document recognizes that "operating according to the highest ethical standards is a prerequisite to being able to deliver on our vision." Furthermore, "the ethical conduct of science and research is a necessary and essential condition precedent without which we jeopardize future food security."

A final note on informed consent for economists: informed consent procedures must be honest and forthright. Some fields may include deception in their work, and often informed consent procedures can become complicated in cases in which participants may be lied to in the course of the research work. For economists, however, this is (for once) an easy answer: we do not deceive in our work. Deception contaminates the pool of research participants because participants who have previously been deceived may no longer believe our incentives are honest, thus endangering the incentive compatibility of our work. And so, failing to obtain consent or providing false information while obtaining consent is not an issue with which we need to grapple: it should not be done.

4.5.2 Respect for Persons: Privacy & Confidentiality

In 2006, the research division of America Online (AOL) decided to release internet search records from a randomly selected 657,000 users from over a three-month period, totally 20 million search queries. Prior to release, the data was de-identified by removing all personally identifiable information (PII), instead including only a random seven-digit number to represent each unique user. The purpose of the release, as Abdur Chowdhurry, head of AOL Research, stated, was to support an "open research community, which is creating opportunities for researchers in academia and industry alike" (Ohm, 2010).

The data were released on August 4, and five days later, Michael Barbaro and Tom Zeller, reporters for the *New York Times*, published a story titled "A Face Is Exposed for AOL Searcher No. 4417749" (Barbaro and Zeller, 2006). In the story, Barbaro and Zeller (2006) write:

> Buried in a list of 20 million Web search queries collected by AOL and recently released on the Internet is user No. 4417749. The number was assigned by the company to protect the searcher's anonymity, but it was not much of a shield. No. 4417749 conducted hundreds of searches over a three-month period on topics ranging from "numb fingers" to "60 single men" to "dog that urinates on everything." And search by search, click by click, the identity of AOL user No. 4417749 became easier to discern. There are queries for "landscapers in Lilburn, Ga," several people with the last name Arnold and "homes sold in shadow lake subdivision gwinnett county georgia." It did not take much investigating to follow that data trail to Thelma Arnold, a 62-year-old widow who lives in Lilburn, Ga., frequently researches her friends' medical ailments and loves her three dogs. "Those are my searches," she said, after a reporter read part of the list to her.

AOL, realizing that its effort to make the data confidential was insufficient to protect user privacy, removed the data on August 7 before the story had even run. However, by that time the data had already been copied and shared across the internet. The data are still out there, for those interested in digging it up (Heffetz and Ligett, 2014). Ironically, the data release had the opposite effect of what Chowdurry and AOL had hoped for. Instead of fostering open science and closer collaboration between academia and industry, the data release and the resulting backlash chilled collaboration. AOL fired the researchers responsible for sharing the data, along with their several of their bosses, and removed any web presence for AOL Research (Ohm, 2010). The incident contributed to a greater wariness on the part of technology companies to make their data open and available to academic researchers.

While AOL was not subject to an IRB, it did have its own privacy policies and procedures. Ostensibly, the company's policies and procedures were followed, but those implementing them appear not to have recognized the risk in releasing the search history data (Zeller, 2006). The AOL story is illustrative of not only the importance privacy and confidentiality play in the principle of respect for persons but also in the potential for failure of those in charge of ethical oversight.

In discussing the right to privacy protection, the terms *anonymity*, *privacy*, and *confidentiality* are often used as synonyms. However, these terms do not mean the same thing and, as Sieber and Tolich (2006) point out, anonymity and confidentiality are mutually exclusive. Defining these terms as they relate to the collection of socioeconomic data is an important first step in cultivating a trusting and secure relationship between researcher and research participant.

Anonymity is when the researcher acquires data about a research subject that is not identifiable information. In economics, online data collection is frequently anonymous. For example, online willingness to pay studies, like Slade et al. (2019), in which surveys and choice experiments are deployed online using a third party. Data are collected absent of any PII and the survey respondents remain anonymous to the researchers and, if there is no compensation for participation, to the third-party survey firm. Similarly, anonymous data can be collected or purchased from companies like Facebook or Google, where researchers have no access to any identifiable information.

While economists sometimes collect and use anonymous data, it is more often the case that data are not anonymous. Examples of this include any time the researcher is involved in face-to-face survey work, if participants are compensated, if participants must sign consent forms, or if the goal is to track participants over time. In the economics lab, data are often collected absent any PII. But when lab participants are paid for participation, they must sign a receipt, meaning their involvement is no longer anonymous, even if their data are anonymous. Similarly, a signature on a consent form means that participation is no longer anonymous, although again there may be no way to identify the individual's data when decoupled from the consent form. When data collected by one researcher are shared with other researchers, IRB protocols typically require that the shared data contain no PII, meaning an individual's participation in the research should be anonymous to the other researchers. Guaranteeing this anonymity can be difficult, as we discuss in detail in Chapter 5.

Distinct from anonymity, privacy is about people, not data (Sieber and Tolich, 2006). Privacy is a person's control over the access that others have to them, their choices, their actions, and so on. In the U.S., privacy is not a Constitutional right, although the Supreme Court has used the Fourth Amendment (protection against unreasonable searches and seizures) to establish a right of privacy from government interference. This has been an important justification for rulings in *Griswold v. Connecticut* (contraception), *Roe v. Wade* (abortion), and *Lawrence v. Texas* (sodomy).[9] Similarly, neither the Maastricht Treaty that established the European Union nor the United Nations Universal Declaration of Human Rights explicitly mentions a right to privacy, although articles in both documents have been interpreted, similar to the Fourth Amendment, to imply a right to privacy, at least from the government. Outside of a right to privacy from government, an individual's right to or expectation of privacy from others is less clear. As Mackie (1977) notes, privacy may be more a feature of our lives that others allow us than a right we inherently have as humans. Because of this, the right to or expectation of privacy can be not only subtle and culturally specific while in some cases legally protected.

While privacy is about people, confidentiality, like anonymity, is about data. In the IRB applications and protocols we have completed, there is always a section about the "privacy of subjects and confidentiality of data." In completing an IRB form and in drafting an informed consent document, the researcher agrees to preserve a research participant's privacy by keeping a participant's data confidential. The details of how data will be kept confidential are typically spelled out in the informed consent document. The confidentiality of data occurs when we make an individual's data anonymous to users of the data.

In a typical IRB protocol and informed consent document for human subject research, the researcher promises to take three actions. First, data will be anonymized, and only the anonymized data will be analyzed. Second, data will be kept secure, either in a locked room or cabinet or on an encrypted drive. Third, data will not be shared with other researchers. If the data are to be shared, then the researcher will need to describe why the data will be shared and how they will ensure confidentiality of the data in the process of sharing.

Confidentiality of data helps assure the privacy of the research participant, thus allowing the participant to feel free to share things about themselves they might otherwise not want to share. The importance of mutual trust is perhaps more of a concern in other professions, such as psychology and medicine, but applied economists may also have similar concerns. To achieve trust, it is imperative to ensure that research participants know their data are protected. That regardless of what they share, the researchers will not share it with outsiders.

A researcher needs to be aware of the situations in which they are considered a mandated reporter. A mandated reporter is a person, typically designated by their profession, who is required by law to report suspected or known instances of abuse, harm, or intended violence, to one's self or others. The situations in which one's status as a mandated reported may be relevant involve cases of child abuse, spousal abuse, planned suicide, or other types of violence. Clarifying with the research participant what constitutes a situation with mandated reporting is another important step in building mutual trust. A researcher must be clear that they are not giving legal advice, but they will seek outside assistance for particular circumstances if there is concern.

4.5.3   Beneficence: Risk–Benefit Assessment

In the summer of 1971, 24 men participated in a two-week prison simulation. Half of the men were randomly assigned to be prison guards while the other half were assigned to be prisoners. The objective of the work, led by Stanford psychology professor Philip Zimbardo, was to evaluate the power of rules, group identity, and behavioral validation. However, Zimbardo's experiment worked too well. What is widely known as the Stanford Prison Experiment quickly devolved into mistreatment and abuse of those who participated (Zimbardo, 2004).

In the experiment, the prisoners and the guards were intended to assume the standard roles within a simulated prison environment. The research team converted a section of the basement in the psychology building into a mock prison, with small cells and a hallway leading to the prison yard. Those selected to be guards were given uniforms designed to de-individualize them, which included khaki shirt and pants and mirrored sunglasses. Those selected to be prisoners were confined to the basement jail wearing baggy smocks and no underwear. Prisoners were to be confined to the mock prison for the entire two-week study period while guards could go home after working an eight-hour shift. There is disagreement about the exact instructions that Zimbardo gave to the guards (Bottoms, 2014; Texier, 2019), but at the very least, they were told to be firm in their exertion of power over the prisoners and to make the prisoners feel submissive, disrespected, and helpless.

Each group rapidly adapted to their assigned roles. Within the first 24 hours of the experiment, the prisoners staged a rebellion, refusing to leave their cells, tearing their clothes, and verbally assaulting the guards. In response, the guards stripped prisoners naked, sprayed them with fire extinguishers, removed bedding from the cells, and refused prisoner requests for the bathroom, instead forcing them to defecate in buckets in the cells. The guards separated "good" prisoners from "bad," isolating those who the guard perceived as instigators of the rebellion. This resulted in the prisoners becoming suspicious of each other over having snitched to the guards. Over the next three days, the guards would arbitrarily strip search prisoners, force them to wear bags on their heads, force them to do push-ups, and deny them food and sleep. Due to the emotional breakdown of several prisoners and the excessive aggression of the guards, the experiment was terminated only 6 days in to the planned 14-day study (Zimbardo, 2004).

There were many ethical violations in the Stanford Prison Experiment, including several related to informed consent. At the start of the experiment, the prisoners underwent mock arrests at their home by real Palo Alto police officers. Those participating as prisoners had not been informed that this would happen. The Palo Alto police took the "arrested" research participants to police headquarters, where they were charged with armed robbery and burglary, were "booked" and Mirzandized, and then transport to the Stanford basement prison (Zimbardo, 2004). Less than 36 hours into the experiment, one participant, a prisoner numbered 8612, began suffering from an emotional disturbance, crying uncontrollably, and demonstrating disorganized thinking and rage. Guards told him at a meeting that he was "weak," and when he returned to the other prisoners, he told them, "You can't leave. You can't quit." It was only after he "began to act 'crazy', to scream, to curse, to go into a rage that seemed out of control" that the researchers permitted him to leave (Haney et al., 1973).

The failure to protect the participants in the Stanford Prison Experiment violates the principle of beneficence. *Beneficence*, as a word, suggests acts and qualities of kindness, generosity, and charity. However, the rules, as pertaining to research with human subjects, go beyond this. The rule of beneficence implores researchers to act morally for the benefit of others, helping them to further their important and legitimate interests, often by preventing or removing possible harms. Beneficence demands that a balance be struck between not causing harm to research participants while maximizing the benefits of research for society. The ultimate intention should be to maximize benefits and improve people's well-being. This can be a challenge for a number of reasons, not least of which is because it is difficult for humans to accurately weight costs and benefits, particularly in the long run.

In most applied economic work, we can assume that there is some benefit and little to no harm. However, in some studies, harm or the perception of harm may exist. One example of the perception of harm is from work that Anna participated in regarding the impact of COVID-19 on food security in Arizona (Acciai et al., 2020). During the IRB review of the protocol, administrative reviewers at HSPP raised the possibility of psychological distress from participants taking the survey. HSPP reviewers were concerned that questions asking a survey participant about their level of food insecurity might cause undue distress to those participants who were in fact food insecure. A compromise was reached in which participants could be asked questions on food insecurity as long as statements and resources were provided at the end of the survey for those participants who might have become distressed through taking the survey.

A second example of potential harm is from an RCT that Jeff help conducted in Zambia, which distributed solar stoves to determine their impact of dietary diversity and deforestation (McCann et al., 2021). The solar stoves were large reflective parabolic dish that concentrated the rays of the sun onto a single point below a cook pot. Here the protocol went through administrative review but during a review by the exempt committee of the IRB a concern was raised about the risk of injury to participants that looked directly into the center of the parabolic dish. The effect would be similar to looking directly into the sun. To reduce the risk of eye damage to solar stove users, the research team proposed providing polarized sunglasses to each individual assigned to the stove treatment as well as educating them on the risk of using the stove when not wearing the sunglasses. This proposal was deemed to sufficiently lower the risk of the project to minimal risk, and the protocol was exempted from full board review.

Other strategies to avoid risk include monitoring participants after the experiment or interview has concluded; developing safety nets for support for any realized risks; excluding vulnerable groups; considering and fully investigating potential, alternative low-risk options; and anticipating the misuse of data or information after collection, although this last strategy implies that we, as researchers, have a duty to what happens with our work once it is out of our hands – no easy feat!

An assessment of benefits is the counterpoint to addressing costs and minimizing risks. In many studies, benefits can be intangible or quite a distance from the research participants. Although "scholars often claim that by contributing to a general body of knowledge" (Israel, 2015) the lives of research participants and the population at large will be improved, it is not clear that this is the case. In fact, the effects and impacts of research work might be uncertain, particularly in the short-term. As such, careful consideration should be given in weighing what the benefits could possibly be – beyond the future, uncertain benefits of the work – especially in light of proximal risks that may exist.

As economists, the process of weighing costs and benefits, with the objective of reducing costs, may seem natural. Most graduate programs in applied economics offer a course on cost–benefit analysis, and in micro theory we spend most of our time trying to maximize utility while minimizing costs or vice versa. Consequently, we may imagine ourselves more suited toward these sorts of assessments than researchers from other fields. However, as detailed in Chapter 2, economists are not immune to hubris. Within an ethical context, ensuring beneficence can often require valuing things without a market price. Furthermore, cost–benefit analyses are not culturally or morally neutral. It is imperative that researchers be careful in weighing these elements, both in the specific work of ensuring beneficence and in making broader determinations about research.

4.5.4 Justice: Recruitment and Selection

In 1989, members of the Havasupai Tribe wanted to learn why the incidence of diabetes within their community was increasing. Genetic links to diabetes had been identified in other tribes, and if a similar gene could be located among the Havasupai, it might provide a tool for addressing risk factors and improving health in the community. Two professors at Arizona State University (ASU), John Martin, an anthropologist, and Therese Markow, a geneticist, worked with the tribe to develop the project. Markow also expressed an interest in expanding the study to include mental disorders, although Martin is said to have recognized that there would be little interest in doing so on the part of the Havasupai (Sterling, 2011).

Nearly 100 tribal members signed a broad consent document to "study the causes of behavioral/medical disorders." As Sterling (2011) notes, most of the participants in the research had not completed high school, and, for many, English was a second language. All the tribe members believed that they were donating blood solely for the purpose of looking for a link to diabetes to improve the health in their community. However, the ASU researchers went beyond this. Determining that the genetic link to diabetes found in other tribes did not exist among the Havasupai, Martin and Markow continued their research into medical disorders. The researchers did not seek additional consent from the tribe before using the donated blood samples to conduct research beyond the original diabetes study. Other researchers at ASU also used the Havasupai samples, without consent, for their work and published papers about inbreeding, alcoholism, and the origin and migration of the tribe from Asia, which contradicts the tribe's religious beliefs about their origin. (Sterling, 2011).

In 2003, the Havasupai Tribe sued the governing body of the public university system in Arizona, the Arizona Board of Regents. The suit listed six charges, including lack of informed consent, violation of civil rights, and intentional or negligent infliction of emotional distress. For the next seven years, ASU vigorously denied any wrongdoing and spent a reported $1.7 million defending itself in the case (Sterling, 2011). Eventually the case was settled, with the Havasupai Tribe receiving $700,000, scholarship funds, and a return of the blood samples. The tribe's experience demonstrates the real harm that research can do to a community.

The case of the Havasupai Tribe demonstrates a violation of the principle of justice. The principle of justice can appear straightforward: treat people all the same. However, the Belmont Report's definition of persons with diminished autonomy already suggests that not all research participants are equal. Children, pregnant women, and prisoners all belong to protected classes in research. There are also researchers who perceive people of different races or statuses to be "less than." The principle of justice is designed to address such biases by acknowledging that certain groups warrant additional protections. It is insufficient to treat people all the same. Rather, the principle of justice should be understood as the notion that equals should be treated equally.

The principle of justice is rooted in combating mistreatment of people, by either inclusion or exclusion in research work. Mistreatment through inclusion occurs when people are included as study participants because they are vulnerable to mistreatment and not because of any genuine interest in creating benefits for the population. The treatment of the Havasupai is an example of this. Conversely, mistreatment through exclusion occurs when people are excluded as study participants because their inclusion could pose some unique challenge, thus excluding the population from receiving the potential benefits of the study. Oh et al. (2015) document the lack of diversity in clinical and biomedical studies, which tend to have study populations with a larger share of white males than exist in the general population.

When applying the principle of justice, researchers must consider the population of interest for a study. Justice, in this conception, applies to classes of people rather than individuals (Mastroianna et al., 1994). In a just study, risks and benefits should be allocated fairly among the population. Fair allocation is best characterized as equity; fairness requires that no single group (e.g. gender, racial, ethnic, socioeconomic) receive disproportionate benefits or bear disproportionate burdens in the process of research. As stated in the Belmont Report:

> The selection of research subjects needs to be scrutinized in order to determine whether some classes (e.g., welfare patients, particular racial and ethnic minorities, or persons confined to institutions) are being systematically selected simply because of their easy availability, their compromised position, or their manipulability, rather than for reasons directly related to the problem being studied.
>
> (United States, 1978)

The principle of justice often becomes complicated when working with vulnerable populations. While individuals should not be forced to participate in a research program, they should also receive fair opportunity to participate. Vulnerable populations are often given additional review by IRBs. Issues of informed consent, in particular the ability to provide consent, as well as issues of recruitment and costs to participation are different with vulnerable populations. Issues of paternalism may exist when applying principles of justice with vulnerable populations. For example, by assuming that a vulnerable population is "too risky" to work with, a researcher fails to give the group the chance to weigh the costs and benefits and risks and opportunities for themselves. It may be the case that minor impositions may have significant benefits and researchers should consider carefully the benefits and burdens of participation. This process can be improved by involving members of the community in making these decisions. Kara (2018) argues that inclusion of community members in research decision-making processes should be done even with non-vulnerable populations. But it is vitally important in these contexts so as to ensure appropriate applications of justice.

Ensuring fairness in the recruitment and randomization of an experiment or other research program may require additional preliminary work to ensure justice. But with deliberative effort requirements of justice are easy to fulfill and are of significant value to the research participants, as well as those who benefit from research products.

4.6 Conclusion

This chapter has outlined the ethical issues involved in data collection focusing on the principles and requirements of IRBs. This includes two parts: (1) the history of and motivation behind these requirements, codes, and regulations and (2) how the the principles of respect for subjects, beneficence, and justice that motivate these codes and regulations are tied to specific practices. These practices include obtaining informed consent from research participants, preserving the privacy of participants and the confidentiality of their data, conducting risk–benefit assessments, and ensuring justice and fairness in recruitment and selection.

Despite these best practices, clear procedures, and regulations, there are some things that cannot be prevented. If someone wants to behave unethically . . . then they will. In particular, this purposeful display of unethical behavior may manifest in two common unethical research problems: fabrication and falsification. In fabrication, nonexistent data or results are created by a researcher. In falsification, data exist but are altered to obtain a specific result. Data or results can also be changed or omitted so that the research is not accurately represented in the research record. In these cases, the regulations, requirements, and codes of conduct do not protect against unethical behavior. And so, as researchers, we must take it upon ourselves to ensure that our work is done ethically and that we protect and ensure the safety of those around us and behave according to the principles and requirements of ethical data collection.

Notes

1 The authors would like to express some hesitancy to the use of participant in this context, as it suggests knowing participation, which in the case of Humphreys's work was not possible.
2 An important note: Green was not involved in carrying out the experiment and claims that he never saw the raw data. However, he signed the journal's authorship form, which certified that he had examined the raw/original data. In Chapter 3, we discussed authorship guidelines, and under most of those, Green would not have qualified as an author, given his contributions. But, without Green's name, the paper likely would not have been published in a journal like *Science*. We discuss this incentive structure further in Chapter 7.
3 Jonsen (2005) raises some of the challenges with this initial charge: "It is not quite obvious what sort of investigation 'identifies' ethical principles (*identify* is a peculiar word: it implies that the principles are lying out there somewhere and can be found by searching, like a treasure hunt)."

4 IRBs go by a number of names, depending on the institution in which they are situated. These include ethical review board (ERB), internal review committee (IRC), or any combination of these terms. For consistency, in this book we refer to them as IRBs.

5 In 2022 the most common specialties on the IRB at the University of Arizona were pediatrics, surgery, pharmacy, and medicine. By contrast, exempt reviewers were from linguistics, marketing, communication, and business/econ.

6 Some Western researchers have increasingly turned to these resources in order to obtain ethics approval in the country in which they are working, in addition to whatever approval is required by their home institution.

7 It almost goes without saying that there were no regulations for nonmedical research programs either, with respect to informed consent.

8 For more on the story of Henrietta Lacks, the contribution of her cells to science, and the fight of her family to receive recognition and compensation for her role, there is no better source than *The Immortal Life of Henrietta Lacks* (Skloot, 2011).

9 Although the current Court seems to be seeking to undermine most, if not all, of these rulings, putting shaky ground under the concept of the right to privacy in the U.S. (*Dobbs v. Jackson*).

5

DATA MANAGEMENT

5.1 Introduction

In the mid-1990s, the Group Insurance Commission (GIC) in Massachusetts released data on approximately 135,000 state employees and their families (Lasalandra, 1997). The GIC was responsible for purchasing health insurance for state employees, and the goal of making these data public was to allow researchers in academia and industry to design and recommend improvements to the state health care system. The release of individual medical data made many people nervous regarding their personal privacy. Dolores Mitchell, Executive Director of GIC, worked to reassure people, stating, "[M]y own records are in there and I care very deeply about security" (Lasalandra, 1997). Prior to the release of the data, GIC made sure to remove what it considered personally identifiable information (PII), such as names, exact addresses (though not ZIP Codes), and Social Security numbers.

Latanya Sweeney, who at the time was a graduate student in computer science at MIT, doubted GIC's assurances of data confidentiality.[1] She purchased a voter registration list for Cambridge, Massachusetts, for $20, which contained information such as individual names, addresses (including ZIP Codes), birth date, and gender (Sweeney, 2002). As the governor of Massachusetts at the time, William Weld had medical records in the GIC data. Weld's birth date, ZIP Code, and gender were public information. Using the voter registration data, Sweeney identified six people in Cambridge with Weld's birthday, three of whom were men, and he was the only one who lived in his ZIP Code. Knowing that Weld was the only man with his birthday in his ZIP Code allowed Sweeney (2007) to search the GIC data and identify Weld's medical records. While GIC had promised to anonymize the data before making it public, Sweeney was able to reidentify that data by combining two different data

DOI: 10.4324/9781003025061-8

sets. This process is known today as a reidentification attack. Once the news of Sweeney's reidentification attack broke, Joseph Heyman, President of the Massachusetts Medical Society, concluded that "there is no patient confidentiality. It's gone" (Lasalandra, 1997).

While the story of Sweeney's identification of Weld is sometimes identified as an extreme example, the opportunity for privacy violations in data is widespread – and the chance to identify people, as Sweeney identified Weld, are hardly uncommon. This is particularly true in the social sciences. As applied economists, we rely on microeconomic data that describe the choices, actions, and attributes of individuals, households, and firms. Ethical norms, and in many cases legal codes, require the de-identification of data when using or sharing it. Laws in many countries, and ethical review boards at universities, require that PII be kept confidential. But making data truly anonymous requires more than just removing names or addresses from a data set, as Sweeney demonstrated by identifying Weld by linking only two data sets.

Another similar reidentification attack was carried out in 2006 by Arvind Narayanan, then a graduate student, and Vitaly Shmatikov, a professor, at the University of Texas at Austin (Narayanan and Shmatikov, 2008).[2] In 2006, Netflix released data from its subscriber database on users' ratings of movies. In order to protect privacy, Netflix removed direct personal identifiers and released only a random sample of all subscribers and only a random sample of the ratings from a given subscriber. The data release was part of the Netflix prize, a $1 million prize for the individual or team that could improve upon Netflix's own algorithm for recommending new movies to subscribers based on a subscriber's past ratings.

The Netflix data contained only four pieces of information: an anonymous user identifier, the movie, the date of the grade, and the grade. Narayanan and Shmatikov combined these data with public data from the movie rating site IMDb.com, which contained a user's IMDb user name, the movies they have watched, their ratings, and the date of the rating. With this combined data set, Narayanan and Shmatikov were able to use an individual's public IMDb rating to identify them and reveal all their ratings in the supposedly private Netflix data. While a person's tastes in movies might not seem to be vital private information, one can imagine someone wanting to keep private their love (or hate) of movies involving topics such as queerness religion, politics, race, and the like.

The objective of this chapter is to understand the challenges of managing and sharing data in an ethically responsible way. We start by discussing the need for data sharing in order to achieve the goal of open science to make research transparent and reproducible. Many researchers are reluctant to share data and code and so the profession needs to consider ways in which to reward data sharing. We then turn to the different types of data that economists use and the unique threats each data type posses to privacy and confidentiality.

The remainder of the chapter shifts focus to the actual how of data sharing and, in particular, the measures that are necessary to ensure shared data preserves the anonymity and confidentiality that is promised to research participants on informed consent forms. What the stories of Weld and the Netflix Prize illustrate is that "removing identifying information is not sufficient for anonymity" (Narayanan and Shmatikov, 2008). A data base administrator or a data set's author must take into account the current and future existence of other data that could be combined in a reidentification attack. This insight has lead to a variety of approaches to ensuring privacy protection in public use data sets. However, the anonymization of data comes with a cost: the more anonymous a data set (the more privacy is protected), the more statistical accuracy is lost. There is a trade-off between protecting privacy and sharing accurate data that social scientists are just now beginning to grapple with.

5.2   The Need for Data Sharing

In 2020, a group of researchers lead by Ariella Kristal attempted to replicate a now-retracted three-study paper (two lab, one field experiment) by Shu et al. (2012). The original study (ironically) was about people's honesty in reporting to a third party in a context where the third party is unlikely to verify honesty. Examples include tax documents and insurance policies, where individuals self-report information and sign their name. The retracted Shu et al. (2012) paper tests for differences in honesty, depending on whether an individual is asked to sign their name at the beginning or end of a document. They report simply having people sign at the beginning of the document increases honest reporting. The replication by Kristal et al. (2020) included all five of the original authors and attempted both direct and conceptual replications of the two lab experiments. None of the results from the original held up under the scrutiny of the replications.

The story could have ended there as an excellent example of ethical research. The original authors conducted several experiments and published their findings. These original authors then engaged with other authors to replicate the original results, and when those original findings did not hold up, they published their new results. The replicating authors write, "Given the policy applications of this result, it is important to update the scientific record regarding the veracity of these results" (Kristal et al., 2020).

However, the fact that there was no attempt, or reported attempt, to replicate the findings of the field experiment in the retracted study raised questions among some researchers.[3] The field experiment involved an auto insurance company that requested policyholders to report the current odometer reading on their insured vehicles. Individuals were randomized into a "sign at the top" or "sign at the bottom" reporting form. In the original 2013 publication, none of the data for the three studies were made available as part of the publication. But all the data were made available as part of the 2020 publication. This allowed a group of researchers unaffiliated with either of the 2013 or 2020 study to take a look at the data. As reported in Simonsohn et al. (2021), several anomalies emerged from just examining the raw data from the field experiment. There were implausible distributions of values, no rounding in self-reported values, and near-duplicate values. These anomalies lead the new group of researchers to conclude that the original data were fabricated. Based on the evidence in Simonsohn et al. (2021), the editors of *Proceedings of the National Academy of Sciences* retracted Shu et al. (2012). It is still unclear who fabricated the data: whether it was the authors who ran the experiment, an individual in the authors' lab, or someone at the insurance company. What is clear is that without the data being shared as part of Kristal et al. (2020), the fraud would not have been discovered.

Communality is one of the scientific norms discussed in the opening chapter. As opposed to secrecy, communality calls for the open sharing of research methods, practices, and findings. It is the foundation of open science. Open science not only contributes to efficiency in producing new scientific research by avoiding duplication and promoting access, but it also makes science more robust by allowing for the identification of bad science and, in extreme cases, falsified results. Data sharing is an integral component of communality to facilitate improvement in the quality and practice of science.

For a data-driven science, like applied economics, there are two key components that must be shared to ensure transparency and reproducibility. The first is data, and the second is code. Code sharing has become relatively common due to journal policies and websites like GitHub. But the sharing of data, beyond the final, cleaned, regression-ready data, remains relatively uncommon for a variety of reasons that we discuss in this section.

5.2.1 Current Practices are Insufficient

As recently as 2010, one could find at least one book on research ethics in social science that encouraged the destruction of data after publication. The justification is that preserving data over time increases the probability that someone other than the original researcher(s) may gain access to the data and be less scrupulous in preserving subject privacy. Oliver (2010) writes,

> Generally speaking it is not necessary to store all of the raw data from a research study, once that study has been written up as a thesis or as a journal article. . . . One might argue that there could be the necessity for another researcher to reanalyse the data in order to confirm the results, and that this is a justification for data storage. However, this could be achieved shortly after the first analysis, thus removing the necessity to store the data. It is possible for another researcher to replicate the research design and to collect more data in a comparable context.
>
> *(p. 90)*

The American Economic Association (AEA) and the Econometric Society instituted data availability policies for their journals in the mid-2000s, so this view was clearly in decline by 2010. But for many years enforcement of data-sharing policies at economics journals was lax.

Perhaps the earliest attempt to replicate results from a set of studies published in a single economics journal was Dewald et al. (1986). The paper was part of a project, funded by the National Science Foundation (NSF), to reproduce existing research that had been published in the *Journal of Money, Credit, and Banking* and improve data availability and transparency. Prior to the NSF grant, the journal's policy established a norm of data sharing by asking authors to make available data upon request. To facilitate the study, the journal's editors adopted a new policy requesting data and code at time of publication. Dewald et al. (1986) were only able to get data from 34 percent of papers published prior to the switch in policy, despite the allegedly established norm of data sharing. Even after the change in policy, Dewald et al. (1986) could only obtain data from 78 percent of papers – a marked increase – but far from full compliance with the explicit policy that data needed to be shared at time of publication.

Though Dewald et al. (1986) published their results in the *American Economic Review (AER)*, not much changed in terms of data sharing in economics for more than two decades (Christensen et al., 2019). It was not until McCullough and Vinod (2003) attempted a similar replication exercise, this time using papers published in a single issue of the *AER*, that editors at other journals began to take notice. McCullough and Vinod (2003) were only able to obtain data from four of eight papers, despite the *AER* having a policy that data be made "readily available to any researcher for the purpose of replication" (Bernanke, 2004). As a result of authors failing to comply with the norms of data sharing, the editors at the *AER* updated the data-sharing policy to require, as a condition of publication, data and code sufficient to replicate results. With the change in policy at the *AER*, most other economics journals, especially those published by associations, followed suit.

However, as is often the case when it comes to ethical concerns, requirements diverge from practice. Stodden et al. (2018) examine 204 papers that were published in *Science*. They find only partial data availability and resistance to sharing when contracted by authors to request data. by authors, when contacted. This results in a somewhat amusing set of excerpts shared from emails with corresponding authors. The authors include 204 papers, which were published in *Science*. Of the authors contacted, 36 percent shared some material, 11 percent were unwilling to provide data or code without "information regarding intentions," 11 percent asked the authors to contact someone else who worked on the article, 7 percent refused, and 2 percent gave reasons they could not ethically or legally share the requested information. Stodden et al. (2018) is well worth reading, if only for the condescending and shockingly ill-informed responses from some of the authors.[4] Consider:

> I have to say that this is a very unusual request without any explanation! Please ask your supervisor to send me an email with a detailed, and I mean detailed, explanation.

Or

> When you approach a PI for the source codes and raw data, you better explain who you are, whom you work for, why you need the data and what you are going to do with it.

Both of these are absurd responses, given the policy of *Science* to make available data and code sufficient for replication purposes upon request after publication. Ultimately, Stodden et al. (2018) conclude that fieldnorms are essential to incentivize data-sharing behavior, suggesting that journal policies may be insufficient in practice, as adherence to the policies remain imperfect.

Further studies support the findings in Stodden et al. (2018). Tedersoo et al. (2021) evaluate data availability in research articles in nine disciplines (biomaterials and biotechnology, ecology, forestry, humanities, materials for energy and catalysts, microbiology, optics and photonics, psychology, social sciences) in *Nature* and *Science*, both of which have requirements for data sharing. The authors find that there was only partial data availability for about 55 percent of papers of the 845 considered. Upon contacting authors, partial availability improved to nearly 70 percent. Tedersoo et al. (2021) report that a number of authors declined to share their data, citing issues of data sharing as well as "certain aspects of [the] request."

Within economics, data-sharing policies are still developing and, for the most part, are not yet mandated, as is the case in *Science* and *Nature*. As of 2022, the journals of the Agricultural and Applied Economics Association (AAEA) still framed/index-framed their data-sharing policy in normative terms: "Authors are expected to submit their datasets and associated documentation. . . . Authors are encouraged to comply with all of this policy, but the editors would prefer partial compliance over non-compliance" (AJAE, nd). In 2015, we along with a set of collaborators attempted to replicate studies in *Econometrica* and the *Journal of Development Economics*, both journals that we considered as having strong data-sharing policies at the time. Yet, we found the data were not available, despite the stated policies. Working with the editors, we were eventually able to get the data from the authors, but the lax enforcement signals that current practices, standards, and incentives for data sharing are insufficient in economic journals, just as in the general-interest science journals. The rules must be enforced before norms will change.

The AEA has recognized this as a problem and in 2018 hired a Data Editor for its journals and updated its Data and Code Availability Policy (AEA, 2020). The new policy states that papers will be published only after data and code have been submitted to the journal and the Data Editor has verified that the results do replicate with the materials provided. To our knowledge, the AEA policy is the most forceful policy among economic journals as it no longer relies on norms for data sharing but mandates data sharing as a condition of publication.

While we admire the AEA for its strong policies and we hope more journals adopt a similarly strong data-sharing policy, it is instructive to consider how other journals might implement such a policy. Successful implementation requires two things: desirability and enforcement. First, for effective implementation, journals must be desirable enough that authors are willing to provide data as a condition of publication. It is costly for authors to construct replication packages for data sharing. If two journals, Journal *A* and Journal *B*, have similar impact factors but only *A* requires data sharing, authors might forgo publication in *A* for publication in *B*.[5] To put it simply, the AEA is able to implement such a strong data-sharing policy because there is extremely high demand to publish in one of the AEA's journals.

Second, for effective implementation, there must be someone verifying and enforcing compliance. The AEA has employed a Data Editor who has hired a team of assistants to run replication code on the shared data and verify the code produces the results in the paper. This might seem like a manageable task, but as the current AEA Data Editor, Lars Vilhuber, reports, the task in fact is enormous, time-consuming, and costly (Vilhuber, 2020). The median size of replication packages his team has received is 2MB, while the size at the 3rd quartile is 30MB and the max is 30GB. The number of files in each replication package is also substantial, with the median number of files at 13 and the 3rd quartile at 39. The median time that it takes an undergraduate research assistant to run the code for one paper and write up a report about the replicability is 15–20 hours (Vilhuber et al., 2022). Few professional associations or journals will have the resources to ensure compliance with forceful data-sharing policies. These implementation issues mean that we as a profession cannot rely on changes in journal policy alone to increase data sharing among researchers. We must also work to understand researchers' reluctance to share data so that we can better encourage data sharing within the profession.

PERSPECTIVE 5.1 DATA TRANSPARENCY BY LARS VILHUBER

The availability of data that underlies research in our papers is key for transparency. When we collect our own data via surveys or work hard to combine many different data sources into a cohesive new data set, the resulting object – let's call it a database – should be made broadly available, because it is under our control to do so. But not all data that we create or reuse can be archived in an open trusted repository. The data may be considered sensitive – now or in the future – and we may not have been given the rights to "post" the data. I will illustrate this with two examples, based on recent articles in economics journals.

In particular, I want to consider here the case when sharing might be considered problematic even when the original data used by the authors is, or was, public. In the U.S., much information surrounding the criminal justice system is public. For instance, when a person is arrested, the names of the officer, the arrested person, and the charge are all public records, even if the person is subsequently cleared of the charge or if the charge is dropped. This information can be scraped from public websites or can be requested via Freedom of Information Act (FOIA) requests. The information is thus public, sometimes subtracting it from the purview of IRBs and leaving it up to the authors to decide what to do with it. However, that does not make the data nonsensitive. Arrest records might be expunged en masse – erased from the database – with a legal requirement for others who may have copied the data to do the same, including researchers. Thus, what was once public information now becomes illegal to retain. This is the issue faced by Ouss and Stevenson (Forthcoming), who therefore cannot make data available that was public when they first scraped it, since mass expungement laws have made large parts of the data they collected illegal to disseminate. Similar constraints may be imposed on data holders through various "rights to be forgotten" laws, such as the European General Data Protection Regulation or the California Consumer Privacy Act.

However, even when the data can be preserved, what researchers do with it might make it more sensitive than most are comfortable simply "posting." Consider Goncalves and Mello (2021a), who took data on police officers obtained via Freedom of Information Act, and "estimate the degree to which individual police officers practice racial discrimination." In other words, they estimate how racist a particular police officer is, based on demographics and observed behavior, where every police officer can be identified from the public records by name.

So what can authors do in these cases? Preferably, they can still preserve the data they had collected and make it available to other researchers on a more restricted basis. For instance, use may be restricted to verifying that the authors' calculations are correct and limited to academic researchers. While such data sharing no longer qualifies as "open" data sharing, it does enable transparency and the verification thereof. In the case of Goncalves and Mello (2021a), the authors deposited their data at openICPSR (Goncalves and Mello, 2021b), with the restriction that researchers wishing to use the restricted data be affiliated with academic institutions, have a data security plan, and demonstrate IRB approval. The authorization process is, for better or worse, out of their hands: neither can the authors withhold approval based on personal bias, nor can they speed up the process or influence its parameters.

A more prosaic workaround when even restricted archiving of data may not be possible is to keep robust personal archives. Journal policies, like the American Economic Association's Data and Code Availability Policy (AEA, 2019), require that authors maintain an archive of their materials when the data cannot be made public, for a minimum of five years. Authors might want to investigate to what extent their own (academic) institution provides mechanisms to preserve robustly such archives, through internal mechanisms or institutional subscriptions to cloud providers.

5.2.2   Why Researchers Do Not Share Data

In 2014, the academic publisher Wiley surveyed 2,250 researchers across disciplines to find out why they were reluctant to make their scientific data publicly available. Researchers responded with over a dozen reasons for why they were hesitant to share their data (Ferguson, 2014). In a well-timed article in *The Atlantic* titled "Scientists Have a Sharing Problem," journalist Maggie Puniewska distilled the many reasons given by researchers for not sharing data down to two: (1) competition and (2) disorganization (Puniewska, 2014). Some of the fears about sharing data are valid, some are self-serving, and some reflect common misconceptions. But we agree with Puniewska (2014) that almost all reasons for not sharing data are typically due to fear of competition from other researchers or disorganization by the researcher.

A common reason given by researchers for not sharing data is the fear of being scooped or outcompeted in making a new discovery (Ferguson, 2014). In economics, this fear amounts to being afraid to share data until the researcher has wrung all the useful information from it. Imagine a researcher collects household survey data containing a variety of information on education, livelihood, and health outcomes. They publish an initial paper, on education, and shares the data per journal policies. The researcher then starts to get to work on analyzing livelihood outcomes. But a second researcher, interested in livelihood outcomes, comes in, takes the shared data, analyzes it, and publishes a paper before the initial research can. The profession is indifferent to who wrote the paper (assuming both livelihood papers were of equal quality). But the initial researcher has expended money, time, and effort only to get scooped before they could fully use the data that they collected. Given that the initial research has not been able to fully internalize the benefits of publication (while fully internalizing the costs of data collection), a natural response would be to stop collecting data. This reaction, the suspension of new data collection efforts, is frequently mentioned in editorials and opinion pieces. For example, Longo and Drazen (2016) worry that science will be taken over by "research parasites" while Gibson (1995) warns of "data vultures" feeding on the data of others. While an individual researcher's decision to stop collecting new data because they cannot fully internalize the benefits of their work seems plausible, it is hard to know how much credence to give to predictions of general equilibrium outcomes in which no new data are collected, particularly in an environment in which so much data are collected with the express purpose of public dissemination for widespread use (e.g., the World Bank Living Standards Measurement Survey (LSMS) surveys or the USAID Demographic and Health Surveys (DHS)).

The second category under which most reasons for not sharing data fall is disorganization. We ourselves fell into this category early in our careers. When we were grad students or young faculty members mostly working on data on our own, our only incentive for organization was to ensure we were efficient in our work.

For the most part, no one was asking to see our data as we wrote our dissertations, and so we kept things only as organized as was necessary to know for ourselves what we were doing. This leads to a pretty clear causal chain in which a researcher keeps their files organized in a way that is only clear to them, and when someone does request the data, the disorganization (or the time required to create order for an outsider) is reason enough to deny the request.[6]

A related reason for not sharing data is a fear of the failure of privacy protection (Sardanelli et al., 2018). While this concern is certainly admirable and valid, it is also a symptom of disorganization because, as we discuss later, there are numerous ways to guarantee privacy – they just require the researcher be organized enough to implement them. Researchers will also claim, with good reason, that it is too costly to overcome the technical barriers, such as data conformity and documentation, to share data. Again, this reason is a symptom of disorganization in the research, or rather the profession's failure to incentivize the researcher to improve on organization.

There are two additional reasons, commonly given, for why researchers do not share data that do not fall into the competition and disorganization categories (Christensen et al., 2019). The first reason is because the researcher has committed some form of research misconduct and they do not want to be found out. Simonsohn (2013) reports using statistical methods to detect what he believed were three cases of fraudulent data. In two cases, the authors eventually made the data available, and Simonsohn was able to confirm fraud. In the third case, the author claimed to have lost the data, leaving Simonsohn unable to confirm if the fraud had in fact occurred. A second reason why a researcher might not share data is because they lack the ownership of the data or the authority to share the data. Economists frequently use administrative data from firms or population data from government agencies. In the former case, the firm may not want to allow the data to be released, and as the researcher does not own the data, there may be little they can do. For the latter, governments often require researchers to access restricted use data by physically traveling to a secure site to use the data. In these cases, often involving Census or Social Security data, the government's need to protect the privacy of its citizens overrides a researcher's desire to contribute to open science. In terms of these final two reasons for not sharing data, there is little one can do to encourage data sharing. But for the vast majority of reasons given by researchers to keep their data private, most can be addressed by changes in a researcher's habits and in the expectations of the profession.

5.2.3 Ways to Encourage Data Sharing

During the 2012 U.S. presidential election, Barack Obama delivered a speech on infrastructure in which he said, "Somebody invested in roads and bridges. If you've got a business, you didn't build that." Obama's opponent, Mitt Romney, used the ambiguity regarding what "that" referred to to claim Obama was telling business owners that they had not built their own firms, inflaming the feelings of many entrepreneurs. Similarly, researchers often think in terms of "their" data, as if they built that data set on their own without any contributions from others. But in reality, building data sets relies on contributions in money, time, effort, and expertise from many people and institutions. Most data collection is funded with grants from the government or private foundations. Students or staff members frequently vet surveys before use, performing quality and logic tests. Enumerators deliver the survey and collect the actual data. Most important, hundreds to thousands of individuals and/or firms consent to having their data collected and used by a researcher. This is not to minimize the researcher's own contribution or to say that the researcher should not feel a sense of ownership of the data. Rather, it is to highlight the collaborative nature of data collection. If the public (i.e., funders, students, research participants) helped contribute to building the data set, then we as "the" researcher should feel some obligation to repay this contribution. One way is by sharing data.

Relying on a norm for data sharing based on a sense of obligation to those who helped contribute to building a data set is insufficient to overcome the reluctance of many researchers to share data (Tedersoo et al., 2021). Thus, we must carefully consider mechanisms to incentivize data collect that overcome the reluctance that exists on the part of the researcher. In the previous section we categorized the reasons for reluctance into competition and disorganization. We also discussed two reasons for reluctance that do not fall into our categories (i.e., fear of being caught in fraud, lack of control of data). For these latter two reasons, incentive schemes to encourage data sharing are unlikely to have much of an impact. But for the other reasons, there are practices that the profession can implement to address the reluctance and make researchers more comfortable with and more likely to share data.

In addressing the fear of competition from data sharing, journals are likely the best institution to provide appropriate incentives. This is because the competition that researchers fear is that other researchers will be able to exploit the data first, publish the results in a superior journal (due to primacy), and capture more citations. One way journals could address researchers' fear of being scooped is to require that authors only release data extracts. A data extract is the portion of the complete data set that is required to produce the analysis in the published paper. In fact, this is what most journals require in their data policy statements. The journal is concerned with ensuring the results published in their journal can be replicated, and thus, their focus, to date, has been on only requiring data sharing that is sufficient to alleviate their concern. Asking authors to submit a data extract, instead of the complete data and cleaning code, incentivizes data sharing because a competing research is unlikely to be able to publish a new paper using only the variables present in an existing paper. In our example of the researcher with household survey data on education, livelihoods, and health outcomes, the data extract accompanying the published paper on education would not need to contain the variables on livelihood and health outcomes. This allows the researcher to then develop the second paper on livelihood outcomes without fear of being scooped. The trouble with journals only requiring data extracts is that it does not allow for the profession to determine if published results are due to *p*-hacking or specification search. If the data extract contains only the variables used in the final analysis, there is no way to determine what other specifications or what other variables were tried in the early analysis. If the goal of open science is to reduce the incentives to commit fraud by ensuring transparency and reproducibility, then the use of data extracts can only be considered half open science. This is one reason why the AEA's new Data and Code Availability Policy requires authors to submit the raw data as well as "the programs used to create any final and analysis data sets from raw data" (AEA, 2020).

An alternative to overcome the reluctance to share data due to competition is a data embargo (Christensen et al., 2019). Data embargoes are a period of time under which the original data is kept private. This provides the research with a time-limited "patent" to the data in which they have exclusive use of that data. The National Institutes of Health (NIH) in the U.S. has established a central repository for genomics data generated by the grants they award. This database, called the database of Genotypes and Phenotypes, has an embargo period, usually one year, in which researchers have exclusive use of the data generated from their grant. This incentivizes researchers to collect new data without fear that "data vultures" will extract all value from the data before the original researchers have a chance to exploit it. The embargo period also incentivizes researchers to get results out quickly instead of letting the data sit on a computer unused – a value to the granting agency. Embargoes are already in use by the AEA and the Open Science Foundation (OSF) for pre-analysis plans. On the AEA RCT Registry, some information about the trial is immediately made public while the researcher can choose to keep other information hidden until the trial is completed. This feature was built into the registry to calm fears that if all the information on a trial was made public at the time of registration, other researchers could come in and scoop the original researcher. A similar feature is available in OSF's registry. While we are unaware of any economics journals that currently implement a data embargo, one could imagine a simple policy whereby replication material is required at the time of publication and then links to the material appear at a set time after publication.

A third way that journals could encourage data sharing by researchers is to establish policies regarding data citation. If researchers fear that sharing data will lead to no new data collection, then one way to address this fear is for journals (and the profession) to reward new data collection. While data citation is still uncommon in economics, the field is changing. Part of the AEA Data and Code Availability Policy is that "[a]ll source data used in the paper shall be cited" (AEA, 2020).[7] One reason for the change of citation standards in economics is due to the introduction of the Transparency and Openness Promotion (TOP) Guidelines from the Center for Open Science (COS), the same group the runs the OSF. Nosek et al.

(2015) introduce the idea of TOP guidelines and establish three levels of journal compliance with these guidelines.[8] The guidelines include establishing citation standards for data, code, and research materials so that the intellectual contribution of those involved in their creation can be recognized and rewarded. TOP provides a sample data citation, as does the AEA Data and Code Availability Policy.

Romer, Christina D., and David H. Romer. 2010. "Replication data for: The Macroeconomic Effects of Tax Changes: Estimates Based on a New Measure of Fiscal Shocks." *American Economic Association (AEA)* [publisher], Interuniversity Consortium for Political and Social Research [distributor]. https://doi.org/10.3886/E112357V1.

A data citation, like any citation, should include author, date, title of the data set, and publisher. In the case of data, the publisher is the location of the data, either in a permanent repository and with some data distributor.

While journals can provide the best mechanisms for overcoming fear of competition, funding organizations have the best institutional tools for overcoming the issue of disorganization. Disorganization arises as a justification for not sharing data because if no one requires sharing reproducible data and code then researchers are unlikely to be more organized than is absolutely necessary for them to complete their own work. Unlike AEA institution journals, most journals will not have the capacity to hire a data editor to verify replicability of data and code. That leaves granting agencies (both private and public) as the institutions that can provide the strongest incentives to encourage researchers to get organized. After publications and citations, generating external funding is typically the most important criteria for promotion and tenure in academia. Much like the NIH requires filing of pre-analysis plans for drug trials and the sharing of data, large governmental and non-governmental agencies could require, as a condition of funding, that recipients develop and execute a clear and organized data management and data availability plan. The agencies would not need to verify that all award recipients adhered to their plans but could engage in random audits to help reduce the incentive to "cheat" on their data management plans.

While funding agencies could provide a strong incentive to get organized, that only partially addresses the problem. There remains the learning of organizational skills. Here, funding agencies could allow researchers to build in some cost for training in methods or skills. Additionally, professional agencies and organizations, like the Berkeley Initiative for Transparency in Social Sciences (BITSS), can (and do) offer workshop and training in organizing data. The combination of pressure from funding sources to obtain training, the availability of training from professional organizations, and mainstreaming open science can help lower the hurdle that disorganization poses to sharing truly replicable and reproducible data and code. To facilitate movement toward this goal, the remainder of the chapter focuses on best practices regarding data management, privacy protection, and creating replicability packages.

5.3 Data Storage and Management

Regarding many practices in empirical science, economics tends to follow the leads and/or mandates of the health sciences. This is true for the adoption of randomized control trials, pre-analysis plans, and IRB. Thus, as economists look to improve standards around data management and data sharing, we can look to current practices in the health sciences. The trends in these fields can help us to understand where our own field is likely headed.

Much of the rules and regulations governing health science research in the U.S. comes from the NIH. The NIH (2020) defines scientific data as "the recorded factual material commonly accepted in the scientific community as of sufficient quality to validate and replicate research findings, regardless of whether the data are used to support scholarly publications." This definition indicates that data must be properly managed and shared beyond what is just necessary for publication, that is, more than just a data extract. In economics, we use scientific data generated by a wide variety of sources, at various levels of aggregation, and with differing needs for confidentiality. Managing the various types of data can be complicated and a natural starting place, when feeling overwhelmed by the task of managing data, is to develop a data management plan (DMP). Such a plan need not be anything formal (unless required by a donor or IRB). At its most basic, a DMP simply provides concrete and actionable answers to the questions laid out in Box 5.3.

BOX 5.3   DATA MANAGEMENT PLAN

1. What type of data will be collected? What is the unit record or unit of observation? How many observations?
2. How will the data be collected? Where will it be stored during the collection process?
3. Where and how will the data be permanently stored? How will backups be provided?
4. How will the data be organized? What is the folder structure? In what file formats?
5. Who gets access to the data? When? How will access be managed?
6. What data will be archived after the analysis is complete? Where and for how long?
7. Under what conditions will the archived data be made available to others? When? Under what license?
8. Who owns the data? Who is responsible for the management of the data, particularly archived data?
9. Are there costs associated with the data management?

DMPs have long been a component of grants required to the U.S. government, including the NIH. In October 2020, the NIH took the requirements for data further, issuing their Policy for Data Management and Sharing. Three things are important about this document. First, it applies to all work done using NIH funding. Previously, the NIH policy had only applied to "large" grants and genomics data. Second, the plan defines not just a data-sharing policy but a data management policy. As discussed earlier in this chapter, a primary reason given by researchers for not sharing their data is the disorganization of the data. The new NIH policy directly addresses this by defining how data should be managed so that it can more easily be shared. Last, the policy provides a strong incentive for compliance. The NIH, as the granting agency, will determine a researcher's compliance with the stated policy, and failure to conform to the policy puts future NIH funding to the recipient institution in jeopardy. Similar to the U.S. Government's requirement for IRB, the failure of individual researchers to comply puts funding for the entire institution at risk. These latter incentives are the types that, as IRBs have shown, can create real, institutional change, at least with respect to stated compliance.

5.3.1 Individual, Personal, or Firm Data

The most common types of data used by economists are individual, personal, or firm data. If these data were generated by a third party as administrative data or as public use data, then the data publisher controls the process of data management and data anonymization. But applied economists frequently engage in their own data collection, generating their data sets through surveys. In this case, the researcher is responsible for data storage and management.

Assuming that the researcher is at a academic or research institution, the researcher will have obtained IRB approval prior to data collection. As part of the approval process, the IRB will typically require the researcher to define a data storage plan. The IRB's interest here is solely in data storage to ensure the privacy of research participants and the confidentiality of their data.[9] In accordance with these policies, two things must be considered:

1. Is the data "sensitive"? Sensitive data require more attention, for example, physical security and/or encryption.
2. How vulnerable are data storage resources? Are there sufficient protections and redundancies to ensure that the data are kept confidential?

Sensitive data are any data where its disclosure could have adverse consequences for the research participant, including not only financial and educational harm but also reputational harm or risk of criminal or civil liability. For economists, who (outside of the lab) collect data on personal or firm income, assets, and consumption, almost all data are considered sensitive.

Prior to the revolution in information and communication technology (ICT), most data were collected on paper and then transcribed to a computer. Security of data focused on the physical storage of surveys or records that might be locked in a filing cabinet or an office. Nowadays, almost all data are collected and stored electronically, either locally (on a physical drive) or remotely (on a server in the cloud). Each institution's IRB will typically have well-defined guidelines for how to ensure storage locations are not vulnerable. These guidelines will likely be strict – but will ensure confidentiality of data and privacy of participants' information.

The guidelines for ensuring secure yet easily accessible digital storage varies from project to project. Yet some practicalities and methods are consistent across data type and storage device. As a general guideline, all data collected on portable devices, such as tablets using computer-assisted personal interviewing (CAPI) software, should be transferred to an approved service as soon as possible after collection and deleted from the portable collection devices.

When we work with local enumerators to collect survey data, we have them upload the data to remote server storage every night and then, after verifying the data are on the server, have the enumerator delete the local copy. The choice of server is typically a function of the CAPI software being used, as the software on the tablets must be able to upload the encrypted data to the server. We also restrict access to the identifiable data on the server to just those researchers who have completed Collaborative Institutional Training Initiative (CITI) training as part of the IRB application. And, it should go without saying, but, with respect to access to these data: all storage devices must be password protected with a strong password.

PERSPECTIVE 5.2 DEVELOPING FORMAL PRIVACY MODELS BY IAN M. SCHMUTTE

Formal privacy models like *differential privacy* give us a tool for quantifying privacy loss associated with a data publication and the trade-off between privacy loss and data quality. The model in Abowd and Schmutte (2019) establishes what (I hope) is a useful framework for working toward the optimal trade-off. Our model assumes that the data provider has high-quality information on social preferences for data privacy and data accuracy. In practice, managing this trade-off requires making decisions and judgment calls, often in consultation with stakeholders. The involvement of economists and other social science researchers is crucial.

For example, the disclosure avoidance system for the 2020 U.S. Census was originally tuned to achieve data-quality targets on a set of tables needed for reapportionment and enforcement of the Voting Rights Act. But the final privacy parameters were determined by interacting with data users, who were able to experiment with "demonstration tables." By running their analyses against the demonstration tables, they could illustrate areas where the system was not meeting their needs and argue for a relaxation of the privacy loss budget or for other changes to implementation.

Before tuning a disclosure avoidance system, it must be developed in the first place. Building practical formal privacy systems depends on the nature of the input data and the desired end uses. Again, the process requires interaction with stakeholders and a detailed understanding of what the data are needed for. On the privacy side, we must determine *what characteristics or properties of the underlying data need to be protected against disclosure.* On the data-quality side, we must determine *what are the most important applications for these data.* With these in hand, we should develop a system for data dissemination that measures the kind of privacy losses that are relevant and the corresponding loss of quality for important applications.

What does this look like in practice? Standard differential privacy can be understood as limiting inference about whether a particular unit appears in the data at all or whether it has a particular attribute. But for data on businesses, it can be the case that the appearance of a business in the data is not considered to be sensitive. Policymakers might also decide that the places and the sectors in which businesses operate are not secrets in need of protection. However, business revenue and operating costs are highly sensitive and should not be disclosed. With these requirements, a standard differential privacy requirement is probably excessive, adding more noise to the data than is strictly necessary.

Hopefully these examples make clear the importance of social scientists' involvement in statistical disclosure limitation and data privacy. Our domain expertise is critical for the successful development and implementation of these systems, and we have a strong interest in them working as effectively as possible.

Once data collection is complete, we transfer the data off of the server used for data collection and into a file backup system like Google Drive, Dropbox, and the like for permanent storage.[10] We use commercial or institutional servers or cloud storage to ensure that the data in those locations is sufficiently encrypted. Once the data are in a permanent storage location, the first thing we do is create a key: a unique identifier for each observation or unit record. We then anonymize the data by separating names, addresses, Global Positioning System (GPS) locations, and other PII, from the rest of the data. We then move the identifiable, private information to a separate password-protected and/or -encrypted folder stored in a different, secure location. Access to the identifiers should be extremely limited. In most cases, only one person needs to have access to them. Separating the identifiers from the rest of the data adds a level of redundancy to the security of that data by ensuring that even if someone obtains access to the data, that data by itself would not identify anyone. The key allows, if it is ever necessary, for the data to be reidentified.

Given that most data collection now occurs electronically, either using CAPI software, being provided administrative data in electronic form, or gathering data on the internet, the storage and management of that data are straightforward. First, one should restrict access to the data during the collection process. Then, after data collection, one again separates any personal identifiers from the data and stores them in a different location. As before, all data should be kept, both the identifiers and the deidentified data, in file backup systems that are encrypted and that require a password to access. Once this is done, one can allow access to the de-identified data to those on the research project with minimal risk that those on the project will accidentally violate the privacy of research participants or the confidentiality of data.

5.3.2 GPS and Remote-Sensing Data

In recent years, economists have begun to use remote-sensing data in a myriad of different analyses. Economists use weather data to help understand human capital formation (Garg et al., 2020), labor markets (Morten, 2019), conflict and institutions (Sarsons, 2015), agricultural production and economic growth (Yeh et al., 2020), intra-household bargaining power (Corno et al., 2020), technology adoption (Tesfaye et al., 2021), and extreme weather impacts (Michler et al., 2019). GPS information has also been used to improve measurement of crop area (Carletto et al., 2017) and, when combined with remote-sensing data, used to improve estimates of harvests (Lobell et al., 2020). Frankly, we are just beginning to explore the potential of remote-sensing data in economic analysis (Burke et al., 2021).

All these new data and new opportunities, however, raise the issue of storage and management of GPS information and remote-sensing data. Although often used by economists as synonyms, Geographic Information System (GIS) and GPS are different systems. GIS is a framework for gathering, managing, and analyzing data. It is rooted in the science of geography and integrates many types of data. One of these types of data comes from the GPS, a satellite-based radionavigation system. GPS is just one of the global navigation satellite systems that provides geo-location and time information to a receiver anywhere on or near Earth. By comparison, another type of data used in GIS is remote-sensing data, which are data obtained about objects or areas from a distance, including aircraft, drones, or satellites.

Generally, economists use GPS data to determine the location of a natural resource (e.g., crop plot, mine), individual, household, firm, or institution and combine this information with remote-sensing data. Most remote-sensing data that economists use is publicly available and is collected, processed, and disseminated by national or international weather or space agencies. As the data are public, no special actions to protect privacy need be taken when collecting or storing the data.

Where privacy concerns arise is when researchers collect GPS data for individuals or households. For example, the specific GPS location where someone lives is sensitive data and requires protection. In some contexts, this might also be true for firm locations, particularly if the firm is engaged in illegal or unregistered activity, such as marijuana farmers or unregistered mines. But in developing countries, many firms operate in legal dark or gray zones in terms of taxation, employment, registration, and compliance. The specific geo-location of these firms may be viewed as sensitive information.

When recording GPS locations as part of a data collection effort, researchers should use similar methods to those described earlier. The GPS information should be included with other identifiers and separated from the rest of the data at the earliest possible stage of the analysis. Care must also be taken when using the GPS information to obtain remote-sensing data. As economists, we rarely download remote-sensing data ourselves. Rather, we rely on colleagues in geography or with GIS expertise to get the data for us. In these situations, we share only the GPS coordinates with the colleague so that there are no other identifiers or data with the GPS information. When we obtain remote-sensing data, we use the key to matching it to the rest of the data set, dropping the GIS coordinates in the process. This provides us with anonymized data for use in analysis. However, as with individual, personal, or firm data, things become more complicated when it comes time to share the data.

5.3.3   Aggregate Data

To this point, we have largely presented data management in cases in which the unit of observation for the data of interest are an individual, a household, or a firm. In these cases, the privacy violation of releasing the data with the PII is obvious. With names of individuals and firms, with addresses, or with GPS coordinates, a user could immediately identify who the data are related to and the confidentiality promised in the informed consent document is lost. Moreover, as we have seen with the case of Governor Weld and the Netflix Prize, releasing data without direct identifiers may not be sufficient to truly anonymize data.

But what if one were to aggregate data that individual-, household-, or firm-level data into an altogether new unit of observation? Would sharing data that reported village-level averages for income rather than individual income data achieve a sufficient level of anonymity for research participants? Could one report country-level averages of profitability for firms in a given industry and be confident that the participant firms whose data underlie the averages would remain anonymous?

Unfortunately, the answer to this query is actually relatively straightforward: aggregating data does not provide sufficient anonymization of data for sharing with other researchers. This comes as a surprise to most people: How could one possible reidentify an individual or firm if all one has is village or county level aggregate values and how would one even know if a given individual or firm is in the data?

One economist who has thought deeply about the issue of privacy in aggregate data is Raj Chetty. Chetty developed the Opportunity Atlas, a Census tract-level database that shows which neighborhoods in the U.S. offer children the best opportunity to get out of poverty (Chetty et al., 2018). The Atlas is based on U.S. Census Bureau data on 20 million children and follows them into their adulthood. The Atlas allows one to see, by parental income, child race, and child gender what neighborhoods provide children with the best potential to achieve a set of outcomes, such as income, while accounting for other factors, including birth rate and incarceration rate. All of the individual Census data that goes into the Atlas is aggregated to the Census tract-level. And most outcome variables are not reported as simple means or medians of the data. Instead, most of the outcome variables are based on ordinary least squares (OLS) regression estimates of the relationship between childhood characteristics and outcomes in adulthood. But even so, as Chetty and Friedman (2019a) show, the use of anonymized individual data to create aggregate data are insufficient to ensure privacy.

Consider the statistical outcome which results from aggregating income for households by reporting only the mean of income (Chetty and Friedman, 2019b). The potential for identification of a specific household arises when the statistic (mean income) changes substantially based on whether a specific household is included or not included in the data. If the population that is being aggregated is relatively large or if the household's income is very close to the mean, the sensitivity of the statistic to inclusion or exclusion of the household will be small. But if a very wealthy household is included in a small group of households, the inclusion or exclusion of that specific observation makes it more likely that someone can infer (1) if the specific household is included or excluded and (2) what the income of that household is likely to be. In the contemporary discussion on privacy protection, privacy is protected if the statistic in question is the same regardless of whether or not specific individual, household, or firm data are included in the data.

Now, consider a concrete example which comes directly from the Opportunity Atlas (Chetty and Friedman, 2019a). The authors of the Atlas want to release estimates from OLS regressions estimated on small samples. Recall that in the Atlas, the unit of observation is the Census tract (effectively, a neighborhood), and results are reported based on parental income, child race, and child gender. The Atlas releases predicted values from an OLS regression of the income percentile ranks of children in adulthood on their parents' income ranks. Based on the economic, racial, and gender makeup of households in a Census tract, the OLS regression results may vary substantially when one includes or excludes a given household.

Figure 5.1 illustrates this idea using hypothetical data presented in Chetty and Friedman (2019a). The figure presents a scatterplot of children's income ranks in adulthood against their parents' income rank for a hypothetical Census tract. The dotted light gray line shows the fit of a simple univariate regression to the data. Reviewing this, we can then ask what the predicted income rank for a child will be if their parent's income rank was at the 25th percentile, which is $\beta_1 = 0.212$. To demonstrate sensitivity, we can add an extreme outlier to the data. When we fit the same regression to the data that includes the outlier the predicted income rank for

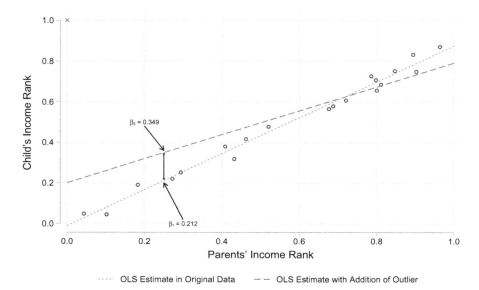

$\beta_2 = 0.349$

$\beta_1 = 0.212$

······ OLS Estimate in Original Data   — — OLS Estimate with Addition of Outlier

FIGURE 5.1   Sensitivity of Aggregate Statistics

Note: OLS = ordinary least squares. The figure shows how sensitive estimates can be to changes in the inclusion/exclusion of a single data point in a hypothetical Census tract. The figure presents a scatterplot of children's income ranks in adulthood against their parents' income rank. We then fit a simple univariate regression to the data and calculate the predicted value of child income rank at the 25th percentile of the parent income distribution (dotted light gray line). To demonstrate sensitivity, we add to the data an outlier point (0,1) marked by an x. We then fit the same regression to the data, including the outlier point, and calculate the predicted value of child income rank at the 25th percentile of the parent income distribution (dashed dark gray line). The figure is adapted from Chetty and Friedman (2019a) using data and code in Chetty and Friedman (2019c) under Modified BSD License and CC BY 4.0.

child with parental income at the 25th percentile is $\beta_2 = 0.349$. Although an extreme example, it illustrates the difference in potential loss of privacy that can occur if an individual, albeit an outlier, is included in a data set. Privacy is only protected to the extent that the aggregate statistics do not vary based on whether or not a specific person's or firm's data were included.

Removing what are traditionally considered PII (names, birth dates, social security numbers, telephone numbers) or spatial identifiers (addresses, GPS coordinates) does not sufficiently anonymize data. Nor does the aggregation of individual-, household-, or firm-level data sufficiently protect privacy. The reason simply is the existence of other data sets. As Latanya Sweeney demonstrated, it is possible to combine "anonymized" health records with voter records to identify Governor Weld. Like Arvind Narayanan and Vitaly Shmatikov showed, it is possible to link "anonymized" Netflix ratings with IMDb ratings to identify individuals. The danger is that by combining data, be it individual or aggregate, with other existing data could result in a person reidentifying the private information present in the data.

5.4 Privacy Protection

The key tenet of modern data privacy is that a given data set should be private enough that one cannot reconstruct the missing information by combining that original data set with additional sources or data sets. We present three hypothetical cases to illustrate how and why the de-identification of a data set by removing explicit PII is insufficient for protecting the privacy of research participants.

Case 1: Consider a data set that contains information on farm households in the U.S. After collecting and analyzing the data, the researcher who collected the data posts it as part of a replication package for a paper. The researcher has removed names and addresses, but the data contain the county in which the farm is located, the number of adults and children in the household, and the farm and nonfarm income of the household. Given population density and county size in rural areas of the U.S., one can imagine an individual obtaining school yearbooks from the public library and determining which families in a given county had the same number of children as a household in the data set. The individual could then use telephone books at the same library to determine which family lived on which street. Finally, that individual could then drive to each address and determine if the family lived on a farm. With this information, the individual would then know the income of that particular family and could make that information public.

Case 2: Consider a nationally representative household survey data set from Zimbabwe that contains information on the health outcomes for individuals in the household. The researcher who collected the data captured GPS coordinates for the households and matched the data to remote-sensing data on rainfall and temperature. After analyzing the data and publishing a paper, the researcher archives the data in a public repository, having removed information on names as well as the GPS coordinates. The data still contain information on what diseases individuals in the household have contracted as well as the age of each household member and the matched time series weather data. Given that the data are nationally representative, rural households in the data set are fairly dispersed, and so an individual could match the time series whether data with the original remote-sensing data to determine in which grid cell a given household was located. Furthermore, the individual could access public voting records, which contain names, biological sex, addresses, and birth year of registered voters. With this information, an individual could identify the names of people in a household and the location of that household in the health data set.

The individual could then determine what diseases the voting members of that household had contracted and could make that information public.

Case 3: Consider a data set on sexual harassment complaints at firms in Canada, which includes the share of female employees at each firm. These data were collected by a graduate student. And, because of the sensitive nature of the data, the graduate student only makes a data extract available to go with published papers that use the data. A faculty member in the department requests to use the anonymized data in exchange for a data citation and the graduate student agrees but only shares a version of the data aggregated by Census subdivisions (municipalities), the International Classification System (ICS) of industries, and the quartile rank of the firm based on the share of female employees. The faculty member conducts their research and, believing the data have been sufficiently anonymized, publishes the aggregate data with the paper. An individual could use the public Directories of Canadian companies to determine the location and types of businesses in each Census subdivision. They could then use the employee directory on a firm's website to generate a rough breakdown of the share of female employees. Based on this information and the aggregate data (which likely contains very few observations in each aggregate "cell") the individual could identify a specific firm and determine the number of sexual harassment complaints at each firm and could make that information public.

Although hypothetical, the preceding three cases, and the real life cases discussed throughout this chapter, illustrate that de-identification of a data set by removing explicit PII is insufficient for protecting the privacy of research participants (Sweeney, 2007). Recall that when economists collect survey data, IRBs require two things. First, IRBs require that participants give informed consent, which includes consent to the use of their data. Most informed consent forms promise confidentiality of the information that a research participant provides. Second, IRBs require that the researcher complete a Protocol for Human Subjects, which includes describing how the researcher will protect the privacy of research participants and the confidentiality of the participants' data. Typically, IRBs only require that data be de-identified prior to analysis and data sharing. Yet, as we have demonstrated, de-identification is insufficient to ensure anonymity of research participants. There is a clear gap between what researchers promise participants (anonymity, privacy, confidentiality) and what we actually provide.

Fortunately, the risk of re-identification is well known to publishers of large, public use data sets like the public-use microdata samples (PUMSs) from the U.S. Census, the American Community Survey (ACS), Statistics of U.S. Businesses (SUSB), the Medical Expenditure Panel Survey (MEPS), the Living Standards Measurement Survey (LSMS), the Demographic and Health Surveys (DHS), the

Opportunity Atlas, and many others. Administrators of these and many other public use data sets are cognizant of the promises made to participants as well as the importance of protecting these sensitive data. As such, administrators for all of these public-use data sets undertake some version of statistical anonymization in order to provide privacy protection that goes beyond simply removing PII. Yet, while the use of these methods is ubiquitous, and sometimes required by law, in large public-use data sets, their use is very uncommon among individual researchers looking to share their data. What this means is that individual researchers are failing to sufficiently protect their research participants' privacy when they engage in data sharing. In the remainder of this chapter, we discuss the most common statistical de-identification methods used by large public-use data sets as well as how individual researchers can use these methods to ensure sufficient anonymization prior to sharing their data.

5.4.1 Statistical Disclosure Limitation

A set of commonly used methods to protect confidentiality in public use data fall under the umbrella of statistical disclosure limitation (SDL), sometimes called statistical disclosure control (SDC). SDL methods include noise infusion, aggregation, record swapping, and suppression. In the spatial dimension, SDL is often achieved through coordinate masking and noise infusion on derived spatial variables. The specific SDL method used is a function of the form of the statistical output, the sensitivity of that output to the inclusion or exclusion of a particular record, and the type of threat to confidentiality that exists (Skinner, 2009).

To understand the how and the what of specific SDL methods, it is important to have a clear understanding of the different types of threats to confidentiality. Computer scientists and cryptographers distinguish between identity disclosure and attribute disclosure (Abowd and Schmutte, 2015). Identity disclosure is when the identity, the PII, of a research participant is revealed in the data themselves or through combining data from multiple sources. This type of disclosure is what researchers are typically thinking about when they de-identify data prior to sharing. Separately, attribute disclosure is when it is possible to infer confidential attributes about a participant from the data or some combination of data. Examples include being able to infer the protected class (race, sexual orientation, religion, disability status, religion, etc.) of a participant. It is uncommon for researchers to consider protecting against attribute disclosure when they are preparing data for sharing.

In working to protect against both types of disclosure, SDL methods evaluate disclosure risk as a probabilistic event. This idea, known as inferential disclosure, is concerned not with the perfect identification of identity or attribute, but with one's ability to infer an identity or attribute with high probability. A person seeking to identify an individual identity or attribute has some prior belief about that identity or attribute. After data are published, the person updates their prior beliefs about the identity or attribute. If the prior and posterior beliefs are small, or the differences are small, then the published data are confidential and preserve privacy. If, however, the difference in prior and posterior beliefs is large, then an inferential disclosure has occurred.

Abowd and Schmutte (2015) point out that addressing privacy issues through inferential disclosure provides two important insights. First, releasing any useful data (data that are not complete noise) results in a nonzero risk of disclosure. Second, certain SDL methods will require that the details of the methods remain confidential in order to be effective. Considering this from the perspective of the economic researcher, SDL inherently distorts the data, which can lead to bias in statistical analysis (Abowd et al., 2019). And, because data providers may be unable to publish SDL critical parameters, it may not be possible to determine the magnitude or direction of the bias (Abowd and Schmutte, 2015). With these insights and limitations in mind, we discuss specific SDL methods.

Suppression

Suppression eliminates entire records or specific attributes of a record from data (Abowd and Schmutte, 2015). Alternatively, specific values can be suppressed and then replaced with inputed values (Skinner, 2009). This is the most frequently used form of SDL and is commonly applied to tabular summaries published by the U.S. Census Bureau. A summary table for a specific Census tract might have missing values in cells for the number of single adults or the number of black or African American males in the tract. Because suppression is often used to deal with outliers or highly sensitive values, the exact suppression rule is generally not published because it could result in inferential disclosure. For users of the data, this means that it is often unclear how the SDL methods might bias the results of an analysis.

Data Swapping

Data swapping exchanges the value of a variable with the value from a different record (Abowd and Schmutte, 2015). The swaps can be done in such a way as to preserve certain characteristics of the distribution of the variable, such as the mean and covariance. However, in general, one cannot preserve the covariances between all variables (Skinner, 2009). Typically, a sensitive record will be identified and certain attributes of that record will be used to locate a "neighbor." Then the sensitive values of the original record will be swapped with the identified neighbor. Frequently, this involves swapping the geographic location of a record so that the sole very wealthy 20-something individual in a relatively poor Census tract will be swapped into a Census tract with many very wealthy individuals across various ages and someone of similar demographics (although either not as young or not as wealthy) will replace the original record. With data swapping, as with suppression, releasing information about the decision rule for when to swap, or where to swap, is typically unpublished. Publication of this information could allow for the reconstruction of the original data set and the reidentification of the sensitive record. Without information on the swapping rules, researchers cannot determine how the SDL method might affect their analysis. Abowd and Schmutte (2015) consider suppression and data swapping "insidious" because neither method allows for data users to determine the magnitude or the direction of bias introduced by SDL.

Modification

Modification involves transforming a variable in such a way as to reduce the detail contained in a specific value (Skinner, 2009). This includes top coding and aggregation. Top coding is similar to winsorizing, which replaces outlier values with some maximum or minimum value. In the case of categorical variables, this top coding might be explicit, such as replacing any household size greater than 9 with the value 10+. Or, in the case of continuous variables, the process may be implicit, replacing all values of income above the 95 percentile with the income value at the 95 percentile. Similarly, aggregation involves coarsening the data (Abowd and Schmutte, 2015). In terms of continuous variables, such as revenue from individual firms, the data can be aggregated up to the ICS industry level. Alternatively, one could group firms by ICS category, calculate the median value for revenues within the group, and then replace each individual firm's revenue with the group median. Or, with individual income data, one could simply report the income quartile into which an individual falls. In terms of categorical variables, one could coarsen the categories. So, instead of reporting age or race and religious denomination, one could report age cohorts or broader religious categories (e.g., Judaism, instead of Orthodox or Reformed).

The degree of modification necessary is determined by the sensitivity of data to individual values. For postmodification, the usefulness or interoperability of the data is determined by the research question one would like to answer. Broad religious categories will be useful for answering some questions but will also limit one's ability to answer other questions. Similarly, top coding of income data can make the data useless in answering certain questions. Piketty and Saez (2003) demonstrate that income inequality in the U.S. looks very different if one analyzes income in publicly available data, such as using the top-coded Current Population Survey (CPS), than if one analyzes restricted data, such as the uncensored IRS income data.

Noise Infusion

Noise infusion adds stochastic perturbation to the values of a variable (Skinner, 2009). This addition of random noise is similar to the existence of measurement error for a variable. Methods for noise infusion are very sophisticated and can be designed to preserve certain characteristics of the original distribution, such as the mean and the standard deviation of a variable, or the correlation between variables (Abowd and Schmutte, 2015). One example of this practice is adding noise to the population counts for each age cohort in each Census block in the Bureau's summary tables. Similarly, in the DHS and LSMS data, noise infusion is used to achieve a degree of spatial anonymity for unit records (Blankespoor et al., 2021). The DHS and LSMS unit record are typically at the household-level. In adding noise infusion in these data, the GPS data are first aggregated to a cluster, often referred to as an enumeration area (EA). The EA centerpoint for this cluster is then perturbed (displaced), such that centerpoints for urban clusters are within a 2km buffer of their true location and rural clusters are within a 5km buffer, with 1 percent of rural clusters displaced within a 10km buffer. The direction of displacement and the distance are both random variables (Perez-Haydrich et al., 2013).

If the variable that has been infused with the noise, and the parameters of the distribution are published, then a researcher could correct for any bias introduced by the mismeasurement. However, in general, the variances of any estimated parameters will remain inflated. But while noise infusion is less problematic for a researcher than suppression, it still limits the types of questions that can be asked. While using LSMS data, Michler et al. (2022) show that the current SDL methods to achieve spatial anonymization does not impact estimates of the impacts of rainfall and temperature on agricultural yields. Conversely, any amount of noise infusion would make a study like Lobell et al. (2020), where remote-sensing is used to measure plot-level agricultural yields, impossible.

Synthetic Data

Synthetic data are similar to noise infusion, but instead of targeting specific variables, all variables are perturbed (Skinner, 2009). Models to generate synthetic data are designed to allow analysis of the synthetic data to generate point estimates that are consistent with those generated from analyzing the confidential data. The synthetic data are drawn from the same data-generating process as the original data so as to preserve the same structure of the original data. The challenge is that a single synthetic data set can typically only preserve the relationships between a limited number of variables. So the original relationships between all variables cannot be preserved. That means that any individual synthetic data set can only be used to answer a limited set of research questions (Abowd and Schmutte, 2015). Alternatively, to address this limitation to some extent, a large number of synthetic data sets can be generated and multiple imputation methods can be used to analyze the original data and bind the bias introduced by the synthetic nature of the data (Skinner, 2009).

While all SDL methods distort data in order to preserve privacy, some SDL methods are more conducive to conducting SDL-aware analysis on. Suppression and data swap, by their very nature, require withholding key parameters of the process, leaving data users uncertain about the accuracy of their analysis.

In contrast, conditional on sensitivity and the exact research question, key parameters for modification, noise infusion, and synthetic data can be released to the public. The publication of these parameters allow for data users to adjust or bound their estimates, lending a degree of certainty to the accuracy of the analysis.

5.4.2 Differential Privacy

The use of SDL methods, like data swapping and imputation, were first used by the U.S. Census in 1990, allowing the Bureau to release for the first time Census block-level data. Since then, the list of SDL methods has grown as the ability to access and analyze data has simultaneously expanded. With the 2020 Census, the Bureau has moved beyond traditional SDL methods and now uses what is known as differential privacy (DP). The precipitating event for the shift from SDL to DP was the demonstration of the database reconstruction theorem (Abowd et al., 2019). The theorem establishes that publishing too many statistics too accurately from a confidential database exposes the entire database with near certainty (Dinur and Nissim, 2003). Abowd (2018) pessimistically calls the database reconstruction theorem the "death knell for traditional data publication systems."

DP is similar to SDL in that neither are a single technique to protect privacy but both are suites of tools. However, DP differs from SDL in that DP techniques allow for the precise measurement of disclosure risk, thereby avoiding excessive data manipulation while meeting anonymization objectives. DP provides a provable guarantee of privacy in exchange for a certain level of noise injected into the data within the constraints of a privacy-loss budget (Dwork et al., 2006). This formal approach to privacy rules is another advantage of DP over SDL in that DP makes explicit the social choice between more privacy protection or more data accuracy. Since the early 2010s, companies like Apple, Facebook, and Google have used DP techniques in preserving confidentiality of user data (Wood et al., 2018). Only recently, however, have economists begun to enter the conversation regarding the right mix of data privacy and data accuracy.[11]

To be differentially private, the published statistic would have to be similar when an individual's information was included in the data to when an individual's information was excluded from the data. The basic idea of DP is to inject enough noise into the data so that a user of the data cannot infer whether a given individual's information is in the data or not. How much noise is required depends on the statistics to be revealed and how sensitive those statistics are to the inclusion or exclusion of individuals. For a statistic such as the number of minority-owned farms in a Census block, DP would require that the published statistic not reveal if an individual was included or excluded from the data. DP gives the individual plausible deniability regarding their participation or lack of participation in a study or database (Christensen et al., 2019). This concept is what underlies the approach taken by Chetty and Friedman (2019b) regarding aggregation of data discussed earlier in this chapter.

To further illustrate the idea of DP, we adapt a common example from the literature (Heffetz and Ligett, 2014). A researcher conducts a DP analysis on a health data set that contains information about patient smoking habits and the occurrence of different types of cancer. The analysis reveals a correlation between smoking and lung cancer. The researcher then publishes a paper stating this correlation. An individual smoker might feel that their privacy was violated, because third parties, like insurance companies, can now infer the probability that the smoker will develop lung cancer and will therefore charge them more for health insurance. However, because the outcome of the analysis would be no *different* whether or not the individual smoker's health data were included in the analysis, the *differential* privacy of the individual smoker has been preserved.

As with SDL, DP protects against inferential disclosure. Imagine two data sets that are exactly the same except that data set $\Theta_{\{A\}}$ contains a record for person A and data set $\Theta_{\{-A\}}$ is lacking that record. DP adds noise to any statistic or analysis so that the probability of getting any given value for that statistic or from that analysis is similar under $\Theta_{\{A\}}$ and $\Theta_{\{-A\}}$. Said differently, with a certain degree of probability, a researcher cannot infer if the statistic or the analysis comes from data set $\Theta_{\{A\}}$ or $\Theta_{\{-A\}}$. Some might object that inferring person A's identity or attribute is not the same as knowing with certainty that person A was included in or excluded from the data set. Or one might argue that privacy is really only violated if the researcher knows for certain that person A was included in the data set. And furthermore, one could claim that the only way to go from inference to certainty is if the researcher knew the method by which the statistic was produced. As a result, one might then conclude that as long as the method for protecting privacy was kept secret, such as the decision rule for record swapping in SDL, then person A's privacy is protected. However, a basic tenet of modern cryptography is that a system is not secure if its security depends on the internal algorithms or methods of the system being kept secret (Wood et al., 2018). Simply hiding the key is not a sure method to keeping something locked.

As DP treats disclosure risk probabilistically, one needs to define the degree of probability with which a researcher can infer if the statistic or the analysis comes from data set $\Theta_{\{A\}}$ or $\Theta_{\{-A\}}$. In DP, a privacy loss parameter, ε, measures the impact that each person's information has on the statistic or analysis, similar to the sensitivity parameter defined in Chetty and Friedman (2019b). The database manager, or the individual researcher looking to share their data, can choose a desired level of privacy protection, ε. The DP algorithm then injects noise into the statistic or analysis to ensure that the probability of disclosure is no greater than ε. In this way, DP can provide a mathematically provable guarantee of a certain level of privacy. Conversely, SDL methods are unable to provide the certainty of a particular level of privacy.

Another difference between DP and SDL methods is that DP is designed in such a way as to allow for the publication of the specific parameters used to infuse noise. This allows researchers to conduct DP-aware analysis, correcting in part for the noise introduced by DP. The major cost of DP is that it requires the specification of a privacy-loss budget. In order to continue to guarantee a certain level of privacy protection, DP must limit the total queries made on the data. Eventually, this privacy-loss budget may be exhausted, at which point data could no longer be used by the public without violating the original guaranteed level of privacy. This hard limit on how many times a data set can be used while maintaining a certain level of privacy is the result of the database reconstruction theorem (Dinur and Nissim, 2003). While detractors of DP view this limit on use as a detriment of DP, proponents point out that this trade-off is not unique to DP and among competing methods DP makes this trade-off explicit. It is then a social choice problem how best to balance privacy and accuracy and prioritize different uses of the data (Abowd and Schmutte, 2019).

As of 2022, DP has only just begun to be adopted by the statistical agencies and the managers of the databases most commonly used by economists. This includes the U.S. Census Bureau, which adopted DP for the 2020 Census, and plans to implement DP in several of the other data sets it publishes (Abowd et al., 2019). The Opportunity Atlas, which is published at the Census tract level, also protects privacy by methods that build on DP (Chetty and Friedman, 2019b). However, to date, public-use household survey data sets used in development economics still rely on SDL to protect participant privacy. And it is exceedingly rare for individual researchers to apply these methods to their data prior to sharing the data.

5.4.3 Implications for Data Sharing

As should be obvious by now, removing PII from data prior to sharing is not sufficient to meet the standards of confidentiality that we promise to our research participants during the process of obtaining informed consent. But as stated at the outset of this chapter, open data is a key part of open science. Applied economic researchers need to grapple with the trade-off between protecting privacy and sharing truly replicable data.

Privacy protection is not trivial, nor is it limited to large public use data sets or censuses of populations. Even a few simple data points can be used to perform a successful reidentify attack (Heffetz and Ligett, 2014). For most people in the U.S., all that is needed is birthday ($d = 365$) and year ($y = 100$), sex ($s = 2$), and a five digit ZIP code ($z = 32,000$). These pieces of data result in more than 2 billion possible combinations, but there are only 330 million people in the U.S. Most individuals are the only person of their sex born on their birth date living in their ZIP code. Given how unique just birth date, sex, and location are, consider of how identifiable an individual is within a data set that includes education, career, household size, farm size, income, race, or any of the other socioeconomic variables typically collected and released as part of a replication data set.

The burden is on us, as researchers who collect, manage, and analyze data to share data in such a way that truly protects the privacy of our research participants. Greely (2007) writes, "It is no solution to say that 'anonymity' means only 'not terribly easy to identify,' . . . or that 'informed consent' is satisfied by largely ignorant blanket permissions." However, for the field of economics it is unclear how best to manage the privacy–accuracy trade-off. Regardless, what is clear is that the current practices fail to satisfy the promise of informed consent regarding the privacy of participants and the confidentiality of data. Without taking what Heffetz and Ligett (2014) term the "naive" approach of refraining from all data sharing, the ethical researcher needs to invest the time and energy to learn how to share data in a truly private way. Fortunately, there are already a growing catalog of user-written R and Stata code for implementing SDL and DP methods (Heffetz and Ligett, 2014; Chetty and Friedman, 2019a). As more and more economists take seriously the need to protect privacy in open data, we hope and believe that the supply of new methods and codes will rise to meet the demand.

5.5   How to Share Data

Sharing data can be difficult and time consuming. It is a challenge to understand how to share data in a way that adequately preserves the privacy of research participants. Additionally, it can take a substantial amount of time to convert disorganized code and folder structures into a truly replicable package. While real, these hurdles are insufficient justification to refrain from sharing data and contributing to open science.

The best way to overcome these hurdles is to proactively develop a data management and sharing plan at the earliest stages of the research life cycle. Funding agencies increasingly require a detailed data management and sharing plan as part of the preliminary project proposal. At the initial idea stage, discussing a data management plan may seem premature, but having a plan in place can help guide the data collection process and streamline the data analysis process. Once a researcher has developed one or two data management and sharing plans, and learned what worked and what did not work, adapting the plans to new projects is fairly straightforward. In our Applied International Development Economics (AIDE) Lab, we have an OSF page (https://osf.io/3vtng/) that outlines standard procedures regarding coding style and data folder structure that are portable across different projects.

While all data management plans vary slightly, all contain the same basic elements. According to to the NIH, a comprehensive data management and sharing plan should:

- identify the data types and resources that will be generated, including the file types and software that will be used to clean and analyze the data.
- propose a timeline for sharing the data and resources, including any embargos.

- determine where the resources will be stored (public or institutional repository), preferably with a DOI address.
- describe how others can access the resources. This entails not just where the data are located but also where the code is located and how the code can be deployed to clean the data and reproduce results.

The plan should also govern the management and sharing of metadata, or data about data, which the NIH (2020) defines as "data that provide additional information intended to make scientific data interpretable and reusable."

5.5.1 Replication Packages

The dual, and simultaneously sought, objectives of open science and data sharing are to create efficiencies in the discovery process while allowing for the verification of past discoveries. Open science makes it easier for future researchers to build on past work without duplicating it. Open science additionally permits for an easier replication and/or reproduction of past work, strengthening the scientific record. *Replicability* and *reproducibility* are often used as synonyms but they have slight different meanings. We discuss these further in Chapter 6, in terms of data analysis but here discuss them with respect to data management.

Replicability is to obtain consistent results across studies that are working to answer the same question but using new data or different methods. This procedure is often called a conceptual replication, an extension, or a verification test. Reproducibility is the degree of similarity (or extent of differences) between the results of measurements with the same data, carried out using the same method. This procedure is often called direct replication or reanalysis (Christensen et al., 2019). To assist with achieving both these goals, applied economists need to create replication packages that include data, code, and implementation details in a README file such that others can replicate and reproduce their work.

In producing a replication package, it is important to distinguish between two different types of reproducibility (Stodden, 2014): computational and statistical. This differentiation is essential because how much data one chooses to share will affect how reproducible one's research is. First, computational reproducibility, what Clemens (2017) calls verification, is when the same procedures are used on the same data to determine if the exact results in a paper can be reproduced. To conduct a verification test requires the data and code, as well as detailed information about software, hardware, and implementation details. Ideally, a replication package that allows for computational reproduction would include the raw data, the cleaning code, and information about software version and hardware type. At minimum, however, all that is required for computational reproducibility is a data extract and the code to produce the tables and figures in the paper. This minimum version of a replication package for achieving computational reproducibility is what is required by most economics journals.

Next, distinct from computational reproducibility, is statistical reproducibility (Stodden, 2014). Statistical reproducibility, or what Clemens (2017) calls reanalysis, is using the same data, or a subsample from the same data, but tweaking the methods and procedures. The goal is to statistically assess the validity or robustness of a result under different permutations. Most empirical research papers check the statistical reproducibility of their findings within the paper itself. In economics, we generally refer to these as robustness checks.[12] To conduct a reanalysis test requires a bit more information than a verification test. One needs both the data and code, as well as detailed information about the choice of statistical tests, model parameters, threshold values, and more. Limiting the replication package to a data extract is not useful in verifying statistical reproducibility because one would like to verify the robustness of results on subsamples of the data and to different choices in data cleaning and variable definition. Thus, both more detailed information and more types of information are required to make a replication package that is statistically reproducible. However, at this time, including sufficient information in a replication package so as to ensure research is reproducible is not the norm in economics and so is infrequently done.

Following the guidelines put out by Jacoby and Luption (2016) for the *American Journal of Political Science* (*AJPS*), a replication package for statistical reproducibility should contain the following: (1) a README, (2) data sets, and (3) software commands.

README

Consider the task of assembling IKEA furniture – a relationship-challenging endurance test in its own right. Now, consider this same assembly task if you were not given directions. A dramatically more difficult ask, to be sure. The directions for assembly are akin to a README file in a replication package. A README file provides the directions for how to take the various components of a replication package and put them together to build the figures and tables in the final paper. README files should be produced as either a plain text (.txt) file or a portable document file (.pdf) file. The README should be readable by as large a set of software types as possible and should not rely on proprietary or pay-for software, like Microsoft Word. Nor should it rely on software that requires an internet connection, like Google Docs. README files should be designed to be widely accessible, as not everyone has the same software programs or shares the same level of internet access.

The README file should contain a list of all the components within the replication package along with a short description of each component. Ideally, one's data analysis workflow (see Chapter 6) will allow for the creation of a single "project" script file that calls and runs all subsidiary script file and produces all tables and graphs. If not, the README should describe which files produce which tables and figures, referencing the number or name used in the published paper. Figure 5.2 provides an example.

Readme Data File for "Money matters: The role of yields and profits in agricultural technology adoption"

Jeffrey D. Michler, Emilia Tjernström, Simone Verkaart, Kai Mausch

15 May 2018

This folder contains the data and Stata programs (version 14) required to replicate the tables and figures in Money Matters as well as the associated appendices. The programs generate all summary tables and figures. In order to construct the final regression tables, some manual editing (and copy-ing/pasting across files) is required, so we do not reproduce them here. However, all relevant numbers are in the regression output generated by the programs files listed below.

The programs are as follows:

- `mm_master_program.do`: Replicates the all tables and graphics in the paper. This program will run all subsidiary .do files.

- `mm_pub_tables.do`: Replicates the regression results in the paper and the appendix. Specifically Tables 3-5 and B1-D1. Plus Figures 2-4 which are generated using regression results.

- `mm_sum_stats.do`: Replicates the summary statistics tables plus MW-tests in the paper and the appendix. Specifically Tables 1-2, 6, and A1.

- `mm_graphs.do`: Replicates Figures 1, A1-A3.

The data are included in `mm.dta`. Several of the programs produce additional data files as inputs into regressions contained in the .do files.

Note that the code requires installing the Stata package -randcoef- as discussed in Barriga Cabanillas et al. (2018) and -tuple-.

References

Barriga Cabanillas, O., J. D. Michler, A. Michuda, and E. Tjernström (2018). Fitting and interpreting correlated random-coefficient models using Stata. *Stata Journal 18*(1), 159–73.

FIGURE 5.2   Example of a README file

Note: Reproduction of a README file for Michler et al. (2019).

the data file is read into a different software program, those labels may be stripped from the data. Fortunately, Stata and similar programs allow one to automatically generate a codebook. So, even if data files contain labels, its a good idea to include a codebook with the data file, in case there is a decoupling of labels from variables.

While including or linking to a data extract is the most common form of data sharing in economics at this time, an ideal replication package would provide the original data source and all information to reconstruct the analysis data set. In fact, Jacoby and Luption (2016) include "analysis data sets" and "information to reconstruct analysis data sets" as two separate components in a replication package. Following the advice of Vilhuber (2022) and speculating on the the trajectory to

Beyond a list and description of the components in the replication package, the README should detail any folder structure required for the data, what is known as the development environment, and the order the files need to be run in. Furthermore, the README should include information on what programs are necessary for replicating the analysis, including any user-written programs, the version of those programs, and whether any manual manipulation of tables and figures is required. One might also include information about the runtime and hardware requirements, particularly if the analysis relies are simulations or big data.

Data Sets

Any replication package should reference the data used in the analysis. For data sets of reasonable size, the data can be directly included in the replication package as a file. For larger data sets, or for those who use internet repositories or an online version control systems like GitHub for hosting replication packages, the data can be archived in a separate location. Data archives, such as Harvard's Dataverse or the Inter-university Consortium for Political and Social Research (ICPSR) at the University of Michigan, can hold data or the entire replication package. Alternatively, for analysis that relies on public-use data sets, the replication package should reference where those data can be obtained and the edition or vintage of the data (i.e., the original download date of the data). Regardless of what type of data are necessary for the replication package, what is crucial is that if the data are not included in the replication package, then the replication package must include citations to the data. These citations should be as detailed as a bibliographic citation. Ideally, the citation will include a digital object identifier (DOI), which is a permanent web address for the location of the data. Placing data in an internet archive automatically generates a DOI for that specific archive entry.

The format a researcher should store their data in, either in the replication package or in an archive, tends to be driven by the standards of the research field. Jacoby and Luption (2016) suggest storing the data as .csv files, which can be read by almost every statistical software. However, if certain types of software dominate the field, then providing data in the software's own format is acceptable. As Figure 5.3 shows, Stata and Matlab dominate among the software programs used by economists.

Although storing data in .csv format makes data readable by many different types of software, the cost is that the format does not allow for any labeling of variables. Because of this, the *AJPS* requires data be accompanied by a codebook that details what each variable measures and what their value means (Jacoby and Luption, 2016). The variable y in economics typically signifies output, but if the variable y shows up in a data set, what does it measure? The output of what? And how is the value measured? In kilograms? Or in kilograms per hectare? One benefit of data file formats like that of Stata is that it allows for the attachment of both variable and value labels. This mitigates the need for a separate codebook. But, if

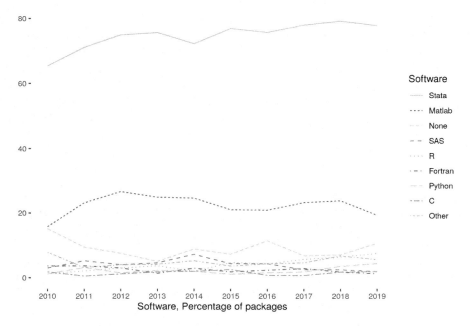

FIGURE 5.3 Software Used by Economists

Note: Figure presents line graphs of the number of papers submitted to the Data Editor of the AEA journals that used a specific software package. Reprinted from Vilhuber et al. (2020) under CC BY 4.0.

come in economics at large, we believe that there is no need to include the original version of the data and a final "analysis data set." Rather, economists should strive to build a replication package that is "push button reproducible." This means that there is a single project or master script file that runs all the code for both data cleaning and analysis.

Beyond format and location of data, a critical decision that researchers need to make is how to protect the privacy of research participants whose data are included in a data set. As should be clear by now, simply removing PII from the data is insufficient to ensure privacy and confidentiality. As of now, there is no standard for how economists should anonymize data prior to sharing them. And so, at present, it is up to the individual researcher to decide how much effort to put into making their data truly anonymous.

Software Commands

Obviously, to be actually reproducible, a replication package must include the software commands used to execute the analysis. As with the analysis data sets, the format of the code or script files is less important then their clarity and detail. We provide more details on organizing a workflow in Chapter 6. Here it is sufficient simply to say that treating your code like a lab notebook is an excellent habit to develop. Script files should include not just what was done (the software commands) but also notes and commentary on why certain actions (commands) were used and the outcome of those actions. A lab notebook without this sort of editorial detail is useless to anyone other than the author, and even the author might have difficulty reproducing their work after a few months or years working on other projects.

As mentioned in the previous subsection, the software commands in a replication package should be organized so as to be push button reproducible. That means that a user needs only to place the data in the correct location and then open up a single script file and click run. That script file will then set up the development environment, with all necessary folders, run all the cleaning code, run all the analysis code, and output all tables and figures in a readable format. Ideally, this overarching project file would even query the archive where the original data are stored and download it to the right local folders. Vilhuber (2022) and the AEA Data Editor's GitHub page include many recommendations and tools to make one's replication package as automated as possible.

5.5.2   *Rapidity of Change*

In applied economics, the norms and standards around replication are changing rapidly. The reasons for the changes are twofold. First, researchers are realizing that the current norm of just providing a data abstract and analysis code to journals, through only self-enforcing mechanisms, is too weak. Even at journals with explicit policies, these policies are often not followed. Second, computing, network, and storage technologies are changing so rapidly, that what is possible to include in a replication package has greatly expanded in just a few years.

Regardless of where the norms and standards for sharing data and code go, we as individual researchers should be guided by one key principle: computational empathy (https://aeadataeditor.github.io/aea-de-guidance/preparingfor-data-deposit.html). Computational empathy means remembering the following two points:

- The replication package is meant to be run by others who have none of the setup, packages, and data, that the original author might have, on computers that may not run the same operating system.
- The replication package should be treated as one of the methods to convey the processes that lead to a manuscript's conclusions. Consider it a teaching tool, targeting graduate students or others who may not be in one's field.

To achieve computational empathy, posting a bunch of data and code online is not sufficient. The author of a paper is the most qualified person on the subject of that paper. This includes all the various components which went into the paper, including the data and code. By extension, this means that whoever is attempting to replicate this work is less experienced and less qualified than the original author. To that end, the author should do all that they can to ensure that their work is replicable, reproducible, and transparent. As methods are changing fast, graduate students or early-career researchers need to be leaders on this front – both with co-authors and in lab or research groups. It is likely that students and early-career researchers will use tools that principal investigators and advisers have not used before. Just in the five to seven years since we completed our PhDs, how data and code can be shared is completely different. When we completed our PhDs the standard was uploading replication packages as .zip files to the author's website or the journal's website. Now data and code can and should be archived on Dataverse or ICPSR and given a DOI. Containers, like Docker, now provide a standardized way to package data, software, and code so that replication packages can be executed regardless of machine or operating system. With these changes in the past decade alone, what the decade to come will hold is sure to be tremendous with respect to advancing open-science practices.

There are also practical considerations for ensuring a comprehensive and usable replication package. Specifically, the pathway to publication will be eased with an appropriately replicable package. Figure 5.4 outlines the process flow of providing replication materials for papers accepted to AEA journals. While the specific process flow is likely to be different at different journals, the broad outlines are instructive. What should be obvious is that making research truly reproducible takes time. It cannot be done by tossing a bunch of data and code files into a folder, zipping it, and then posting it online. Early-stage decisions about data management and workflow need to be made with the end product (paper and replication package) in mind.

As for current resources on practicing open science and creating optimal replication packages, we recommend a few sources. First, the AEA Data Editor maintains a GitHub web page that contains guidance and resources for putting together a replication package that meets the current highest standards in the economics profession (https://aeadataeditor.github.io/). Additionally, BITSS maintains a web resource with advice and links to a variety of tools for building replication packages (www.bitss.org/resource-library/). While these specific resources and their contents may change as standards for replication packages increase, so will the available resources. Learning and using these tools is a long-term investment in terms of career success but also for making science better.

5.6 Conclusion

Open data are a cornerstone of open, ethical, and reproducible research. Yet, open data presents its own ethical challenges. Simply sharing data violates promises of anonymity made to the research participants whose confidential information is in the data. The applied economics profession is just beginning to grapple with the trade-offs between more accurate data and more privacy protection. New methods

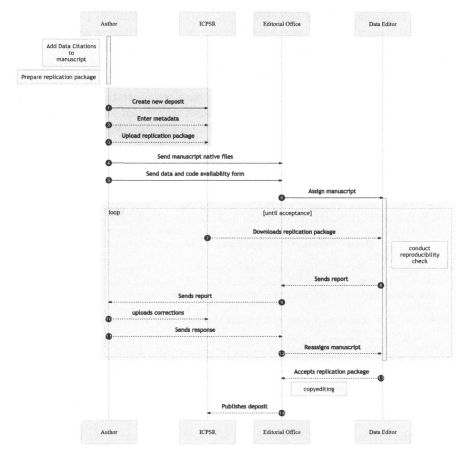

FIGURE 5.4   Replication Process Flow at American Economic Association Journals

Note: ICPSR = Inter-university Consortium for Political and Social Research. The figure presents the approximate flow process for providing replication materials for papers accepted to AEA journals. Reproduced from https://aeadataeditor.github.io/aeade-guidance under CC BY 4.0.

of privacy protection, like SDL and DP, offer opportunities to better protect the privacy and confidentiality of research participants. But these methods are not yet the norm in the profession.

De-identification, which is what IRBs typically require for data, does not provide the anonymity that informed consent forms promise. The language on informed consent forms needs to change so that it truthfully represent what sorts of privacy protection can be guarantee. But we echo Heffetz and Ligett (2014), in cautioning against an alternative of reverting to a norm of closed, private data sets. Currently the field is left with the unenviable choice between our commitment of anonymity to our research participants and our commitment of openness to the scientific community.

As a profession, we are still working to arrive at the optimal allocation. As individual researchers, we must keep learning and keep adapting new methods. We are learning to create better replication packages and practice computational empathy in their creation. All the complexities and complications of data management offer an opportunity to learn and practice better science – in line with available technology – rather than be a burden. As such, as researchers, we must take it upon ourselves to ensure that our work ensures the privacy and confidentiality of the participants in our research while simultaneously ensuring that our work is replicable and reproducible for others in the community.

Notes

1 Sweeney is now the Daniel Paul Professor of the Practice of Government and Technology at the Harvard Kennedy School and in the Harvard Faculty of Arts and Sciences.
2 Dr. Narayanan is now an associate professor of computer science at Princeton University, and Dr. Shmatikov is now a professor of computer science at Cornell University and Cornell Tech
3 Kristal et al. (2020) did not completely ignore the field experiment. They report in their paper that they found large differences in the baseline data and conclude that the initial randomization failed in some way. They did not pursue the reanalysis any further.
4 It is worth highlighting that the official data sharing policy of *Science* reads:

> All data necessary to understand, assess, and extend the conclusions of the manuscript must be available to any reader of Science. All computer codes involved in the creation or analysis of data must also be available to any reader of Science. After publication, all reasonable requests for data and materials must be fulfilled. Any restrictions on the availability of data, codes, or materials, including fees and original data obtained from other sources (Materials Transfer Agreements), must be disclosed to the editors upon submission.

5 Anecdotally, one of the authors can speak to a co-author suggesting exactly this due to the "onerous" requirement.
6 The policy also encourages citation of software packages, another relatively uncommon practice in economics.
7 We discuss TOP guidelines in detail in Chapter 7.
8 This is to say that IRBs are (generally speaking) unconcerned with data management practices.
9 Obviously, one could cut out this step if the server used for data collection was also the server for permanent data storage. The only reason we use different locations is that the server we use for data collection is not our university's preferred (and institutionally paid-for) cloud storage service.
10 See the symposium at the 2019 AEA Annual Meeting (Abowd et al., 2019; Abraham, 2019; Chetty and Friedman, 2019b; Ruggles et al., 2019).
11 See more about robustness checks in Section 6.4.

6

DATA ANALYSIS

6.1 Introduction

In the humorous and enlightening *How to Lie with Statistics*, Darrell Huff (1954) writes:

> Despite its mathematical base, statistics is as much an art as it is a science. A great many manipulations and even distortions are possible within the bounds of propriety. Often the statistician must choose among methods, a subjective process, and find the one that he will use to represent the facts.

This ability to choose among a variety of appropriate methods has come to be known as "researcher degrees of freedom." But while different methods may be acceptable for answering a single research question, Huff (1954) warns that "when there are many reasonable explanations you are hardly entitled to pick one that suits your taste and insist on it." Huff's book exposes numerous absurd but real-life examples of statistical manipulation used to justify or defend a variety of political or corporate positions. These include sampling with a built-in bias, not clarifying if the average is the median or the mean, not reporting if differences are statistically significant, and graphs with misleading scale or vague labels. Huff also discusses the difficulty in determining when someone is actually lying with statistics or are just incompetent at statistics.

The challenge of determining when misreported statistics are the result of a deliberate desire to deceive or simple sloppiness is important to Huff's legacy as a debunker of bogus analysis. As Gelman (2012) reports, Huff went on to pen a manuscript titled *How to Lie with Smoking Statistics*, which was commissioned by the Tobacco Institute to debunk the statistical evidence that

DOI: 10.4324/9781003025061-9

smoking caused cancer contained in the Surgeon General's 1964 *Smoking and Health* report. The Surgeon General's report was based on a preponderance of evidence from numerous studies, conducted by numerous scientists, using numerous methods, over many years. Huff received a fee of $10,000 from the Tobacco Institute, (approximately $100,000 in 2023, similar to the amount Alan Krueger got from Uber). He worked to undermine the conclusion of the report by raising doubts about the statistical accuracy of individual studies, supplemented with his writerly wit and anecdotes draw from other, non-tobacco studies. Some of his criticisms of specific studies were valid, although many were simply based on conjecture about how a study could have been done differently. The book was never published and was only uncovered as part of the release of documents following the 1998 Tobacco Master Settlement Agreement (Reinhart, 2014). Huff, who died in 2001, was never asked about his involvement with the Tobacco industry, thus leaving us to try to determine if the contents of *How to Lie with Smoking Statistics* represent Huff's deception or his incompetence.

In this chapter, we explore the ethical issues facing applied economists when doing data analysis. The challenge, as Huff's work demonstrates, is in determining when and why a researcher made a particular choice in the analysis. Was it the right choice? Were there other options? Was a different choice initially made, then reversed once the results were known? Was the choice made to lead to a specific result? The multiplicity of decisions that researchers must face when conducting analysis has been termed either "researcher degrees of freedom" or, more literarily, "the garden of forking paths" (Gelman, 2012). The "great many manipulations and even distorations" (Huff, 1954) that are possible in data analysis is why in Chapter 3 we advocate for the use of pre-analysis plans to guide research.

In this chapter we begin by discussing the value of setting up a workflow to manage the entire analysis process, from reading in raw data to producing publication-ready tables and figures. The goal of establishing a workflow is to standardize the process of research across projects. This not only allows for easier collaboration but also helps ensure that research is reproducible – both by one's future self and by future researchers. We then discuss specification searching, or the process of settling upon a given method or model for analyzing data. At its most extreme, specification search can entail the falsification of results. But more common are concerns around the *post hoc* generation of hypotheses after results are known (HARKing) and reanalyzing data until one arrives at a predetermined result (*p*-hacking). Although a pre-analysis plan can (and should) guide one's research, Nosek et al. (2012) note that data manipulation is possible through motivated reasoning in complex and ambiguous situations – such as empirical data analysis.

We follow the section on specification search with two related discussions. The first considers the ethics around the standards for reporting significant results in applied economics. Expanding on ideas presented in Ziliak and McCloskey (2008), we examine the value of tests for statistical significance in understanding and valuing results. The second discussion considers the processes and practices of replication and reproduction. This subsection examines the value of these practices for science, writ large, and how applied economists can ensure that we undertake best practices in this domain.

The objective of this chapter is to provide insight into the ethical dilemmas that arise everyday when we make choices during the analysis of data. Relying on the scientific method, and always reflecting on the when and why a decision is made, is key to ensuring one is engaged in ethical research. As Hotelling et al. (1948) write, "too many people like to do their statistical work as they say their prayers – merely substitute in a formula found in a highly respected book." While we continue to advocate for pre-analysis plans and similar methods of accountability, by understanding how researchers can influence the outcome of their studies we can better navigate along the garden of forking paths.

6.2 Workflow

Workflow is common jargon in manufacturing, management, and software development, but the concept is extremely useful for applied economics research. At its most basic, a workflow is a repeatable series of actions necessary for completing a task. Henry Ford's assembly line for automobiles is a workflow: standardized, repeatable activities that produce the same result every time. At its most powerful, a workflow not only allows for the reproduction of an output using the same inputs but also allows for portability and interchangeability of the process. Ford's main assembly line was at the Highland Park Plant in Michigan, but Ford established production lines throughout the U.S., Canada, Europe, and South America, all producing the same car. Additionally, the complex and skilled production of cars by hand was simplified into a set of simple, repetitive processes in which one line worker could be interchanged for a different line worker. The result was a replicable and reproducible workflow for the assembly of the Model T.

A workflow for cleaning and analyzing data, and producing tables and figures, is the key to ensuring replicable and reproducible work – both for oneself while working and for others later. Establishing a workflow should be undertaken as a first step, prior to cleaning data. Trying to build a reproducible workflow midway through the cleaning or analysis results in time lost to figuring out what was done previously, where files are, where code is saved, and the like. The sign of a good workflow management system is that when a project is opened, one is immediately able to figure out where all the files are, what the files do, and the order in which they must be run. This should be true regardless of if the project belongs to you or to someone else.

The objectives of a workflow should be to create accurate, efficient, simple, standardized, automated, usable, scaleable, interchangeable, and portable results. The final goal is to be able to replicate a paper or other piece of research with a single push of a button (somewhat obviously called "push button replication"). To achieve this goal, a successful workflow takes all the steps that go into the process of creating a final research project and consolidates them into a single stream of work. This makes it easier for a researcher to complete their own work and share that work with peers and colleagues. Ideally, having established a workflow for a single project, the structure of that workflow can be adapted, with minimal cost, to new projects.

The first principle of a reproducible and replicable workflow is that data should be treated as immutable. ***Do not ever edit raw data.*** Important corollaries are do not edit your raw data manually and do not edit your raw data in Excel; do not overwrite your raw data; do not save multiple versions of the raw data. Code in a workflow should move the raw data through a pipeline from cleaning to final analysis. And for that to be possible, it is imperative to start with *raw* data. To this end, data should be stored separate from code or other files that manipulate data or otherwise analyze data.

The second principle of a reproducible and replicable workflow is the use of a version control system, such as Git. Version control is simply a system that records every time changes are made to a file so that one can examine any specific version of the file at a later date. When we were in grad school, prior to learning about Git, we saved every version of our code with the date attached. So we had computers full of files like `analysis_20130823` and `analysis_20130825`. The problem with this system is that it is nearly impossible to tell what changed between the two versions. Version control systems track and save changes to the code in the background in a single file, allowing you to go back in time and examine any version. So there is no need to save multiple versions of the same file. Additionally, the way version control tracks changes allows for very simply comparison of what has changed from one version to the next.

Figure 6.1 provides an example using GitHub Desktop, which is a graphic user interface for Git.[1] GitHub Desktop displays only the section of code that has changed, highlighting line deletions in red, line insertions in green, and even highlighting the specific bit of text that was added or removed. Many of the software interfaces for Git allow for cloud storage and syncing across multiple machines, making collaboration with other researchers extremely easy. Building workflow upon a version control system provides a natural structure for ensuring research is reproducible and replicable.

Beyond these two principles, the specific details of a workflow will vary from project to project and person to person. We recommend Christensen et al. (2019) and Gentzkow and Shapiro (2014) as good references with specific instructions and ideas for workflow construction and formatting. However, there are a set of best practices that can be incorporated into any workflow:

1. Create a development environment.
2. Streamline your coding script files.

```
15    15
16    16    *  TO DO:
17     -    *  match fies variables to lsms panel variables
      17  +    *  complete
18    18
19    19
20    20    ****************************************************************

           @@ -152,12 +152,19 @@ restore
152   152       gen           wave = -1
153   153       lab var       wave "wave number"
154   154
155    -/*  generate country variable
      155  +*  generate country variable
156   156       gen           country = 3
```

FIGURE 6.1   Example of Version Control

Note: Sample version control code. Figure by the authors. The upper, darker shaded line at 17 and 155 were deleted (notice the -) and replaced with the lower, lighter shaded lines (notice the +). Lines 21 to 151 are suppressed since no changes occurred.

3. Generate a master file.
4. Use a consistent style.

Implementing these best practices requires planning, organization, documentation, and execution. As mentioned earlier, building the workflow prior to undertaking any coding will save time and headaches later in the data analysis process.

First, creating a development environment allows for your workflow to be portable from one computer or user to another. A development environment is simply the folder structure in which data and code live. At its best, the code itself will generate the development environment, creating all the necessary folders and placing all the necessary files in those folders, like an installer package for a piece of software. At a minimum, a development environment should be obvious, easily described, and readily understood. Using an online repository like GitHub allows users to "clone" a project, bringing along the folder structure and all the code onto a new machine.

A good development environment has a clear folder structure, effective naming conventions, makes use of relative paths, and includes a comprehensive README. Figure 6.2 demonstrates a sample file structure for a simple workflow. A root folder, "main folder name," should be the primary folder. Within that folder, subfolders might include a "raw" folder that includes raw data, "do-files" that include cleaning and analysis files, "temp" that may include temporary or intermediate files, "clean" that includes the regression-ready data, and "output" that includes results, such as graphs and tables, as well as other output, such as presentations or shareable data files.

A good development environment should easily expand to accommodate complexity while still being easy to navigate. Projects that are more complex, either

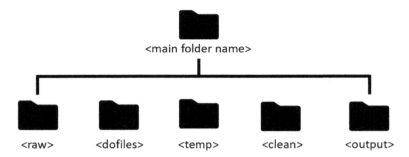

FIGURE 6.2 Suggested Folder Structure

Note: A sample suggested folder structure for raw, do, temp, clean, and output files. Figure by the authors.

with more data, more required data cleaning, and/or more regressions, will call for more levels in the folder structure. But one should not confuse more levels with more complexity. Consider an example: in our research for the World Bank, we use survey data collected in multiple countries over multiple waves or rounds with multiple modules in a given survey. As an example, the "raw" folder will contain a folder for each country, each country folder will contain folders for each round of the data, and each round folder will contain the data from each module. So while there are multiple countries, rounds, and modules, the folder structure remains the same across countries and across rounds. That structure would then be repeated in the "temp" folder so that cleaning code inputs raw files from the folder raw/ country A/round 02 and outputs the cleaned version of them into temp/ country A/round 02. Gentzkow and Shapiro (2014) provide a tremendous reference for more details on creating an effective development environment, including the value of automation, directories, keys, abstraction, documentation, and management.

Second, within your folders, it is essential to consider the organization of files themselves. Obviously, efficient and clear code is an integral part of a workflow. To this end, code files, be they Stata do-files, R-script files, or Matlab M-files, should *do* only one thing. Variables should be cleaned in a single file, and the cleaned data saved in a new folder, such as "temp." A different script file should then merge the cleaned individual data files. Yet another script file should read in the merged data and conduct all the analysis.

Again, more complex projects will require more coding and thus more script files containing that code. But even for extremely complex projects script files can and should remain streamlined. To achieve this, we like to organize our script files into folders that clone the folder structure of the raw data. We have a single script file to clean each raw data file and give the script file the same name as the raw data file it cleans. We then give decipherable names to the intermediate script files that merge cleaned data. Each project requires a slightly different folder and file structure, but we try to be as consistent as possible across projects. This allows us to jump from project to project without spending costly time scrolling through code trying to figure out what it does.

Third, it is important to generate a master or overall project script file. This master script file serves a single purpose, which is to run all the subsidiary script files for the project, compiling everything together in its entirety and outputting all the results. This saves you and other researchers the time of trying to figure out what coding files need to be run in what order within a replication package. A master script file allows one to achieve the objective of a successful workflow: push-button replication.

All of our projects contain such a master script file, which we often label, somewhat blandly, "projectdo." This "projectdo" file defines the root directories for each user so that the code in all of the subsidiary files knows where to look for the data without having to change directory paths in every file. When possible, the "projectdo" file creates the development environment itself, downloading the data and placing it in the correct folders. It also installs or loads any user-written packages so that the code does not break when it tries to use a package that the current user does not have installed on their machine. Finally, it runs all of the code in the proper order, placing intermediate data files in the "temp" folder and outputting any tables or figures in the "output" folder. In our more complex World Bank projects, we have intermediate master files that are run from the overall "projectdo" and that themselves run files lower down the chain. In projects with hundreds of individual script files, subsetting these files by using intermediate "master"-type files can be an efficient way to execute complex and/or complicated projects while keeping the code and file structure simple and clear. However, the relative pathway for the main directory should be set up in the main "master" file.

The final best practice for creating a good workflow is a consistent coding style. Coding should include documentation within each script file that describes details about the project and file, what the file does, what it assumes the user has, and what must still be done on the file. Such documentation should be clear and concise, with a focus on design and purpose, not mechanics. Headings should label what is being done in a particular section, although following the recommendation from earlier, a single file should not have more than a few sections. Spaces and tabs should be used liberally in order to make reading code easier. Comments can be helpful for clarifying and sharing what is intended to occur in a code block and clarifying what actually occurred. As mentioned in Chapter 5, when writing code, one should be guided by computational empathy, always remembering that the code is meant to be run by others who have none of the context that the original author might have.

As with the other best practices, the goal is to build and implement them so that the resulting workflow is portable and interchangeable. For coding style, this means using the same style on every project (portable) and having all of our students use the same style (interchangeable). This makes it easy for us to review code written by each other and by our students for any project. It also makes it easy for students to review each others' code. Figure 6.3 shows a piece of sample code in our own house or lab style. Every file starts with a preamble containing information about who wrote the file and when it was edited, along with what the file does and what data or packages the file assumes the user has access to. The preamble is always followed by a section that sets up relative path locations for input data, outputs, and log files. After the setup comes the actual content of the file with plenty of white space and notes to allow a user to easily read and comprehend what the code is doing. Finally, all files conclude with some end matter, describing the variables, ordering them, and then saving the data in a new location.

Ethical applied economic research requires that data analysis is replicable and reproducible. Making work replicable and reproducible requires a clear workflow. Building a workflow should be undertaken as a first step in the analysis process and doing so can save time and increase efficiency throughout a project. Every project will be different, but setting up a structure for workflow that is portable and interchangeable is well worth the effort as it will make one more efficient and make one's work more easily reproducible by others.

6.3 Specification Search

It was a question of the ethics of specification searching that first brought us to the quandaries of ethical research. As we detailed in Chapter 1, the case of Brian Wansink that initially drew our attention to the too often ill-defined arena of research ethics in applied economics. Although there were myriad issues with Wansink's work, as graduates students, what concerned us most were the questions about specification search. We wondered how we were to understand best practices for good, thorough econometric work versus data dredging or HARKing. It was clear, under scrutiny, that Wansink's work revealed signs of statistical manipulation, with data diced and sliced such that the results that were ultimately published were as likely to be false positives or Type I errors as real effects. But where were the lines? How could we be sure we were not specification searching in our own work?

The process of specification search is succinctly and humorously summarized in the XKCD comic in Figure 6.4. Specification search can go by many names, but broadly it is any misuse of data analysis to present patterns as statistically significant when there is no real underlying effect. Advances in computing power and data availability, to some degree, influences the rising concern about specification search among applied economists – a reduced cost of running regressions makes finding any sort of significant relationship possible. The lower cost of compute time, combined with the increased competition for publication, creates a strong incentive to find some way to find important, flashy, publishable, and newsworthy results.

```
1     * Project: WB Weather
2     * Created on: May 2020
3     * Created by: jdm
4     * Lasted edited: 12 June 2021
5     * Edited by: alj
6     * Stata v.16
7
8     * does
9         * cleans WB data set for IHS3 cross section
10        * outputs .dta LSMS household data ready to merge with weather data
11
12    * assumes
13        * Extracted and "cleaned" World Bank Malawi data (provided by Talip Kilic)
14        * customsave.ado
15
16    * TO DO:
17        * complete
18
19
20    * **********************************************************
21    * 0 - setup
22    * **********************************************************
23
24    * define paths
25        loc     source  =   "$data/household_data/malawi/wb_raw_data/data/ihs3cx/ag"
26        loc     root    =   "$data/household_data/malawi/wave_1/raw"
27        loc     export  =   "$data/household_data/malawi/wave_1/refined"
28        loc     logout  =   "$data/household_data/malawi/logs"
29
30    * open log
31        log     using       "`logout'/ihs3cx_hh_clean", append
32
33
34    * **********************************************************
35    * 1 - clean household data
36    * **********************************************************
37
38    * load data
39        use             "`root'/SEC_2A", clear
40
41    * generate unique ob id
42        gen             plot_id = hhid + " " + plotnum
43        lab var         plot_id "unique plot identifier"
44        isid            plot_id
45        *** there are 5,203 unqiue plots
46
47    * rename variables of interest (plotsizes)
48        rename          s2aq4 plotsize_self_ac
49        rename          area plotsize_gps_ac
50        sum             plotsize_self_ac plotsize_gps_ac
51        *** mean values are 1.5 (gps) and 1.7 (self-reported)
52
53    * **********************************************************
54    * 2 - end matter, clean up to save
55    * **********************************************************
56
57    * prepare for export
58        compress
59        describe
60        summarize
61        sort plot_id
62        customsave , idvar(plot_id) filename(AG_SEC2A.dta) ///
63            path("`export'") dofile(2008_AGSEC2A) user($user)
64
65    * close the log
66        log close
67
68    /* END */
```

FIGURE 6.3   Sample Coding Style

Note: Sample coding style, as used by the authors. Figure by the authors.

FIGURE 6.4 Significant

Note: From XKCD, with permission obtained from creators.

Although changes in computing power and data availability have increased the opportunities and incentives for specification search, concerns about the unconstrained search for significant results was raised by Edward Leamer (1978, 1983) in the late 1970s and early 1980s. The issue was raised again a few decades later by Peter Kennedy (2002). Leamer (1983) proposes that we "take the 'con' out of econometrics," echoing the idea in Leamer (1978) that we should be open and transparent in our work: "Sinners are not expected to avoid sins; they need only confess their errors openly." Kennedy (2002) furthers these ideas suggesting that we "take sinning out of the basement." He recommends ten "rules of sinning," or the ten commandments of applied econometrics (see Box 6.3).

Transparency and open science are the best practices to employ in one's research. We can state this even more simply: just be honest about the methods used in one's economic analysis. In the following subsections, we discuss several types of specification search, which occur along a spectrum, from clear wrongdoing to more ambiguous behaviors. This includes outright falsification of results, as well as HARKing and p-hacking. We also provide recommendations for avoiding these actions in one's own research.

BOX 6.3 THE TEN COMMANDMENTS OF APPLIED ECONOMETRICS, PARAPHRASED FROM KENNEDY (2002)

1. Use common sense and economic theory, with work rooted in careful thinking, expertise, and good statistical practice.
2. Avoid Type III errors, which occur when a researcher produces the right answer to the wrong question. Be guided by relevance.
3. Know the context and ask questions to learn it. Do not perform "ignorant" statistical analyses.
4. Inspect the data; clean data, check data, and 'get a feel' for them.
5. Keep it sensibly simple, finding a method not to impress readers or deflect criticism but appropriate for the data and context.
6. Use the "interocular trauma test," looking long and hard at the findings to ensure they are logical and make sense.
7. Understand the costs and benefits of data mining: do not worship any single statistic and do not hunt down statistical significance.
8. Be prepared to compromise, considering the balance between approximations and reality.
9. Do not confuse statistical significance and meaningful magnitude: there is more to research than precise point estimates.
10. Report a sensitivity analysis – or multiple analyses!

6.3.1 Falsification

The ethical problem of fabricating data, as Michael LaCour did in the retracted LaCour and Green (2014) are clear cut. But the practicalities of working with data can present fuzzier ethical questions. Replication studies are often put forward as a solution to the problem of inconsistent or unethical data analysis (Coffman and Niederle, 2015). However, "replication failure is common to both honestly conducted science" (Wible, 2016). As Huff point out, it can be difficult to determine if the failure was due to a desire to deceive or was sloppiness or an innocent mistake.

In Chapter 4 we defined both fabrication and falsification. Fabrication involves the making up of data while falsification is the manipulation of results. In recent years, there have been several high profile incidents of social scientists fabricating their data, such as in the retracted studies by LaCour and Green (2014) and Shu et al. (2012). In those studies, the authors generated fake data and then engaged in "truthful" or at least accurate statistical analysis of that fabricated data. It is harder to point to incidents of falsification of results based on real data. It is not clear why this is the case. Maybe such actions are more difficult to detect? Or such actions are harder to get away with so fewer attempt it? Or maybe if one is going to falsify results it is easier to arrive at the same false results by fabricating the data?

If the results from surveys of economists and other academics are to be believed, very few researchers engage in either fabrication, falsification, or other types of specification search or, at least, few are willing to admit it in an anonymous survey. List et al. (2001) report that slightly more than four percent of economists admit to falsify results. Necker (2014) reports that less than 3 percent of economists admit to fabricating data while 7 percent report falsifying or manipulating results. In a meta-analysis of other papers based on surveys of researchers, Fanelli (2009) reports between 2 and 7 percent of researchers admit to fabrication or falsification.

Based on the self-reported behavior in List et al. (2001), Necker (2014), and Fanelli (2009), falsification is not only nonzero but also not endemic in the profession. Yet applied economists might not view all forms of falsification as equally bad. In fact, List et al. (2001) distinguish between research "felonies," such as outright falsification, and research "misdemeanors," including things that today would be considered HARKing or p-hacking. Many more economists admit to "misdemeanor" behavior (10 percent) than to "felony" behavior (4 percent). List et al. (2001) describe the sort of rationalization one might engage in to justify "misdemeanor" behavior: "an inflated t-ratio here, an undeserving co-author there – who really is hurt by such behavior? Academic economists, after all, do not have patients."

In the absence of a bright-line rule, how are applied economists to determine what constitutes falsification or results? How does one judge what is a "felony" and what is a "misdemeanor?" Consider an example of rounding numbers: Diaconis and Freedman (1979) calculate the probability of a table of rounded numbers add up to 100 percent. When rounding numbers to the nearest 0.001 in a table with four categories, the chance that the table will sum to exactly 100 is 2/3. This probability shrinks exponentially as the number of categories increase. As the authors note, "failure to add to 1 occurs so frequently that if many sums of proportions add to exactly 1 in a reported set of tables, one begins to suspect the reporter of forcing the proportions to add to 1" (Diaconis and Freedman, 1979).

This observations links with Benford (1938), who investigates the behavior of leading digits in "naturally" occurring or "real-life" data, such as the area of rivers, atomic weights, street addresses, death rates, all the numbers printed in an issue of *Reader's Digest*, and so on. Benford (1938) demonstrates that this naturally occurring data follows the theory of the leading digit law. The leading digit law is an observation that in many real-life data sets, the leading digit is likely to be small. Figure 6.5 shows the distribution of first digits, according to the leading digit law. Each bar represents a digit, and the height of the bar is the percentage of numbers that start with that digit.

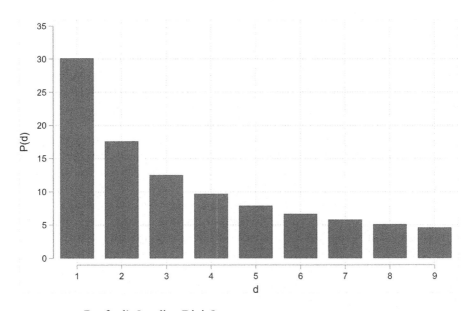

FIGURE 6.5   Benford's Leading Digit Law

Note: The graphs shows the distribution of first digits, according to the leading digit law. Each bar represents a digit, and the height of the bar is the percentage of numbers that start with that digit. If all digits appeared with equal probability, they would be equally sized bars at 11.1 percent. Figure by authors.

However, when Diaconis and Freedman (1979) examine Benford (1938), they show that when Benford presents how frequently the numbers 1 to 9 occur as the first digit in a number, the frequencies of occurrence in each of the categories of data all sum to 100. This, as we know from Diaconis and Freedman (1979), is a highly improbable event. Thus, it seems likely that Benford rounded the numbers so that they would sum to 100. As Diaconis and Freedman (1979) show, the rounding did not occur randomly, but Benford, either consciously or unconsciously, rounded numbers toward the value predicted by theory. So 4.775 was rounded down to 4.7, which more closely aligns with the theoretical prediction of 4.6. Similarly, 12.26 was rounded up to 12.4, which more closely aligns with the predicted value of 12.5.

The results in Benford (1938) were falsified through a simple process of selective rounding. The question is, Would applied economists today view the rounding in Benford (1938), or a similar, apparently innocuous, manipulation of results as a "misdemeanor" or a "felony?" Does such falsification demand a correction or even a retraction of the associated paper? It is not clear that the profession has consensus on just how much falsification is acceptable. Similarly, the profession lacks a well-defined approach to identifying falsification of research, or dealing with falsification, beyond clear instances of fabrication.

6.3.2 HARKing

A traveling man paused at a village to rest, sitting down under a tree. In front of him was a large barn, the side of which was covered with small painted circles with a bullet hole in the center of each one. The traveler jumped up with amazement, wondering, "Who was this local sharpshooter?" He knocked on the door of a nearby house and inquired if they knew who the marksman was. A man in a cowboy hat came forward, and the traveler asked, "How do you manage to hit the bull's-eye every time?" The man in the cowboy hat smiled and simply said, "There is nothing to it! I love to shoot – so I shoot at the side of the barn. And then I take a piece of chalk and draw a circle around each hole."

This story, known as the "Texas sharpshooter fallacy" and illustrated in Figure 6.6, is an example of HARKing or "Hypothesizing After Results are Known." Kerr (1998) coined the term HARKing and defined it as "presenting a *post hoc* hypothesis in the introduction of a research report as if it were an *a priori* hypothesis." That is, HARKing occurs when researchers determine their results and then add or remove hypotheses, without acknowledging this process. This goes against the typical process of the scientific method in which hypotheses are made, analyzed, and then confirmed or not. HARKing is contrary to this process because it involves rewriting the hypotheses of the investigation so that it confirms the results in the data. Although Kerr (1998) himself was hesitant to label HARKing as unethical, there is growing consensus that HARKing is, at worst, unethical, representing one form of scientific misconduct, and at best, bad science.

FIGURE 6.6 The Texas Sharpshooter Fallacy

Note: The Texas Sharpshooter making his mark. Illustration courtesy of Dirk-Jan Hoek by CC BY 2.0.

The primary reason that HARKing is problematic, is that it results in hypotheses that are only confirmed, never allowing for research that produces null results or unconfirmed hypotheses. HARKing means that one's research only ever proves oneself correct – at least seemingly so. The result is a limited or biased scientific record, similar to the file drawer problem, discussed in Chapter 3.

Rubin (2017) defines three forms of HARKing, which occur on a spectrum from the most to the least likely to harm scientific progress. We follow Rubin (2017) in naming convention for each of these types:

1. **CHARKing:** occurs when researchers create new hypotheses based on their empirical results, and then report those results as though they were tests of *a priori* hypotheses. Hypotheses are *constructed* after the empirical results are known.
2. **RHARKing:** occurs when researchers conduct a *post hoc* literature review in order to find previously published hypotheses, which can be presented as *a priori* hypotheses. Kerr (1998) euphemistically refers to this as "empirically-inspired scholarship," as hypotheses are *retrieved* after the empirical results are

known. This type of HARKing sometimes occurs in the process of publication when reviewers seek further discussion and explanation for findings.
3. **SHARKing** occurs when researchers remove hypotheses from their work that do not fit their empirical results. Kerr (1998) refers to this as "suppressing loser hypotheses" as hypotheses are *suppressed* after the results are known.

Regardless of the exact type of HARKing, there are potential consequences but thankfully, many, relatively easy solutions. The first solution set comes from Commandments 1 and 2 in Kennedy (2002):

- Be guided by common sense and economic theory.
- Avoid Type III errors by asking the right questions.

If research is guided by economic theory, researchers are unlikely to be able to engage in HARKing. Research that sets out to test a theory will, of necessity, define the empirical design of that research. One cannot design an experiment or an econometric approach to test the theory of firm behavior under price uncertainty in Sandmo (1971) and then, if the theory is rejected, construct or retrieve a new hypothesis, or suppress the original hypothesis. In fact, using theory as a starting point from which to build empirical tests is likely to result in an interesting, and publishable outcome regardless of whether the theory is rejected or not. Similarly, starting empirical research by first ensuring that one is asking the right or relevant question helps reduce HARKing by increasing the likelihood that any empirical result will be interesting. Finding that markets in developing countries are complete is just as interesting as finding that they are incomplete. As Benjamin (1992) and LaFave and Thomas (2016) demonstrate, finding evidence of either outcome can get one published in *Econometrica* as long as the research question is interesting and relevant. Testing theory and asking interesting and important questions provides a firm footing for empirical research and by extension a framework for presenting conclusions that will be interesting regardless of the sign or significance of the coefficient of interest.

The second solution to HARKing is one which we have discussed extensively in Chapter 3: pre-analysis plans (PAPs). A PAP can guide one's research and provide justification (and cover, as needed) for explaining findings in the set of final results. PAPs can not only mitigate HARKing but can provide a way to frame unexpected empirical results or and changed perspectives as exploratory work. Hollenbeck and Wright (2016) discuss this idea in the context of ethical exploratory analysis, what they called "THARKing," or *transparently* HARKing. This is opposed to their definition of "SHARKing," or *secretly* HARKing.[2] As Hollenbeck and Wright (2016) write, "there is never any justification for the process of SHARKing, we argue that THARKing can promote the effectiveness and efficiency of both scientific inquiry and cumulative knowledge creation." THARKing can be a natural extension, facilitated by effective use of PAPs.

In general, the consequences of HARKing are less significant than those of fraud. The act itself, too, is often less deliberate – although still requires consideration and action by a researcher, and should be discouraged. But, luckily a careful research design and planning can mitigate the negative potential outcomes of HARKing.

6.3.3   p-*hacking*

For decades, the idea of *p*-hacking, alternatively called data dredging, data snooping, data butchery, significance chasing, and selective inference, among others, was known, though unnamed in the scientific community.[3] Stigler (1987) wrote about it decades before the term was actually coined: "The more you torture your data, the more likely they are to confess, but confession obtained under duress may not be admissible in the court of scientific opinion." While the term was formally coined in 2004 (Nuzzo, 2014), uncertainty persists: What exactly is *p*-hacking?

We have already alluded to the practice of *p*-hacking in the XKCD comic (Figure 6.4). The scientists test and test and test different colors of jelly beans until they find the relationship they want – a color of jelly bean that causes acne. This testing and retesting is at the heart of *p*-hacking. It describes the conscious or subconscious manipulation of data so as to produces a desired *p*-value. *p*-hacking is typically done by taking full advantage of the researcher's degrees of freedom, that is, the ability to test a variety of plausibly appropriate approaches and select the one that gives the desired result. These decisions might include how variables are constructed, selection of variables, the transformation of variables, the selection of econometric model, the inclusion or exclusion of control variables, and the calculation of standard errors, among a variety of other choices that might get a researcher to the result they want.

It can sometimes be difficult to differentiate between various types of specification searching and the difference between *p*-hacking and HARKing can be vague. To some degree, this vagueness is definitional: both involve the selective reporting of results. To distinguish between the two types of specification search, we like to focus on the process. In HARKing, tests are run and then hypotheses are changed to match the empirical results. In *p*-hacking, more and more tests are run in order to ensure that the empirical results align with the original hypotheses. HARKing is essentially an *ex post* process, while *p*-hacking is the ongoing and deliberate misuse of data analysis to find patterns in data that can be presented as statistically significant. In doing these repeated analyses, the risk for false positives (Type I error) – and thus finding the desired results – dramatically increase.

p-hacking violates a basic tenant of the frequentists approach to hypothesis testing as laid out by Ronald Fisher. As Brown et al. (2019) note, "scientific exploration begins from a position of ignorance. Compelling alternative hypotheses are unknown." Because one starts from a place of ignorance, applied economists can use null hypothesis statistical testing (NHST) and have a degree of confidence when the null is rejected. The major cost of this approach is that, because one starts from a place of ignorance, nothing can be inferred when the null is not rejected. When researchers engage in p-hacking, they have reversed the process. Instead of starting from a place of ignorance, the researcher starts by searching for a particular, predetermined answer to their research question. They are trying to prove the alternative hypothesis instead of disproving the null hypothesis. While a software package will readily calculate the p-value for researchers trying to prove the alternative hypothesis, the result can only be viewed as descriptive. Since the researcher violated the tenants of Fisherian NHST, the p-value has no positive content.

Unlike falsification and HARKing, it is reasonably straightforward to determine the degree to which p-hacking occurs in published applied economic research. This is because p-hacking involves manipulating results to achieve a specific outcome from a statistical test. Abel Brodeur and his various co-authors, have been at the forefront of efforts to identify the extent of p-hacking in published papers. Brodeur et al. (2016) review 50,000 hypothesis tests published in 641 articles in three of the Top Five economic journals: the *American Economic Review*, the *Journal of Political Economy*, and the *Quarterly Journal of Economics*. They found evidence that 10 to 20 percent of tests are misallocated, meaning there are more results that are marginally significant and fewer results that are marginally insignificant than one should expect. Brodeur et al. (2016) interpret this as evidence of p-hacking: "researchers inflate the value of just-rejected tests by choosing 'significant' specifications." More recently, Brodeur et al. (2020) examine 21,000 hypothesis tests published in 25 economics journals to determine the extent of p-hacking. The authors found that the frequency with which p-values are inflated to become marginally significant varies substantially by econometric method.

> In the [instrumental variable] IV literature . . . a significant result is almost 5 *times* more likely to be published than an insignificant IV result. In the [difference-in-difference] DID literature, a statistically significant result is 4.2 times more likely to be published. For RCTs, a significant result is only 1.9 times more likely to be published. For [regression discontinuity design] RDDs, a significant result is 2.8 times more likely to be published.

Additionally, Brodeur et al. (2020) find that other disciplines exhibit more p-hacking in published work than economists. And, while many associate the problem of p-hacking with younger researchers trying to get tenure, Brodeur et al. (2016) document that older researchers are actually more likely to engage in p-hacking behavior. We explore the consequences of p-hacking as related to publication bias in Chapter 7.

As with HARKing, there are ways to avoid the practice of p-hacking. First, consider again the commandments of Kennedy (2002), specifically 7 and 9:

- Understand the costs and benefits of data mining.
- Do not confuse statistical significance and meaningful magnitude.

Commandment 7 highlights the fine line that exists between what qualifies as *p*-hacking and what is exploratory or data-driven research. As Kennedy (2002) points out, the phrase "data mining" used to be viewed as a cardinal sin in empirical work. It was viewed as allowing the data to drive the hypothesis (HARKing) or as mining the data for a specific significant result (*p*-hacking). More recently, with the advent of machine learning (ML), the phrase data mining has been rehabilitated as a term in applied economics. However, even in the context of ML, it is not always clear what qualifies as *p*-hacking and what is data-driven research, as the XKCD comic in Figure 6.7 demonstrates.

Weighing the costs and benefits of data mining, or trying to decide what qualifies as *p*-hacking and what qualifies as exploratory research, is a challenge. As Kennedy (2002) writes, "these two variants [of data mining] usually are not mutually exclusive and so frequently conflict in the sense that to gain the benefits of the latter, one runs the risk of incurring the costs of the former." Where the cutoff is will be a function both of the research question and of the researcher. Some research questions may be less defined and require more exploration or testing of the data. Some researchers, particularly graduate students and early-career professionals may need

FIGURE 6.7   Machine Learning

Note: From XKCD, with permission obtained from creators.

to explore more as they learn how to formulate well defined, testable hypotheses. Both of us ran many more regressions when we were graduate students than we do now. We were not trying to *p*-hack but rather just learning by doing in terms of how regressions worked and how results respond to variations in specifications and controls. Usually a bit of reflection can reveal one's own intentions. If someone asked, "Why are you doing this?" could you answer truthfully?

"Why are you doing this?" is also at the heart of Commandment 9 but with a different "this." As was mentioned regarding HARKing, the strongest papers are ones that ask an interesting question. Similarly with *p*-hacking, if one has an interesting question the significance of the coefficient of interest will not make or break the study. Rather, as Leamer (1996) argues, interesting research questions are rarely characterized by sharp nulls because all such hypotheses are surely false. The effect size is almost certainly not exactly equal to zero. Kennedy (2002) also emphasizes the importance of careful interpretation of findings to make sure that they make sense and that to get them, one has not had to "hunt statistical significance with a shotgun." Finding a significant result is not necessarily the same as finding as important result. Although statistical significance is not the end all and be all, thoughtful consideration, based on careful inference and planning, should be used to ensure that results are not just significant but substantive. This is the point Gelman and Tuerlinckx (2000) raise when discussing Type M errors. We will return to the issue of significance versus magnitude in Section 6.5.

As with HARKing, the second solution to *p*-hacking is a clear pre-analysis plan. Any analyses that follows the PAP can be clearly distinguished as part of the original plan, and any exploratory research is clearly documented as such. The guiding principle of a PAP should be to document when in the research process, and for what reason, a particular model emerged (Laitin, 2013). Even without a PAP, this sort of direct approach to documenting the when and why of certain variables, specifications, and tests can help mitigate fears that a certain result was dug out of the data after a long search.

Another way to help mitigate the effect of *p*-hacking, at least in terms of interpreting hypothesis tests, is to employ corrections for multiple inference. Testing multiple hypotheses (as in Figure 6.4) can give rise to either the family-wise error rate (FWER) or the false discovery rate (FDR). The former is the probability of making at least one false discovery among a family of comparisons, while the latter is the probability of making at least one false discovery among the discoveries already made. In general, one should make such corrections whenever one is testing multiple versions of a variable or a model related to a single theory or hypothesis. Being direct and documenting how many tests one ran by correcting for MHT helps address worries that numerous specifications were tested and then discarded before settling on the "right" one. Michler and Josephson (2022) provide more details on exactly when and how to apply corrections for multiple inference.

Ultimately, the implications of *p*-hacking are such that the reliability of research and credibility of the scientific record are undermined through work that fails to accurately represent true findings. As researchers, we should proactively work to avoid falsification, HARKing, and *p*-hacking through careful research design, planning, and transparency in the presentation of results.

6.4 Robustness Checks

A common exercise in empirical studies in economics are "robustness checks," in which a researcher examines how their main regression coefficient estimates behave when the regression specification is changed in some way. This is a typical practice in empirical economics papers, but if there is one takeaway from the preceding section on specification search, it is that one should not just run a bevy of models or test a bunch of variables simply because one can. Rather, one should be guided by a PAP and/or by economic theory to justify why a specific robustness check was done.

However, robustness checks can feel like a myriad of additional tests presented only for the sake of proving that the test was done. As Huntington-Klein (nd) writes, "it is easy to feel like robustness tests are things you *just do*." For example, in one of Jeff's papers based on an RCT, a reviewer asked, unsatisfied with the results from the 100-plus regressions already presented in the paper, for a robustness check in which logs of the variables were taken. The paper had already been through one round of review. In the second round, the reviewer writes, "I would also be curious to see specifications with logarithms." No justification or reason, other than personal curiosity, was given for why the reviewer doubted the results given the 11 tables of robustness checks already present in the appendix. Jeff and his co-authors appealed to the editor, arguing that, given the large number of robustness checks already done, they "need[ed] better justification from the reviewer" than simple curiosity before the authors spent "costly time in providing these results." The editor was not persuaded, and so Jeff and his co-authors added 84 more regressions (seven new tables) to the appendix. Four of the 84 tests resulted in a variable changing from significant to not significant when logs were taken. In the end, the additional robustness checks were "things you *just do*" in order to get the paper published.

As with choosing a specification, one should undertake robustness checks cognizant of a researcher's degrees of freedom when choosing regressions, variables, and tests. Huntington-Klein (nd) offers the following questions to consider when making a decision about whether or not to do a robustness test:

1. My analysis assumes A.
2. If A is not true, then my results might be wrong in way B [estimate too high/estimate too low/standard errors too small/etc.].
3. I suspect that A might not be true in my analysis because of C.
4. EITHER: D is a test of whether or not A is true,
   OR: D is an alternative analysis I can run that does not assume A, allowing me to see how big of a problem B is.

5. If it turns out that [A is not true OR B is a big problem], then I will do E instead of my original analysis.

He argues that "if you can't fill in that list, don't run the test!" Like all of one's analyses, the robustness checks performed should be carefully motivated and should not simply be present for the sake of existence. Every additional test should be about examining potentially critical assumptions, not just about testing every possible iteration. Robustness checks provide a mechanism to document the sturdiness of estimates as well as to examine alternative estimates, in case key assumptions do not hold. They should not be fishing expeditions or an attempt to test all possible iterations, or, as in the case of Jeff's reviewer, be motivated by simple curiosity without some underlying justification why the check itself in interesting, important, or necessary. This is because running additional tests are not costless. They come at the cost of the time it takes to run them. But more important, they come at the cost of statistical power, because with every new test one should correct for that fact that one is engaged in multiple inference.

There are two approaches to conducting robustness checks: vary the specification or vary the data. Varying the specification is known as the multianalysis approach. It takes the data as given and varies the specification or model (Simonsohn et al., 2020). Varying the data is known as the multiverse approach. It takes the model as given and varies the data that are feed into the model (Steegen et al., 2016). Michler et al. (2021) provide a useful example of both. In their paper, the authors estimate the correlation between remotely sensed rainfall and the agricultural productivity of farmers in sub-Saharan Africa. Michler et al. (2021) argue that there are innumerable ways that one could construct a rainfall metric (mean daily rainfall, total seasonal rainfall, number of days without rain). They also highlight that there are numerous different remote sensing sources from which one could get the rainfall data. Because researcher degrees of freedom are extremely large in their setting, the authors present results in the form of specification curves (see Figure 6.8). In these curves, Michler et al. (2021) vary both the specification (multianalysis) and the data (multiverse). Doing both helps define a robust set of outcomes that do not depend on a single choice regarding how a variable or model is defined.

Figure 6.8 presents a specification curve for a single country (Ethiopia) and a single rainfall variable (mean daily rainfall) using data from Michler et al. (2021). Each panel presents results from a different specification. The top panels present variations on specifications in which rainfall enters linearly: weather only, weather plus household fixed effects, weather, household fixed effects, and measured inputs. The specifications in the bottom panels are similar to those in the top except they add a quadratic term. Each panel includes 120 regressions, with each column representing a single regression. Within each panel, Michler et al. (2021) vary the data. For a given model, they test how results vary based on (1) the statistical disclosure limitation (SDL) method used to

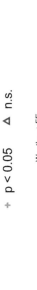

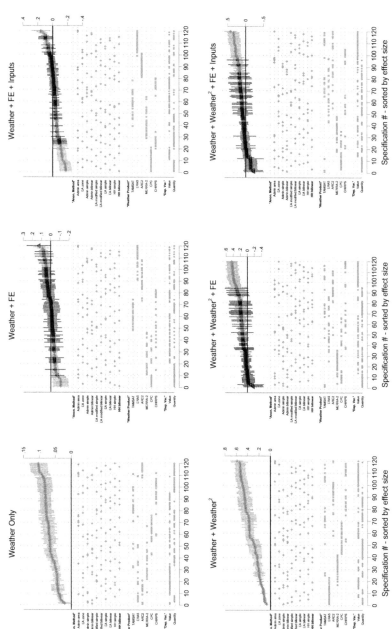

FIGURE 6.8 Specification Curve for Mean Daily Rainfall in Ethiopia

Note: Light gray bars represent significant results while black bars are not significant. The specification curves are produced from data and code in Michler et al. (2021) under CC BY 3.0 IGO.

preserve privacy in the production data, (2) the source of the remote-sensing data, and (3) how they measure agricultural production. Each of these choices regarding what data to vary and how to vary it was based on an exhaustive literature review and was actually prespecified in a PAP (Michler et al., 2019). By presenting results from both the multiverse and the multianalysis approach in the form of a specification curve, one can quickly tell how changes in assumptions regarding data and model affect the results.

If you feel a bit lost in a world where data and specifications are shifting around, do not worry. In the following two subsections, we discuss both the multianalysis approach and the multiverse approach to robustness checks in more detail. Throughout, we use Figure 6.8 as an example.

6.4.1   Multianalysis Approach

The multianalysis approach to robustness checks was coined by Simonsohn et al. (2020) with the goal of addressing issues of noise and bias in empirical papers. In this type of analysis, the data are taken as given, and the analysis is varied around this immovable point. Christensen et al. (2019) provide a thoughtful description of the multianalysis approach as well as several examples.

Simonsohn et al. (2020) motivate their multianalysis approach by noting that in empirical research, there is a near infinite set of specifications that could be run. Which specifications actually get selected from this larger set depends on the researcher. Thus, there is the potential for "author effects," as Neumark (2001) noted were present in research on the impacts of minimum wage laws. The multianalysis approach tests a number of different plausible models on the same data and then presents the results in the form of a specification curve. The point is not to demonstrate the validity of a single model but to show the robustness of results to different assumptions about how to model the data-generating process. As Simonsohn et al. (2020) note:

> Competent researchers often disagree about whether a specification is an appropriate test of the hypothesis of interest and/or statistically valid for the data at hand. . . . Specification curve analysis will not end debates about what specifications should be run. Specification curve analysis, instead, will *facilitate* those debates.
>
> *(Emphasis in the original)*

Simonsohn et al. (2020) develop a formal model, which demonstrates that the sample of specifications presented in any paper provides only a noisy approximation of all possible tested or potentially tested analyses. As such, the results in any paper are not a random sample but a selected or contrived sample, based on researcher preferences, biases, and so on. As a result, the specifications presented are not statistically independent. The multianalysis approach resolves this by making the noise and selection more transparent, eliminating arbitrary inclusion decisions, and permitting cross-specification statistical inference.

Consider our example drawn from Michler et al. (2021) and the ways in which the authors use the multianalysis approach. Recall that in Figure 6.8, each panel presents a different specification while each regression in a panel is from a different combination of the data. By looking at the pattern of results across panels, one can determine the effect that changing the econometric model has on the results. Comparing the specification with weather only to the specification that adds the square of weather, the sign and significance of coefficients do not change, though the magnitude of the linear weather term is much larger when its square is added. Looking across the specifications, adding household fixed effects changes the sign and significance of many estimates, although there is little effect on the magnitude of estimates. Adding inputs to the fixed effects specifications has little effect relative to the weather and fixed-effects specifications.

From a cursory examination of the specification curves in Figure 6.8, one can quickly deduce what assumptions about the data-generating process the results are robust to and what assumption they are not. Looking between the top and bottom panels shows that the relationship between rainfall and agricultural productivity is linear – including the quadratic term has no meaningful affect on the sign or significance of estimates. Looking between the left and center panels shows that the relationship between rainfall and agricultural productivity is substantially effected by time-invariant household characteristics – including household fixed-effects results in rainfall being uncorrelated with agricultural productivity. Ultimately, when presented as a specification curve, the multianalysis approach allows readers to identify trends that indicate what results arise simply from chance and what results are robust to different modeling assumptions.

6.4.2 Multiverse Approach

The multiverse approach to robustness checks was first coined by Steegen et al. (2016). This name is inspired by the concept of multiple coexisting realities, each represented by a different construction of the data. In contrast to the multianalysis approach, the multiverse approach holds the specification constant and then varies the data used in the model. Christensen et al. (2019) include details on multiverse analysis, including a detailed accounting of Steegen et al. (2016).

In the multiverse approach, the idea is to create multiple universes by taking multiple samples from the analysis dataset. There are multitudinous choices that a researcher makes when cleaning data and constructing variables, and this leads to degrees of freedom for the researcher. This can result in selective reporting or cherry-picking of results. The multiverse approach conducts the same analysis across a large set of alternative versions of the data that correspond to all reasonable combinations of data cleaning and construction choices. In Steegen et al. (2016), the authors consider a study of the effects of fertility on political attitudes. There are multiple reasonable ways to measure fertility and the choice of how to define this variable might affect the outcome. They find that, while there are good arguments for selecting any single definitions of fertility, one of the definitions results in substantially more significant results. It would be extremely tempting to present in a paper the one variable definition, from the many plausible variable definitions, that produces the strongest results. The goal of the multiverse approach, like the multianalysis approach, is to enhance transparency. By presenting results from multiple, reasonable ways to define the variable, the authors allow the reader to decide which definition they prefer and draw their own conclusions.

With this in mind, consider again our example drawn from Michler et al. (2021) and the ways in which the authors use the multiverse approach. Each panel in Figure 6.8 presents 120 different universes of data. By looking at the pattern of coefficients within a panel, one can see how sensitive the results are to changes in the data. In the two left panels, every universe of data produces positive and significant outcomes, although the size of the coefficient varies. In the remaining four panels, results are sensitive to choices made by the researcher regarding what remote-sensing source the data come from and how the outcome variable is defined. For the specification that includes weather and household fixed effects, using rainfall data from NOAA's Climate Prediction Center Unified Gauge-Based Analysis of Global Precipitation (Chen et al., 2008) or NASA's Modern-Era Retrospective analysis for Research and Applications (Bosilovich et al., 2016) tend to show that rainfall is negatively and significantly correlated with agricultural productivity. But rainfall data from the African Rainfall Climatology version 2 (ARC2; Novella and Thiaw, 2013) and the European Centre for Medium-Range Weather Forecasts' ERA5 (Hennermann and Berrisford, 2020) tend to show that rainfall is positively, although not always significantly, correlated with agricultural productivity. Rainfall drawn from other remote-sensing sources tends to show no significant relationship between rainfall and agricultural output.

Specification charts offer the opportunity to, in very little space, present results from a large set of possible variations in the data. A reader can quickly discern if results are sensitive to alternative definitions of variables or alternative draws of the data. Looking within the panel of results from the specification using weather and household fixed effects shows that by carefully selecting the source of the rainfall data the unscrupulous researcher could "find" exactly the relationship they wanted: positive, negative, or none.

As with the multiverse approach to robustness checks, the goal of the multianalysis approach is to increase transparency in cases in which there are many researcher degrees of freedom. Christensen et al. (2019) observe that "a fuller assessment of the robustness of results could cross these two approaches, examining results along pairs of data-analysis combinations." This is exactly what Michler et al. (2021) achieve – presenting over 700 results in a single figure to assess the robustness of the relationship between rainfall and agricultural productivity to different assumptions about the model and data.

6.5 Reporting Standards

In trying to diagnose what ails applied economic analysis, it is easy to focus on issues like HARKing and p-hacking. However, these are really symptoms of an ailment, not the ailment itself. The root cause of these symptoms is the incentives to publish research in a discipline where a p-value of less than 0.05 is often seen as a necessary condition for publication. Part of the reason for this situation is that applied economics research tends to rely on Fisherian NHST. If the null is not rejected, one cannot simply infer that the null is true or that the alternative hypothesis is false. This has the effect of focusing attention on research that can reject a null with a high degree of confidence. But, as Imbens (2021) observes, statistical significance in empirical results is "widely used, widely misunderstood, and widely decried."

While the focus on rejecting nulls is justifiable from a frequentists approach to statistics, there is little justification for the profession's fixation on the cut off of $p < 0.05$. In fact, Fisher (1956) writes that "no scientific worker has a fixed level of significance at which, from year to year, and in all circumstances, he rejects hypotheses; he rather gives his mind to each particular case in the light of his evidence." This is hardly the situation that prevails in applied economics today. The profession's focus on a "fixed level of signifiance" has given rise to concerns about the use of p-values in evaluating research for publication. Accordingly, there is ongoing debate about how statistical results should be presented.[4] The debate is rooted in questions about what we learn from the inclusion of p-values in results.

Imbens (2021) identifies three primary issues with p-values broadly and, implicitly, their use in the discussion and publication of results: (1) p-values to test sharp null hypotheses frequently do not answer the question of interest in most empirical studies; (2) even when one wants to test a sharp null, p-values may not be the most useful statistic for a test; and (3) the abuse of p-values, specifically the cutoff of $p < 0.05$. Imbens (2021) argues that the first is most compelling, but perhaps the most discussed is the third. In this chapter, in fact, we argue exactly that.[5]

PERSPECTIVE 6.1   READING YOUR RESULTS HONESTLY BY JASON KERWIN

When analyzing data, I always try to take an honest view of what my results imply and discern whether there's a real signal or if we are just looking at noise. In a perfect world we would have pre-analysis plans for everything we do, but this is not feasible in economics: too much of what we study comes from public or secondary data sources, so you cannot credibly commit to having specified your analyses in advance. Our goal as data analysts is thus to examine the results in the same way we would if we did have an analysis plan. That does not mean hewing to strict rules about how you should pick control variables; it means you need to think about the big picture of what your results are telling you.

For example, I was recently looking at a table of the effects of an intervention on a number of related outcomes. One of them showed a significant effect (at the 10 percent level). My co-authors and I had an extensive discussion about how the treatment – which really did affect other outcomes of interest – might have moved this one. We discussed potential models that could explain the effects. But then we looked at the table again with fresh eyes and reassessed. One p-value below 0.10 out of many in the table is totally consistent with random noise. Could the intervention have moved this outcome? Sure – but our data did not provide compelling evidence for that.

Sometimes my robustness checks help tell me whether we are really seeing a signal, or just finding patterns in noise. When working on robustness checks for another paper, we found that some of our results varied quite a bit based on sample selection choices. These could matter for real, but they also indicate that any patterns of effects we were looking at were fragile and that our confidence intervals (which we were already bootstrapping) were understating the true uncertainty in our estimates. We chose to focus our discussion of the results on effects that were not just statistically significant but also bigger than the variations induced by changes in the sample.

Magnitudes matter, too: sometimes a treatment causes a truly robust and statistically significant effect but it is tiny. Think of a treatment that reduces the rate of missed doctor's visits from 4 percent to 3.9 percent. The takeaway is sometimes that the treatment did little, or effectively nothing, depending on the specific context. This is sometimes called "economic significance": Does this effect actually matter? A different way of interpreting the results is to think about the effect sizes we can rule out – for example, maybe we can show that the change in missed doctor's visits is no bigger than 0.2 percent. But no mechanical rule will suffice in all cases. As a researcher, you have to bring your judgment to bear. Are these results meaningful in magnitude? Why?

Being honest about my results means that my work generates a lot of null results: even when I find some statistically significant effects, I often interpret them as not being meaningful. Given the well-known "null result penalty," this could be bad news in two ways. First, it might mean that I have trouble publishing a paper. Second, it means that the scientific record will be skewed by missing data. I have a simple solution to both of these problems: I always try to publish my null results. How to deal with the null result penalty? Sometimes nulls can be included in a paper that also presents statistically significant treatment effects, making it easier to convince reviewers to publish the paper. In other cases, the null itself is interesting and can be published on its own. At the design stage of a project, we should be focusing on research designs that are interesting irrespective of the specific results. A new state policy not changing the targeted outcome is important to know! Publishing my nulls makes being honest with my data much easier. There's no penalty for not finding stars; we are searching for scientific truth, not hunting for low p-values.

6.5.1   Conducting Statistical Inference

The standard frequentists approach to conducting statistical inference is to calculate the standard error on a point estimate. This involves taking care to ensure that the standard errors are correctly calculated so that inference is robust to violations of assumptions about the distribution of the error term. The common framework for thinking about the mistakes that one could make in drawing inference is committing a Type I or Type II error. As a reminder:

- **Type I error** or **false positives:** when one rejects a true null hypothesis.
- **Type II error** or **false negatives:** when one fails to reject a false null hypothesis.

Each type of error is associated with an error rate, or the probability of committing either a Type I or Type II error. The Type I error rate is known as the significance level (α), which standard practice fixes at 0.05. The Type II error rate is known as the power of the test (β), which we typically set at 0.20.

While Type I and Type II errors are a standard feature of econometric texts, the statistician Andrew Gelman (2004) claims that he has never made either of these types of errors. He writes,

A Type 1 error occurs only if the null hypothesis is true (typically if a certain parameter, or difference in parameters, equals zero). In the applications I've worked on, in social science and public health, I've never come across a null hypothesis that could actually be true, or a parameter that could actually be zero. A Type 2 error occurs only if I claim that the null hypothesis is true, and I would certainly not do that, given my statement above!

Similar to Gelman, Guido Imbens (2021) argues that for most applied economic research, we are not interested in the rejection of a zero effect alone, meaning that a p-value may ultimately be uninformative. This argument combines two issues: (1)

p-values that test sharp null hypotheses do not often answer the question of interest, and (2) p-values may not even be the most useful test statistic for examining sharp null hypotheses. Typically we are interested in the magnitude of estimates and the uncertainty around those estimates, as well as their robustness to identification concerns.

Gelman and Carlin (2014) argue that a better framework for thinking about the mistakes that one can make in drawing inference is the Type S and the Type M error. A Type S error, or sign error, is when the sign on the point estimate is in the opposite direction of the true effect. A Type M error, or magnitude error, is when the magnitude of the point estimate over- or underestimates the true effect size. As with Type I and Type II errors, one can calculate the error rate or probability of committing Type S or Type M errors. While not commonly presented in applied economics papers, these error rates are easily calculated using software provided by Gelman and Carlin (2014).

The goal of thinking in terms of Type S and Type M errors is to shift the focus away from testing sharp null hypotheses reported in the form of p-values and toward quantifying the uncertainty around a point estimate. One way to operationalize this thinking is to calculate the error rate for Type S and Type M errors, as in Gelman and Carlin (2014), but there are numerous other ways more common to applied economics. One, which Michler and Josephson (2022) argue for in their review of recent advances in inference, is the reporting of confidence intervals rather than p-values or the stars that signify certain p-value cutoff. As Romer (2020) writes, "In contrast to reporting a point estimate and whether it is statistically significantly different from zero, reporting a confidence interval provides information about the full range of possible values of the parameter." Even adhering to a fixed cutoff like 95 percent, a 95 percent confidence interval provides a richer set of information than a single p-value or the stars signifying $p < 0.05$. A confidence interval provides information regarding the likely range of the magnitude of the point estimate (Type M) as well as how likely it is that the sign on the coefficient is correct (Type S). The specification chart in Figure 6.8 illustrates this point by showing the range of signs and magnitudes that results can take under different modeling assumptions, although the figure also color-codes results with $p < 0.05$.

A second way that Michler and Josephson (2022) suggest to shift the focus away from a specific p-value cutoff is the bootstrapping of asymptotically pivotal statistics. Before explaining further, a couple of definitions may be useful. First, the term *bootstrapping* is derived from the idiom "to pull yourself up by your own bootstraps," that is, to use existing resources to improve your situation. The bootstrap resamples from existing data in such a way as to mimic that underlying data. Second, an asymptotically pivotal statistic is a parameter whose probability distribution does not depend on unknown parameters. So, the standard error of a point estimate is not pivotal but the t-statistic is pivotal. Bootstrapping asymptotically pivotal statistics provides refinement to statistics calculated following asymptotic theory, as the distribution function of the bootstrapped statistics converges to zero more quickly than the conventional approach. Thus, a bootstrapped t-stat will be more precise than one calculated using asymptotic theory.

Generally, bootstrapping is a straightforward way to derive estimates of parameters of interests, in which a researcher uses their existing data to draw a new sample, a procedure which is repeated many times. The bootstrap distribution represents the distribution of these derived samples. This distribution provides a good approximation of the "true" distribution of the data. The pivotal statistics derived via bootstrapping provide more accurate estimates than standard asymptotic approximations. As such, Michler and Josephson (2022) advocate for using the bootstrap when conducting inference for a paper's primary results and suggest further that results based on standard asymptotic approximations should be presented as robustness check or not at all.

Asymptotically pivotal statistics, such as the t-stat, are used to calculate both p-values and confidence intervals, so there is nothing about bootstrapping them that inherently connects to Type S and Type M errors. Rather, the process of bootstrapping focuses attention on the uncertainty inherent in statistical estimates. This is because the process of bootstrapping involves drawing numerous samples from the data (Michler and Joesphson, 2022, suggest 10,000–15,000) and then drawing the distribution of these samples. The numerical process of drawing random samples and plotting the distribution highlights that the test statistics used for inference are probabilistic values with their own range of uncertainty. So, presenting point estimates in combination with confidence intervals based on bootstrapped t-statistics shifts attention away from the number of stars on the estimates and instead focuses on transparency, directing attention to the uncertainty around those estimates.

6.5.2 Cult of Statistical Significance

Presenting results using confidence intervals based on bootstrapped t-stats helps address the first two issues Imbens raises regarding p-values: tests of sharp nulls are typically not that interesting, and even when they are a p-value may not be the best criterion. The third issue he raises is about the general abuse of p-values, by which he means the importance that the profession attaches to $p < 0.05$ (Imbens, 2021). But Imbens is far from the most vocal critic of the abuse of p-values. That distinction belongs to Stephen Ziliak and Deirdre McCloskey, who coined the phrase "cult of statistical significance" to refer to the strict adherence to a "fixed level of significance."

In their book *The Cult of Statistical Significance: How the Standard Error Cost Us Jobs, Justice, and Lives*, Ziliak and McCloskey (2008) provide numerous examples of how statistical significance testing is a barrier to (quality) empirical research. Throughout the book, Ziliak and McCloskey focus on the negative feedback loop in which economists draw conclusions based on p-values and statistical significance, policymakers make decisions based on those conclusions, and so authors, reviewers, and editors focus solely on p-values as the basis for a paper's potential for relevance or impact. The abuse of p-values arises from a desire to say something important but misunderstands what makes something important. As Ziliak and McCloskey (2008) write,

> The textbooks are wrong. The teaching is wrong. The seminar just attended is wrong. The most prestigious journal in your scientific field is wrong. . . . Fit is not the same thing as importance. Statistical significance is not the same thing as scientific finding. R^2, t-statistic, p-value, F-test, and all the more sophisticated versions of them in time series and the most advanced statistics are misleading at best.

Ziliak and McCloskey are often portrayed as advocating for the abolition of p-values. And at times this can seem like the only resolution to their critique of the cult of statistical significance. Yet in all of their writing on the topic, Ziliak and McCloskey advocate for simply de-emphasizing Fisherian NHST and reemphasizing alternative methods of assessing significance (McCloskey and Ziliak, 1996; Ziliak and McCloskey, 2004, 2008). In this, their position does not differ that much from Gelman (2004) or Imbens (2021): p-values are overemphasized and are often not the best way to answer an economic research question.

Since the publication of Ziliak and McCloskey (2008) many journals have decisively moved away from allowing authors to use p-values and stars in the presentation of results. Both *Econometrica* and the *American Economic Review* (*AER*) discourage or ban the use of stars to designate statistical significance. The instructions for authors submitting to *Econometrica* request that authors "please do not use asterisks or bold face to denote statistical significance. We encourage authors to report standard errors and coverage sets or confidence intervals" (Econometrica, nd). The *AER* (*nd*) takes a harder line in their guidelines for accepted articles, commanding "do not use asterisks to denote significance of estimation results. Report the standard errors in parentheses."

Journals, editors, and professional associations in other applied fields have gone even further. In 2014, the editor of *Basic and Applied Social Psychology* (*BASP*) banned Fihserian NHST, writing "prior to publication, authors will have to remove all vestiges of the NHSTP [null hypotheses statistical testing procedures] (p-values, t-values, F-values, statements about 'significant' differences or lack thereof, and so on)" (Trafimow and Marks, 2015). In 2016, the American Statistical Association (ASA) issued a statement that, in part, read:

> Underpinning many published scientific conclusions is the concept of "statistical significance," typically assessed with an index called the p-value. While the p-value can be a useful statistical measure, it is commonly misused and misinterpreted. This has led to some scientific journals discouraging the use of p-values, and some scientists and statisticians recommending their abandonment, with some arguments essentially unchanged since p-values were first introduced.
> *(Wasserstein and Lazar, 2016)*

This last statement seems to imply that a statistical test should be completely banned because some misuse or misunderstand it. As Imbens (2021) points out, this would be like the AEA or AAEA banning the use of instrumental variables or some other specific statistical approach just because some researchers apply it poorly.

So, if Ziliak and McCloskey are not in favor of banning *p*-values and stars, as *BASP*, the ASA, *AER*, and *Econometrica* have, what do they recommend? In their conclusion, Ziliak and McCloskey (2008) make seven recommendations, which we condense and paraphrase in Box 6.5.2. At their most concise, Ziliak and McCloskey (2004) recommend researchers ask the following of every paper they read: "[D] the paper focus on the *size* of the effect it is trying to measure, or does it instead recur to irrelevant tests of the coefficient's *statistical* significance?" (emphasis in the original).

This returns us to the issue of committing Type M and Type S errors. We cannot simply focus on what is significant, but what is important, what has economic significance. We must make a case for everything we include in a regression or analysis, not simply what ends up being significant. In considering the presentation of results, think broader: present more information, not less; work to be guided by ideas of economic significance and the implications of findings for policy; try to find a new light to illuminate the path, rather than the "stars" which have guided us for so long.

BOX 6.5.2 ZILIAK AND MCCLOSKEY'S (2008) STATEMENT ON THE PROPERTIES OF SUBSTANTIVE SIGNIFICANCE

1. Sampling variance is something interesting, but a low variance is not the same thing as scientific importance. Economic significance is the chief scientific issue in economic science.
2. No uniform minimum level of Type I error should be specified or enforced by journals, governments, or professional societies.
3. Scientists should prefer power functions and operating characteristic functions to vague talk about alternative hypotheses.
4. Hypotheses should be tested against explicit economic or other substantively significant standards.
5. Hypothesis testing should be sharply distinguished from significance testing.
6. Quantitative measures of magnitude (oomph) should be brought back to the center of statistical inquiry.
7. Fit is not a good all-purpose measure of scientific validity, and should be deemphasized in favor of inquiry into other measures of error and importance.

6.5.3 Null Results

As applied economists, there are entire units of us within the U.S. Government Economic Research Services (ERS) at the U.S. Department of Agriculture, Bureau of Labor Statistics at the Department of Labor, the Economic Analysis Group at the Department of Justice, the Office of Economic Policy at the Department of the Treasury, and others. This means that we are doing more policy facing work than your typical quantitative social scientist. As such, we need to be more attentive to the range of conclusions that an estimate may produce. A single-point estimate is not going to sufficiently elucidate the full scope of implications of a policy: we need to think in terms of Type M and Type S errors, not Type I and Type II errors, if we are to be effective at affecting policy. Similarly, a null effect should be rigorously examined to ensure that the impact of that policy is truly a null.

Researchers often report estimates, whether in the main results or as robustness checks, which are not statistically significant As Andrews and Kasy (2019), Brodeur et al. (2020), Ziliak and McCloskey (2008), and others report, there is a bias in the publication process toward significant – that is not null – findings. While standard Fisherian NHST has its benefits – it reduces to one number the probability of committing a Type I error – there are costs. The primary cost is that statistical inference is not possible on a nonsignificant result: we can say it is not significant but we cannot say much more than that. The logical thing to do when faced with this state of affairs is to refrain from offering any interpretation of a null result because it is uninformative. In the extreme, researchers bury null results in a file drawer. However, an insignificant result does not necessarily mean that it is unimportant. Abadie (2020) argues, "failure to reject [a hypothesis] may be highly informative," and non-significant results may be "more informative than significant results in scenarios common in empirical practice in economics."

There is a growing body of research that highlights just how informative null results can be (Abadie, 2020; Andrews and Kasy, 2019; Brown et al., 2019; Imbens, 2021; Kasy, 2021). In short, if researcher-readers are Bayesian, each time they come across the published results of a significance test, they will update their prior beliefs about the likelihood that the result is true. Abadie (2020) argues that "for the parameters of interest in empirical studies in economics, there is rarely any reason to put substantial prior belief on a point null hypothesis." Furthermore, the size of the data sets used in applied economics have grown so large that most studies have sufficient power to detect parameter values even a small distance from zero. These two features of contemporary applied economic research means that most will have strong priors for rejecting the null. Thus, when the Bayesian researcher comes across a nonsignificant result, this will be surprising and cause the reader to update their priors. Abadie (2020) and Kasy (2021) show that in many empirical settings, a null result will cause a larger change in beliefs for the reader than if the null had been rejected.

It may be safe to assume academic researchers act as limited-information Bayesian agents who have sufficiently clear priors and a strong understanding of nulls and posterior distributions. However, Brown et al. (2019) argue that those working in public policy and doing policy-relevant work may require further information in order to distinguish insignificant findings from unimportant findings. They recommend that researchers test null results to ensure that they are "true nulls" and then provide sufficient contextualization of just how surprising is the null finding. This can include various *ex ante* and *ex post* calculations, including power calculations and simulations. Brown et al. (2019) develop several tests for investigating a null finding, particularly helpful for economists evaluating the policy implications of a program.

However one goes about communicating the informativeness of nulls, Brown et al. (2019) stress three principles economists should keep in mind when working on research specifically designed to inform policy:

1. Scientific findings and policy decisions should not be based simply on if a p-value passes a specific significance threshold.
2. "Proper" inference mandates the complete reporting of results and full transparency in method, estimation, and findings.
3. Statistical significance – p-values or other metrics – does not measure the size of an effect and thus cannot capture the *importance* of a result.

Abadie (2020), Imbens (2021), Kasy (2021), and Ziliak and McCloskey (2008) promote the same principles, suggesting that surprising results, which might lead to changes in policy or other large shifts in optimal decisions, are absolutely necessary to publish, especially if they are null findings.

6.6 Replicable and Reproducible Research

The ultimate goal of all the practices and recommendations discussed in this chapter is to allow one's data analysis to be replicable and reproducible. While the beginning of this chapter focused on various types of specification search, the underlying assumption was that these sorts of practices are detrimental to science because findings will fail to be reproducible and replicable. That is, unethical behavior undertaken in data analysis fails to show the same results when reexamined by researchers other than the original authors. The goal of conducting robustness checks is to show that results do not hinge on a single idiosyncratic choice made by the authors, a choice that different researchers reasonably might not make. Similarly, reporting standards that fixate on $p < 0.05$ creates incentives for p-hacking, meaning authors are more likely to make data cleaning and data analysis choices that a disinterested or skeptical researcher would not make.

Recall from Chapter 5 that replicability refers to obtaining consistent results across studies that are working to answer the same question but using new data or different methods. Reproducibility refers to the degree of similarity (or extent of differences) between the results of measurements with the same data, carried out using the same method. Within these broad categories are narrower activities, such as verification tests or reanalysis (see Table 6.1).

Conceptually, the simplest form of replication is verification. Verification involves trying to replicate the results of existing research using the same data and same methods. At its most basic, verification can simply be a test that the data and code shared as part of a replication package do what they are supposed to do: produce the tables and figures in the published paper. While a verification test may be informative regarding any mistakes that were made in the code, it is more

---

PERSPECTIVE 6.2   HIDING BEHIND CUTTING-EDGE TECHNIQUES BY SEONG DO YUN

Big data, machine learning, high-performance computing, and artificial intelligence. Nowdays it is no longer surprising to find economists who are applying these techniques to their research. The major agricultural and applied economics departments offer courses focusing on these areas. There are numerous job candidates emphasizing their specialty in these areas every year. As more and more researchers uses these cutting-edge techniques, I want to bring three inconvenient factors out from behind the scene and into discussions of ethics in applied economic analysis.

Where is the economics? Let me raise this old question in every quantitative economics analysis. We are living in the era of causal inference, and a credible identification strategy is the most important element in applied economics. In general, economic data or data for economic analysis do not mechanically fit the needs of these necessity. In addition, unfortunately, all the cutting-edge data techniques described earlier are based on the best prediction performances rather than a proper identification strategy. Suitable identification improves the prediction, but the opposite is not necessarily true. Ironically, the importance of an economic foundation becomes more important when emphasizing the necessity of heavy data-driven approaches. In most cases, it is right to say that my machine learning results support the economic theory rather than reveal unknown new relations in the economic theory. Watch any of Susan Athey's online lectures on machine learning in economics to gain an appreciation of the necessity of economic theory to make sense of machine learning results.

Big means really big. It should be no surprise that computationally feasible does not necessarily mean scientifically meaningful. If someone is running an ordinary least squares regression with ten observations, for example, an averagely trained economist will definitely raise a question about its statistical credibility. Surprisingly, a similar situation does not often happen in big data or machine learning work in applied economics. One of the most popular machine learning techniques in applied economics is random forest because of its direct usability in many software packages. Surely, trees can grow at any length with any size of data. Is it, however, really sufficient to take a few hundred observations to use random forest or any other machine learning algorithm? A close friend who works at Amazon once complained to me that he lacked sufficient data for his machine learning application. His data set was about 0.3 million observations.

Exempted from replicability? A few decades ago, there was a big boom in the computable general equilibrium (CGE) model in operational research. The normal length of a journal article was not sufficient to include all equations, even in a simple CGE model, and they were generally omitted. Not surprisingly, their models were criticized as a black box and their replicability questioned. Consequently, CGE articles in the major applied economics field journals have become scarce nowadays. The complexity of a method or model does not exempt the authors from providing replicable data and code.

Big data or heavy calculation-based approaches mentioned earlier are not a free pass to ethics in data analysis and modeling efforts. With cutting-edge techniques, do not bury the weakness of the methods behind delusive terminologies. Without a rigid theory-driven specification or good identification strategy, falsification, HARKing, or p-hacking are still valid threats. If the analysis does not require parallelization or cloud computing resources to handle the data size, machine learning or big data analysis is likely not a good method. Longer appendices or supplemental information is a new trend in our profession. There is no loner any excuse to hide behind the complexity of a method when it comes time to making research replicable and reproducible.

TABLE 6.1 Types of Replications and Reproductions

Compared to original study	*Procedures: same*	*Procedures: different*
Using the same data	Verification	Reanalysis
Using different data	Direct replication	Extension

Note: Table is adapted from Christensen et al. (2019).

likely to produce a correction to the original research article than produce its own separate research paper. That said, finding mistakes in high-profile research has resulted in new publications. One such case is a paper by Reinhart and Rogoff (2010) which purported to show the benefits of government austerity measures. In trying to verify the results, Thomas Herndon, a graduate student at the time, found basic errors in Reinhart and Rogoff's Excel spreadsheet. As Herndon et al. (2014) detail, fixing the coding mistakes produces the exact opposite results of those originally published in Reinhart and Rogoff (2010).

Typically more interesting than a verification test is an attempt at reanalysis. While it uses the same data, reanalysis differs from verification in that it goes beyond just checking for coding mistakes and instead tries to reproduce the results while making different coding decisions along the way. Huntington-Klein et al. (2020) show just how sensitive results can be to apparently innocuous coding decisions. They had seven different researchers replicate the findings of two published studies that claim to identify causal effects. Huntington-Klein et al. (2020) find large differences among the replicators in the decisions made regarding data preparation and analysis, many of which would typically not be reported in a publication. The subjectivity of decision-making throughout the research process – researcher degrees of freedom – results in significant differences in findings.

Direct replication is when a researcher sets out to follow the data collection and analysis procedures used in a previous study but in a new context. A direct replication is basically a robustness check conducted by another researcher. It asks the question, Is one able to find similar results to a study, with the same methods but in a different context? Most direct replications occur in the context of lab experiments, either in economics or psychology. This is likely because of the lower cost of conducting an experiment in the lab, compared to the field or to collecting observational survey data. Additionally, the artificiality of the lab lends itself to replication in which everything is kept the same except for the subject pool. One of the most replicated studies in recent years has been the lab experiment conducted by Fischbacher and Föllmi-Heusi (2013). In their experiment, the authors have participants roll a die in private and report back what number they rolled. Higher numbers earn the participant more money. Although the experimenters do not know what number the participants actually rolled, they do know the probability of rolling any given number and therefore can calculate the share of participants that lie. In their lab experiment, which involved university students in Switzerland, they find that only 20 percent of participants lie to the fullest, which is the rational thing to do in the context of the experiment. The study has since been replicated at least 90 times and in numerous different settings (Abeler et al., 2019). To take just one example, Arbel et al. (2014) replicate it among college students in Israel and find that, among females, higher levels of religiosity correspond to greater levels of honesty. In their meta-analysis of replications of Fischbacher and Föllmi-Heusi (2013), Abeler et al. (2019) find that participants across all these studies lie at much lower rates than economic theory suggests, thus confirming the findings of the original study.

Extension studies seek to test the boundaries of existing findings by seeing if they reproduce in different contexts with different methods. It asks the questions, Is one able to find similar results to a study, with similar methods but in a different context or with a different research question? Many follow-up studies to a seminal paper could be considered extensions, as they explore the bounds of the original findings. One example, from our own research, in an extension study of the seminal paper by Suri (2011) on heterogeneity in the returns to adoption of hybrid maize in Kenya. As of 2022, the study has been cited over 900 times both for its importance in proposing a new estimation method but also for providing insights into an ongoing empirical puzzle regarding why profitable technologies do not get adopted. Michler et al. (2019) is an extension of Suri (2011) because it adopts and extends her estimation method and then applies it to a new context: that of improved chickpea in Ethiopia. They find that the solution to the empirical puzzle that Suri found for hybrid maize adoption in Kenya does not explain the empirical puzzle of improved chickpea adoption in Ethiopia. Thus, Michler et al. (2019) provides evidence on the extent to which Suri (2011) can be used to explain the adoption of different crops in different contexts.

Replication and reproduction of existing research is an essential component of the scientific process and open science practices. As Christensen et al. (2019) write, "replication enables science to be self-correcting, so that even when individual studies get it wrong, scientific communities eventually get it right." The process encourages work to exist within a scientific community, rather than simply within a single researcher's portfolio. The principles and practices of open science discussed throughout this book, such as ensuring replicability and reproducibility, help address concerns related to misreporting or other unethical behavior. But these principles can also help bring research practices and culture in line with the Mertonian norms that make up the "classical scientific ethos" as discussed in Chapter 1 (Miguel, 2021). Open science further serves to address biases, conscious and unconscious, that can make their way into research work. Nosek et al. (2012) shows among psychologists, even absent any data manipulation, there is a prevalence of motivated reasoning in complex and/or ambiguous situations – and statistics are definitely complex and often ambiguous. Although unconsciously undertaken, motivated reasoning ultimately biases scientific findings. As such, practicing open science by making research transparent works to ensure that biases are, if not eliminated, well documented; that misconduct is not present; and that research is in line with best practices for open inquiry and investigation. The process allows for self correction, revision, and adaptation of the scientific record – all moving toward truth and knowledge.

At present, the incentives for transparency in applied economics are too low. Currently, ensuring data and code allow for results to be replicable and reproducible is, by and large, not required for publication. Furthermore, the incentives that exist to replicate research by others may distort which works are replicated.

Those interested in conducting a verification test or reanalysis may do so because they are dubious of an original findings. And, perhaps accordingly, direct replications tend to receive the most attention when they overturn an original finding. Editors could play an important role in restructuring incentives to promote verification and reanalysis by promising to publish replications and reproductions of papers previously published in the journal, regardless of the results. Christensen et al. (2019) suggest a number of other potential tools. These include (1) replication audits, which work to provide systematic evidence on the extent of replication issues through large-scale investigations involving multiple studies, and (2) crowdsourcing to provide open peer collaborations for multiple researchers on replication projects.

In order to uphold the quality of the scientific record, as well as to eliminate unethical behavior in research, and to eliminate the influence of bias, open science and research transparency, through facilitating replication and reproduction of one's work are essential. Researchers must ensure that work is reproducible, replicable, and transparent. Christensen et al. (2019) serve as a tremendous reference for more detail on these topics from the value of these practices to their actual implementation.

6.7 Conclusion

The objective of this chapter has been to share an overview on the decisions and choices made during the data analysis stage in the research life cycle. The goal is to help readers understand and appreciate how researchers can influence the outcome of studies – almost inadvertently, through our biases, preconceptions, and standard practices. As Huff (1954) writes, "it is not necessary that a poll be rigged – that is, that the results be deliberately twisted in order to create a false impression." Throughout this chapter, we have shown that work does not deliberately need to be p-hacked, HARK-ed, fabricated, or falsified in order to be unethical or biased. There are a multitude of ways in which our biases, conscious and unconscious, may affect the outcomes of our work.

The keys to combating the potential for unethical data analysis are the principles of open science. These include (1) a clear, understandable workflow; (2) transparency in how specifications or models were arrived at; (3) carefully motivated robustness checks; (4) thinking in terms of Type M and Type S errors, not just in terms of $p < 0.05$; and (5) ensuring your research is reproducibility and replicability. With every new paper (and every revision to an existing paper), the process repeats and the temptation to sin in the basement reappears. Remember, Hotelling et al. (1948), who wrote that "too many people like to do their statistical work as they say their prayers – merely substitute in a formula found in a highly respected book." So, do more than worship your work, instead consider Huff's preaching (though not his practice) to think critically and be transparent. Sinners need not avoid sins. "They need only confess their errors openly" (Leamer, 1978).

Notes

1 Git is one of several version control systems while GitHub Desktop is one of many graphical user interface (GUI) for using Git. The system/software structure is similar to R and RStudio or LATEX and Overleaf. Some of the many other GUIs for Git include Bitbucket, Fork, GitKraken, and SourceTree.

2 In this alphabet soup of acronyms do not confuse Hollenbeck's and Wright's "SHARK-ing" with Rubin's (2017) "SHARKing."

3 As with HARKing, there are lots of different names and variants for this behavior. In this chapter, we simply refer to it as "p-hacking" for parsimony.

4 See the symposium on statistical significance published in the *Journal of Economic Perspectives* (Imbens, 2021; Kasy, 2021; Miguel, 2021).

5 Relatedly, Imbens (2021) argues that detecting p-hacking is an issue altogether different from addressing p-hacking. Detecting p-hacking is a problem of statistics. Addressing p-hacking requires addressing the incentives for p-hacking, such as publication bias, and creating behavioral change by de-emphasize the importance of "fixed levels of significance." We discuss publication bias and ways to address p-hacking in Chapter 7.

PART IV

Sharing Research

7

ACADEMIC RESEARCH DISSEMINATION

7.1 Introduction

In late 2021, Kenneth Judd, an economist at the Hoover Institute at Stanford, took to the internet to complain about the treatment a paper of his had received at the hands of James Heckman and Harald Uhlig, then editors of the *Journal of Political Economy* (*JPE*), one of the Top Five journals in economics (Judd, nd). The short version of the dispute, according to the Judd, follows:

1. In 2012, Judd and two co-authors (Yongyang Cai and Thomas Lontzek) submitted a paper to *JPE*.
2. In 2014, Monika Piazzesi, co-editor at *JPE* rejected the paper based on two reviewer reports. Judd emailed Heckman appealing the decision. Heckman allowed the authors to resubmit the paper as a new submission, with him, not Piazzesi, as editor.
3. In the winter of 2014/2015, Judd requests that Heckman speed up the review process so that the paper can be published ahead of one of the co-authors entering the job market.
4. In 2015, as the second review process continues, Judd made public comments critical of Piazzesi's handling of the initial paper. Heckman threatened to reject the paper if Judd did not stop in making his comments.
5. In 2017, Judd removed his name from the paper, which was accepted in 2018 and eventually published in 2019.

The email correspondence documenting the dispute between Judd, Heckman, and Uhlig was published by Judd (nd) on his website.

DOI: 10.4324/9781003025061-11

There are several interesting takeaways from this case that illustrate the the ethical issues around the dissemination of research in academic settings. First is simply the time lag between initial submission and final publication. The paper was first submitted in November 2012, meaning the initial idea, project development, data analysis, and so on, all happened prior to that date. According to Judd's emails, the paper was rejected in November 2014 based on the recommendation of two reviewers. The paper was then resubmitted to *JPE* as a new submission with Heckman as editor in late 2014. The authors received a revise and resubmit decision with six reviewer reports in late September 2015. The revised version of the manuscript was submitted in December 2017, which was accepted in May 2018. Although accepted for publication, the paper was not published online until September 2019 and was printed in the December 2019 issue (Cai and Lontzek, 2019). From first submission to publication online took six years and ten months! While not an ethical issue itself, the long timeline to publication creates incentives that can lead to unethical behavior, which we discuss in Section 7.3.

The second takeaway is what we consider the unethical (or at the very least unscientific) process by which the paper was published. Without weighing in on the quality of the article and whether or not the review process was fair, the interactions between Judd and Heckman seem to violate any notion that publication is based on the merits of a paper. After having a paper rejected, Judd went behind the back of one co-editor, Piazzesi, to use his influence with a different co-editor, Heckman, to get a second chance (Judd, nd). Then, after a year in review with Heckman as editor, Judd pleaded with Heckman to accelerate the review process so that Lontzek, a graduate student, could have an accepted paper prior to entering the job market (Judd, nd). If Lontzek did not land an academic job, Judd or another faculty member was going to have to continue supporting Lontzek instead of hiring a new student (Judd, nd). As Gelman (2022) notes in his blog about the emails, "to ask the decision to be made because it's 'like winning the lottery' [for a grad student]? What does this say about the field of economics, or maybe academia more generally? And to plead for journal acceptance to save a third party from having to pay someone's salary?"

Heckman is not any more ethical or scientific in his handling of the matter. As Judd continued emailing to beg for a quick and favorable decision, Judd also started publicly criticizing Piazzesi for her initial decision. Heckman responded by telling Judd if he continued to criticize a fellow editor, Heckman would reject the paper, regardless of its merits (Judd, nd). Even Uhlig, the managing editor, was drawn into the frey, telling Judd that the editors at *JPE* were doing Judd a favor by reversing the original decision to reject the paper (Judd, nd). In what appears to be a quid pro quo, Uhlig and Heckman emphasize that their special treatment of Judd's submission needs to be met with silence regarding Judd's criticism of Piazzesi, or else the paper will not get publish (Judd, nd). None of those involved seem to be troubled by using connections to get a second hearing for the paper or making publishing decisions based on someone's grant budget.

The third takeaway is the claim of publication bias that Judd raises to explain why Piazzesi rejected the paper. In his initial email to Heckman, Judd argues that his paper was rejected not because of its quality or import but because of the reviewers' dislike of the specific method used for the analysis (Judd, nd). Because the initial reviewer reports and Piazzesi's reject letter are not publicly available, we cannot judge the accuracy of Judd's claim. But, if one were to assume his characterization of the rejection is accurate, this is a very serious allegation. Note that he is not alleging that the paper was rejected because the method used was wrong. Rather, that it was rejected for reasons of politics, in which only one of two equally valid methods is viewed as acceptable not due to merit but to personal preferences. If editorial decisions are made in such a way, and we have no proof beyond Judd's claim, it would be evidence of publication bias.

The final takeaway concerns issues of authors. Ultimately, Judd felt that he had to remove his name from an article, in order for it to be published. As he characterizes it, the paper, and the careers of his younger co-authors, was being held hostage by Heckman and Uhlig (Judd, nd). One could obviously view the situation in a completely different light: Judd is threatening the careers of his young co-authors because he has an ax to grind with Piazzesi. Regardless of who one wants to blame, the email exchange highlights a situation in which authorship was determined by interpersonal politics and not scholarly contribution.

Before we discuss in greater detail all the ethical issues raised by the Judd-Heckman emails, we must first discuss the issue of plagiarism which, unlike many topics in this book, is reasonably clear and straightforward. The issue of plagiarism includes ideas around copying, self-plagiarism, and text recycling. Following this, we address the ethics involved in the process of academic publishing, from the perspective of an author and from the perspective of a reviewer. We raise concerns around the rising prevalence of predatory journals and conferences, while highlighting other recent trends in publishing including preprints and short papers. This more general discussion of the publication process and its ethical considerations is followed by some specifics on the ethics of publishing and the process of publishing in economics, highlighting what has become known as the tyranny of the Top Five. We conclude the chapter with a discussion of publication bias and we revisit the conversation about authorship initially begun in Chapter 3.

7.2 Plagiarism

Plagiarism is when someone appropriates and uses the thoughts of someone else, without giving appropriate credit. At base, plagiarism is a form of cheating since it misrepresents the work of some else as if it was your own. Plagiarism takes the intellectual property (IP) of one person and passes it off as the IP of another. As discussed in Chapter 3, two institutions exist to help protect against plagiarism: the legal code that governs IP and the social norms that govern professional conduct. The categories of things that may be plagiarized includes thoughts or ideas, processes such as code, results, words, and more (Comstock, 2013).

The Oxford University Press has a helpful blog post which iterates six types of plagiarism (Oxford, 2021):

1. **Paraphrasing:** Without citing sources, if someone paraphrases the work of someone else, then they have plagiarized. If properly attributed, then paraphrasing is not plagiarism – but rewriting something as though it was completely created by the author, when, in reality, it derives ideas from other sources, is plagiarism.
2. **"Patchwork" or "mosiac":** Similar to paraphrasing, someone may patchwork or mosaic the work of someone else, by copying and pasting pieces together from various texts, in order to create "their own" text. This might also include paraphrasing.
3. **Verbatim:** Perhaps the most commonly known – and most easily identifiable with modern software – verbatim plagiarism occurs when someone copies text directly from a source, without citation or attribution. This is also one of the most easily avoided types of plagiarism. Per Oxford (2021): "This can be avoided by quoting the original source with quotation marks or using an in-text citation."
4. **Source-based plagiarism:** Simply citing sources is insufficient for avoiding plagiarism. One must make sure that sources are cited correctly, following the appropriate style and field standards. Source-based plagiarism may occur if someone makes up a source or deliberately cites the conclusions incorrectly or contrary to the actual conclusions of the source. This latter point is important, as it touches on both falsification and plagiarism.
5. **Global plagiarism:** A sort of plagiarism which most may associate with "copying," global plagiarism occurs when an individual passes off work that they did not do as their own. Consider if someone submits homework that was actually completed by a sibling: this is global plagiarism.
6. **Self-plagiarism:** One of the most difficult types of plagiarism to understand – and commensurately, to avoid. Self-plagiarism can range from reusing key phrases from previous work to publishing the same paper in multiple outlets. Among the six types of plagiarism, self-plagiarism is the only type where there is gray area around what is ethical.

None of the first five types of plagiarism is tolerated in research, nor are the more extreme forms of self-plagiarism. The Office of Research Integrity at the U.S. Department of Health and Human Services (DHHS) considers plagiarism a form of research misconduct, on the same level as falsification and fabrication of research. The Office of Research Integrity considers research misconduct to have occurred if (1) the act was committed intentionally, or knowingly, or recklessly; (2) it can be proven by a preponderance of evidence; or (3) the action represents a significant departure from accepted practices (Comstock, 2013).

Important in this definition of research misconduct is that there are two parts: actually plagiarizing and deciding to plagiarize. Oliver (2010) notes that the latter may actually be a graver misconduct than the former. He writes that "we may need to reflect on whether a person stands condemned of an act of plagiarism alone, or whether it is the proven intent to plagiarize which is the key offense." Of course, it is impossible to get into the mind of another, and so intent in cases of plagiarism can be difficult to accurately discern. But, as in conducting ethical research along other parameters, an important component is to make the decision to conduct work ethically – to deliberately decide to not conduct unethical work. Plagiarism is no exception to this.

Getting data on the extent of plagiarism is difficult. One reason is that few journals or editors keep systematic records of plagiarism. We asked an editor at the *American Journal of Agricultural Economics* if they had data on the number of submissions that were identified as plagiarized. The editor responded that the journal has historically not run submissions through plagiarism software and so there is no way to determine if plagiarism is a problem or not. At the time of this correspondence (2020), one of the editors was using their own research funds to pay the cost of using plagiarism software to check submissions at the journal. But, since the software is not integrated to the submission system, editors only check if they suspect plagiarism, giving rise to lots of false negatives or Type II errors. An editor at a different journal, one owned by a large academic publisher, responded to our inquiries by saying the large academic publisher had plagiarism software integrated into the submission system so editors got a report for each submission. However, the journal did not keep statistics on plagiarism cases, since the software often identifies "plagiarism" by matching the submission to an earlier versions of the paper "published" as a preprint, working paper, or conference paper. Thus, the software produced a lot of false positives or Type I errors, making it difficult to determine when a submission was actually plagiarized.

A second reason why it is difficult to quantify the extent of plagiarism in the field is that editors are loath to make any identified cases public. Enders and Hoover (2004) sent questionnaires to 470 editors at economics journals and received 130 responses. In inquiring about how editors would respond to a clear case of plagiarism:

- 90 percent said that they would likely or definitely notify the original author that their work had been plagiarized.
- 78 percent said that they would likely or definitely ban future submissions to the journal from the plagiarist.
- 47 percent said that they would likely or definitely notify the plagiarists department chair, dean, or provost.
- 30 percent said that they would likely or definitely issue a public notice of plagiarism.

Enders and Hoover (2004) were inspired to undertake the survey because of their own experiences identifying plagiarism. In email communication that they include in the paper, one of the authors (Enders or Hoover) was asked to review a paper that plagiarized their own work. They notified the editor, who responded that the paper would be rejected, that the plagiarizer banned from future submissions, and that the editor might contact the plagiarizer's dean. But, after consulting the editorial board, the following rejection letter was sent to the plagiarizer:

> Dear [plagiarizer], Thank you very much for your submission. Unfortunately, after careful review, we have decided that we cannot accept [the paper] for publication in [journal]. We appreciate having had the opportunity to consider your work and hope that you consider our journal for future submissions.
>
> *(Enders and Hoover, 2004)*

Because of the fear of litigation and of "ruining someone's career" the editor and the journal took no other action than to reject the paper. Plagiarism was not given as the reason for rejection, and the plagiarizer was invited to submit more papers to the journal.

In the absences of quantitative evidence on plagiarism, Rosser Jr. (2014) provides a number of anecdotes based on his experience as an editor at the *Journal of Economic Behavior and Organization* (*JEBO*). He notes several cases of egregious unethical behavior, including cases of reviewers stealing ideas from proposals which they reviewed; situations of "authors" publishing papers with abstract, introduction, and conclusion changed – but all else the same as an already-published paper; and "authors" wholesale republishing a paper in a different journal in another language. He also raises cases of copied words and phrases, galley proofs changed to remove attribution of responsible parties, and potential miscommunications that bordered into plagiarism.

As Enders and Hoover (2004) and Rosser Jr. (2014) observe, it is important to recognize that plagiarism is not simply copying words – although that is likely the most common type of plagiarism. In fact, plagiarism can include and encompass idea theft. This is not necessarily the type of idea or project theft as described in Chapter 3, but rather reading an idea and then presenting the concept as your own, without attribution. The distinction here is subtle but important and relates to the sources of one's inspiration. Many if not most of our ideas are not born in a vacuum but arise from reading the work of others. As Wilson Izner puts it in a well-known witticism, "when you steal from one author, it's plagiarism; if you steal from many, it's research." When writing, one should carefully consider the ideas presented and give attribution to the source of those ideas. Adding a citation is like paying a debt – or, more kindly, extending credit – to those who originally developed that idea. So, pay your academic debts and give out kindnesses by citing sources!

7.2.1 Self-plagiarism

In 2011, Bruno Frey, then a professor at the University of Zurich, came under fire for a series of publications about who survived the *Titanic* disaster and why. In his coverage for the *Wall Street Journal*, the journalist Christopher Shea noted the striking similarities between four papers that appeared in *JEBO, The Proceedings of the National Academy of Sciences, Rationality and Society*, and the *Journal of Economic Perspectives* (*JEP*; Shea, 2011). In a scathing letter to Frey, David Autor, editor of *JEP*, called the papers "substantively identical," Frey's actions "ethically dubious and disrespectful" and a violation of the editorial agreement signed with the American Economic Association (AEA) (Autor, 2011). Autor published the correspondence in *JEP*, and Frey was banned from publishing in AEA journals. However, no correction or retraction was issued for the paper (Frey et al., 2011). Ultimately, Frey lost his job at the University of Zurich, after a review determined he engaged in publication misconduct when he had failed to sufficiently acknowledge previous works (Winckler et al., 2011).[1]

Typically, cases of self-plagiarism are not as straightforward as with Frey, nor are the punishments for self-plagiarism as severe. In fact, some economists and social science researchers do not consider self-plagiarism to be true plagiarism, since plagiarism is theft and one cannot steal from one's self (Cronin, 2013). Rosser Jr. (2014) writes that "legally and ethically, what has come to be called 'self-plagiarism' is not true plagiarism, which involves intellectual property theft of some sort." Others argue to the extent that self-plagiarism is the recycling of one's own text and ideas, it is simply an efficient way to build a research portfolio (Neville, 2005; Hexham, 2013; Vermeulen, 2012). In support of this position, some point out that although the term *self-plagiarism* was coined in 1893 (Anonymous, 1893), widespread use of the phrase is relatively new. Green (2005) argues that self-plagiarism only "became an important issue as a result of the development of a tool for its discovery," that is, the rise of plagiarism-detection software. Callahan (2013) argues that self-plagiarism is a moral panic created by senior scholars, with its victims being junior scholars who now have to vary their text in ways their seniors did not while developing more unique ideas for papers than their seniors had to.

In evaluating the arguments of those who think concerns about self-plagiarism are overblown, it is useful to distinguish between three types of conduct that are frequently lumped together as self-plagiarism. The first and mildest type of conduct that might be considered self-plagiarism is known as text recycling, which is reusing sentences or phrases from one's own previously published works. The second practice has been referred to as salami slicing (Roig, 2015), which is publishing multiple papers that are slight variations on one's own previously published works. The third and most egregious practice is what Frey did – publish substantially the same paper in multiple journals while hiding this fact by not citing the other papers. These three practices represent different degrees of unethical behavior.

Personally and professionally, we do not consider text recycling, within reason, self-plagiarism. What qualifies as "within reason," is a bit like Supreme Court Justice Potter Stewart's famous utterance: "I know it when I see it." Obviously, Frey publishing substantially the same article in four different journals is not within reason, even if all the papers had cited each other. We agree with Hexham (2013), who writes:

> Authors often develop different aspects of an argument in several papers that require the repetition of certain key passages. This is not self-plagiarism if the work develops new insights. It is self-plagiarism if the argument, examples, evidence, and conclusion remain the same without the development of new ideas or presentation of additional evidence.

The value of a paper is not found in how innovatively it can say something but rather how innovative is the something that it says.

Because it is not obvious where text recycling edges over into unethical behavior, we believe it is good practice to change, adapt, or in some way modify text published in one place before it is published elsewhere. In our own practice, we try to vary our writing and word choice in each new paper, even when papers share the same data or methods. But, for some things, like describing a survey sampling frame, there are only so many ways to write it. In these cases, it is worth following the advice of Deirdre McCloskey: be concise and avoid elegant variation (McCloskey, 2019a).

Despite the protests of Green (2005), Neville (2005), Vermeulen (2012), Callahan (2013) and others, we believe that self-plagiarism, in the form of duplicating ideas or only tweaking them slightly, is a serious breach of research ethics in applied economics. While authors may not be able to steal from themselves, we believe that publishing papers that do not show growth and advancement over previous studies is unethical because it seeks to get twice the credit for a single idea. While it has always been common for researchers to build on their previous work and ideas, there is an important distinction between creating a research portfolio of complimentary ideas and self-plagiarizing. The distinction lies in how previous work is used and cited by current work.

An example from our own experience as a reviewer helps illustrate this point. In reviewing a paper in 2020, one of us discovered extensive similarities between the paper under review, call it the submitted paper (SP), and an old paper, call it the working paper (WP). Several facts muddied the water regarding the exact relationship between the SP and the WP. First, the author list for the SP overlapped with the WP, although there was an author on the SP that was not listed on the WP. Second, the text in the SP had clearly been revised in terms of grammar, syntax, and punctuation such that the SP was very similar to but not identical with the WP. Third, the WP was at the time part of a departmental working paper series. Fourth, the SP frequently cited the WP as "previous findings" in support of the results in the SP.

These facts lead to several questions. What was the relationship between the SP and the WP? Was the SP simply an updated version of the WP, now ready for peer review and publication? If so, then why was the updated version citing its older self as corroborating evidence? Or, were the SP and the WP distinct pieces of research? If so, then why were the framing, wording, context, and many of the results so similar between the two? As we wrote in the review:

> If the two articles are in fact different, then the authors have clearly violated [journal] policy on ethics in publication: [link to policy]. If the two articles are in fact the same, the ethical violation is not as severe, though it is still unethical to cite an earlier version of a paper as evidence in support of the findings in an updated version of the same paper.

While it is common for a published paper to cite results from a longer WP version of itself, this was not how the SP treated the WP. The SP did not refer to the WP as a place to find additional results but as independent research that confirmed the findings of the SP. Either the authors had recycled an inordinate amount of text between two papers on a similar topic or they had engaged in self-plagiarism by trying to get two publications from the same research idea and insight.

We raised these concerns with the editor, who requested clarification from the authors. The authors responded that the SP and the WP were indeed distinct papers, with the WP about to be published in a different journal. They also apologized for the substantial amount of text recycling and, in their revision, rewrote and/or rephrased the sections that had substantial overlap with the WP. By clarifying the relationship between the SP and the WP and removing and revising the sections with recycled text, the authors addressed the primary ethical concerns raised in the review process. The paper no longer recycled substantial portions of other work, and the citations made to the published WP clarified how the two were related. As Autor notes in his letter to Frey, the primary problem was that Frey failed to cite the other papers. "Had you chosen to inform us of the *JEBO* and *R&S* articles prior to the publication of your *Journal of Economic Perspectives (JEP)* article, we would of course have no grounds for complaint" (Autor, 2011). But, as Autor also notes in his letter, the resolution of the self-plagiarism by citing the other papers would have resulted in *JEP* declining to publish the paper, since it provides no new insights. This outcome was exactly what Frey was trying to avoid by not citing his other work. Unlike Frey, in our case, the SP did cite the related paper. But like Frey's case, once the WP was published, the SP provided little to no new insights. The authors were engaged in salami slicing, making it an easy decision to reject the SP.

There is some debate among economists about whether salami slicing is inappropriate or if it makes research more approachable and readable. However, the Office of Research Integrity at DHHS considers it a type of research misconduct since it distorts the scientific record. Per *Nature* (2005), salami slicing wastes the time of editors and reviewers on papers that make little contribution. Hiding the fact that one is salami slicing by not citing all the papers that are slight variations denies peer reviewers the opportunity to assess if something is a meaningful contribution to the literature. The practice of salami slicing presents an distorted picture of the state of knowledge in a field since it cuts a single piece of evidence into many pieces and then presents them as if they were a set independent pieces of evidence. Salami slicing is driven by the "publish or perish" imperative, which we will go more into depth in (Section 7.3), – but the focus on quantity versus quality serves only to dilute the overall quality of the scientific record, and, in some cases, pushes researchers to engage in misconduct.

Cary Moskovitz, who directs the Text Recycling Project at Duke, has developed a set of guidelines to help researchers and editors understand and identify self-plagiarism in practice. O'Grady (2021) describes when the practice of text recycling is ethical, legal, and tips on how to present such text transparently. A full set of these recommendations is reproduced in Box 7.2.1.

BOX 7.2.1 BEST PRACTICES FOR RESEARCHERS IN TEXT RECYCLING

1. Authors should recycle text where consistency of language is needed for accurate communication.
2. Authors may recycle text so long as the recycled material is accurate and appropriate for the new work and does not infringe copyright or violate publisher policies.
3. Authors should be careful not to recycle text in ways that might mislead readers or editors about the novelty of the new work.
4. For most unpublished work, authors hold copyright and can recycle from that work without legal restriction.
5. Most publishers require authors to transfer copyright to the publisher. Authors' rights to recycle from their own published works are then limited by copyright laws, which differ by country. Publication contracts may, however, let authors retain some rights to recycle. These rights are contractspecific and differ markedly across publishers. Authors should know what their signed contract allows.
6. If the amount or type of recycling exceeds what copyright law and the signed contract allows, authors should obtain permission from the publisher of the source document.
7. Authors should be transparent with editors, informing them about the presence of recycled material upon submission.
8. Authors should be transparent with readers by including a statement notifying readers that the document contains recycled material.
9. If the authors of the new work are not identical to those of the prior work, the corresponding author of the new work should obtain permissions.

Modified from "Text Recycling: Best Practices for Researchers" by the Text Recycling Research Project licensed under CC BY 4.0.

The differing views of what constitutes self-plagiarism and how serious it is creates a complicated path for addressing it. But, as with plagiarism, considering the two parts of plagiarism (deciding to plagiarize and actually plagiarizing) can provide guidance for effectively avoiding self-plagiarism. Interrogating why one is considering adding or deleting a citation, or why one is copy text from an earlier paper, sheds light on one's motives. As ethical researchers, we should always seek to be transparent in our work, not just how one did the work but why certain decisions were made in the work.

7.3   The Process of Publishing

Incentives exist for researchers to plagiarize because, for most researchers, publishing is necessary to advance one's career. This is the case for researchers working both inside and outside the academy. Publishing raises one's profile as a researcher, provides a mechanism for researchers to contribute to the scientific record, allows for the expansion, communication, and discussion of ideas, and provides opportunities for interacting with new perspectives and insights. When it comes time for promotion, tenure or to name fellows of professional associations, one's research record, in the form of published papers, is typically the dominant factor. But, as Edwards (2015) observes, there is more to be gained than our own success and contributions to the scientific record:

> The dissemination of research is an important first step on the path toward knowledge translation and practice change. Presenting research at professional meetings allows for more rapid dissemination of research findings. . . . Where appropriate, researchers [should] develop targeted messages for key stakeholders regarding their research, to enhance knowledge translation, and knowledge users can facilitate this process through systematic reviews, guideline development, and communication through practice networks.

The presentation and publication of research is the first step on the path to broader impact.

But there is a dark side to placing so much focus on publications. During a panel discussion in 1972, Hannah Arendt expressed her frustration with the focus on publications:

> This business of publish or perish has been a catastrophe. People write things which should never have been written and which should never be printed. Nobody's interested. But for them to keep their jobs and get the proper promotion, they've got to do it. It demeans the whole of intellectual life.
>
> *(Arendt, 2018)*

If publish or perish is the imperative for researchers, it distorts incentives for researchers. Instead of working to publish sound, important scientific work, researchers end up working to publish anything they can to advance their career and avoid perishing. While we may purport to be – and may truly be motivated by contributing to the scientific record and sharing our work – the act of publishing is more complex than that.

The why of publishing is obvious to most researchers, even those new to the field, but the how of publishing is often less clear. And, because of the distorted incentives the publish or perish imperative introduces, the how of publishing is a process not just of logistics but also of ethics. There are many parties involved in the process, each with their own objectives and ethical standards. There are (1) the authors who, absent plagiarism, wrote the article; (2) the editor, the person at the journal who is managing the publication process and who will ultimately make the final decision about publication; and (3) the reviewers, the people that give feedback and make recommendations about the submitted article. In the following subsection, we discuss the process both from the perspective of authors and reviewers. The role played by editors is outside of our experience, and so we refer the reader to Belle-mare (2022a) and the essays in Szenberg and Ramrattan (2014).

7.3.1 Publishing as an Author

The process of publishing a paper can be complicated, confusing, frustrating, and opaque, especially when starting out in a field. This combination of complicated, confusing, and frustrating gives rise to opportunities where authors might be inclined to make choices or take shortcuts that are ethically dubious. Add to this the fact that the publication process is often opaque, and author might be unable to determine the ethical implications of their choices. To simplify the process of publication from the author's perspective, we break the process down into six stages (see Figure 7.1). We discuss each stage in this process, focusing on the ethical dilemmas an author might face at each stage.

Somewhat obviously, the publication process starts with having a paper ready to be published. However, when a paper is actually ready for submission is subjective. Bellemare (2022a) suggests that the ideal time to submit one's work is when "the marginal cost of polishing starts exceeding the marginal benefit of doing so." While an author could reasonably measure their marginal cost of polishing, many of us lack the gift for divining how anonymous reviewers will reward an additional unit of polishing. In our experience working with a variety of co-authors, we typically submit a paper when we are simply so sick of looking at it that nothing else can productively be done. Admittedly, not the best approach.

Since it is difficult to determine where the marginal costs equal the marginal benefits, knowing when to submit a paper creates a dilemma for authors. Submit too late and someone else might have beaten you to the idea. Submit too early and the paper might be rejected for being incomplete or unpolished. Because of the publish or perish imperative, authors have strong incentives to submit papers too early. Authors may send out an early version of a paper to an out-of-reach journal, knowing the paper will

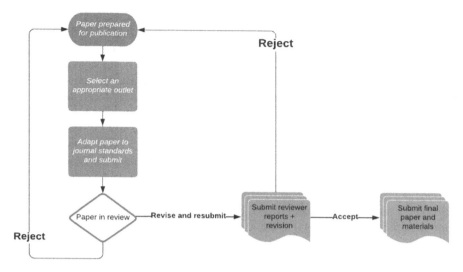

FIGURE 7.1   Process of Academic Publication

Note: The process of academic publishing. Image by the authors.

be rejected but hoping to get comments that can be incorporated prior to submission to a more achievable journal. This practice is so common, especially among graduate students, that *AER* lists it among the "DON'Ts" in its tips for authors. We believe that such action, while not unethical, is in poor form. It wastes editor and reviewer time. A more fruitful approach is to present the early version of the paper at conferences and seminars and request comments from friends, colleagues, and mentors.

Once the author has determined the paper is ready, the next stage is to submit the paper to an appropriate journal. Ideally, an appropriate journal, or a rank-order list of multiple journals, would have been discussed during the writing process. As with determining when a paper is ready, what qualifies as an appropriate journal is somewhat subjective. We always believe that the first journal we send a paper is an appropriate journal, only to be told by reviewers that our beliefs were wrong. Again, the uncertainty about what journals qualify as appropriate creates a dilemma for authors. Aim too high and the papers may spend years racking up a string of rejections. Aim too low and the impact of the paper, both on the field and one's career, may be diminished. As we have advanced in our careers we have honed our skills in figuring out what journals our research fits into best. We still get more rejections than acceptances. But we get far fewer desk rejections – when the editor does not even send the paper out for review – than we used to.

While finding an "appropriate" journal for new papers is a subjective and ongoing learning process, there are two things that one should never do when submitting a paper. First, never submit to a predatory journal. Predatory journals portray themselves as rigorous academic outlets yet will generally publish anything, with minimal or no peer review, in exchange for a publication fee. We discuss these journals (and conferences) more in Section 7.3.3. Second, never simultaneously submit a manuscript to multiple journals. Simultaneous submission of one paper to multiple journals is not unethical in itself, since some fields allow for it. But in economics, simultaneous submission is not the norm and is expressly prohibited in the submission guidelines for many journals.

Perhaps the most difficult stage in the publication process for authors comes after one has hit the "submit" button: the waiting process. The first hurdle that the paper must clear is the editor, who will either decide to send it out for review or will desk reject the paper. Desk rejections typically occur for one of two reasons. First, the paper was not an appropriate fit for the journal, either because the paper topic was outside the aims and scope of the journal or because the editor determined the topic of the paper was not important enough to meet journal standards. Second, a paper will be desk-rejected because it was at too early of a stage or was too unpolished to merit review. Desk rejections often come with a letter from the editor explaining the decision, though frequently not offering much feedback. One good thing about a desk rejection is that it tends to happen relatively quickly. The fastest we have had a paper desk rejected is on the same day we submitted it – a clear indication that we had failed in identifying an appropriate journal. That said, we have also waited for 61 days before getting a curt note from the editor that the paper was rejected but without providing a specific reason.

Alternatively, the editor may decide to send the paper out to reviewers. After the editor has received reports from the reviewers, the editor will either decide to reject the paper or allow for the paper to be revised and resubmitted. Most submissions end in a rejection. This is because, no matter the quality of any given submission, there are numerous other quality submissions competing for the limited space in a journal. Just how fierce the competition is varies from field to field. For development economists, the World Bank Development Impact Blog publishes a "State of Development Journals" each year (McKenzie, 2022). Table 7.1 tracks submissions to the top development economic journals over the last six years. The most prominent journals get well over a thousands submissions each year, or 4-plus submissions a day. Given space constraints in journals, this mass of submissions means acceptance rates are extremely low. Table 7.2 tracks acceptance rates at the same journals. For most journals, acceptance rates are less than 10 percent. This stiff competition for space in journals incentivizes authors to engage in many of the unethical practices we discussed in Chapter 6.

If the paper is rejected based on the reviewer reports, there are differing views on what to do with the reports that come with the rejection. One of our advisors took the position that there was little value in investing time addressing reviewer concerns unless there was the possibility of acceptance at that journal. However, the pool of relevant reviewers at field journals is not that large, meaning it is possible to draw the same reviewer at two different journals. In fact, one of us has been asked to review the same paper at three different journals. After we saw the same paper, essentially unchanged, for the second time, we strongly suggested that

TABLE 7.1 Submission Numbers to Development Journals by Year

| | Annual Number of Submissions | | | | | |
	2016	2017	2018	2019	2020	2021
Development Engineering	n.a.	49	54	37	46	52
Development Policy Review	n.a.	235	267	262	298	416
Economic Development and Cultural Change	421	434	459	460	567	325
Journal of African Economics	424	421	420	447	537	523
Journal of Development Effectiveness	91	n.a.	132	105	185	1427
Journal of Development Economics	1,313	1,344	1,504	1,475	1,849	1,889
Journal of Development Studies	1,100	1,277	1,255	1,296	1,572	1,587
IZA Journal of Development and Migration	61	74	68	61	66	72
World Bank Economics Review	400	449	493	523	649	547
World Bank Research Observer	50	n.a.	89	n.a.	70	72
World Development	2,300	2,362	2,864	2,756	4,352	3,531

Note: Table is reproduced from data in McKenzie (2022) and relies on the journal-reported total number of submissions received each calendar year. Data for the *World Bank Research Observer* is unavailable for 2017 and 2019.

the authors should incorporate the comments and that it was poor form to ask others to review the paper when the author had ignored previous comments. Having taken the time to provide helpful comments, it is frustrating to see the same paper again, unchanged. Paul H. Rubin and Antony W. Dnes, editors at a "second-line" journal, also encourage authors to spend time with previously received reviewer comments. Not to do so is "both a scientific and a strategic error" (Rubin and Dnes, 2014). We strongly recommend taking reviewer comments from rejections seriously, especially when there is general agreement among the reviewers on where improvements can be made.

Instead of an outright rejection, an editor may offer a reject and resubmit. This occurs when the paper has a good idea, but it is not at a level acceptable for the journal. The manuscript will have to undergo a major overhaul before it is reconsidered. When the resubmission is made after a reject and resubmit, it typically goes out to different reviewers than saw the first submission.

TABLE 7.2 Acceptance Rates at Development Journals by Year

	2016	Annual Acceptance Rate (%)				
		2017	2018	2019	2020	2021
Development Engineering	n.a.	23	30	15	21	33
Development Policy Review	n.a.	20	18	17 to 20	15	15
Economic Development and Cultural Change	5.7	9	5	9.5	8.9	7.5
Journal of African Economics	7.5	6	7	5.8	3	4
Journal of Development Economics	6	9	5	9.55	8.9	7.5
Journal of Development Effectiveness	25	n.a.	24	21	22	17
Journal of Development Studies	11	12	9.5	9.9	8	6
IZA Journal of Development and Migration	31.1	32	28	16	14	16
World Bank Economics Review	5 to 7	6.2	7	6.5	4.3	4.7
World Bank Research Observer	18	n.a.	13.5	n.a.	11	10
World Development	9 to 12	13.5	12	11	9	9

Note: Table is reproduced from data in McKenzie (2022) and relies on the journal-reported total number of submissions and acceptances each calendar year. Data for the *World Bank Research Observer* is unavailable for 2017 and 2019.

Conversely, if a revise and resubmit is offered, the author has the opportunity to make revisions to the paper before it is sent back to the same reviewers. When making the requested revisions, the authors *should* do these as quickly as possible, as getting a paper to publication should be one's first work priority. What the author *should not* do it is to incorporate the comments received, make one's paper significantly better, and then submit the paper to a different (better) journal. This is unethical because it wastes reviewer resources and is disingenuous to the editor. The world of applied economics is small. If an author does this, word is likely to get out and a person's reputation will rightfully be tarnished.

After revisions are made on a revise and resubmit decision, the paper is sent back to the same reviewers for consideration. Editors do not want to waste reviewers' time, so a definitive decision on acceptance or rejection typically comes after the first round of revision. However, the review process may repeat a few times, with reviewers asking for new modifications or adjustments. In some cases, a new reviewer may even be added. The most rounds of revisions we have gone with a paper is four.

In fact, we have had four rounds of revision for multiple papers. But multiple rounds does not necessary mean a long lag to publication. One of our papers that went four rounds took 586 days from first submission to final acceptance. But another paper that went four rounds took only 367 days from first submission to final acceptance. By contrast, we have had a paper accepted after one round of revisions, although the time between first submission and final acceptance was 376 days.

The publishing process in economics is long and spots in top journals, even top field journals, are hard to come by. This situation creates incentives for authors to manipulate statistics to help improve the chances of publication by obtaining results that are statistically significant. It also incentivizes authors to engage in salami slicing or self-plagiarism in order to get as many potential publications out of a single research question. Publishing a paper ethically means being honest and transparent in one's analysis. It also means trying to publish the best paper possible by avoiding salami slicing and improving the paper when one gets reasonable reviewer comments.

7.3.2 Publishing as a Reviewer

The peer-review process is designed to assess the validity, quality, originality, and overall contribution of a papers submitted for publication. Editors expect reviewers to give their approval to the ultimate inclusion of a particular paper in the scientific record. By reviewing and approving a paper for publication, reviewers bestow upon papers a degree of credibility and accuracy in its methods, analysis, and results. The ultimate purpose of peer review is to maintain the integrity of science by eliminating invalid or poor quality papers. And while peer review is not perfect, editors rely on reviewers to scrutinize, criticize, and evaluate the papers under consideration for the journal.

Several ethical issues arise in the review process simply because of the way the review process is structured. Authors submit manuscripts to editors, who then solicit anonymous feedback from colleagues or competitors of the author. The anonymity of reviewers insulates them from criticism and retaliation, thus allowing them to speak freely and openly in their review to the author and in their comments to the editor. But anonymity can be a cover for unethical behavior on the part of the reviewer. In the extreme, a reviewer, by having an early look at a paper, could steal the idea and hold up the paper in review while they work to get a similar competing into publication.

More common ethical issues arise from journals using either the single-blind or double-blind review process. Historically, economics journals were double-blind, meaning that the author does not know the identity of the reviewer and vice versa. If one is reviewing for a double-blind journal, the expectation is that this dual anonymity holds. However, most authors present their early research at conferences and seminars. This, combined with the recent trend to post idea and hold of articles, makes it more and more likely that a reviewer knows the identity of the author. If one happens to know the identity of the author, one may want to disclose this to the editor. But accidental violations of author anonymity have become so common that the social norm in the profession is simply to maintain impartiality in the review. What one should not do is immediately conduct an internet search for the paper title so as to identify the author. This is extremely tempting, and we ourselves have done it in the past. But it is a violation of the agreed-on review procedures and journal policies. One should make a good faith effort to maintain the double-blind review process.

Because it is difficult to maintain author anonymity, more and more economics journals are moving to a single-blind process, meaning that the author does not know who the reviewer is, but that the reviewer knows the identity of the authors. Single-blind review does away with what many now view as the fiction of double-blind review. But single-blind review introduces its own ethical issues. Knowing the author, reviewers may have conflicts of interest (COIs), which should be disclosed to the editor. Reviewers may be friends of the author and therefore inclined to provide an overly favorable review. Alternatively, reviewers may be competitors with the author in terms of grants and publication space and therefore inclined to provide an overly harsh or unfavorable review.

A great deal can – and has – been said about being a good reviewer. It is a skill that is improved with practice. Good resources on being a reviewer and writing an effective report include Oxford (2015), Stiller-Reeve (2018), Wallace (2019), and Bellemare (2022a), although there are many others. In terms of writing a good review, obviously do not ask for things we have warned against earlier in the book. This includes useless robustness checks, demanding results have $p < 0.05$, and so on. It is perhaps easiest to simplify the recommendations on how to be a good reviewer into a few bullet points:

1. Focus the evaluation on the quality of the research in the paper.
2. Provide constructive, doable suggestions.
3. Clearly describe the what and why of fatal flaws.
4. Do not ask the authors to change their paper to be a different paper.
5. Avoid providing a lengthy list of typographical errors, unless they significantly inhibit the ability to understand the paper.
6. Be timely in accepting/rejecting a request from the editor, and in turning in the review.

In following these recommendations consider, above all, the golden rule: "review for others as you would have others review for you" (McPeek et al., 2009). When acting as a reviewer, one should strive to be quick and helpful – even if the recommendation is to reject. If a pathway to publication seems impossible, even after revisions, then it is best to recommend rejection. Remember, the role of a reviewer is to provide quick assistance to the editor and helpful comments to the authors and to enhance and extend the scientific record through their service.

PERSPECTIVE 7.1   NOVELTY AND BORROWED MEASURES BY HOPE MICHELSON

To achieve fresh insights in our own analyses, applied economists often incorporate measures that originate in other disciplines: satellite measures of crop yields; wet-chemistry or spectrometry-based calculations of soil quality; DNA fingerprinting of seeds to assess varietal purity; GPS measures of field sizes. We are eager magpies.

Our readiness to deploy new measures is a strength, contributing to new economic insights and new areas of research: satellite-based measures of night-lights have provided new ways to quantify economic activity; measures from air-quality monitoring sensors help us document the effects of indoor and out-door air pollution on household health; satellite-based rainfall measures pro-vide information about agricultural conditions in regions of the world where data are scarce. This is important applied work, the future of our discipline.

To use borrowed measures requires care and diligence; we need to know what we are doing, and we need to communicate that rigor to those who evaluate and consume our work. Currently, the scrutiny of the measures we borrow mostly resides with the researchers themselves. Economist reviewers are generally not equipped to evaluate measures from analytical chemistry or from remote sensing, for example. In my experience as an author, a reviewer, and an editor, it is rare for a reviewer to scrutinize these measures or even to ask about them – their source, their limitations, their quality.

Responsibly borrowing methods or data products from outside economics also requires humility. One good way for economists to evaluate their adopted measures and strategies is through establishing and investing in true interdis-ciplinary collaboration. A few months ago I met with an academic soil scientist and longtime collaborator to present lab-based measures of soil nutrients from a panel of plots whose soils we had sampled repeatedly over a five-year span. Our pH measures suggested considerable variation over time. The economists on our team wanted to link these differences with other observed farm and household characteristics to study potential relationships between biophysical and economic outcomes. However, my soil scientist collaborator flagged these same-plot fluctuations as biologically implausible: "pH simply does not change like that over that timescale," she said, "not without significant intervention."She speculated that differences in lab testing protocols were the true source of what we were seeing in plot-sample pH over time. She was right – and we went back to the drawing board, disappointed but grateful.

Without our soil science colleague's observation and concern, we might have published those incorrect measures of pH, along with a corresponding analysis that used them as dependent or independent variables. And it's un-likely a reviewer for an economics journal would have flagged as implausible the magnitude of these variations.

How do we encourage responsible and ethical use of borrowed measures? As a reviewer, I look for interdisciplinary collaboration and co-authorship as a strong signal that deployed measures were verified by the home discipline. I also ask in some cases for documentation of the analytical error and discussion of the measurement process and validation efforts. The authors and principal investigators of a study bear the responsibility for validating any measurement they use. Even so, reviewers and editors should also push for careful documentation and discussion of these points to encourage norms of careful and collaborative use.

7.3.3 Predatory Journals and Conferences

Until now we have focused on the process of publishing papers. However, there are generally two parts of the academic dissemination process: presentation at conferences and publication in journals. In some fields these different mechanisms can be weighted the same – that is, inclusion in a conference or preceding is just as valuable as a publication. That is not the case in economics. Conferences provide a foundation or first step for work in progress, which is ultimately headed to an academic journal. Presenting at a conference provides a chance to get feedback and input prior to formal peer review.

While presenting at or publishing in a prestigious outlet is a great boost to one's career, the wrong outlet can send a negative signal about the quality of one's work. What qualifies as the wrong outlet varies depending on where one works and the audience one is trying to reach. The *American Journal of Agricultural Economics* (*AJAE*) is probably the wrong outlet if one is trying to get tenure in the economics department at the University of Chicago. But publishing in the *AJAE* would send a strong signal about the quality of one's work for those of us in departments of agricultural and applied economics at Land Grant Universities. Similarly, for those looking to communicate research to researchers in other fields, policymakers, or business leaders, will have their own appropriate conferences and publication outlets.

However, there are some outlets for research that are always the wrong outlet. These are known as predatory journals and conferences. As Grundniewicz et al. (2019) note, "the publish-or-perish culture, a lack of awareness of predatory publishing and difficulty in discerning legitimate from illegitimate publications fosters an environment for predatory publications to exist" and, if the amount of emails we get from these predatory outlets is any indication, to flourish. The intense incentive to present research at conferences and publish it in journals in order to receive promotion and tenure can result in researchers taking shortcuts in disseminating their findings. Predatory journals and conferences take advantage of this situation to exploit researchers for monetary gain.

As Grundniewicz et al. (2019) detail:

> Predatory journals and publishers are entities that prioritize self-interest at the expense of scholarship and are characterized by false or misleading information, deviation from best editorial and publication practices, a lack of transparency, and/or the use of aggressive and indiscriminate practices.

In short, predatory journals charge publication fees to authors without providing the review and editorial services associated with legitimate journals. Predatory conferences charge researchers registration fees without providing the scholarly interactions expected from legitimate conferences (Josephson and Michler, 2018).

To avoid these predatory outlets, one needs to be able to identify them. Distinguishing predatory from legitimate is typically obvious, given how blunt predatory techniques in soliciting submissions can be. Any journal that sends an email asking for the reader to submit an article is almost assuredly a predatory journal. As we saw in Tables 7.1 and 7.2, legitimate journals receive a large number of submissions and reject a majority of these submissions. Editors at legitimate journals have no need to send email requests for more submissions. Furthermore, these solicitations tend to have obvious grammar, spelling, or typographical. These mistakes are deliberate, and well thought out. They are a filtering mechanism to to ensure only gullible or desperate researchers respond. As we rotate who among the two of us is first author and corresponding author, we frequently get auto-generated emails addressed to the other. One of us even recalls an email sent by a journal editor named "Adolf Hitler" requesting submissions.

Jeffrey Beall, a former academic librarian, used to maintain a list of predatory journals and publications known as Beall's List. However, there was some controversy around Beall's methodology and potential conflicts of interest, which led to Beall electing to shut down the website in 2017 (Basken, 2017; Silver, 2017). Absent a comprehensive list of predatory journals, it is often easier to define the set of legitimate journals one might publish in and then sticking to that set. One way to identify legitimate journals is to look for those affiliated with a professional association, like the AEA, the Econometrics Society, the Agricultural and Applied Economics Association (AAEA), or the International Association of Agricultural Economics (IAAE).[2] Another way to identify legitimate journals is to look for who publishes the journal. Most legitimate journals are published by university presses (University of Chicago Press, MIT Press, University of Oxford Press, etc.) or by large for-profit publishers (Wiley, Elsevier, Springer, Taylor & Francis, etc.). A final way to identify legitimate journals is to interrogate the name of the journal. Most legitimate journals have concise names (*Econometrica*), specific names (*Food Policy*), or are named after the association (*Journal of the Association of Environmental and Resource Economists*). Predatory journals tend to have elaborate names that are extremely broad and vague about what research they contain. Some indicative examples include the *Journal of Applied Economics and Business*, the *Journal of Business Management and Applied Economics*, the *International Journal of Agriculture and Environmental Research*, and the *Journal of Global Innovations in Agricultural and Social Sciences*.

It used to be that if a journal had an article-processing charge (APC) it was a sign that the journal was predatory. However, as Bellemare (2022a) discusses, changes in the publishing industry have resulted in more open access journals and more journals with APCs. So, a journal charging an author thousands of dollars to publish a paper is no longer a good indicator to determine if the journal is predatory or legitimate. Although when the invoice for a $3,750 APC arrives it often feels like one is being taken advantage of.

Predatory conferences can be more difficult to identify because even legitimate conferences send out calls for submissions. Additionally, conference websites for some of the smaller or regional conferences can look decidedly homemade. Finally, the names of legitimate conferences can have extended names, such as the Joint Pan-African Grain Legume and World Cowpea Conference, which we attended in 2016. Grove (2017) warns that "'predatory' conferences now outnumber official events organised by scholarly societies." Predatory conferences may be more flagrant violators of ethical norms than predatory journals, as they simply charge researchers to attend what are essentially imaginary events (Josephson and Michler, 2018). As part of his reporting on predatory conferences, Grove (2017) attended an event organization by the World Academy of Science, Engineering and Technology (WASET). The organization held 183 events in 2018. In one London hotel, WASET held 387 "conferences" in a single day. Researchers who show up to these events often find that they are the only one attending their "conference" and have thus been booked into a session with researchers from other disciplines ostensibly attending a different "conference." Prior to the COVID-19 pandemic, WASET had planned to run 140,000 "conferences," or about 390 "conferences" a day.

Ultimately the best metrics of which journals and conferences are appropriate comes from experience and knowledge. With that said, there are a few rules of thumb when evaluating if a journal (or conference) is the right outlet:

- Does the journal (or conference) have a formal editorial or review board, and if so, are members or their institutions familiar to you?
- Does the publisher (or host) have policies or practices for digital preservation?
- Does the publisher (or host) have a "fleet" of journals (or conferences) and the home page for all appears the same?
- Is the journal (or conference) clear about the submission process and about what fees will be charged?
- Is the journal (or conference) promising a quick turnaround or decision?
- Does the journal (or conference) have a nonstandard measure of standing, for example, "view factor" instead of impact factor.

There are numerous other sources which provide a good method for evaluating whether or not a outlet is predatory. This includes an excellent post from Idaho State University (ISU, nd), which includes email images highlighting "red flags," and Leonard et al. (2021), who identify ten simple rules for avoiding predatory publishing scams.

Predatory journals and conferences continue to exist because they rely on the naïveté of researchers and the publish or perish imperative. Those who publish in or present at these outlets are often tricked into it, thinking they are engaging with a reputable journal or conference. This is particularly the case for older or younger researchers – or for those outside of the "club," for example, researchers in developing countries or those working outside the research-oriented Western university environment. Awareness campaigns, such as Think, Check, Submit, and the references and resources in this chapter can help address researcher naïveté. Simple steps and strategies such as these can easily address the researcher side of this problem.

More difficult to address is the institutional environment which creates an incentive structure or belief system that the quantity of publications can offset a lack of quality. Researchers may struggle to publish in traditional outlets or find that producing quality research is too time consuming. Such a researcher may decide that the personal benefits outweigh the negative effects of publishing in a predatory journal. The consequences of using predatory outlets for one's research can feel abstract – after all, what does it *really* mean to corrupt or damage the scientific record. However, the negative externalities from predatory outlets affect not just the rest of the profession but the wider public as well. Research published in these journals or presented at these conferences increases the noise-to-signal ratio regarding what we know about a topic. They sow uncertainty and doubt about what works and what does not work. The misinformation that ends up published in predatory journals can metastasize into deadly and widespread real-life harm. This was never more true than during the COVID-19 pandemic (West and Bergstrom, 2021): misinformation published in predatory journals spread like wildfire throughout the world, creating misinformation networks and costing lives.

Grundniewicz et al. (2019) tell a very personal story to one of the authors about the dire consequences of predatory publications. Their mother ("Jane"), diagnosed with breast cancer, had exhausted all standard treatments. Working with her alternative-medicine practitioner, Jane decided to pursue a therapy of vitamin infusions based on recently published research. The opportunity gave her hope until her son-in-law realized that the publication came from a predatory journal and, as such, had not been credibly tested or vetted: a devastating realization for a woman fighting for her life and trying to find *anything* that might put the cancer into remission.

It is imperative as researchers that we focus not just on publishing but on publishing well. The dissemination of our work is essential for the advancement of science, and so we need to ensure that we are actually assisting in that advancement with our publications – rather than just moving ourselves forward. There is little that we as a scholarly community can do to directly reduce the supply of predatory outlets. But we can work to reduce the demand for these outlets. On an individual level, one should not attend predatory conferences and one should not publish in predatory journals or serve as a reviewer or editor for them. As a field, economics should work to reduce the publish or perish imperative. Josephson and Michler (2018) provide a number of concrete examples. These include (1) reducing the time to publication, (2) rewarding authors for publishing in a greater diversity of (legitimate) journals, (3) rating work based on economic impact not just statistical significance, and (4) clarifying author contributions to papers. We address each of these issues in the remainder of the chapter.

7.3.4 Publishing Trends

The process of publication can feel like a static component of the life cycle of research – the same for generations – with its own, recurrent ethical conundrums, including when to submit, where to submit, how to deal with rejection and revision, and more. However, even though much in publishing is the same as it has been for decades, there are a number of new trends designed to reduce incentives to engage in unethical behavior.

Registered Reports

A recent trend in economics has been the use of registered reports to help reduce the incentive to specification search. Registered reports are when an outlet peer reviews and accepts for publication a paper before the data on which that paper will be based is even collected. In this way, papers are published based on the question, theory, and methods, rather than results themselves. In addition to reducing the incentive to p-hack, many hope that registered reports will be a solution for publication biases.

The process of publishing a registered report typically follows that of a normal paper – with a few notable exceptions. First, researchers develop an initial idea, around which they design a study. At this point, rather than carrying out the study, the authors submit the study design for peer review at a journal. The registered report undergoes the peer review process and is either accepted or rejected, based on the merits of the idea. If the study design is accepted, the researchers then proceed with the study and write up the results – that is, they complete the report. The now completed paper is submitted for a second stage of peer review, in which the reviewers assess if the plan, as laid out in the initial proposal, has been followed. The key is that in this second stage of peer review, the reviewers are not to judge if the findings themselves are significant or interesting – only the quality of the implementation of the research design. The report is then published as a standard research paper. Figure 7.2 shows this general timeline.

FIGURE 7.2 Timeline for Registered Reports

Note: Figure is from COS (nd) website. Reprinted under CC BY 4.0.

Registered reports are still relatively uncommon at economics journals. However, early results indicate that these reports are working as intended. However, registered reports are hardly a panacea to all research misconduct. Chambers and Tzavella (2022) review eight years of life science and social science use of registered reports, finding that early impacts are "promising." They find that registered reports are more likely be different from *a priori* hypotheses, to be computationally reproducible, and receive more citations. However, Chambers and Tzavella (2022) raise a number of important questions about registered reports that science will need to consider. These include, Are registered reports perceived differently than articles? Do they differ in other ways, beyond perceptions? Are there career consequences for those writing registered reports? What contributions are registered reports making to theory and applications – as well as to the broader scientific record – in the long term? As registered reports become more common in economics it will be important to engage with these questions.

As Chambers and Tzavella (2022) detail, registered reports began in the life sciences and are still somewhat more common there. Within economics, registered reports were pioneered at the *Journal of Development Economics* (*JDE*). Bogdanoski et al. (2018) provide some preliminary insights about the experience at *JDE* and are working to improve the process. As of 2022, only five papers have been published as registered reports, and 25 have been accepted at a stage 1 phase, pending final review of the completed report (McKenzie, 2022). Currently, the Center for Open Science (COS) lists nine economics journals that accept registered reports. These include the *JDE*, as well as *Q Open*, the *Journal of Behavioral and Experimental Economics*, the *Review of Finance*, and the *Journal of Political Economy: Micro*. However, thus far, the practice is still quite young, and it will be interesting to see the results that emerge from the widespread use of registered reports in the discipline.

Preprints

Working papers are relatively common in economics, and organizations like the National Bureau of Economic Research (NBER), the Institute of Labor Economics (IZA), the World Bank, and others, have working papers series to which economists, and others, regularly contribute. Furthermore, conferences will frequently post pre-publication versions of papers that have been presented at meetings. What is more recent, however, is the publishing of this work by an author, without "organizational" coordination, on a centralized website. Such prepublication papers are not properly "working papers" because they are not part of any published or affiliated series. Rather, they are "preprints," meaning prepublication and therefore pre–peer review.

The trend toward posting pre-prints is facilitated by easy access to the internet and by the long lag times between submission and acceptance of a paper. The most common preprint sites for the quantitative or mathematical sciences is arXiv, which is a "free distribution service and an open-access archive for 2,300,823 scholarly articles." The website is clear to note that "materials on this site are not peer-reviewed by arXiv." Preprints and working papers offer an opportunity to "claim one's turf" on a certain research question. It also provides an opportunity for informal peer review and dissemination of knowledge, which can be helpful for career progression as well as attaining grants. Since allowing economics papers to be posted to arXiv in 2017, the populating of the site has grown substantially for the field (see Figure 7.3).

However, there are some considerations to keep in mind when debating whether or not to post a paper prepublication, either to arXiv or in a working paper series. The first is that there are a few journals – although increasingly rare – which will

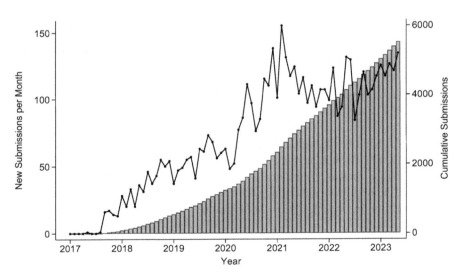

FIGURE 7.3 Monthly Submissions to arXiv Using ECON Topic Label

Note: Figure displays the number of new submissions per month on to arXiv using the ECON topic label plus the cumulative number of submissions. The figure is created by authors using data from arXiv: https://arxiv.org/archive/econ.

not accept work that has been published elsewhere, even if that "publication" is in a preprint service, working paper series, or website. This encourages researchers to consider outlets for their research before posting them. Another reason is that preprints may represent a risk to quality academic publishing as they have not been through the process of peer review. They may dilute the scientific record and – in some cases – be used by unknowing parties as the "final" word on the matter, even though they are not peer-reviewed or published. In this way, when others cite invalid, poorly vetted, or false facts from pre-prints – harm could be done, similar to damage done from the predatory publication movement. Ultimately, it is up to the researcher to decide whether publication of a preprint or working paper is appropriate for their work.

As a lesser concern, others cite the idea that working papers may simply die as working papers. While this is a preferable outcome to the "file drawer problem," in which the paper is never seen (formally published or informally), it is still of concern that there may be multitudinous papers simply sitting, never published, in the working paper format. Baumann and Wohlrabe (2020) reviewed working papers, looking to track them to publication. They found, however, that of the 28,000 papers they study, while about 67 percent end up in a journal, another 8 percent are released as a book chapter, and a staggering 25 percent are not published. While there are some explanations, often authors do not fully understand or are able to completely uncover "where" these working papers have gone. By and large, however, these results do suggest that most preprints make their way, ultimately, to publication.

Short Papers

Another recent trend in publishing, particularly in economics, is the attempt to move to shorter papers. The increasing length of economic papers has been noted in numerous outlets, both academic and journalistic. Card and DellaVigna (2014) provide an instructive, though now somewhat dated, example from the Top Five journals in economics. Figure 7.4, which reproduces a figure from Card and DellaVigna (2014), provides evidence of just how long papers have become in the economics profession. From a median length of about 15 pages in 1970, the median length of papers in these journals was about 50 in 2012. Figure 7.4 also reports the standardized length of papers in the *AER*, which shows no increase or decrease in length relative to the four other Top Five journals.

There is no disagreement that papers in economics have gotten much longer. Where writers disagree is about the reasons for the increased length, the interpretations about the benefits/costs of longer papers, and the solutions to the "problem" of long papers. Some view the increased length as an outcome of authors trying to substitute length for importance in papers, while others view it as a natural outgrowth of the field's shift from theory to applied micro, while still others blame reviewers and editors for requesting ever more robustness checks. In terms of benefits and costs, Bloem (2018) does not see a problem, because the added length often goes to addressing concerns

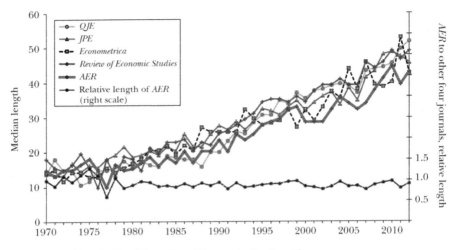

FIGURE 7.4   Standardized Lengths of Papers in the Top Five

Note: The measures of page length are standardized to take into account the differences over time and between journals in the number of characters per page of text. Shorter papers, comments, replies, and notes are also excluded. The 2012 page lengths are based on articles published before November 2012. Figure is reprinted from Card and DellaVigna (2014) Copyright American Economic Association; reproduced with permission of the *Journal of Economic Perspectives*.

by skeptical readers about causal claims in applied micro papers. Conversely, Kimball (2018) argues the elasticity of reading a paper is large, meaning fewer people read long papers, thus impoverishing the economics debate.

What people see as the cause and the effect of longer papers determines their solution to the "problem" of longer papers. Different journals have taken very different approaches to capping the length of papers. Some journals lack page or word limits, while others have page or word limits of a length that require little to no enforcement. The editors of the journals published by the Econometric Society, which include *Econometrica*, *Quantitative Economics*, and *Theoretical Economics*, issued a joint statement that acknowledged the increased length and promised to "try to stop, and in fact try to reverse the trend and bring down the paper length (including online appendices)" (Imbens et al., nd). It is unclear the effect this policy has had on published paper length. The approach by editors at the *AER* and the *Journal of the European Economic Association* (*JEEA*) has been more draconian. According to Card and DellaVigna (2014), editors at these two journals imposed (strictly) enforced page lengths of 40 pages in 2008 and 2009. These policies led to a sharp decline in the length of submissions at both journals. Interestingly, Card and DellaVigna (2014) infer that the composition of submissions to the *AER* did not change; rather, authors shortened their papers by an average of 22 pages to fit within the page limit. By contrast, at the *JEEA* the composition of papers changed, with authors of long papers submitting their work to different journals that did not impose a page length.

Several new journals as well as legacy journals have introduced a short-paper track to help combat the increasing length of economic papers. Short-paper tracks at traditional journals, or exclusively short-paper journals, tend to limit word count to less than 6,000 words, which is about 12 pages, plus a limit of five exhibits (tables or figures). Additionally, many short-paper tracks or journals have an expedited review process, with papers being either rejected or conditionally accepted at the end of the first round.[3] These short papers differ from "letters" journals like *Applied Economics Letters* or *Economic Letters* and from comments and corrections published at traditional journals. These letters and comments are typically very short, limited to about 2,000 words or four pages.

There is a growing list of short paper journals or journals with short-paper tracks. Among the former are *AER Insights*, the *Journal of Urban Economics: Insights*, and the *Journal of the Agricultural and Applied Economics Association (JAAEA)*.[4] Other journals have introduced a short-paper track, where authors can submit a short paper that undergoes an expedited review process. Journals with short-paper tracks currently include the *Review of Economics and Statistics*, the *Economic Journal*, the *Journal of Public Economics*, and the *Journal of Development Economics*.

At this time, it is unclear how serious editors will be in trying to shorten papers. It is also unclear how short papers will impact the profession. Will authors take to the idea? Will they be able to effectively communicate important economic insights within the page limits? Will readers cite short papers at similar rates to longer papers, or will there be a discount for short papers? Despite whether longer papers are a problem in economics, the number of journals and associations that have created space for shorter paper speaks to the perception that there is an appetite for shorter articles.

7.4 Publishing in Economics

On February 28, 1953, James Watson and Francis Crick, building on work by Rosalind Franklin, discovered the double helix structure of DNA. They wrote up their discovery, which was published as a two page paper in *Nature* on April 25, 1953 (Watson and Crick, 1953). An unattributed quip cited in Hadavand et al. (2021) jokes that "if Watson and Crick had to deal with economics publishing, their article would have been 70 pages long and taken three years to get into print." The quip expresses a common sentiment in economics: our papers are longer in length and take significantly longer to publish, relative to other disciplines. However, the quip is wrong in assuming Watson and Crick's 1953 work, if sent to an economics journal of the time, would have metastasized into a long paper during a cumbersome review process. John Nash's 1950 *Econometrica* paper on the bargaining problem was eight pages (Nash, 1950). George Akerlof's (1970) *Quarterly Journal of Economics (QJE)* paper on the market for lemons was 12 pages long. Clearly economists did not always write long papers. So what has changed?

A common culprit blamed for the increasing length in both pages and review time is the shift in economics from theory to more applied work. The rise of empirical economics has often been dated to the work of David Card and Alan Krueger on minimum wage effects and to the tools for estimating causal effects by Guido Imbens and Joshua Angrist in the early 1990s. Others place this shift with the rise of randomized control trials, such as those done by Abhijit Banerjee, Esther Duflo, and Michael Kremer in the early 2000s. Whenever it started, applied economic research has come to dominate the pages of most journals. However, the slowdown in time to publication was noted by Ellison (2002) at a time when the credibility revolution was just underway. As he documents, review times began to increase in the late 1970s and early 1980s (see Figure 7.5). And as we saw in Figure 7.4, page length also began to climb around this time.

Recently, Hadavand et al. (2021) detail these trends by evaluating 241 articles published in three of the Top Five economics journals. These authors investigate whether economic papers are longer in review and longer in length, compared with other disciplines, as well as whether papers differ based on the number of authors. The comparisons made by Hadavand et al. (2021) confirm that in economics, our papers are longer, take significantly longer to publish, and have fewer authors,

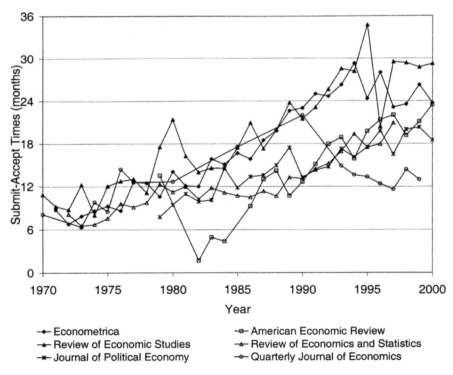

FIGURE 7.5 Mean Submit–Accept Times for Papers

Note: Image from Ellison (2002) shows the change in mean months from submission to acceptance at six general interest journals. Reprinted with permission of the *JPE*.

relative to other disciplines. "An economics article that is at the 50th percentile of time to acceptance would be at the 85th percentile of times to acceptance in the other social science journals and at the 97th percentile in the two natural science journals" (Hadavand et al., 2021). Lybbert et al. (2018) find similar trends in the *AJAE* finding that agricultural and applied economics mimics the trends in economics: in more recent years, papers have been longer, include more tables, figures, and equations, and also have extensive appendices (often hosted online). The edited volume by Galiani and Panizza (2020) provides a variety of explanations and analysis about the causes and consequences of these trends in publishing in economics.

Several ethical issues arise from the long lag in economics between submission and acceptance. These relate to how long publication timelines distort author incentives in an environment where researchers feel like they must publish or perish. If one must publish to advance one's career in the field, and if acceptance rates for most journals are in the single digits, and if papers are in review for years, then is it any wonder some researchers resort to unethical behavior? Such behavior can include engaging in *p*-hacking to help ensure a paper has flashy results so that once in review, it is more likely to be accepted. Or authors may try to maximize the number of publications from a single research project by engaging in self-plagiarism or salami slicing. Or still yet authors may submit papers to predatory journals in an attempt to substitute quantity of publications for quality of publications.

The differences between publications in economics and other disciplines beg a question about the *value* of such differences. That is, do economists gain from longer review times or from writing longer papers? It is not possible to compare across disciplines, but Hadavand et al. (2021) make efforts to examine the return to scholarly output via citations. The authors find that the length of time in review correlate with larger impact: 51 percent of articles that require a third round of revision have greater scholarly impact than the 27 percent of papers that only go through two rounds. Hadavand et al. (2021) find only small, although still significant, correlations between a fourth round of review and more citations. They fail to find that longer articles or those with more authors are cited more often. The result that longer time in review, measured by multiple rounds of review, leads to more citations may suggest that we, as researchers, should complain less when another round of review is requested.

There are several margins that extend the time of papers in review. These include (1) the number of times a paper is submitted or resubmitted in the review process before publication, (2) the time the paper is with editors and reviewers considering the paper for publication, and (3) the time the paper is with authors making revisions. Hadavand et al. (2021) suggest that it is this first margin (number of submissions) that is productive in terms of improving scholarly impact. However, it is the third margin (time with authors) that they find to be the greatest drag on review times in the discipline. Figure 7.6 shows, by decile of slowness, the main contributors to publication slowness. In the fastest deciles,

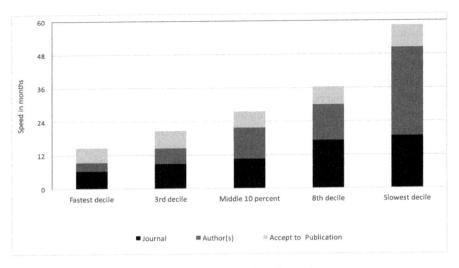

FIGURE 7.6   Contributions to Slowness, By Decile of Speed.

Note: Contributors to slowness time to publication acceptance, by speed decile. Image from Hadavand et al. (2021), reprinted with permission of the authors.

where the time from submission to publication is less than 24 months, it is time with editors and reviewers that make the largest contribution to slowness. But starting with the middle decile, authors themselves are the major contributors to the slowness in publishing their papers. In the middle decile, papers stay with authors for about ten months, while in the slowest decile papers stay with authors for more than two years.

Hadavand et al. (2021) conclude that "over half the variation in lags in acceptance arises from authors spending more time on revisions." They also conclude that this time is not productive in terms of future impact. Hadavand et al. (2021) consider a number of characteristics or traits of both the authors and the papers that might correlate with scholarly impact and time in review. They find that the characteristics of the authors do not increase time spent in review significantly, but the characteristics of the paper do. Most notably, theory papers are managed in fewer rounds. This raises an important caveat to the length of time with author – as theory papers take less time, it may be the case that reviewers of empirical papers request more regressions, robustness checks, and similar data-based changes, which take a significant amount of time to complete. We cannot know, based on the analysis in Hadavand et al. (2021), what the characteristics of the reviews are – and so cannot fully understand if the authors are simply dragging their feet or if all the time a paper is with the authors is truly necessary. Among the other characteristics that Hadavand et al. (2021) examine, length of the paper itself does not matter for review time, although papers with fewer authors are often handled more quickly.

Given the pressure to publish, what solutions could address the slowness problem in economics? We acknowledge that a not insignificant amount of time comes from authors themselves. But there are a number of ways that time to publication could be reduced along all three margins that Hadavand et al. (2021) consider (number of resubmissions, time with journal, and time with author).

First, there are several strategies that journals already implement to reduce the number of rounds that a paper is in review. Short papers undergo a shortened review process, with papers either rejected or conditionally accepted after one round of review. Editors at *Economic Inquiry* have long offered a *no revision* option to any paper submitted to the journal. The *no revision* option was instituted by Preston McAfee when he took over as editor in 2007. His initial review of the process found that the policy significantly reduced the time to publication for papers and did not lead to a reduction in the quality of publication (McAfee, 2010). The editors of *Economic Inquiry* continue to offer this option today.

Second, there are a variety of strategies that journals have adopted or could adopt to reduce the time papers are with reviewers or with editors. The most common of these is to pay reviewers for their time. Several journals, including the *World Bank Economic Review* and the journals published by the AEA, pay reviewers for submitting timely reviews. Other journals, such as the *Journal of Agricultural and Resource Economics* (*JARE*), have experimented with the policy. Thompson et al. (2010) report on a natural experiment they conducted as editors of *JARE*. They find that a nominal payment to reviewers can expedite review times, although the time reduction is modest. Thompson et al. (2010) note that this modest reduction in reviewer time "affords editors time to pursue other editorial duties besides reminding reviewers that their reports are due or past due."

Building on the findings in Thompson et al. (2010), Hadavand et al. (2021) argue that "monetary incentives merely shift a few delayed reports across the margin to qualify for payment." Instead of monetary incentives, Hadavand et al. (2021) recommend limiting reviewer time, either through behavioral nudges to encourage faster reviews or firmer penalties for lagging reviewers. Chetty et al. (2014) report on the results of an experiment conducted by the editors of the *Journal of Public Economics*. Reviewers were randomized into four groups: a control group had a six-week deadline for submitting their review; a treatment group with a four-week deadline; a cash incentive group that got $100 for hitting the four-week deadline; and a social incentive group that would have their turnaround times made public.

Figure 7.7 summarizes of the results the experiment. While all groups responded strongly to reminder emails, more than 50 percent of reviews in the control group did not return their reviews by the six-week deadline. The four-week treatment group got their reviews in earlier than the six-week control group; however the difference of time in review between the two groups was 13.5 days, or essentially two weeks. As with the control group, more than 50 percent of reviews were outstanding at the four-week deadline. The cash incentive group tended to turn their reviews

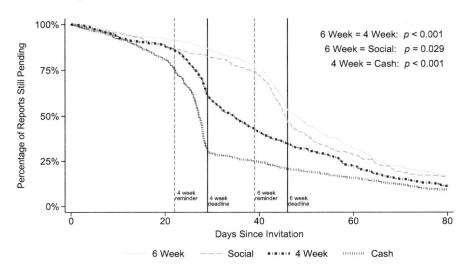

FIGURE 7.7   Incentivizing Faster Review Times

Note: Figure reports 'survival curves' by treatment group. Each curve plots the percentage of reports pending versus the days elapsed since the reviewer received the invitation. The solid vertical lines depict the six-week deadline and the four-week deadline. The dashed vertical lines depict the reminders sent one week before each deadline. Figure is adapted from Chetty et al. (2014) using data and code in Chetty et al. (2019) under Modified BSD License and CC BY 4.0.

in right on time. The median time to review for this group was 27.2 days, or almost exactly four weeks, which was eight days quicker than the four-week treatment group. Not surprisingly, the social incentive treatment group turned reviews in significantly earlier than the six-week control group, though the magnitude of the effect was modest (two days). Chetty et al. (2014) conclude that shorter deadlines are a cheap and effective way of reducing a paper's time in review, although a majority of reviewers still miss the deadline. For journals interested in ensuring compliance with deadlines, cash incentives are extremely effective.

Instead of encouraging reviewers to submit reviews quickly, Hadavand et al. (2021) explore ways journals and editors could try to punish delinquent reviewers. Editors could "fire" a reviewer if a review is not returned immediately after the deadline. However, this does nothing to shorten the time in review, since the editor must then find a new reviewer and provide a new deadline. Furthermore, firing a reviewer comes with no cost to the reviewer. Instead, editors could impose an embargo on paper submissions for reviewers who have been fired. Since most researchers review for journals they would like to submit to, a threat to deny new submissions unless reviews are submitted in a timely fashion might have substantial force.

Turning to reducing time with editors, Hadavand et al. (2021) argue that there is no excuse for a paper to sit with editors. Editors at journals are frequently paid for their time. Particularly in Top Five economics journals, where editors earn between $32,000 and $65,000 a year. Besides remuneration, adding more editors could help reduce the time a paper takes to receive an editorial decision. Lybbert et al. (2018) examine a century of changes at the *AJAE*, including the quadrupling of editors over that time. However, they also note that at the time in which the journal decided to move to four editors, there were half as many papers submitted as there are today – perhaps an argument to further expand the number of co-editors. In either case, as with the margin of times in review, the time spent with editors and reviewers is not the most significant contributor, by and large, to the lengthy review times seen in economics.

The third margin that extends the time of papers in review is the time the paper is with authors making revisions. As Hadavand et al. (2021) note, longer time with the author is not necessarily productive time, as the length of time a paper stays with the author is uncorrelated with the number of citations. There could be several reasons for why this time does not result in improved quality of final papers. It may be that authors are too busy with other, newer, projects and are procrastinating or backloading the completion of revisions (Akerlof, 1991). Or it may be the case that procrastination results in lower quality research. Alternatively, it could be that authors lack the time or the skills to make high-quality revisions, taking many months to make only minor improvements.

In all three cases, the economic profession could benefit from journal policies that shorten the time authors are allowed to revise a manuscript. If authors are procrastinating, then resubmission deadlines, like reviewer deadlines, would make completing the task a higher priority. If procrastination results in lower quality research, deadlines would help authors produce better papers. And, if authors lack the time or the skills to make high-quality revisions, a resubmission deadline might help them pull the plug on the paper sooner and look for a different, more appropriate journal to submit to.

There is scant evidence one way or that other that a resubmission deadline helps shorten the time from submission to publication without harming the quality of the papers. However, Hadavand et al. (2021) report on the effects of the *AJAE*'s policy. Unlike most journals in economics, the *AJAE* includes a "soft" deadline for resubmission in their decision letter. Authors are asked to resubmit their manuscript within six months of the editorial decision. The mean submit-to-acceptance time at the *AJAE* in 2020 was ten months, with the 90th percentile at 22 months. While the mean paper clearly misses the six-month deadline, the *AJAE*'s submit-to-accept time is substantially lower than other top field journals, and only one field journal had a mean value of less than 22 months.[5] Despite this relatively short turnaround time, the *AJAE*'s impact factor in 2019 (3.44) was nearly identical to the average impact factor of the other six field journals (3.67). A soft deadline seems like an effective path for shortening the long publication times in economics without impacting the quality of research.

Publishing papers in economics is unique from publishing in many other disciplines. Our papers are longer in length, and they take longer to publish. The time it takes to both write and publish an economics paper adds to the existing pressure to publish or perish. These pressures create incentives for research misconduct. As discussed, there are a number of low-cost policies that editors and journals could implement to help reduce this pressure by reducing the length of time from submission to publication. The applied economics profession should be attentive to and aware of how the long publication times impact researchers, especially early-career researchers, and should work to help reduce this pressure, thereby reducing the incentives to engage in research misconduct.

7.4.1 Tyranny of the Top Five

Economists, including ourselves, often talk about the Top Five journals, meaning the *AER*, *Econometrica*, *QJE*, *JPE*, and the *Review of Economic Studies*. All five are highly cited general-interest economic journals. For most economists, publishing in these journals is the pinnacle of their professional careers, since these are the journals that have published groundbreaking papers that win researchers Nobel Prizes. As Kenneth Judd (nd) wrote in one of his emails to James Heckman, "a *JPE* paper is like winning the lottery."

Despite the allure of the Top Five, there is a dark side to fetishizing publication in a small set of journals. It drives unethical behavior, like Kenneth Judd, for those trying to get published in the journals. It also gives editors at these journals power to influence the careers of others based solely on their whims, as James Heckman demonstrated. For those trying to get research published in the Top Five, it can often feel like a club dominated by the elite and therefore impossible to break into. As we write this, Daron Acemoglu has two papers forthcoming in *Econometrica*! But, as McAfee (2010) argues, "the causality actually runs the opposite direction – people who publish a lot wind up hired by top departments." Here the enduring example is John List, a graduate of University of Wyoming and former member of our department at the University of Arizona who is now head of the economics department at the University of Chicago and has about 30 Top Five publications, or slightly more than one a year throughout his career.

The dark side of our profession's focus on a small set of top journals has been termed the "Tyranny of the Top Five" by no other than James Heckman. Heckman and Moktan (2020) provide evidence for what has long been anecdotal concerns about the undue influence that the Top Five exert on the careers of economists. This influence shifts incentives, in a negative way, as describe in Chapter 2. Heckman and Moktan (2020) document that the perceived value of the Top Five has real consequences for tenure and promotion, and state that, "for rational career-oriented economists who prioritize tenure and career advancement, given the current incentives, academic careers should be little more than quests for publication in the T5 [Top 5]." They find that there are strong incentives for career advancement for researchers to aim strategically – and perhaps to the detriment of other publications – at the Top Five, at least for those in the 35 top-ranked economics programs in the country.

Heckman and Moktan (2020) further document that the Top Five journals are not the "top" in terms of overall scholarly impact. With the exception of the *QJE*, the Top Five are not the journals with the top five impact factors, based on 2-, 5-, 10-, 15-, and 20-year impact factors. And, with the exception of the *AER*, the Top Five are not where the "top" economists (based on citations) published their articles from the years 1996 to 2017. Heckman and Moktan (2020) conclude that Top Five publications serve as a signal to tenure committees and external letter writers "through channels that are independent of publication quality."

Aside from changing incentives for young researchers with respect to publication outlets, Top Five journals also exhibit issues with "incest." Heckman and Moktan (2020) document that those with connections to journal editors are more likely to be published in those journals – and that the Top Five are no exception. As such, connected researchers are likely to fare better in publication – and thus ultimately in their careers. These connections can come through formal or informal networks. As Pressman (2014) notes, "journal editors are human, and reciprocity is a fundamental, deep-seated human trait. Editors are more likely to help those they know and those who have helped them." This is exactly what played out between Judd and Heckman. Despite Judd feeling like he was mistreated, he was actually given an opportunity that economists not connected to the University of Chicago would likely not have.

Beyond the human inclination to help those that they know, editors exhibit an influence on the research which is published, thereby influencing the research that is actually done. In the Top Five, which have long editor tenures, it may be the case that researchers choose to pursue research programs which are likely to be of interest to current editors. This is a point Judd makes in his emails to Heckman: that his paper was rejected not because of any quality issues but because it used a specific method that the editor in charge of the manuscript, Monika Piazzesi, disagreed with on some ideological grounds (Judd, nd). The implication of Judd's accusation is that in order to get published in the *JPE* a researcher needed to use Piazzesi's preferred methodological approach and that other, scientifically valid, approaches would be rejected out of hand. Heckman and Moktan (2020) conclude that

[a]n overemphasis on T5 [Top Five] publications perversely incentivizes scholars to pursue follow-up and replication work at the expense of creative pioneering research, since follow-up work is easy to judge, is more likely to result in clean publishable results, and hence is more likely to be published. This behavior is consistent with basic common sense: you get what you incentivize.

Because of the perverse influence that the Top Five hold in economics, there have long been calls to change the incentives, or at the very least, to shift the evaluation of researchers away from the current weight placed on publications in these journals (Heckman and Moktan, 2020). Bardhan (2003) writes about the difficulties in publishing in these journals for people in "periphery" fields, in particular in his subfield of development. He notes that it may damage careers to go shopping around for a place to submit – that is, to submit and resubmit papers to all the Top Five before ultimately "settling" for a field journal. He encourages people evaluating researchers for promotion and tenure – as well as for young researchers themselves – to take a wider perspective on where papers *should* go for publication.

For those existing in the field of agricultural and applied economics, concerns about publishing in the Top Five may seem somewhat remote. Unlike other fields in economics, like macroeconomics, industrial organization, health economics, or international development, the field of agricultural and applied economics has its own separate departments at universities. While most economists, regardless of their field of research, go through tenure and promotion in a college of arts and humanities, social science, or in a business school, agricultural and applied economics departments tend to exist in colleges of agriculture or life science. This shifts expectations about promotion and tenure requirements and, by extension, expectations about where one should be publishing.

Similar to other fields within economics, there is a perceived hierarchy of publications in the field of agricultural and applied economics. As the flagship journal of the AAEA, *AJAE* is generally considered the most prestigious in the field. But, as with the Top Five general interest journals, the *AJAE* is not always the top by impact factor. For several years, Marc Bellemare, on his blog, has tracked the Top Five journals in the field based on impact factor. Table 7.3 lists the Top Five by impact factor over the last four years. While the *AJAE* is frequently in the Top Five, it is not always there and it has not been the most cited journal in any of the last nine years. While the career consequences of not publishing in the *AJAE* are

TABLE 7.3 Top Five in Agricultural and Applied Economics

2018	2019	2020	2021	2022
FP (3.11)	FP (3.79)	FP (4.19)	ARRE (5.18)	CJAE (11.35)
AJAE (2.46)	ARRE (2.98)	AJAE (3.03)	AEM (4.76)	ARRE (6.62)
ARRE (2.02)	AJAE (2.53)	AEPP (2.78)	FP (4.55)	FP (6.08)
JAE (2.00)	JAE (2.51)	ARRE (2.75)	AEPP (4.08)	AEPP (4.89)
AE (1.73)	AE (2.42)	AEM (2.65)	AJAE (4.08)	ERAE (4.45)

Note: Table is reproduced from data in Bellemare (2022b) and related blog posts for each year. Values in parentheses are the journal's impact factor, calculated on the basis of calendar year citation numbers. Definition of journal abbreviations in order of appearance: *FP – Food Poicy, AJAE – American Journal of Agricultural Economics, ARRE – Annual Review of Resource Economics, JAE – Journal of Agricultural Economics, AE – Agricultural Economics, AEPP Applied Economic Perspectives and Policy, AEM – Aquaculture Economics and Management, CJAE – Canadian Journal of Agricultural Economics, ERAE – European Review of Agricultural Economics.*

not as dire as for those in top 35 departments not publishing in the Top Five, we know of numerous cases where students and pre-tenured faculty have been told by senior colleagues that an *AJAE* would make their tenure case easier. Despite the perception that an *AJAE* can be a necessary condition for tenure in agricultural and applied economics departments, there are numerous excellent and successful scholars without an *AJAE* at top departments. In terms of ethical considerations, as one moves up in the field, they should consider if they are explicitly or implicitly instituting their own tyranny of a particular journal when evaluating young professionals.

7.5   Publication Bias

Publication bias reflects an ethically problematic trend in publishing toward an overabundance of statistically significance results. The outcome of publication bias is that the published literature does not reflect the truth. If there is a tendency to publish only significant results, then what readers see are the true significant results plus many false positives (Ioannidis, 2005). Left out of the published literature – hidden out of sight from readers in some researcher's file drawer – are the true non-significant results plus the false negatives. If all results were made public, say, in a hypothesis registry, then readers could determine the probability of publication as a function of a study's results and correct for it (Andrews and Kasy, 2019). Absent knowing the conditional publication probability, it is impossible to precisely determine the magnitude of publication bias and how much it distorts what we know.

Consider an example of publication bias in the medical field, reported by Turner et al. (2008) and Turner et al. (2022). In Turner et al. (2008), the authors obtain data on all 74 Food and Drug Administration (FDA) approved clinical trials of 12 antidepressant drugs between 1987 and 2002. They then match the trial data and FDA decisions for these studies to published journal articles. In Turner et al. (2022), the authors update their original study by adding data on 30 trials of four new antidepressants since 2002. As Figure 7.8 shows, of the 74 trials in the original study, 37 were viewed by the FDA as having positive results, meaning the drug was efficacious. All but one of these 37 positive results trials (97 percent) was published. By contrast, 37 trials were viewed by the FDA as having negative results, meaning the drug was not efficacious or the study was underpowered. Of these trials, only 11 percent were eventually published. As Turner et al. (2022) shows, publication bias seems to have diminished over time. Of the 30 trials in the new study, 7 out of 15 trials with negative results were published. The overall body of evidence regarding what works and what does not work has grown. In the earlier study, only 54 percent of trials were ever written up and published. In the later study, 73 percent of trials were written up and published, providing a more accurate view of drug effectiveness and ineffectiveness.

While the trends toward increased publication of negative or null results is encouraging, both Turner et al. (2008) and Turner et al. (2022) document a

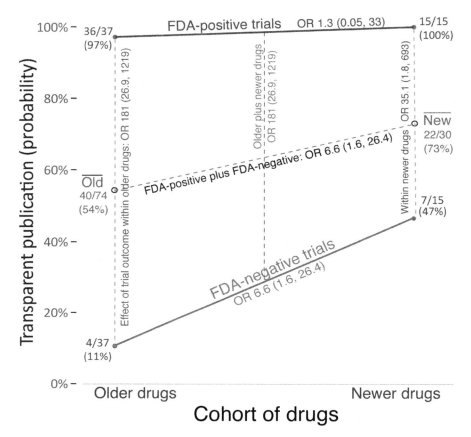

FIGURE 7.8 Effect of FDA Regulatory Decisions on Publication

Note: The figure illustrates the effects of trial outcome and cohort (older vs. newer antidepressants) on transparent publication. For FDA-positive trials (top line), transparent reporting was already nearly 100 percent. By contrast, within FDA-negative trials (bottom line), transparent reporting increased substantially. This resulted in an increase in transparent reporting for all trials regardless of outcome (dashed oblique line). Reprinted from Turner et al. (2022) under the Creative Commons CC0 public domain dedication.

disturbing tendency for negative trial results to be published in a way that conveyed a positive outcome, contradicting the FDA decision. In Turner et al. (2008), 11 of the 37 trials with negative results (30 percent) were published in such a way as to convey a positive outcome. In Turner et al. (2022), 2 of the 15 trials with negative results (13 percent) were published in such a way as to convey a positive outcome. If someone was to view only the published literature from the older trials, it would appear that 94 percent of the trials were positive when in fact only 51 of all trials were positive (Turner et al., 2008). This distortion of the literature has improved, slightly, in the new studies. If one were to only view the published literature, it appears that 71 percent of trials were positive, when in fact only 50 percent of trials run produced positive results (Turner et al., 2022).

At its root, publication bias is just a specific form of sample selection bias. If only papers with significant results get published, then the sampled (published) evidence is not representative of the true population of evidence. As Ioannidis (2005) and Christensen et al. (2019) detail, there are several contributors to this form of sample selection bias. First is the human-induced bias we discussed earlier in relation to editorial preferences, where editors may prefer to publish papers with significant results and reject papers with null results (Card and DellaVigna, 2020). Second is the decrease in acceptance rates at journals noted by Card and DellaVigna (2013), which increases competition and strengthens the incentive to arrive at a significant result. Third is that "hot topics," such as the minimum wage debate discussed in Section 3.4.1, increase the number of teams working on the topic as well as the number of tests run, leading to more false positives (Christensen et al., 2019). Additionally, researchers on hot topics may feel the competitive pressure to produce new, surprising, and significant results in order to get published. A fourth contributor to publication bias is the existence of underpowered studies, which lead to more false positives, since any significant result in a low-powered study is more likely to be the result of intentional or unintentional p-hacking than the discovery of a true null (Ioannidis et al., 2017). Fifth is researcher degrees of freedom, which allow researchers to search across many different specifications to arrive at significant results (Casey et al., 2012).

A number of recent papers have worked to document the extent of publication bias in economics (Brodeur et al., 2016; Christensen and Miguel, 2018; Ioannidis et al., 2017; Vivalt, 2019; Blanco-Perez and Brodeur, 2020; Brodeur et al., 2020). While some of these were mentioned in Chapter 6, their conclusions regarding the implications for publication bias are worth discussing here. The earliest among this recent group is Brodeur et al. (2016), who document evidence of publication bias in three of the Top Five journals (the *AER*, the *QJE*, and the *JPE*). The authors construct a database of 50,000 tests reported in papers published in these journals between 2005 and 2011. They convert reported p-values on these tests into z-statistics ($p = 0.05$ becomes $z = 1.96$). Since z-statistics have a standard normal distribution, this transformation allows for easier visualization of the fat tails (small p-values) in published results. Assuming the null hypothesis is true, in the absence of publication bias, a distribution of z-statistics from published papers would be monotonically decreasing. If the null is true and journals publish all results equally, there would be many papers with insignificant results (small z-statistics) and fewer significant results (large z-statistics). Conversely, if journals prefer to publish significant results, the distribution of z-statistics would be monotonically increasing: more significant results are more likely to be published. What Brodeur et al. (2016) find is neither of these outcomes but rather a two-humped distribution, with a dearth of reported p-values just below the $p = 0.05$ significance level. Brodeur et al. (2016) interpret these missing, slightly insignificant results as evidence of authors p-hacking, so as to produce significant and therefore publishable results. This two-humped distribution provides evidence of publication bias in journals and evidence of authors *p*-hacking in order to fit the editorial and reviewer demand for significant results.

Brodeur et al. (2020) extend this work to twenty-five journals, looking at differences in publication bias by journal prestige and by empirical method. Figure 7.9 reproduces their key finding regarding different methods. Similar to their previous results in Brodeur et al. (2016), Brodeur et al. (2020) find a two-hump distribution for studies that employ difference-in-difference and instrumental variable methods. There is a peak in the distribution just above $z = 1.96$ and a trough of missing marginally in significant values. By contrast, this two-hump distribution is muted for studies using randomized control trials and almost absent in studies using regression discontinuity design. Published papers using these latter two methods are also more likely to have insignificant or borderline significant results. While publication bias is less in studies using random controlled trials (RCTs) and regression discontinuity designs (RDDs), Brodeur et al. (2020) are clear that all the methods demonstrate evidence of publication bias. This supports findings in Vivalt (2020) and in Kasy (2021), who write that "there is ample evidence that publication is selective, albeit to different degrees and ways across various empirical fields."

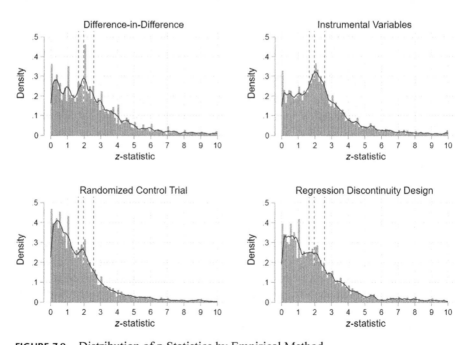

FIGURE 7.9   Distribution of z-Statistics by Empirical Method

Note: The figures display histograms of the distribution of *z*-statistics by statistical method. Vertical lines demarcate traditional significance levels. Figure is adapted from Brodeur et al. (2020) using data and code in Brodeur et al. (2022) under CC BY 4.0.

While it is clear that publication bias exists in economics, what is less clear is how to solve this ethical problem since the exact source of the bias is not necessarily clear. As discussed earlier in this section, there are several factors that can contribute to publication bias. The relative importance of each of these factors is unknown, and therefore, developing concrete solutions is a challenge. That said, recent years have seen a number of interesting proposals to reduce publication bias in economics, from the very theoretical to the very practical.

A more theoretical, meaning potentially less practical, solution is laid out by Frankel and Kasy (2022). The authors develop a model of publication in which the value of a published paper is that it informs public policy. With this as the objective of publication, Frankel and Kasy (2022) derive an optimal decision rule for publishing a paper: journals should publish extreme results that shift the prior beliefs of readers. While the optimal decision rule in this setting is decidedly selective in that it prioritizes one type of result over the other, its priority is publishing surprising and meaningful results, not just statistical significance results. Thus, Frankel and Kasy (2022) provide a microeconomics model for the arguments put forward by Ziliak and McCloskey (2008), Gelman and Tuerlinckx (2000), and others. A surprising result might be a significant result but could also be a nonsignificant result. What matters is creating a change in the prior beliefs of the reader.

A potentially more practical solution is to strengthen the peer review process. We state "strenghten" because as it stands now peer review does not reduce p-hacking and may in fact contribute to its prevalence (Brodeur et al., 2020). If editors publicly direct reviewers to reduce the weight they place on statistical significance, then this could reduce the incentives for authors to p-hack, since they know that reviewers will not penalize them for nonsignificant results. Blanco-Perez and Brodeur (2020) study the effect of just this sort of directive, which was issued by the editors of eight health economics journals in 2015. They find that, post-statement, the number of tests rejecting the null hypothesis decreased by 18 percentage points.

In addition to editorial statements, numerous other potential solutions have been proposed by economists studying the problem of publication bias. Proposed solutions include de-emphasizing statistical significance (Ziliak and McCloskey, 2008), pre-analysis plans (Olken, 2015), registered reports (Chambers and Tzavella, 2022), and pre-results or null-results journals (Kasy, 2021).

Publication bias is widespread in economics and despite awareness of the issue, there seems to be little evidence that the problem is improving over time (Brodeur et al., 2020). While researchers have proposed a number of different ways to address publication bias, there is uncertainty about the root cause of the problem, and therefore, little agreement about how best to solve it. Until the profession agrees on how to bring about systematic change to reduce publication bias, we as researchers need to ensure our work as authors, reviewers, editors, and readers is ethical. As authors, one should prespecify research whenever one is looking to make causal claims. One should also avoid "sinning in the basement" (Kennedy, 2002) or at least confess when one has sinned. As a reviewer or editor, one should not demand a paper have significant results in order to be published. One should also interrogate papers during the review process to ensure significant results did not arise due to p-hacking. As a reader, one should be attentive to the presence of publication bias and remember the importance of not just Type I errors but also Type M and Type S errors.

7.6 Revisiting Authorship

Before concluding this chapter, we return to some of the ideas from Chapter 3 and team building as it relates to authorship. Ideally, discussions of authorship occur at the project development stage, but we recognize the reality that many of these conversations do not actually happen until one is writing up the results or preparing the manuscript for publication.

There are two important considerations when it comes to authorship: first, what it takes to be included as an author and who gets on this list and, second, what is the order of those listed authors. While the former seems more complicated and fraught with tension, the latter can be a significant hurdle, in particular on larger teams where contributions may vary from acquiring funds to data cleaning to analysis to actually writing. Depending on the policies and practices within a team, each of these may constitute authorship and may rate a different place in the list of authors. The Contributor Roles Taxonomy CRediT author statement is designed to help resolve issues about who qualifies as an author. The AEA's Author Randomization tool is designed to help resolve issues of author order.

In economics, where there are not strong social norms about what constitutes authors and author order, it is often up to the discretion of the members of the team to ascertain what merits inclusion and placement in an author list. Membership on an author list should be an ongoing conversation, had at the outset of a project as well as before publication. We also encourage lead investigators (professors, project leads, etc.) to lay out clear policies on authorship for those who work with them. We have an authorship statement for our research group/lab, which we distribute to students we work with at the beginning of each new academic year. Our authorship statement reads, in part:

> Authorship is a privilege, and a critical component of the scientific process. When you make a significant intellectual or material contribution to a project, then you will typically be an author on the manuscript. Nonetheless, there have often been considerable resources and effort devoted to a project before you were involved, and thus others may also deserve authorship credit.
>
> Authorship (including order of authors) is always discussed before a manuscript is submitted from the lab. In fact, we encourage these conversations to happen early in the project, so everyone is clear on their role (and the terms of

authorship). As a general rule of thumb, to be considered for authorship you need to substantially contribute to at least two to three of the following:

1. Intellectual development of the idea and/or research design.
2. Funding for the work through proposal development and writing.
3. Significant time analyzing data and preparing it for publication.
4. Manuscript development including outlining and text writing as well as contributing to figures and tables.

There are many additional tasks and efforts that go into the publication of a paper. This includes doing background literature searches and/or reviews, data collection, data cleaning, analysis at the direction of a principal investigator, editing of or commenting on a manuscript. In the economics profession, none of these rate authorship credit, though these contributions are acknowledged in footnotes to the paper. We will work to ensure discussions about authorship occur early in the project so that we are all on the same page regarding expectations.

We frequently revisit the topic of authorship during the course of a research project. Initially foreseen co-authors may not end up substantially contributing to the work, and, conversely, substantial contributions from new project members will be appropriately recognized. Students should understand that they may not be first author on work (even their thesis) if it is not written up in a timely manner. This can be a problem once students have graduated from the program and move on to other employment or study. Again, we will work to ensure expectations for the timing of publication are clearly documented.

(Josephson and Michler, nd)

We encourage our students to revisit the concept of authorship, carefully consider their contributions to a project, and not assume authorship is guaranteed simply because they played some role sometime during the life of the project. Although the understanding of effort might be a difficult conversation, it is an important component of being part of a team.

To ease this conversation, there are a number of possible tools that teams and individuals can use. Some journals require the submission of a CRediT authorship statement and include author contributions at the conclusion of an article. While far from universally adopted, CRediT author statements are becoming more common in economics papers and we frequently use this model with student co-authors. The idea of the CRediT author statement is to move away from the vagueness of *authorship* and toward an understanding and appreciation of *contribution* to the final paper. Providing more information, as the CRediT statement recommends, is a way to better assess contribution, as well as to avoid cases of ghost authorship or unfairly uncredited authors. Table 7.4 presents the fundamental components of the CRediT author statement, adapted from Allen et al. (2019).

TABLE 7.4 CRediT Author Statement

Term	*Definition*
Methodology	Conceptualization; generation of ideas; creation of research objectives; development or mapping of methodology; creation of models
Software	Work in coding and programming; software development; implementation, writing, and testing of code
Validation	Verification of the overall replication/reproducibility of research findings and results
Formal analysis	Use of statistical, mathematical, computational, or other methods to analyze data
Investigation	Participation in the research process itself, in particular performing experiments or data collection
Resources	Provision of materials, samples, participants, instrumentation, computer resources, or other analytical tools
Data curation	Management activities to produce metadata, scrub data and maintain research data
Writing – original	Preparation, creation, and/or presentation of the research for publication in the initial draft phase
Writing – review & editing	Preparation, creation, and/or presentation of the research, specifically critical review, commentary or revision, in the pre- or post-publication stages
Visualization	Preparation, creation and/or presentation of the research findings, specifically visualization/data presentation
Supervision	Oversight and leadership responsibilities around planning and execution of research
Project administration	Management and coordination responsibilities for the planning and execution of research work
Funding acquisition	Acquisition of financial support for the research

Note: Table is adapted from Allen et al. (2019).

The order of authors can have a significant affect on the perception of contributions to a project and the rewards reaped by contributors. However, absent a generally agreed upon method for author order lists, it can be difficult to determine what an individual contributes to a paper. As was discussed in Chapter 3. Typically authorship in economics fluctuates between two trends: either lexicographic or non-lexicographic, in which the first author is lead author, making the primary contribution to the paper. Taxonomies like CRediT or the AEA random author ordering are designed to help clarify or equalize authorship credit. Absent strong norms regarding author ordering, we encourage the practice of including some statement about contribution in a footnote to the paper.

Before concluding this discussion, it is imperative to recognize that not all authors will be viewed as contributing equally, even if authors are listed alphabetically, randomly, or contributions are detailed using CRediT. As documented by Sarsons et al. (2021), female authors frequently and systematically have their contributions to papers downgraded when it comes to promotion and tenure. We often rely on authorship order to help us understand more about the authors who wrote the piece. That is, in the absence of strong signals of researcher quality, the members of the community may consciously or unconsciously rely on characteristics of the individual to make judgments. This can affect people's careers and have broader outcomes for people's livelihoods. As such, authorship order is worth careful, ethical consideration – beyond contribution alone.

PERSPECTIVE 7.2   CO-AUTHORING WITH GRADUATE STUDENTS BY MARIA MARSHALL

Co-authoring with graduate students has always been a pleasure. It is one of the positive and quantifiable outcomes that come from mentoring graduate students. I have found that how I mentor and publish with master's students is quite different from how I mentor and co-author with doctoral students.

Co-authoring with master's students for me is straightforward. Master's students typically work on well-established projects where in most cases the data have already been gathered. They demand a more hands-on approach for two reasons. First, they are on a tighter timeline to finish their theses. Second, they have less experience with the research process. Turning their theses into publishable manuscripts usually requires that we work on the publication once the student has left my institution. In most cases, I've worked without the student to turn the thesis into a publishable manuscript. I've found that in most cases, that has required that I rewrite substantial portions of the thesis and/or reanalyze the data. At this point, we have a dilemma, should the student be the first author on the article? The idea for the thesis is usually generated jointly (unless it was already an established project), the data are usually provided by the mentor, the mentor guided the modeling process and provided substantial feedback on both the data analysis and the writing. In my opinion, if the mentor then must distill the thesis into a publishable manuscript by rewriting and/or also reanalyzing the data, then the student should be the second author. However, if the student does the work of making the thesis a publishable manuscript, then they should be the first author. At that point, I also encourage students to be the corresponding author so that they gain that experience.

Co-authoring with doctoral students can be less straightforward. On one hand, we ask that their dissertations be their contribution to the academy. Some mentors believe that doctoral students should sole author publications as a signal that they can do research independently. On the other hand, most are working as research assistants on projects that provide ideas, data, and funds for the dissertation essays and, almost more important, for my students, constant and substantial feedback on their ideas, models, results, and writing.

In all cases where students have worked with me on a research idea but I was not their dissertation supervisor, those students have always been first authors on joint publications. I have always followed standard practice and my doctoral students have also always been first authors on all published articles that were based on their dissertations. However, in most cases I have also been a co-author. I have had a case or two when doctoral students I am mentoring wanted to be the sole author. However, these discussions were usually started by the students well into the draft process of the essay. For example, recently, the discussion came about as I noticed that they had started using "I" instead of "we" in the draft of the essay I was editing. It made me realize that I had taken for granted that the article would be co-authored as the article was based on my funded project, I had worked with the student on survey development, led the data collection process, and provided substantial feedback on data analysis and article drafts. Nevertheless, it reminded me that when two or more individuals are working on a manuscript, contributions to the manuscript should be detailed and authorship should be discussed at the beginning of the project.

7.7 Conclusion

Bellemare (2022a), in describing how to write a paper, notes that "the greatest sin an academic writer can commit is the sin of omission, which consists in leaving important information out of a paper." The second greatest sin an academic author can make is the sin of commission, which is actively engaging in unethical publication practices, such as Judd and Heckman. The goal of academic writing and the publishing process should not just be to publish an ethical manuscript but to ethically publish an ethical manuscript. A manuscript should be transparent about how the research it represents was conducted. And readers should be able to be confident that the published paper passed through the stages of impartial peer review and represents a unique and original piece of research.

Of course, the complications and complexities of the publishing process, exacerbated by the publish or perish imperative, can make ethical publishing difficult. There are strong incentives to engage in self-plagiarism, salami slicing, predatory publishing, specification search, or to use one's connections to help a paper through the review process.[6]

In terms of the life cycle of a research idea, most of the previous ethical issues arise in a private setting, where one is working alone at a computer or with a small group of collaborators. To this extent, the ethical issues facing the researcher are primarily personal. When one sets down the road to present or publish a paper, the research enters the public sphere, increasing both the risks and rewards of unethical behavior. When one tries to publish a paper one is seeking reward in the form of recognition and citations for one's work. But by making one's work public, one runs the risk of having their unethical deeds brought to light. One would hope that these benefits and costs balance in such a way as to incentivize ethical behavior. But as the examples throughout this chapter reveal, the field of applied economics often finds itself in a low-level equilibrium or completely off the equilibrium path. As we have stressed throughout this book, adhering to transparency in one's work and actions can help blunt incentives to sin by either omission or commission.

Notes

1 Frey and his coauthors were also accused of adapting ideas from a paper from a different author from 1986 without citing that paper. This would be the plagiarism of ideas, if they were aware of the paper at the time that they wrote their own.
2 Another identifier of a legitimate is a journal's membership in communities such as the Committee on Publication Ethics (COPE), or its presence in curated indexes such as Web of Science or being listed in the Directory of Open Access Journals.
3 This, of course, correspondingly limits the opportunity for revision that, in turn, limits the type of paper that is ultimately published through these mechanisms.
4 Although we should note that from our own experience *JAAEA* has yet to start imposing this strict word and exhibit length. A paper Jeff published in the first issue was almost 7,800 words and included six exhibits, not counting the 15 pages and seven exhibits in the online appendix.
5 The field journals Hadavand et al. (2021) consider are the *Journal of Development Economics*, the *Journal of Econometrics*, the *Journal of International Economics,* the *Journal of Labor Economics*, the *Journal of Monetary Economics*, and the *Journal of Public Economics*.
6 One issue, worth consideration, on which we do not touch in this chapter is whether the publishing process itself is ethical, given the existing economic and financial structures of publishing houses. For more about this, see the relevant discussions in Sent and Klamer (2002) and Gershman (2014).

8

DISSEMINATION BEYOND THE ACADEMY

8.1 Introduction

In the "first hundred days" of his presidency, Franklin D. Roosevelt introduced to Congress 15 major bills designed to stabilize an economy that Herbert Hoover's laissez-faire policies had left to wallow (Schlesinger Jr., 1958). Many of these pieces of legislation are well known to American high school students by their acronyms: Civilian Conservation Corp (CCC), Tennessee Valley Authority (TVA), Federal Emergency Relief Administration (FERA). But potentially the most important piece of legislation was an amendment tucked into the Agricultural Adjustment Act (AAA; Ahamed, 2009). And, among all the luminaries in Roosevelt's cabinet, potentially the most important advisor during this hectic time was an obscure agricultural economics professor at Cornell: George F. Warren.

The amendment to the AAA allowed Roosevelt to devalue the U.S. dollar relative to gold and print currency without gold backing, effectively giving the President the authority to take the country off of the gold standard. At the time, abandoning the gold standard was anathema among economists and politicians alike. Although the Great Depression had begun in 1929, in the intervening four years all of the major industrial powers had continued to tie the value of their currency to gold. The outcome of this policy was a vicious cycle in which demand for consumer goods was depressed, which caused consumer prices to fall, which raised the real cost of borrowing by firms, which resulted in firms reducing production of consumer goods, which caused prices to fall even further. As long as economies maintained the gold standard, the only way prices could rise again was as a result of increased economic activity. But the only way economic activity would increase was if prices first started to rise (Ahamed, 2009).

DOI: 10.4324/9781003025061-12

Cutting through this Gordian knot of macroeconomic theory was the applied work of George Warren on agricultural commodity prices. In his book *Wholesale Prices for 213 Years: 1720–1932*, Warren showed that far from being an immutable standard, gold prices, and, by extension, all other prices, fluctuated with discoveries of new gold deposits (Warren and Pearson, 1932). When new discoveries were made, this increased the supply of gold, which reduced the price of gold, which reduced the real cost of borrowing by firms, which resulted in firms increasing economic activity, which caused consumer prices to rise: a virtuous cycle. Thus, the way to restart economic activity was to raise the price of gold by devaluing the dollar.

Warren, who had advised Roosevelt on how to manage the then Governor's apple orchards at Hyde Park, was called to Washington D.C., to advise the now President on the heretical notion of abandoning the gold standard (Stanton, 2007). Over the protests of many in his cabinet, Roosevelt took the U.S. off the gold standard on 5 April 1933 (Schlesinger Jr., 1958). For the remainder of the year, Warren meet with Roosevelt for breakfast each morning to decide on what the price of gold should be for that day. Slowly the policy began to have an effect, with prices rising 10 percent in 1933. The virtuous cycle kicked in, and the recovery began to feed itself. By the end of Roosevelt's first term, industrial production had doubled and GDP rose by 40 percent (Ahamed, 2009). Warren made the cover of *Time* magazine in November 1933.

The consequences of one's research can be unexpected, far-reaching, and long-lasting. As an agricultural economist, whose work included monographs titled *Alfalfa*, *An Apple Orchard Survey of Wayne and Orleans County, New York* and *Dairy Farming*, it is unlikely Warren expected to end up setting gold prices with the President over breakfast. Once Roosevelt accepted Warren's policy recommendation about leaving the gold standard, there was a ripple effect, and by the end of 1933, all the major industrial powers had also abandoned the gold standard (Ahamed, 2009). While the gold exchange standard was reestablished at Bretton Woods after World War II, it only lasted until 1971, and the idea of a gold standard has not been part of mainstream economic, political, and policy discourse since then.

The story of George Warren demonstrates the breadth and depth of impacts that applied economists can have on government policy. While many of us hope that our work will affect policy and improve people's lives, few economists spend time studying the ways in which economic research gets turned into policy (Nelson, 1987). Few applied economists would seek to credibly estimate the impact of a change in policy on an economic indicator without having studied and read up on the most recent methods for causal identification. Thus, it is surprising the applied economists would seek to have their research impact policy without first coming to an understanding of the "mechanisms by which economic writings and research are translated into public policy results" (Nelson, 1987).

One must also consider that the trajectory of the impact of one's work may occur in ways beyond our control and outside our influence. As a researcher looking to influence policy, it is important to evaluate how the findings from one's research could be used by others. While researchers do not have complete control over how others might use their work, researcher can work to frame the conversation about their work through carefully considered communication. In particular, researchers should consider the various audiences that might engage with the work, the appropriate format for communicating to that audience, and the specific content of that communication.

In this process, a researcher is inherently considering the potential *impact* of their work. The word impact can mean different things to different groups of people, particularly people in different positions or types of work. For academic economists, impact can be not only the effect estimated in their paper but also the citations that the paper gets and, somewhere down the road, a change in policy. For a government economist or an economist at a think tank or lobbying firm, impact is likely to mean a change in policy resulting from direct contact with government decision-makers. For agricultural extension specialists, impact may be providing actionable answers to a farmer's question about which risk management tools to adopt. In each of these cases, what impact means and how impact is achieved is a function of the audience one is trying to reach.

In this chapter, we start by discussing communication as an art form, one that benefits from inherent skill but still requires deliberate practice. We detail how effective communication arises from considering audience, genre, and composition. Next we discuss the role of the media in dissemination of research beyond the academy and a number of ethical considerations which arise when working with the media. We then delve into the relationship between research and policy, including different models of how this relationship can work. We complete the chapter by discussing the rapidly changing environment of research discussion, including some thoughts on social media platforms.

8.2   The Art of Communication

Communication is often referred to as an art, suggesting a process of creation and development of a final product that is cultivated through imagination and skill, rather than following a formula or through rote memorization and implementation. But claiming that communication is an art does not mean that it simply requires inspiration and talent. It also requires deliberate practice to train and hone one's skill.

The author Annie Dillard, in her book *The Writing Life*, describes the moment of inspiration in an vision of her Smith-Corona typewriter erupting, the keys becoming a smoking caldera sending sparks throughout the house (Dillard, 1989). The vision provides the impression of inspiration as a dangerous event that can catch the author unaware and easily overwhelm them. Elsewhere in *The Writing Life*,

Dillard describes finishing a book in a cabin heated only by a wood-burning stove. The cabin lacked wood split to the right size for the stove, and she was so cold she could not write. In what is an extended metaphor for the writing process, Dillard describes learning to split wood to heat the stove. The initial failures followed by days of repetition that keeps her warm while outside. Eventually, through practice, she learns how to split wood ("aim past the wood, aim through the wood; aim for the chopping block"), allowing her to split enough wood to heat the cabin and finish the book.

In a different context, James Humes, speechwriter for five presidents, also emphasized that communication is an art - more than just an inherent skill, requiring attention and practice. Humes is best known as the author of the plaque left on the moon by the Apollo 11 astronauts. "Here men from the planet Earth first set foot upon the Moon July 1969, A.D. We came in peace for all mankind." A simple and clear sentence derived from NASA's declaration of policy and purpose. Humes believed that "the art of communication is the language of leadership" and that mastering effective communication is essential to being a good leader. He underscored that communicating is more than simply exchanging information. It involves synthesis and clarification in order to influence others to change how they think and act.

While much of one's time as a researcher is spent writing, few of us became applied economists because we wanted to be writers. Through simple practice – splitting wood – most of us learn to become competent academic writers. Still, developing one's skill and ability in communication outside of academia comes as a challenge to many academics, if for no other reason than that we simply lack practice. Despite this challenge, there are numerous reasons why a researcher should put in the necessary effort to effectively communicate research beyond the academy. Some researchers may need to as part of their formal job description. Others may believe that the research they do should reach a broader audience. Others may be contacted by a journalist, seeking their expertise. It may be the requirement of a grant, particularly taxpayer-funded grants. Or, a researcher may simply be self-interested and hoping to raise their profile. Regardless of the precise reason, the overall objective is similar: the desire to reach and influence non-academics with ones research.

Learning the art of effective communication requires three things: (1) reading a lot, (2) writing a lot, and (3) revising a lot. As numerous books on writing point out, being a good reader is a key input in to being a good writer. One does not need to exclusively read master prose stylists, like Joseph Conrad or Virginia Woolf. Rather, one just needs to read a lot, both the good and the bad, and be a good reader, paying attention to what makes some writing good and other writing bad. Having learned what works and what does not work by reading, one then needs to write a lot. Every day is ideal; or, as Pliny the Elder put it: *nulla dies sine linea*. The goal should be to get words on a page, to follow the unfurling of one's thoughts wherever they go. One need not worry about quality in the preliminary stages. It is later, once words are written on a page during the final, and most time consuming step, that quality should be considered, during the process of rewriting and revising. This is probably the most difficult for people, since few of us are taught the craft of revision in school.[1]

Learning to communicate well is an ethical imperative for researchers, maybe as important as learning how to correctly analyze data. Ineffective communication can lead to results being misunderstood, recommendations being misapplied, and research dollars being misspent. A well executed but poorly communicated research idea is wasteful and inefficient, leaving the scientific records, and possibly the world, needlessly impoverished. Beyond learning how to communicate well, selecting how one communicates is key to being effective in getting one's ideas across. The selection of the how involves deciding upon three things: one's audience, one's genre, and one's composition.

8.2.1 Identifying an Audience

When engaged in the process of doing research it can be easy to forget that we are doing this work for someone other than ourselves. Even when it comes time to write a paper based on the research, it is often a safe assumption that the audience is someone much like oneself. But, as one prepares to communicate applied economic research outside of academic journals, considering who one's audience will be is critical. As Doherty (2022) observes, identifying and understanding to whom we are addressing our work can help to dictate not just how (genre) but also what (composition) we communicate.

When looking to communicate one's research outside of an academic setting, the first step is to determine *who* the audience actually is. For applied economists, there are several potential audiences with whom we may interact. Of course, other researchers are likely chief among our "typical" audience. Beyond the academy, audiences for applied economics work may include various bodies in local, state, or federal governments; stakeholders, including research participants; members of industry; people working in the media; or even the public at large. Some work may have more than one audience.

Once the audience for the work has been determined, the next step is to determine how to frame what one plans to communicate. Consider the metaphor used by Daniel Kahneman and Amos Tversky (1981) in their classic study of framing effects on decision-making:

> If while traveling in a mountain range you notice that the apparent relative height of mountain peaks varies with your vantage point, you will conclude that some impressions of relative height must be erroneous, even when you have no access to the correct answer. Similarly, one may discover that the relative attractiveness of options varies when the same decision problem is framed in different ways. . . . The susceptibility to perspective effects is of special concern

in the domain of decision-making because of the absence of objective standards such as the true height of mountains.

Just as Kahneman and Tversky were concerned about framing in decisionmaking, the goal of researchers in disseminating their work outside of academia is to influence the decision-making of their audience. Thus, understanding how an audience responds to different ways of framing the research is important to effectively influence the audience.

The process of framing the research for an audience involves deconstructing the information in the research into facts, concepts, and morals (Searing and Searing, 2016b). Facts are things that can be, but might not currently be, objectively known and incontrovertible. The amount of carbon that humans put into the atmosphere last year is a fact, as is the amount of carbon humans will put into the atmosphere ten years from now. The former is objectively known now and will remain so ten years from now. The later is not at this time objectively known but will be ten years from now. Concepts are definitions of an idea or issue, the specificity of which depends on the context and audience. The definition of value as "something of worth" may be sufficient in many contexts while in other contexts a more specific definition, such as value as "the price of something," may be required. Morals are strongly held beliefs about what ought to or should be done. Within and across different contexts there can be both intra-moral conflict as well as inter-moral conflict. Intra-moral conflict would be a disagreement about the amount of money to be spent on public education. Inter-moral conflict would be a disagreement about whether funds are better spent achieving equitable educational outcomes or improving efficiency in educational outcomes.

One might like to think of facts, concepts, and morals as objects that lack ambiguity. But, as the Kahneman and Tversky metaphor shows, what qualifies as each of these is context- and audience-dependent. In their edited volume, Searing and Searing (2016a) provide a "workbook" to help economists and those in public policy to frame their research in terms of facts, concepts, and morals. The workbook provides a structure for defining what is a fact for the audience under consideration and what might be factual issues for said audience – such as the uncertainty about future carbon emissions. A similar structure is applied to defining the concepts most pertinent to the research as well as identifying what concepts may be unfamiliar to the audience and what definitions the audience might disagree on. Finally, the workbook provides a structure for clarifying that moral considerations are likely to be present in the audience and how intra- and inter-moral conflict will influence how the audience reacts to the research.

In deciding on how to frame one's research for an audience, and what are the factual, conceptual, and moral issues, it can be helpful to answer the following questions:

1. Who is this work for?
2. What does the audience need? What do they want?

3. What does the audience already know about the subject of the work?
4. What is important to the audience – and what is not important?
5. What should the audience learn or think after engaging with the work?

Deciding on an audience is just the first step in becoming an effective communicator of one's research outside of the academy. Having settled on an audience, the next step is to frame one's research for that audience. Framing is important because it sets the terms or boundaries for how an audience receives the research and, ultimately, how they use the research. Clarifying what the factual, conceptual, and moral issue will be for the audience will help the researcher guide the audience on how to understand, interpret, and use the research. Knowing the audience and how to frame the research allows one to think about and select the most appropriate genre for presenting the work.

8.2.2   Selecting a Genre

As academic researchers, most of the writing we do is in the genre of an academic applied economics paper. This genre has a fairly strict structure: introduction, theoretical framework, data, empirical framework, results, conclusion. It also has a well-known tone or authorial voice: formal, first-person plural, present simple tense. But, when looking to communicate to an audience outside of the research community, it is important to be able to share research in a variety of different ways. This involves selecting the appropriate genre for the audience one is communicating with (Doherty, 2022).

What format is most appropriate to use is audience and context dependent. It might be a presentation, infographic, policy brief, blog post, radio interview, podcast, or some other format altogether. What is important is that the information comes to the audience with a structure and in a tone with which they are familiar and comfortable. The ability to write a good policy brief or create a good infographic or generate a helpful presentation is not easy – although researchers often think that if they can write a whole research paper, then *obviously* they can easily master these other genres. But, as with any type of writing, mastering other forms is an art that requires talent along with practice and time to cultivate and develop. As Oliver (2010) observes that it is not easy to go from one style and format to another while preserving fidelity to the original academic work.

The U.S. Department of Agriculture (USDA) Economic Research Service (ERS) has a tremendous set of various formats which speak to a wide spectrum of audiences at a variety of levels of detail (composition). This is part of their mission: ERS shapes its research and outputs to serve those who make or influence public policy and program decisions, including the White House, USDA policy officials, the U.S. Congress, other federal agencies, state governments, local officials, and industry groups. In addition to a set of data products, ERS publishes online research reports, pieces in its magazine *Amber Waves*, and data visualizations.

Consider two examples from ERS. Both were published as part of *Amber Waves*: Whitt et al. (2022) is a written brief, and Zeng and Dong (2022) is an infographic. Both pieces are drawn from larger, more academic-style research papers by the authors – but the material has been reframed into a different genre so as to better communicate the information to a specific audience. Whitt et al. (2022) present information about financial health indicators for family farms and how these farms weathered the COVID-19 pandemic. In about 12 paragraphs, supplemented by five images, the authors share a set of statistics and indicators on this topic.

The text and accompanying image in Table 8.1 demonstrates several characteristics of a good brief. First, it defines a concept (operating profit margin) that might be unfamiliar to the audience. It contextualizes this term before discussing how many small family farms earn no profit while midsize and large farms tend to earn a profit. Facts relevant to the overall topic, the size of family farms earning a profit in 2020, is presented in the remainder of the paragraph. In these sentences, the authors include additional details that provide greater context in order to help the reader better understand the main facts. In this case, that means comparing the 2020 statistics, which represent information during the very abnormal period of COVID-19, with 2011, a somewhat "normal" year. This information is illustrated with a graphic (see Table 8.1) and expanded on in a subsequent paragraph (not presented here). The entire text of the piece is available through the ERS and is worth a read, as a strong example of effective communication of technical information in a different genre.

Turning to Zeng and Dong (2022), the authors extrapolated away from the text of their more academic paper and instead created an infographic to present information on the U.S. soybean agricultural trade multiplier in 2020. We present the entire infographic here in Figure 8.1. While the infographic contains some text, it is largely numbers and images. As appropriate, definitions of concepts are provided; consider the description of the multiplier effect that appears near the bottom center of the graphic. But the concepts and facts are presented in an even more concise way than those in Whitt et al. (2022). While some information is lost to the necessary consolidated composition of the infographic genre, it distills the important points on a topic to a single image that is easily digestible by the audience. Researchers often express concern over loss of information in changing the genre in which they present their research output, but in fact, it is not so much as loss as it is adapting to the needs of the audience. That is not to say such translation is easy – frankly, it can be quite difficult.

Both Whitt et al. (2022) and Zeng and Dong (2022) are good examples of how to communicate complex information in different genres. This takes skill and practice and patience – and attention to the audience which is likely to interact with that information. Relatability and clarity are key. To some extent, this is achievable

TABLE 8.1 Data Visualization with Text and Graphic from Whitt et al. (2022)

Small family farms were most likely to have an operating profit margin (OPM) that indicated higher risk of financial problems from 2011 to 2020

Percent of farms with OPM of less than 10 percent (high risk)

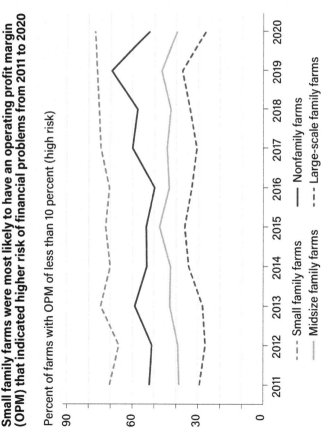

Small family farms ---
Midsize family farms ——
Nonfamily farms ——
Large-scale family farms ---

Operating profit margin – the share of gross income that is profit – is one way to gauge a farm's financial performance. Many small family farms do not earn a profit and even lose money farming (42 percent in 2020 and 39 percent in 2011). In contrast, most midsize and large-scale family farms earned a profit. In 2020, 83 percent of midsize family farms earned a profit compared with 82 percent in 2011. For the large-scale family farm category, 88 percent earned a profit in 2020, compared with 85 percent in 2011. However, most small family farms earn gross income from farming (94 percent in 2020 and 96 percent in 2011), and nearly 100 percent of midsize and largescale family farms earned gross income from farming in 2020 and 2011.

Notes: **Operating profit margin (OPM)** = 100 times (net farm income plus interest paid minus charges for unpaid labor and management) divided by gross farm income. OPM ratios are not calculated for operations with zero gross farm income. **Family farms** are farms in which the principal operator and their relatives (by blood or marriage) owned more than half the business's assets. **Small family farms** have gross cash farm income (GCFI) of less than $350,000. **Midsize family farms** have GCFI between $350,000 and $999,999. **Large-scale family farms** have GCFI of $1 million or more. **Nonfamily farms** are farms in which the principal operator and people related to the principal operator do not own a majority of the business. The principal operator is the person who makes day-to-day operating decisions for the farm.

Source: USDA, National Agricultural Statistics Service, and USDA, Economic Research Service, 2011–2020 Agricultural Resource Management Survey.

FIGURE 8.1 Infographic on the US Soybean Agricultural Trade Multiplier by Zeng and Dong (2022)

Note: Infographic by Zeng and Dong (2022), drawn from information from the Agricultural Trade Multipliers data product of the Economic Research Service.

simply by taking the time to ensure that what is being presented is truly *for* that audience – not just repurposed and repackaged to achieve some goal or mandate of the researcher. As Bellemare (2022a) writes, researchers should talk *with* others, not *at* them.

8.2.3 Defining the Composition

Researchers have a ethical responsibility to clearly and effectively communicate their work. Kara (2018) points out that "as a presenter of research, you have a great deal of power; perhaps more than you realize. As always, power brings with it ethical responsibility." As researchers it is in our power to decide who we share our research with (audience), how we frame that research (genre), and what parts of the research we share (composition).

Researchers looking to be effective communicators need to ensure that their work is understandable and interpretable to a broader, nonacademic audience. This means crafting a message appropriate for the audience that contains content that is useful, understandable, and digestible to the audience in a form that is accessible to the audience. This must be done carefully since "your presentation may conceal as well as reveal" (Kara, 2018).

When one thinks about the process of composition, one typically thinks about a composer or, maybe, more generally, any writer or painter, sitting down to their work writing or painting. Composition, after all, refers to the individual's decisions about and processes for creating the final product as well as the final product itself. Yet, having identified the audience and selected the genre, defining the composition is more frequently a process of revision than of putting new thoughts down into words. When it comes time to disseminate one's research to a nonacademic audience, one typically already has an academic article or some other technical document that contains all the details and results. One then only needs to revise this material so that it speaks to one's identified audience and conforms to one's selected genre.

In his book, *The Craft of Revision*, Donald Murray (2012) provides a useful guide on how to revise and rewrite one's work with a purpose. Revision is not just editing but the judicious, purposeful, and deliberate subtraction and addition to an existing text. Murray (2012) organizes his book around a set of goals a writer wants to achieve in the revision process. These include rewriting with focus, with documentation, and to develop.

Rewriting with focus involves selection, emphasis, and clarity. A presentation, infographic, policy brief, blog post, radio interview, podcast, or whatever genre one is communicating in will almost always need to be shorter and more concise than the original, more technical research paper. Thus, the process of composition is frequently a process of reduction and censorship; it involves eliminating the unnecessary in order to focus on the one central idea that one is trying to communicate. The maxim "say one thing" is the rule for rewriting with focus.

The goal of rewriting with documentation is to ensure that, for whatever one is working on, the piece satisfies the audience's desire for concrete details. This involves the selection of facts that are accurate, specific, significant, and fair. Rewriting for accuracy and specificity is not just ensuring the numbers are correct and labeled but that they are presented in a way that is honest and true. Recall the number of different ways Huff (1954) could "lie with statistics" through simply adjusting the presentation of a statistic or how it is labeled. Rewriting for significance addresses the issues raise in Ziliak and McCloskey (2008). Are the facts that one is presenting not just statistically significant but also economically significant? Rewriting for fairness requires being cognizant that as the author one gets to choose what to reveal and what to conceal (Kara, 2018). Being fair in what information gets cut and what stays in is an important ethical decision when revising research for dissemination in an new genre.

Rewriting for development addresses the tendency of academic researchers to make the mistake in thinking that communicating with audiences outside academia requires making the research superficial. Since the audience is not academic and frequently unfamiliar and uninterested in the technical aspects of research, it is all too easy to fall into the trap of making one's nonacademic work shallow and cursory. The techniques of development combat this issue by encouraging one to rewrite and to develop with information, with authority, and with clarity. Do not just provide a statistic but lead the audience to an understanding of why the information is important. This involves speaking or writing with authority but also with clarity so that one does not come across as condescending. Key to achieving this goal is to put meaning in context.

In their workbook for ethically framing research, Searing and Searing (2016a) provide a structure for verifying that one has achieved one's goals during the process of revision. This involves visualizing how one's research will be received by the audience who reads or listens to the research being communicated. The first is visualizing what it would be like to be in the audience receiving this information. Would one be shocked? Angry? Enlightened? Confused? Searing and Searing (2016c) call this "expected reciprocity analysis." The second visualization is to imagine the headline an audience member might write to describe the research. As the researcher, would one be happy with this headline? Proud of how one's research is being reframed? Or embarrassed if one's friends or acquaintances saw the headline? Searing and Searing (2016c) call this *"New York Times* analysis." The final visualization is to imagine how you, the researcher, will feel after sharing the research. Will one be proud of the work? How will this impact one's professional standing? Searing and Searing (2016c) call this "self-appraisal analysis."

Communicating one's research beyond the academy is an art, and becoming a better artist requires dedication and practice. Identifying an audience, selecting a genre, and defining the composition are all steps to becoming a better communicator. Like Annie Dillard splitting wood, it takes time to master each of these steps. Deciding to be an effective communicator is not just a useful skill for improving one's professional career, it is also an ethical decision. As the authority on one's own work, the researcher is in a position of power and gets to decide how to frame the research and what to reveal and conceal. Making those decisions with an eye on how the research will be received and used by an audience is an ethical imperative.

8.3 Working with the Media

For many economists, communicating with a journalists is the most efficient way to amplify one's research and/or share one's expertise. While numerous forms of communication have emerged over the last 20 years, journalists working in print, radio, television, and new media still have incredible reach in getting a message out to the public. One can spend hours in meetings with stakeholders and government officials and still not have the same impact on policy as one well-timed interview. Taking advantage of opportunities to disseminate work through new and traditional media can be a rewarding experience for researchers (Baron, 2010). Because of this, working with the media is an important part of disseminating one's research beyond the academy.

However, there are risks to trying to get one's research picked up by or communicating as an expert with a news outlet. Once one's work is out in the public eye, the researcher no longer has control of the narrative. And this can have potential negative implications. There are several ways that the composition of one's research, and the conclusions one would want a reader to draw from it, could be adapted and altered for a broader audience. First, one's work or knowledge could be distorted or exaggerated in a way that, to most academic researchers, would appear clearly unethical. Second, one's work or knowledge could be adapted or expanded upon in a way that places the research in a new context or repackages it for a new audience, which the researcher may feel is inappropriate but may not be obviously unethical.

Distortion, exaggeration, or other misuses of one's work is, for many researchers, at the front of their mind as they consider disseminating work or speaking with the media. Consider, from Huff (1954):

> The distortion of statistical data and its manipulation to an end are not always the work of professional statisticians. What comes full of virtue from the statistician's desk may find itself twisted, exaggerated, oversimplified, and distorted-through-selection by salesman, public-relations expert, journalist, or advertising copywriter.

This quote lays the blame at the feet of the user of the statistic. However, as discussed in the previous section, it is the responsibility of the researcher to ensure that research is presented in a genre and with a composition that fits the audience.

The fierce debate surrounding the replication of Edward Miguel and Michael Kremer famous deworming study (Miguel and Kremer, 2004) is an example of exaggerated differences created, primarily, by journalists. As part of their work on research transparency, the research group International Initiative for Impact Evaluation (3ie) funded a series of replication or reanalysis studies. One of theses focused on the original Miguel and Kremer study. In their re-analysis, Davey et al. (2015) find that "the original data provide some evidence, with a high risk of bias, that a school-based drug treatment and health-education intervention improved school attendance, and no evidence of effect on examination performance." They also found that "the effects on school attendance varied according to format of analysis." The replicators did not claim to have found major issues in replicating the original findings, only that there were ways to analyze the data such that one could make the main results of Miguel and Kremer (2004) go away. As Chris Blattman (2015) writes in his blog post about the replication, "to be quite frank, you have to throw so much crazy sh*t at Miguel-Kremer to make the result go away that I believe the result even more than when I started."

Blattman's reading of the replication was fairly representative of the reaction of economists, as demonstrated in two long blog posts summarizing differing views of the replication (Evans, 2015; Özler, 2015). However, the coverage of the replication and its results by the news media was quite different. The headline in *The Guardian* was "New Research Debunks Merits of Global Deworming Programmes" (Boseley, 2015). In coverage by BuzzFeed News, science writer Ben Goldacre highlighted "major flaws" in the original research and claimed that the different results presented by (Davey et al. (2015) using different methods was "definitely problematic" (Goldacre, 2015). Coverage by Vox, which framed the story as how "some of the results fell apart" under reanalysis, mentioned five times that deworming pills do not improve school or exam performance (Belluz, 2015). This is a claim never made in Miguel and Kremer (2004), the last line of whose abstract reads: "we do not find evidence that deworming improved academic test scores."

In addition to distortion or exaggeration in media coverage, one may wonder: What if my work is misused by others? Ziliak and McCloskey (2008) ask researchers to consider the potential negative impacts their research might have. Even if a researcher does not intend for their work to be used for policy – or used in a certain way – it may still be used in that exact way. And so, it is all the more important that work be clear and not exaggerated so that distortions from future use by those outside of the research community are mitigated.

In a world where misinformation runs rampant, it is necessary that we, as researchers, have done all that we can to ensure that our work is correctly represented. While not the goal of the art of communication, making sure that one's work is correctly represented is surely a necessary condition to influence policy in the way one intends. Misinformation can arise for any number of reasons, be they willful, accidental, based on ignorance or in partisanship, or just simple care-lessness. Misinformation is often drawn out of misrepresentations, sometimes of flawed research, but other times using work out of context, stretching or distorting findings, or altogether rejecting or ignoring findings. While the onus of accurately representing research is on the individual using that work, it behooves researchers to view enabling the translation of findings to policy and action as their ethical-lyrooted responsibility.

Beyond distortion or exaggeration, which researchers can take steps to mitigate, another concern among academics considering dissemination of research is the repurposing or repackaging of that research for a new audience. In a piece in the *Chronicle of Higher Education*, Doherty (2022) describes the case of a book about the role of recently freed Black women in the American labor movement, written by the journalist Kim Kelly (2022) and published by an imprint of Simon & Schuster. An excerpt of the book, printed in *The Washington Post*, described research by Tera Hunter, Edwards Professor of American History and Professor of History and African American Studies at Princeton University. In the *Post* excerpt, Hunter was not cited or quoted, seemingly because attributions to her work were eliminated during the editing process (Doherty, 2022). This incident instigated discussion among academics, provoking the question among some: Why would a journalist be writing this particular book when an academic had already published several books on the topic? This discussion evolved to include a debate about whether a staff writer for *The New Yorker* was appropriately qualified to review an academic book on the restitution of African art (Doherty, 2022).

The incident reflected the fear among academics that their research would be co-opted by journalists and popular-press authors in ways that the original re-searchers might not be comfortable with. This fear was combined with the worry that academics might not receive sufficient recognition for their work. The *Post*'s removal of direct reference to Hunter's work, plus the title of Kelly's book, *Fight Like Hell: The Untold History of American Labor*, reaffirmed these fears. After all, the original research had been done by Hunter, not Kelly, and Hunter had in fact told the history of freed Black women in the American labor movement in two dif-ferent books published by academic presses (Hunter, 1998, 2006).

Kelly's book and the response of academics to it evince a conflicted under-standing of expertise. In the academy, expertise typically is defined as "extensive knowledge of a particular field of study," which is credentialed through the con-ferring of degrees (Doherty, 2022). As academics ourselves, it is easy to give pri-ority to this definition of expertise. Yet, expertise can exist in other forms beyond scholarly knowledge of a subject. Effective communication is an art, an art that requires practice to cultivate and develop – to become an expert in. And, while it is important that scholarly expertise be appropriately attributed, this does not preclude journalists or others, with expertise in communicating technical ideas to a lay audience.

Publishing by a journalist for a wider audience can *feel* redundant to an academic when, in fact, the shift in the central idea and the change in presentation is a creative endeavor that itself requires expertise. Doherty (2022), a professor and a journalist, addresses this head on:

> But a title like "untold story" isn't merely a marketing gimmick: It also reflects the existing knowledge and expectations of a book's audience. Many readers outside the academy may be unacquainted with ideas that are considered well known in academic circles. While some of those readers might seek out scholarship on their own, many more of them will have their interest piqued by a trade book or a magazine article that refers to that scholarship. In some sense, then, journalists and critics are on the same team as academics: The former are helping spread the latter's ideas beyond the academy's walls.

There is art in the process of communication and as academics we should recognize the expertise that journalists and professional writers have in this area. Working together to accurately convey complicated concepts to a broad audience can have substantial impact, not just on the careers of those involved in the work but on the public at large. One just needs to think of the success of *Freakonomics* (Levitt and Dubner, 2005) or *The Book of Why* (Pearl and Mackenzie, 2018), both co-authored by an academic and a professional writer.

The preceding two stories, *Worm Wars* and *Fight Like Hell*, address two different concerns academics have about working with the media: distortion and re-purposing of research. And the two stories, as presented, appear to lead to two different conclusions. The lesson from the exaggeration around the deworming study seems to imply caution or demurral when approached by journalists. By contrast, the lesson from the repackaging of research for a new audience seems to be that academics should welcome the opportunity to work with journalists. Both lessons are important when it comes time to disseminate one's research to a broader audience. One should be cautious, because the narrative can be bent and distorted.

It is worth noting that both of these cases are rare. In most scenarios, researchers papers are not just "picked up," but rather, researchers are contacted by a person from the media who is interested in an expert opinion, which is built from the work of that researcher. While these rare cases may caution researchers, there are real opportunities for fruitful collaboration. And, importantly, the operative word here is collaboration: co-production of new media that speaks to an audience in a genre and with a composition that they understand. This collaboration can sometimes mean co-authoring a piece with a writer, but more often means sitting down with a journalist to provide background, context, expertise, and detail to help the journalist produce an accurate and thoughtful piece of reporting. To facilitate the learning of this skill, most professional associations provide trainings, both to academics and to members of the media.

Just (2017), in a presentation at an early-career mentoring workshop sponsored by the Agricultural and Applied Economics Association (AAEA), provides tips for becoming a effective communicator of one's research to nonacademic:

1. Decline requests, if necessary. Say "no" or "I don't know," if it is the right response!
2. Ask for time to prepare, if needed.
3. Stay on message.
4. Stay simple.
5. The person from the media will share when he or she is recording.
6. A department, college, or university press office can be an asset.

Most of these points are clear and simple and require no elaboration. However, it bears reiterating that researchers have the discretion to engage with whomever they wish. Journalists have their own code of professional ethics, which, generally, are aligned with researchers' ethics as well. However, unscrupulous or biased media sources are increasingly of concern around the globe. If a researcher feels uncomfortable talking to a journalist – for whatever reason – one can simply decline. Like anytime someone says "no," it is a complete sentence: no justification, explanation, or reason is required. While academics can play an important role in making the news less biased, it is important for researchers speaking with the media to also consider the motivations of the journalist – and to ensure that the ethics and objectives of both parties are aligned.

Most universities or agencies that employ economists have communications departments which can assist researchers in communicating with the media. Communications offices can be a tremendous asset. At our current university, we have both a college press liaison and an Office of University Communications. Where we did our PhD, the department was large enough that it had its own communications specialist. These offices provide trainings for communicating with the media, resources that help researchers to prepare for interviews, and can connect researchers with media sources and journalists and vise versa. In recent years, these offices have taken on a greater role in framing and directing how researchers communicate with the media. While they can be helpful in training researchers, the mission of all these offices is to advance the reputation and priorities of the unit that it represents. The increasing importance of managed and branded communication suggests a shift in the incentives of universities and other research institutions. Coverage from the press may lead to benefits for the institution, which drive them to encourage researchers to obtain more coverage. While there are merits to this, it may divert researchers away from their first essential work: the research itself. There could also be pressure to encourage researchers individually or as units to shift their research topics, encouraging people to chase more "interesting" topics which are "trendy" or "worth covering."

As incentives change, researchers may observe benefits beyond simply seeing their research disseminated to interested parties. There may be career benefits, in which one finds themselves elevated or otherwise receiving praise for these interactions. This is perhaps not unexpected. Particularly in colleges of agriculture, in which many applied economists work. Expertise across the college varies dramatically and so it might be easiest for a dean who has a PhD in plant science, for example, to best understand the work of an applied economist when is it presented to them on the evening news. There are also benefits to this sort of recognition at the field level. The AAEA has a weekly "Members in the News" message, which is disseminated to the membership. This has the role of raising the profile researchers whose work is having an impact beyond the academy. But it also encourages researchers to court media attention by realigning their research to better comport with what might interest the media.

It is not unethical for an individual researcher to change their research interests or time allocation in order to take on a larger role in communicating their work and expertise with the media. But, there is an ethical consideration here: As a profession, do we want career advancement and reward to be based on interactions with the media? Do we want to judge research based on the ability to generate news? After all, before (and after) his downfall and dismissal from Cornell, Brian Wansink generated quite a bit of media attention.

Of course, researchers seeking to disseminate their work or expertise hardly think that they will be or become Brian Wansink (nor should they). Instead, in communicating with the media, consider advice from Kamau (2019): "your work as a scientist is important. Media coverage of your research is not just a lark – it is a valuable way to conduct outreach, which in turn can help you to make a real, measurable difference in the world." In communicating with the media, work to continue to present the appropriate genre, audience, and composition for one's work and strive to share one's findings and expertise appropriately and ethically.

8.4   The Research and Policy Relationship

Some of the objective of speaking with the media – or communicating beyond the academy at all – is to ensure that our work has an impact on the lives of people.

PERSPECTIVE 8.1   MAXIMIZING IMPACT THROUGH THE NEWS MEDIA BY DAVID L. ORTEGA

Engaging with the news media can raise awareness of one's research and expertise and provides an opportunity to inform and educate the public. Agricultural and food economists played a vital role in helping consumers make sense of the pandemic-related supply chain disruptions that affected the agri-food sector. The pandemic disruptions and subsequent inflationary period have made individuals start paying attention to where their food comes from, how agricultural and food supply chains work, and realize the interconnectedness of global agricultural and food markets.

As academics, many of us are accustomed to sharing our knowledge in the college classroom and to one another, but there is a broader audience yearning for information. The news media can allow our insights and research to reach individuals outside our institutions and professional organizations. Beyond good communication skills, engaging with the media requires understanding each other's goals and comparative advantage. Academics are often looking for ways to disseminate information, and news outlets are looking for credible sources of information. The alignment of these two interests can result in the effective dissemination of information and credible reporting. While research papers and studies are sometimes featured in the media, many of the interactions are about analyzing or providing insights into current events. Having a rich knowledge base and expertise is essential and improves the quality of communication by establishing credibility.

But simply having relevant expertise is not enough. Understanding and communicating with one's audience in a relatable and effective way are sometimes equally important. This type of communication is very different from how applied economists engage with an academic audience. Unlike academic lectures that are often filled with discussions of model specifications, issues of identification, and robustness checks, journalists are interested in big-picture analysis that they can incorporate into their reporting. Not all interviews lead to a media appearance. An academic that can meaningfully describe or explain a topic or share insights into a current event is much more likely to be featured than one who spends their time talking to a reporter about the precision or significance of a point estimate.

While institutions or organizations can help communicate one's research through press releases or feature stories, other outreach efforts like social media and blog posts can help get a scholar's work noticed. These outlets often force academics to distill complex analysis and information into more relatable terms. Working with journalists or reporters can take on many forms, from a quick email exchange to recorded and live TV interviews; the type and level of preparation needed will vary accordingly. The media environment is fast-paced and engaging with reporters often requires quick turnarounds given their tight deadlines. Referring colleagues when one is unable to meet a specific deadline or when a request falls outside one's area of expertise can help foster media engagements.

Working with the media can be very rewarding. Interactions with reporters can provide unique insights into specific topics and even spark new research ideas.

When applied economists talk about "impact" they typically mean the causal effect of X on Y. But, the actual "impact" of our work is far wider – ranging from the impact on other researchers in the field to impact on policy. Among researchers in the social sciences, there is the perception that economists have an enormous (some say disproportionate) impact on policy (Hirschman and Berman, 2014). Despite this, Robert H. Nelson (1987) a longtime government economist, notes that few economists spend time learning how policy decisions are actually made or how to more effectively influence policymakers. Hirschman and Berman (2014) observe that economists are often ineffective at actually effectively influencing policy. In Nelson (2016), the author reflects that little has changed in the last 30 years. Presuming that economic research should influence policy, by making policy better or more effective, it is then an ethical question to ask, "[W]hat must be accomplished for economists and economics to have policy effects?" (Hirschman and Berman, 2014).

Traditionally, economic researchers have taken a laissez-faire approach to how research shapes policy (Nelson, 1987). Many simply think "knowledge shapes policy" and leave it at that. Boswell and Smith (2017) note that "notions of 'impact', 'engagement' and 'knowledge exchange' are typically premised on simplistic, linear models of the policy process, according to which policymakers are keen to 'utilize' expertise to produce more 'effective' policies." As an alternative to this laissez-faire approach, Boswell and Smith (2017) propose several different models of the relationship between research and policy. Figure 8.2 is a simplified visual representations these four models.

The first model of research to policy interaction is the typically linear, supply-driven, academic perspective: research impacts policy. Research can lead to adjustments in policy through a diffuse and incremental process, one that is almost inactive for any single researcher. The second interaction is a demand-driven model, in which potential policy (and often related politics) shape the creation of

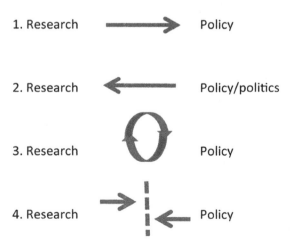

FIGURE 8.2   Research and Policy Interactions

Note: Figure provides a simple representation of four ways for modeling the relationship between research and policy. From Boswell and Smith (2017) under CC BY 4.0 International.

knowledge and its ultimate use, similar to what was discussed in Chapter 2. The third model is one of coproduction, designed as a feedback loop between research and policy. The fourth and final model is one of autonomy, in which impact is achieved through only the selective observation of signals between those interested in creating research and those interested in making policy.

In the following subsections, we connect the first three of these research and policy models to different careers and thus different perspectives on these interactions. For the first model, we consider the academic economist, employed by a university. For the second model, we consider the government economist or one working at a think tank. For the third model, we consider economists, often academic economists, working in Cooperative Extension. We use this framing because different jobs held by applied economists effectively designate different objective functions, dependent on those jobs. While we can assume that all economists are rational, utility-maximizing individuals, who (for the sake of this discussion) are seeking to increase their "impact" in the field, what that impact is, and how it weighs into an objective function, varies based on one's job. For an academic economist, it may be based on reads and citations, while for a government economist, it may be based on policies influenced. Either are valid models with respect to the specific objective function. We are all seeking impact with our work – but how it is achieved and how it is measured is likely to vary.

Regardless of which model for research and policy one works with, it is important to keep in mind the warning from Boswell and Smith (2017):

> The highest impact research is that which serves to re-shape the social world it seeks to describe. This implies that models to promote engagement with knowledge users need to be attentive not just to the complex pathways to research impact, but also to the very real ethical implications of research influence. . . . Not only can the impact agenda affect the practices of social science, as is widely recognized in social science literature; social science can also instigate new policy problems. Proponents of policy impact should have a care what they wish for.

Regardless of which job one holds in the profession, as one seeks to shape and reshape the surrounding world with one's research, one must be considerate and cognizant of how one goes about it.

8.4.1 Research → Policy: The Academic Economist

The first model we consider is one in which research impacts policy. The model takes an enlightenment perspective, in which policymakers will eventually be enlightened by the research. It is an implicit assumption of this model that policymakers will draw the "right" conclusions from the research and implement the "correct" policy. Research results in adjustments in policy through a diffuse and

PERSPECTIVE 8.2   WHAT WE WRITE ABOUT WHEN WE WRITE ABOUT IMPACT BY JEFFREY R. BLOEM

The words we write matter, and therefore, we should never write the word *impact* when we write about our empirical results. This claim may be surprising. A large portion of applied economic research can correctly be characterized as "impact evaluation." Moreover, the public often asks applied economists to assess the economic "impact" of important events – such as pandemics, recessions, wars, and so on. So, why should applied economists never write the word *impact* in their papers or reports?

The problem with writing the word *impact* is two-fold. First, the word *impact* means too many things to too many people within and outside the applied economics profession. For example, applied microeconomists use the word *impact* to indicate the difference between some treatment and the unobserved counterfactual, macroeconomic modelers use the word *impact* to mean "predicted changes," and policymakers often use the word *impact* to mean "outcome" or even "output." All these interpretations of the word *impact* are very different. Second, writing about "impact" is central to the task of much of modern-day applied economics. A substantial portion of applied economics research – particularly the sort that aims to inform policy decisions – could plausibly characterize results as the impact of some event or phenomena on some outcome of interest. The interaction of these two factors produces a communication problem with ethical implications. Simply put, this common word many applied economists use regularly is, at best, unclear and, at worst, misleading.

What does the word *impact* actually mean? *Webster's* dictionary defines the word *impact* as "to have a direct effect on" and implies a causal definition. Modern-day applied economics, of course, has a lot to say about causality and our ability to estimate causal relationships with real-world data. One consequence of the perceived obsession with causality among modern-day applied economists is the associated obsession with writing causal language even when doing so is not econometrically justifiable. This misrepresentation of empirical results is just as ethically problematic as performing subpar statistical analysis because both lead the researcher to obscure the truth from the reader.

If applied economists should never write the word *impact*, then what words should we use instead? Everyone who writes the word *impact* has a particular definition in mind and, presumably, has a reason why that definition fits well within the context of their writing. Therefore, anytime a researcher uses the word *impact* to describe results from applied economic analysis there is an alternative word or phrases that can be used to both more accurately and more clearly describe the results.

For example, as an applied microeconomist most of my research is interested in understanding causal effects, but not all of my research is able to credibly estimate causal effects. This informs how I write about the results of my analysis. When I can justifiably estimate a causal effect, I use the phrases "average treatment effect," "average treatment on the treated," or "intent to treat effect," depending on which is most appropriate. To the contrary, when I cannot rule out all plausible sources of bias due to omitted heterogeneity, I use variations of the phrase, "estimated differences associated with the treatment/policy/event." An important lesson that I learned early in my career is that causality is not a binary concept where a researcher can either identify causal effects or they cannot. In many cases, interesting and policy-relevant questions lead to analysis that is not able to credibly estimate causal effects but can rule out some important forms of possible bias. This does not mean the analysis is worthless, but it does require that I write about the results in an accurate and clear way.

Although communicating our results accurately and clearly is an important topic for applied economists in general, the issue is magnified when applied economists write for a policymaker audience. This is because policymakers are (a) likely not technically trained or subject matter specialists and (b) relatively time-constrained. Thus, if policymakers read our work at all, they will likely just read the words that researchers write and ignore the details of an identification strategy and the underlying assumptions of a regression specification or model. Moreover, they will probably only read the summary or introduction of any particular article or report. Therefore, it is imperative that we write accurately and clearly up front when we write about our empirical results. Applied economists in the U.S. Federal Government must generally comply with the Plain Writing Act of 2010, which requires that writing in public documents be "clear, concise, well-organized, and follows other best practices appropriate to the subject or field and intended audience." Applied economists in any sector can benefit from following the spirit of this law, and avoiding the word *impact* when writing about empirical results is a good place to start.

incremental process, with a body of research evidence for or against a policy accumulating over time. Changes to a policymaker's understanding of the issue are often conceptual and these result in policy changes through knowledge creep and other less active processes (Boswell and Smith, 2017).

The research to policy model relies on the idea that research can influence policy over long periods, through gradual shifts in perceptions and ways of thinking on the part of the policymakers. Nelson (1987) observes that it is possible that research might contribute to what eventually become significant shifts in policy, but that this is not typically how policy formation occurs. Sure, there are famous test cases, such as John Maynard Keynes's influence on fiscal policy and Milton Friedman's influence on monetary policy and regulation. But these cases are so well known because they are so rare. Rather, Boswell and Smith (2017) suggest that the lack of directly observable or measurable impact of this model of diffusion allows it to persist, at least among academics.

Additionally, this slow rolling model reflects, in part, the common academic economist's perception that policy is not something they do but rather something that their research suggests or implies (Nelson, 1987). Consider the frequent scenario when reading an applied economics paper: one is drawing toward the conclusion, and then, suddenly, a section titled something along the lines of "policy implications." Taking up a couple of paragraphs to a page, the section seems out of step with the rest of the paper. It reads as almost perfunctory, designed to connect the carefully identified regression results to some, often distant, theoretical or potential policy. These sections are often added, at the last minute, in order to make the research results more applicable or satisfy real or perceived demands by reviewers or editors. As frequently as not, these section weaken an otherwise good paper by capping what had been rigorous analysis with a set of conjectures on how, maybe, in some way, that the author will take no action toward implementing, the findings could affect policy.

An approach to policy impact that views research as only implying or suggesting policy relevance is a failure of audience, genre, and composition. Writing a policy recommendations section in an academic paper develops no clear pathway or trajectory for that work to actually come to be read by the relevant policymaker or stakeholder. To impact policy requires more deliberate work than just publishing a paper in an academic journal.

One reason why this diffuse, indirect model is attractive to academic economists is that it reflects the set of incentives faced by most academics. They (we) measure impact differently from those in other professions and are commensurately rewarded differently. In particular, academics tend to measure the impact of their own research in terms of papers published, citation counts, and media coverage. While academic economists often claim their research is "policy-relevant" and they will include potential "policy effects" of their findings, this is typically a hypothetical impact, at best, and a wishful afterthought, at worst.

Although the research to policy model is the default model that most academics have in their head, the implications of this can be that, in fact, research has little to no impact on policy. Boswell and Smith (2017) suggest ways to improve the link between research and policy, or in their words "close the gap." They suggest that expectations for achieving impact on policy ought to shift away from individual researchers and toward the collective diffusion of more diverse bodies of work. This would involve supporting and encouraging multiple authors, potentially from multiple fields, to synthesize a body of evidence and formulate concrete and actionable policy messages. In agricultural and applied economics, especially for those academics and Land Grant Universities with federal funding, these sorts of collaborative bodies already exist in a variety of forms. But outside of this field, the diffuse, enlightenment model taken by many academics is unlikely to actually affect policy, and so a more considerate and cognizant pathway for achieving impact is essential.

8.4.2 Research ← Policy: The Government Economist

The next model we consider is one in which policy shapes research. The model is inherently political in that government entities are directing or driving research for both tactical and strategic purposes. Policymakers may be tactical in what research they request, as a way of either generating evidence to support pregiven policy preferences or as a way of delaying the decision-making process to provide "breathing space" (Weiss, 1979). Alternatively, instead of asking for specific research on a specific issue or question, policymakers can act strategically, setting long-term research agendas or informing the ways governments respond to research (Boswell and Smith, 2017). This latter, strategic approach, was discussed in Chapter 2 in terms of induce innovation.

Since this second model is political, it is often presented in a negative light, with political power driving research with the sole goal of justifying and protecting the status quo power structure. That, however, is overly simplistic. While this model can clearly be interpreted as "representing powerful interests directing the research agenda," it can also be interpreted as "mission-driven, policy-oriented research" (Boswell and Smith, 2017). The model itself is agnostic to the ethical implications of what it describes. The policy to research interaction could be a pronativism politician seeking research to justify their racists, anti-immigrant views. But it could just as well be a legislative majority allocating funds to research technologies to substitute for carbon-burning sources of energy. The model reflects how a policy-oriented perspective can and will shape a research agenda.

Unlike the first model, where research influences policy through a slow diffusion process, influence in this second model is rooted in access to power. For economists, the ethical consideration is how to respond when policy or politics provide the research question. For academic economists, they can choose to accept or forgo such assignments for policy-drive research. Or they can choose to accept or forgo government and think-tank funding that seeks to induce innovation in research toward a specific outcome. But many economists and other researchers working throughout the federal government, at think tanks, and at other nonacademic institutions do not have this luxury. In fact, nearly a quarter of professional economists work in the U.S. Federal Government. Add to this the number of economists employed by state and local governments, by lobbyists, think tanks, and other nonacademic bodies which seek to influence politics and policy.

There are clear ethical issues raised when one is in a position where the job is to do politically driven research. However, these positions also provide economists with a tremendous opportunities to influence policy at many levels of government. As Dr. Susan Offutt (2016), who has worked for USDA (ERS), the Office of Management and Budget (OMB), and the Government Accountability Office (GAO), observes, "no policy proposal or pronouncement is legitimate without an analysis that purports to show that it will be effective." It is the role of government economists to provide this support, through policy-directed research. This power to provide a research-based justification for a policy raises its own ethical questions. As Nelson (2016) writes:

> Can a good end justify a questionable means? That is to say, the economist in government is accorded a certain amount of prestige and thus decision making influence – because at least some people in government defer to the scientific status of economists. In practice, asserting that a policy recommendation is technically grounded in economic expertise increases the likelihood that the argument will be heard and perhaps even followed. But what if the policy recommendation is actually grounded in little more than ordinary common sense?

Nelson, who spent most of his career as an economist in the Office of Policy Analysis at the U.S. Department of the Interior, provides an illustrative example from his involvement with federal energy leasing in the early 1980s. In this case, the Pauley Group had purchased a federal oil lease in California in the 1960s but had not developed it and had surrendered it back to the government in the early 1970s. However, by the mid-1970s, after the OPEC-driven rise in oil prices, the Pauley Group sought to reclaim the lease back. Its attempts to do so failed in court, and so it subsequently sought help from Congress, through special legislation, to return the lease to the company. The Pauley Group, through legal, although perhaps not ethical, back-channeling and lobbying had managed to garner support for the legislation from both the Democratic congressional delegation from California and the Republican presidential administration, including the Secretary of the Interior. Nelson, hearing about the legislative attempt to override the court decision, notified NBC News, which ran a story on the issue, effectively killing the legislation. Nelson (2016) acknowledges that he knew he was making an ethical decision in following his own personal conviction, against the position of both his immediate and ultimate boss, the Secretary of the Interior and the President. The lease was then put back up for auction was was resold for $25 million. Nelson (2016) writes, "in a certain sense it was a contest between my values as an individual (and as an economist) and the conventional political standards of Washington" and notes that these sort of choices are standard for economic professionals in government, and an integral part of their work.

Hirschman and Berman (2014) argue that economists must be embedded in the political power structure if they are to effectively direct and drive research in order to influence policy. And, when one is in a position of power, all decisions become ethical decisions, because the choices made by those in power effect those who lack power. Offutt (2016) acknowledges this, writing "consequences for other people are apparent in policy choices, and economists have a hand in identifying what they are." This, she suggests, is the crucial ethical considerations that policymaking economists face. It is the responsibility and opportunity of government economists to evaluate the consequences and outcomes of a policy and then make appropriate recommendations. In this work, when research questions may be driven by a policymaker, Offutt (2016), following Thompson (1983), suggests consider three questions:

1. Would the decision maker have acted in the same way, regardless of the advice received?
2. Could the advisor have reasonable foreseen any adverse consequences of the decision?
3. Could harm have been prevented if the advisor had taken an active role criticizing the decision or the process by which the decision had been reached?

To answer these questions with certainty is difficult, but posing them is critical for making ethical decisions as a policymaking economist.

An appreciation of the circumstances in which these sorts of ethical challenges arise are helpful for preparing an economist to face them when they do. Perhaps due to the directionality of this second model, in which research is directed by policy questions or political influence, ethical issues and considerations for government economists arise in a different way than for the standard academic economist model. But, as Offutt (2016) writes, "the existence of ethical challenge is not a defect of public service but rather part of its essence."

8.4.3 Research ↔ Policy: The Extension Economist

The third model that we consider is one of coproduction of research and policy. As in the second model, the coproduction model still sees research as being deeply influenced by politics. But the model also allows for academic research to direct and shape policies. Thus, the model represents a more complex interrelationship between knowledge production and knowledge use. Ideally, the model represents are mutually constructive coproduction of both research and policy, in which there is reciprocity between all parties. As Jasanoff (2004) writes in her book *States of Knowledge*, "states are made of knowledge, just as knowledge is constituted by states."

The first model discussed relies on the assumption that researchers are asking the right questions for policy, and the second model relies on the assumption that policymakers are asking the right questions of researchers, so to does the third model rely on a key assumption: that of performativity (Boswell and Smith, 2017). The idea that economics is performative is best expressed by Callon (1998), who argues that "economics, in the broad sense of the term, performs, shapes and formats the economy, rather than observing how it functions." MacKenzie (2008) documents the performative nature of economics in his book on finance theory and markets, *An Engine, Not a Camera*, arguing that economic theory does not describe how financial markets work but shapes how financial markets work. Performativity is key to the coproduction model because it means one cannot disentangle research from policy and vice versa. The two are mutually reinforcing. In the case of finance, economic research described ways that financial markets could or should work, policymakers then adapted that research to design regulations for those markets, which created problems that then required new research to fix (Cassidy, 2010). An inescapable conclusion of the coproduction model is that research, be it economic, social science, or bench science, itself produces social problems that require policy responses (Boswell and Smith, 2017).

While the model of research driving policy was representative of the academic economist, and the model of policy driving research was representative of the government economist, the model of coproduction is representative of economists working in Cooperative Extension.[2] The Land Grant University system in the U.S. was established by the Morrill Act of 1862. Located in every state, the objective of these schools was and is to educate the next generation of farmers and engineers by fulfilling the three-fold mission of research, teaching, and Extension (Croft, 2019). Land Grant Universities operate the U.S. Cooperative Extension Service (CES) in partnership with federal, state, and local governments. CES provides nonformal education to agricultural producers and communities through networks across the country. According to Croft (2019), there were CES offices in more than 3,000 U.S. counties and territories.

Agricultural, or Cooperative Extension operates within a knowledge system which encompasses research and agricultural education. Through Extension, Land Grant institutions conduct research that is then translated into practical information for stakeholders, including government agencies, agricultural producers, small businesses, consumers, and families. Extension specialists also listen to stakeholder questions and concerns, which they then bring back to the university or experiment station to seed ideas for new research. According to the USDA's National Institute for Food and Agriculture (NIFA), the hallmarks of an extnesion program include openness, accessibility, and service. Extension is driven by public need and demand, focused on improving lives through education, technology, and development. Inherent to Extension is the role of outreach, communication, and ongoing engagement. In order to serve the stakeholders, sustained communication is required, based on mutual understanding of a shared objective. In order to achieve this, Land Grant Universities dispatch extension specialists to convey knowledge and share research, based on the demands and needs of the communities in which they work. This relationship is represented by the cyclical framework of coproduction, in which stakeholders (the policy) are able to provide feedback to specialists (the research) so that all parties are served through a mutual and ongoing relationship. Again, it is worth noting, that other economists engage in similar models when doing outreach. So, although these relationships are not unique to Extension, we consider CES to be a pioneer in these collaborations.

The co-production relationship is often viewed – or at least conceived – as the ideal relationship between research and policy. Although as Boswell and Smith (2017) note, it is not without its issues, as problems can be created through power imbalances in the structure of relationships. Further, Extension itself, because of its mission to communicate academic research to non-researchers, has struggled to gain credibility in both the research and policy spheres. Timm (1949), in his introduction to extension economics, writes that "there was the trying task of winning professional prestige from fellow scientists on one hand and in the eyes of the "dirt farmer" on the other." However, as disseminating research beyond the academy to achieve policy impact becomes ever more important, Cooperative Extension is perhaps best positioned to capitalize on this opportunity, at least in terms of turning applied economic research into agricultural and environmental policy action. Extension, definitionally, is communication as an extension of one's own research and that research is driven by the needs of constituents and stakeholders of state-funded universities.

8.4.4 Research → | ← Policy

The final model of research and policy interaction described by Boswell and Smith (2017) is of separate spheres. In this model, research and policy exist in autonomous realms, each operating with a different set of objectives, logic, and meanings. This is sometimes described as the two communities thesis, in which a boundary or gap separates researchers and policymakers (Caplan, 1979). While this model might not seem to parallel reality, in terms of what we know about politics, policy, and research, one need only read Nelson (1987, 2016), Offutt (2016), and others to know that research and policy do often operate in autonomous spheres. Nelson (1987) in particular documents how little researchers know about the process of policymaking and how infrequently policymakers digest documents produced by researchers.

While the separate spheres model is pessimistic about the ability of research to impact policy and vice versa, the model does not require that research and policy never reach each other. Rather, in this model the process is not deliberative. Instead of a defined relationship, as is implied by the other models, there is a sort of selective signaling between the two separate realms. Researchers will filter some information from the noise of politics and policy debates. Similarly, policymakers will internalize some of what is learned from research. In this model, journalists, consultants, and lobbyists can play the role of filter or communicator between researchers and policymakers (Lindquist, 1990). Boswell and Smith (2017) suggest that the implications of the separate spheres model are that researchers should consider how their questions and research may be driven by signals picked up from politics or policy. At the same time, researchers should consider the perspective of policymakers and try to understand the how and the why of why some data or results get picked up by policymakers and why other data and results do not. It is worth interrogating, on both sides, how these forms of indirect communication works between the separate spheres.

While we have connected previous models to specific work done by applied economists, in this model, where there is no direction relationship between research and policy, we do not connect this model with a specific type of economic work or profession. Rather, this pessimistic model of research and policy interaction provides warning or caution for all economists, regardless of where they sit. First, despite the separate spheres, the model does not give cover to researchers who want to claim that they never imagined their work could influence policy. Whether or not we directly seek to influence policy in our work, regardless of the system of knowledge transfer between spheres, there is an exchange and diffusion of knowledge and information between realms. To pretend otherwise is to abdicate responsibility for the influence one's research has on those who interact with it. Second, because of the separate spheres, researchers need to be humble about claims that their work had an "impact" on policy. The indirect communication pathways that the separate spheres model represents assumes a specious causality between research and policy, making any rigorous demonstration of research impact on policy a fools errand.

We have quoted from George E.P. Box before: "all models are wrong, but some are useful." In reviewing the four models of research interaction with policy presented in Boswell and Smith (2017), none offers a complete and definitive representation of reality. Rather, researchers and policymakers should take a synchronistic view of the models. Each model has strengthens and weaknesses, and each shines light on a form of research and policy interaction. Depending on the researcher, the policymaker, the information trying to be communicated, and the policy under consideration, any of the four models may be the operative one. In looking to effectively disseminate research so as to influence policy, applied economists need to be aware of the context and audience and adapt their communication to match the relevant model of how research and policy interact.

8.5 Changing and Dynamic Communications

The communications environment is changing. Some of this is driven by technology, some is driven by responses to the COVID-19 pandemic, some is simply driven by the nature of innovation and the passage of time. Regardless of the underlying mechanisms, the method by which researchers can effectively reach stakeholders and other interested parties has expanded and is likely to continue to expand throughout one's career. Staying abreast of these trends and the changing dynamics of communication is important as one seeks to disseminate research beyond the academy. In this section, we describe a few recent trends in communication.

Journal articles are the stalwarts of academic communications. Among the Top Five journals in economics, three have been published for over 100 years (the *Quarterly Journal of Economics*: 1886, the *Journal of Political Economy*: 1892, the *American Economic Review*: 1911) while the other two are approaching 90 (*Econometrica*: 1933, *Review of Economic Studies*: 1933). The *American Journal of Agricultural Economics* has also been around for a century (first published in 1919 as the *Journal of Farm Economics*) and many other journals in the field of applied economics are many decades old. Even with the changing trends in publications discussed in Chapter 7, academic publications are likely to remain the primary mode of research dissemination for years to come. But the process of disseminating the work contained in academic papers to a broader audience is shifting dramatically. Social media, particularly Twitter, has broadened researchers' networks, so that they now interact with researchers, policymakers, and stakeholders, many of whom they may never have met. Recent work is suggestive, although far from definitive, that articles promoted with a thread on Twitter receive more citations than those that do not receive similar treatment (Klar et al., 2020; Ladeiras-Lopes et al., 2020; Luc et al., 2020). The informality of social media, combined with the ability to reach a wide audience, may be a winning combination for those looking to increase their reach and communicate to different groups.

More informality is a broad trend within the communication environment. For many years, written briefs – short distillations of academic papers or white papers – were considered the best way to reach stakeholders. With easier access to typesetting and photo-editing software, briefs have become more like brochures than the text-heavy short papers that they were previously. Easy-to-use graphic design software have made the creation of infographics an easy way for quick communication to stakeholders. More recently, visual presentations and short videos have become popular, as can be seen in the plethora of TED-sponsored talks.

The lockdowns resulting from the COVID-19 pandemic had a major impact on how people communicate in all areas of life. For researchers, the pandemic moved conferences, meetings, and data collection to online or remote venues. The improvement in video conference calling technology likely means that some meetings or events that used to be conducted in person will remain remote. This allows those looking to disseminate their research to meet with a much broader audience than previously. Where one once had to physically travel to where stakeholders and governments agents worked or convene everyone in a central location, one can now bring people together while everyone remains at their desks. This not only saves time and money but also allows for greater access to these events for those who used to be unable to afford such travel.

While the appropriate genre for communication will always be audience dependent, the online environment dominates and defines the new context of communication. As such, one must ensure that their points can be as effectively communicated online, as they could be in person. This is something many students are already adept at doing. Anna regularly teaches freshman who are already accustomed to presenting and communicating in the online environment and who have already developed well honed video and photo skills. This suggests that younger applied economists will be similarly adept at this – but it will be a task for the rest of us to keep up with the changing environment. There is almost always a new type of media, a new way to reach people, and a new trend to which researchers interested in communicating with stakeholders must stay abreast.

8.5.1 Academic Social Media

Since 2000, the growth of social media has been the most important change in communicating research to those outside of readers of academic journals. Academic social media, in the form of blogs, Twitter, Facebook, and the like, provides an online community in which academics and others in the field (or those interested in the field) can connect and network. Although many remain skeptical, social media can add value to academic work in a number of ways. Social media provides a professional network, which allows researchers to join a wider conversation, beyond one's typical network of colleagues and co-authors. Social media also provides a way to find and share resources one might not otherwise encounter. Finally, it allows one to engage in social self-promotion through sharing one's research and insights. While social media can add value to one's research in all these different ways, it is far from an unalloyed good. Social media can be a place where misinformation lives and is spread. It can bring out the worst in people, in terms of angry rants, misogyny, racism, and other forms of prejudice (Wu, 2020). Social media can also be used to exaggerate, distort, distract, or cover up research that is shoddy or problematic. The promises and pitfalls of engaging with social media means that researchers need to weigh the ethics of whether or not to join and, if one has joined, the ethics of how one should participate in social media.

The first ethical consideration researchers must make is whether or not to join social media, either by starting a blog or creating a profile on a social media platform. In the early years of social media, the obvious answer to whether or not to join seemed to be "no." Social media was seen as more of a pitfall than a promise. Stories about professors being denied tenure or fired for blogging or posting, both about controversial and non-controversial topics, were common (Johnson, 2005; Kaplan, 2015). However, this pessimistic perspective has changed over the years (Nature, 2011). McKenzie and Özler (2014) present evidence that blogging raises the profile of the blogger and increases the number of abstract views and downloads of a blogged about paper. An editorial in *Nature* goes further than just claiming social media engagement can be beneficial. The editorial argues that it is an ethical imperative for researchers to engage in social media so as to combat the spread of misinformation by "getting the right facts out there, and citing and linking to the best, most trustworthy sources of information" Personally, we are more inclined toward (Bellemare, 2022a) position on the question of whether or not to join social media: "if you do not feel you have time for social media, that is fine."

If one does choose to join social media, the next ethical consideration researchers must make is how to participate in social media. One should be clear about why they are using the platform and have a plan for using it, including strategically following others and using the account with some regularity (Crew, 2019). Bellemare (2022a) suggests three ways that using social media can not only benefit the researcher but the research community. First is that engaging in social media can make one a better writer and researcher. Distilling complex research into the genre of a blog post or Twitter thread helps one clarify the key concepts and results from an academic paper. Encountering new research by others can spark new ideas for research projects and build new collaborations.[3] Second is the ability to define oneself as the scholar one wants to be. McKenzie and Özler (2014) show that blogging changes readers' perceptions about the blogger and the blogger's institution. Third is the ability to engage in self-promotion through blogging or posting about one's research. The Altmetric Manifesto highlights the roll of social media, particularly Twitter, for increasing the impact of research:

> Twitter citations are also uniquely conversational, reflecting a broader discussion crossing traditional disciplinary boundaries. . . . While Twitter citations are different from traditional citations, our participants suggest that they still represent and transmit scholarly impact . . . offering faster, broader, and more nuanced metrics of scholarly communication to supplement traditional citation analysis.
>
> *(Priem et al., 2010)*

At its best, social media posts about new research represent a "curating" and "informing" of a broad audience that extends far beyond the academy.

Unsurprisingly, researchers on social media are often not at their best. Studying research articles in the field of dentistry, and contra Priem et al. (2010), Robinson-Garcia (2017) note that they "see much presumably human tweeting almost entirely mechanical and devoid of original thought, no evidence of conversation, tweets generated by monomania, duplicate tweeting from many accounts under centralized professional management and tweets generated by bots." They acknowledge that some accounts exemplify the ideal of research dissemination via social media, but this represents fewer than 10 percent of posts. In an striking example from the paper, Robinson-Garcia (2017) discusses the top tweeted scientific dental paper, titled "Acetaminophen: Old Drug, New Issues," written by A. Aminoshariae and A. Khan, and published in the *Journal of Endodontics* in 2015. The paper was tweeted 264 times by U.S.-based accounts. A closer look, however, raised concerns. Robinson-Garcia (2017) documents that 193 of the tweets (73 percent) came from a single account, with 65 of those tweets simply reading "Paracetamol research: [URL]." Of the remaining 71 tweets about the paper, 58 came from another single account. These two accounts were responsible for all but 15 tweets about the paper. And these two accounts often retweeted each other, with effectively the same information repeated over and over. Robinson-Garcia (2017) outlines a number of similar cases, highlighting how much of the "engagement" with a paper is by single issue tweeters, professional or hired social media managers, bots, or duplicate tweets.

Like many things in life, what one gets out of social media is a function of what one puts into it. The evidence in McKenzie and Özler (2014) suggests that regularly writing blog posts can raise one's profile. The evidence in Robinson-Garcia (2017) suggests that the limited number of characters in a Tweet does little to raise interest in or awareness of one's research. In light of these findings, it can make sense to treat interactions with social media as part of professional service. Bellemare (2022a) writes, "they [conversations between colleagues] are now taking place on social media, and have *de facto* become public goods and thus a form of professional service." Thinking of interacting with social media as service helps keep time spent on various platforms to a reasonable amount and helps ensure that it is not interfering with other work.

That said, we prefer to think of social media as not just professional service but as the last stage of the research process – the opportunity for disseminating one's research beyond the academy. Social media posts may not directly result in more citations from other academics, but it is a low cost way to engage in outreach or diffusion of one's research to nonacademics. While not a direct measure of economists' influence on policymakers, Michael Bailey, Theresa Kuchler, and Johannes Stoebel have shown in a series of papers how social media networks influence everything from home purchases to technology adoption to COVID-19 precautions (Bailey et al., 2018, 2020, 2022). Social media networks also influence flows of labor and goods, which in turn influence migration and trade policy (Bailey et al., 2020, 2021). As the editorial in *Nature* argues, diligent use of social media helps push "the most relevant and trusted information to the top" so that journalists, policymakers, and other stakeholders have access to it when it comes time to make decisions on policy (Nature, 2011).

There are several practical considerations in creating and maintaining an effective professional social media presence. Most of these are common sense: present oneself as one would on a professional website; identifying one's self as an academic or researcher; include one's credentials; use a professional handle; use a head-shot with a clear view of one's face; adhere to any requirements from an employer regarding making public statements; keep content centered around work and research; do not post anything that one would not want to be forever in the public record.[4] To as great a degree as possible, keep one's account professional and work to minimize personal perspectives or political opinions.

However, presenting oneself professionally online does not mean that researchers need to eschew controversy altogether. In fact, economic research can be very controversial. Crew (2019) advises that it is important to have a plan, if posting something controversial. And one should consider what might qualify as controversial for one's social media audience. For example, the scientific consensus is that burning carbon is the primary cause of climate change and that genetically modified foods have no negative health effects, and many have health benefits, relative to non–genetically modified organism (GMO) food. But these scientific facts are often not shared by the population at large. According to Funk (2020) about half of American adults think that GMO foods are worse than non-GMO foods. So, the facts that most in the profession agree upon may be perceived differently by one's social media audience.

Social media is part of the atmosphere of professional economists and is likely to continue to be moving forward. Whether one selects to engage is at one's discretion, but it should be done with clear eyes about the opportunities and costs, as well as a clear set of objectives or goals for that engagement. Treat social media as part of one's dissemination plan for one's research. As Bellemare (2022a) cautions:

> I can think of a few examples of academics who are Very Online People, but whose CVs are woefully short on publications. Social media use will not be penalized by those who will judge your professional accomplishments if it is clear that you prioritize your research. But if it becomes clear that you should have spent your time more productively away from social media and your research has suffered for it, you are likely to be penalized. Social media is a complement to good research – not a substitute for it.

In engaging with social media, make sure that one's work is still at the forefront – and the time on the platform and being a "good follow" does not replace the main objective, which should be to be a good researcher and scholar.

8.6 Conclusion

In a shifting communication environment, with barriers to sharing thoughts, research, or other work seemingly moving to zero, the way in which researchers communicate and disseminate findings from research is also changing. Opportunities to promote one's self and one's research are seemingly boundless. This has resulted in the emergence of a number of important considerations for researchers when weighing various pathways for disseminating their research beyond the academy.

What all these innovations have not changed, though, is what constitutes effective communication. Communication is an art, and like any art, it requires practice to perfect. The keys to effective communication are identifying one's audience, selecting the appropriate genre for that audience, and then defining the composition or content of the communication. Rewriting is an important part of practicing the art of communication and in ensuring one's writing is effective.

The goal of all this effort is to be able to share one's research and expertise beyond the academic community and to extend the impact of one's work. The media, both traditional and new, can play an important roll in amplifying one's research. But, like at every stage of the research life cycle, misalignment of incentives creates ethical issues. The objective of journalists may not be the objective of researchers. This should not stop researchers from working with journalists, it just requires a frank assessment of the objective of each party and a clear understanding of where things can go wrong.

Similar, too, the objective of policymakers need not be the objectives of researchers. There are a number of different ways in which researchers and policymakers can work together or work at cross purposes. Frequently, academic researchers adopt a laissez-faire approach to research's impact on policy while researches in the governments or think thanks may take a much more hands on approach, using policy to drive research. The work of Cooperative Extension presents a third way for research and policy to interact through the coproduction of research. Finally, researcher and policymakers may choose to refrain from direct interactions, allowing journalists and other intermediaries to filter communication. None of these models should be seen as exclusively or exhaustively descriptive. Rather, each model shines light on a possible form of research and policy interaction.

For applied economists, the end of the life cycle for a research idea is having an impact on the lives of the people in our community. Unless one happens to be giving advice to a future president about apple orchards, it makes sense for the applied economist to use every tool available to them. This includes not only effective and appropriate use of traditional forms of communication but also adopting new technologies and platforms, like social media, to broaden one's professional network. Social media presents its own promises and pitfalls. But, with careful consideration about what one wants to accomplish, social media is just one more tool for disseminating one's research and sharing one's knowledge and expertise. In interacting with journalists, policymakers, or social media, honesty, candor, and transparency will always serve as good guides.

Notes

1 Books that we have found useful in our own writing are Donald M. Murray's *The Craft of Revision* (Murray, 2012), Strunk and White's *The Elements of Style* (Strunk and White, 1999), William Zinsser's *On Writing Well* (Zinsser, 2006), Stephen King's *On Writing* (King, 2000), Anne Lamott's *Bird by Bird* (Lamott, 1995), and of course Dillard's *The Writing Life* (Dillard, 1989).

2 Although Extension is practiced all around the world and is one of the most important methods for disseminating agricultural information to farmers, we limit our discussion of extension to the U.S. Additional resources on ethics and extension include Taylor (2019), and Taylor and Zhang (2019) on educating future economists to work in Extension; Barry (1993) on coordinating research, extension, and outreach in the profession; and various chapters from different editions of the *Handbook of Agricultural Economics,* including Anderson and Feder (2007) and Everson (2001). It is also worth noting that other economists, not in Cooperative Extension, also use similar practices, when engaged in outreach.

3 More than one contributor to the text boxes in the book first came to our attention through social media.

4 Between 2010 and 2018, the Library of Congress archived every public post on Twitter. But, as of 1 January 2018, the Library only acquires tweets "on a very selective basis."

PART V

Conclusion

9

ON BEING AN ETHICAL APPLIED ECONOMIST

9.1 Introduction

In *Capital*, Karl Marx concludes the first chapter, on commodities, with a section titled "The Fetishism of Commodities and the Secret Thereof." In his often convoluted prose, Marx (1867) writes:

> A commodity appears, at first sight, a very trivial thing, and easily understood. Its analysis shows that it is, in reality, a very queer thing, abounding in metaphysical subtleties and theological niceties . . . The form of wood, for instance, is altered, by making a table out of it. Yet, for all that, the table continues to be that common, every-day thing, wood. But, so soon as it steps forth as a commodity, it is changed into something transcendent. . . . This I call the Fetishism which attaches itself to the products of labour, so soon as they are produced as commodities, and which is therefore inseparable from the production of commodities.

Marx's theory is that things, a table in this example, have an intrinsic "use value" and a "labor value" that reflects the amount of labor that went into producing the object. But, when it comes time to exchange this thing as a commodity, its "exchange value" need not have any connection to the physical properties of the object. In exchange, a commodity becomes a fetish object because individuals believe that the object is worth something outside of its direct use value or labor value. In exchange economies, commodities "appear as independent beings endowed with life, and entering into relation both with one another and the human race" (Marx, 1867).

Discussions of ethics and, in particular, research ethics, often suffer from the same sort of fetishism. We all have our own intrinsic moral or ethical values. These value systems often reflect our social upbringing and how we as individuals have

DOI: 10.4324/9781003025061-14

synthesized what we have been taught by family, religion, culture, and other influential sources and experiences. But even for individuals who adhere to some well defined ethical construct, like the Catholic Catechism or the Nicomachean Ethics, ethics and morality are still defined at the individual level by their use value to that individual. How the individual produces those values, the cost that individual bears in turning ethical and moral concepts into lived actions, can be thought of as the labor value of that individual's moral or ethical code.

But something happens when society begins to regulate or impose ethical behavior. In the same way as commodities become fetishized, ethical codes quickly become fetish objects. The codes can become an end onto themselves, devoid of any connection to an individual's moral or ethical values. Discussions of research ethics become a "dull and tedious quarrel," to use Marx's phrase, about compliance or noncompliance with a certain regulation. Ethics becomes a thing that researchers think about only during the formal process of ethical approval. At the extreme, researchers mediate and express their interactions with others – the IRB committee, research participants, collaborators – in terms of compliance with established ethical codes. This is, unfortunately, frequently the state of affairs at present. Refrains of "It received institutional review board [IRB] approval" are often heard when concerns about the ethics of a study are raised, as though simply receiving approval for a protocol ensures ethical behavior in practice. This is a natural consequence of the fixation on code, rather than actual ethical behavior.

Ultimately, the fetishism of research ethics as compliance to ethical codes of conduct impoverishes research ethics. Throughout this book we argue that ethical considerations are enmeshed in each stage of the life cycle of a research idea. Ethical considerations begin as one forms an initial research idea and ethics need to be designed into any project from the start. Ethical considerations extend far beyond the IRB approval process, playing a crucial role in how one manages and analyzes data and disseminates results. No code of conduct or institution can or should govern ethics at all of these stages. Where codes, and institutions to enforce those codes, are useful are at points of high risk or potential danger throughout the life cycle, such as working with research participants, conflicts of interest, professional conduct, and publishing findings. But we, as researchers, should relate to these codes with a mindset of ethical conduct, not just ethical compliance.

To that end, we conclude our practical guide to research ethics not with a code of conduct or an economist's oath, but rather with a set of four virtues that we set of rules have found to have a high use value. These are: fairness, respect, care, and honesty. We believe that promoting virtues for the individual is an effective way to be an ethical applied economist. These virtues have proven useful to us both personally and professionally. Keeping these virtues in the forefront of our mind when we face ethical issues has helped us avoid fetishizing ethics. But these virtues are *individual* virtues. We do not present them as a code or universal system that all researchers should adhere to. We agree with Burris (2008) that "the logic of virtue promotion is inconsistent with the enforcement of rules that fetishize formalities or treat the subject as bad or amoral, if not idiotic." The following four virtues may have value to the reader, or maybe there are more valuable substitutes, or maybe there are complements that we have not mentioned. What is important to remember is not to make commodities of these virtues, lest they be transformed from useful markers of ethical conduct into fetish properties.

9.2 The Ethical Applied Economist

In Chapter 1 we introduced the idea of ethical pluralism, which sees complementarity between outcome-based, rule-based, and virtue-based ethics. Through this book, we have focused on the norms, duties, and outcomes or ethical considerations that arise while doing applied economic research. We have left virtues mostly undiscussed. But to be an ethical applied economist, one cannot simply focus on achieving compliance with a set, rules or on the outcomes of one's actions. Rather, the ethical applied economist must also embody a set of moral values, what we call virtues, and the actions that one takes when confronted with ethical problems. As any economist knows, the word *value* can mean many different things. To avoid confusion, and reflect our focus on the applied aspect of economic research, we discuss moral values in terms of virtues, which are simply embodied values. Virtues are not just things that we hold dear or "value" but are moral values in action. Virtues have motivating power. For our purposes, virtues are not overly aspirational (as are moral values), and virtues are not too prescriptive or specific (as are standards, principles, or rules). The following four virtues, adapted from Schroeder et al. (2019), have proven to be effective as operating guides when striving to do the right thing at all times, although particularly in ethically challenging situations.

9.2.1 Fairness

Our first virtue is fairness, which Rawls (1971) conceives as justice. Rawls's theory of justice as fairness comprises two principles. The first of these is that each individual has the same indefeasible claim to equal basic liberties. The second of these is that when economic and social inequalities exist, they must satisfy two conditions: (1) each individual has fair equality of opportunity, and (2) inequalities work to the advantage of the worst-off. The latter of these conditions is an egalitarian form of Pareto optimality, known as the difference principle (Lamont, 1994).

In describing the concept of justice as fairness, Pogge (2006) distinguishes between four types of fairness. The first type is commutative fairness, sometimes referred to as fairness in exchange. Commutative fairness refers to the equity of transactions between parties. Commutative fairness is only possible when both parties are at liberty to enter into an arrangement free of coercion. With respect to research ethics, fairness in exchange is an important principle when collaborating on a research project with colleagues, enrolling research participants into data collection, and working with journals to publish papers. Commutative fairness is essential in any collaboration, but particularly collaborations where there is a potential power imbalance, such as working with graduate students, nonacademic collaborators, or local partners. Collaborators not in a position of power, such as graduate students working with their advisor, should receive fair compensation for the work they put in, both in terms of money and in terms of authorship credit. Similarly, fairness of exchange in data collection means that research participants receive some benefit to themselves or their community from their involvement in the research. Consider an experiment testing the impact of solar stoves on deforestation and dietary diversity. In this context, commutative fairness meant giving all participants, both treatment and control, an equal chance of receiving a stove at the end of the experiment (McCann et al., 2021). In dealing with journals, which tend to have power over authors, fairness in exchange means that the journals do not exploit the need for authors to publish but instead provide adequate editorial, review, and publication services. The principal of commutative fairness means that predatory journals and conferences as unethical. Communicative fairness means working to ensure equality and equity, in practice and implementation, between engaged entities.

The second type of fairness described by Pogge (2006) is corrective or restitutive fairness. Corrective fairness requires righting a wrong. For research ethics, corrective fairness would be redressing a valid grievance by a colleague who was not given proper authorship credit. In Josephson and Smale (2021), corrective fairness is returning to households and individuals who were not adequately informed of their rights as research participants during the consent process and ensuring that these entities do provide informed consent and desire to participate in the research. Corrective fairness can also mean issuing a correction to a paper, or retracting it, if one realizes that mistakes were made in the data analysis (Thompson and Newmaster, 2021). Corrective fairness means making adjustments when wrongs are recognized.

The third type of fairness is distributive fairness (Pogge, 2006). Distributive fairness deals with the division of resources among qualifying recipients (Schroeder et al., 2019). Broadly, distributive fairness is concerned with equality of access to scarce resources. Issues of distributive fairness are often raised by critics of randomized controlled trials (RCTs). The concern is that RCTs do not satisfy the principle of distributive fairness because they provide a treatment to a random subset of a population and not the subset of the population that is most in need of the treatment (Ravallion, 2014; Abramowicz and Szafarz, 2020). More generally, distributive fairness is about the consideration of one of the central principles of microeconomics: the allocation of scarce resources. Schroeder et al. (2019) provide an example to distinguish between distributive and commutative fairness, in the context of the famous de-worming RCT of Miguel and Kremer (2004). Commutative fairness would argue that participants in the RCT are owed access to the drug after the study, as their time and effort contributed to the study overall. Distributive fairness would, based on the Universal Declaration of Human Rights (UN, 1949), argue that once the effectiveness of the deworming medication has been proven, all human should have access to it. Concern for ensuring distributive fairness is one reason why McCann et al. (2021) choose to distribute solar stoves to both treatment and control at the end of the experiment. Distributive fairness means working to ensure equitable access to scarce resources.

The final type of fairness that Pogge (2006) identifies is retributive fairness. Retributive fairness deals with the punishment for violations of social and moral rules. This type of fairness typically falls under punitive or criminal law and thus is typically not something an individual researcher would engage in. Yet, both universities and professional associations have codes of conduct, and violations of those codes are often adjudicated by faculty committees or committees of one's professional peers. We have sat on these committees and have reflected on what retributive fairness means when others violate professional codes of conduct. Retributive fairness means ensuring reasonable punishment, when violations to moral, social, and ethical rules do occur.

When thinking about fairness as a virtue and how we want to embody it in our research, we ask reflective questions about the equity of our research. Is the research question relevant to the population we would study? How will we ensure that the population will benefit from the research? Are members of the research team adequately rewarded for their contributions? Are our research participants adequately informed to make decisions? Are there any involved in the research process that might lack representation to seek retributive justice? Many of these ethical questions are difficult to answer and they go far beyond what is required for compliance with IRBs. But, we believe that the ethical applied economist should be concerned about fairness in their research and endeavoring to answer these sorts of questions as part of conducting ethical research.

9.2.2 Respect

In one respect, we already discussed the principle of respect for persons in Chapter 4. However, there we focused on how respect for persons relates to data collection and compliance with IRB regulations. Going beyond the principle of respect for persons, we believe that respect is a valuable virtue for the ethical applied economist. By respect, we do not mean a sense of admiration for a person, as in we respect Caesar Chavez or Rosa Parks. Rather, as a virtue, respect is about acknowledging the rights of people to make decisions with which one disagrees.

Respect means allowing a research participant to withdraw from a study, regardless of circumstance, even if the withdrawal reduces the power of the study below what one had prespecified. It means not imposing one's will or views about a certain analytical approach on colleagues, collaborators, or students. All of us, as experts in our field, have strongly held opinions and beliefs about the right way and the best way to go about answering a research question. But economists can and do disagree about how to tackle a particular research question. Anyone who has read through a reviewer report knows how difficult it can be to accept that criticism of one's preferred method as valid. And it can be hard to write a response to a reviewer report that is genuinely respectful and to not just focus on compliance with the demands of editors and reviewers.

Respect involves respecting not only the opinions or decisions of others but also their time. Providing sufficient documentation so others can replicate one's work is showing respect for people's time. Achieving both respect for opinions and for time can be especially difficult for faculty members when working with student collaborators. As a PhD economist, it is all too easy to view one's students as students and not as future colleagues. One must respect the opinions and the time of students, acknowledging that they may be more read up on the latest advances in an estimator. It is inherently respectful of a student's time to ensure that they are doing work that helps them learn how to do their own research.

But respect is not simply ceding responsibility for decision-making to others. As Schroeder et al. (2019) note, "while it may be difficult to imagine a situation where [a researcher] is accused of being too fair, it is possible to be accused of being 'too respectful.'" If one observes a colleague treating students in a degrading or demeaning way, it would be too respectful to conclude, "well, everyone's management style is different," and then simply allow that colleague to continue. How to embody respect is particularly difficult when working across cultures. As an example, how does one approach research on female genital cutting? Does one try to respect those who practice it and avoid making value judgments (Bellemare et al., 2015)? Or does one report incidences of female genital cutting as a recognized illegal human rights abuse and risk creating tension and disorder in local cultural institutions (Luc and Altare, 2018)? How to strike the balance between imposing one's own moral code on others and being complicit in human rights abuse can be difficult. Ultimately, a successful balance will depend on the researcher and the context they are working in, and may mean not undertaking the research at all if moral or ethical gaps cannot be closed.

9.2.3 Care

Our third virtue is care. We can care in two ways: we care *about* – or value – something and we care *for* – or protect – something. Both meanings often go hand-in-hand. As applied economists, we care for our research (design, analysis, results) and care about those involved (colleagues, participants, readers). Care may also mean that we feel responsible for how the research is interpreted or used, the welfare of all those involved in the process of research, and its dissemination.

In terms of demonstrating care for those involved in research, this can take many forms. For faculty, care can be demonstrated by creating an inclusive work environment for students and colleagues. Any time we bring in a new student to work with us, we start by sharing with them a document about how we as principal investigators work to foster an inclusive work environment. This includes statements about nondiscriminatory conduct, responsible conduct of research, leave and self-care, and dealing with imposter syndrome (Josephson and Michler, nd). It also includes information about coding procedures and authorship policies. With this information, students are informed about our work culture and environment on multiple planes, and we demonstrate care through equipping students with this knowledge. Considering research participants, demonstrating care involves ensuring that informed consent procedures are tailored to the local context in terms of language, literacy, and culture. With respect to readers or those who interact with one's research, care means being transparent and precise about research findings. Overcomplicating or overselling findings, in order to hide flaws in methods or weaknesses in results is not demonstrating care for those who read, cite, or make use of one's research.

Research misconduct itself can be considered a lack of care for others. Producing knowingly false or fraudulent results shows a lack of care for the reputation of the economics profession, for the journal one publishes in, for the institution one works for, and for the colleagues and students in one's care. The fallout from the scandal surrounding Brian Wansink shows a lack of care for those with whom Wansink collaborated, in particular his former students, who, as an advisor and mentor, he was supposed to protect (Lee, 2018).

We also demonstrate care for research itself, which means being attached to the research question, method, and findings, as well as having a sense of responsibility for how the question is framed, the method implemented, and the findings used. For the research question, care involves being invested or committed to the idea. If one does not care about the research question, meaning one finds it boring, uninteresting, or unimportant, then one is not likely to invest time and effort into answering it. The end result is shoddy, and perhaps incorrect, research. But if one cares about the research question, one is more likely to take care to ensure the research design is well crafted and ethical. One is less likely to take shortcuts in data collection, management, and analysis. By extension, if a research project is conducted with care, and one has taken care to implement a rigorous and ethical research design, then one is more likely to care about how the findings are interpreted and used.

There is some possibility that one can care too much, meaning one fails to be disinterested. This usually involves being too attached to the potential impacts one's research may have at some point in the future. In applied economics, projects often take years to move from initial idea to published paper. This investment of time and energy can result in researchers caring too much about the outcome of the project. Having spent years on research design, data collection, data cleaning, and the analysis, it can be difficult to end up with a bunch of null results. Because one cares so much about the research, it can be tempting to engage in *p*-hacking or other forms of data manipulation to turn null findings into significant results so as to get the paper published in a top tier journal. One way to combat this temptation is to recall that care and respect for all those involved in the research are key parts of being an ethical applied economists.

Manipulating results because one is too attached to the outcome comes at the expense of demonstrating care and respect for students, colleagues, and research participants, whose reputations and well-being may be hurt because one decided to engage in research misconduct. It also shows lack of care for those who may be affected by the policies that may result from one's research. While recognizing this does not remove the temptation, it helps one reflect on the costs and benefits of one's research decisions.

9.2.4 Honesty

The last virtue that we find helpful as an operating guide is honesty. Unlike fairness, honesty does not require a complicated definition. However, like the other virtues, the scope or extent to which one should be honest requires some discussion. At its most basic, honesty means not lying. This is perhaps the most basic prerequisite for conducting ethical research (Schroeder et al., 2019). But telling lies, through acts of commission, is only part of honesty in research. The other part of honesty is avoiding leaving out salient information through acts of omission. Honesty is not deceiving people by presenting outright falsehoods as well as not obscuring or hiding questionable or unethical actions.

For these reasons, honesty is often reframed in discussions of research ethics as transparency or a commitment to open science. While transparency covers a lot of what we mean by honesty in economics research, we believe it too often narrows the focus to the stages in the research life cycle involving data collection, management, and analysis. Honesty also encompasses integrity in developing research ideas, working with colleagues and students, dealing with publication, and disseminating research beyond the academy. Thus, avoiding acts of commission and omission involves approaching research, and all those involved in the process, with transparency and integrity. In our research, we work to prioritize clear and open communication, which means sharing and exchanging information in a way that is neither patronizing nor condescending. It requires practicing the art of good communication.

Honesty in conducting research encompasses behavior including not wasting research funds, not falsifying or manipulating data, not engaging in specification search, not plagiarizing work by others or previous work by oneself, not putting one's name on research that one did not contribute to, sharing data and code, and ethically addressing all the other numerous issues discussed here and in other books on research transparency (Christensen et al., 2019). Honesty in working with others involved in the research process means not deceiving funders; not marginalizing students, colleagues, and partners; not deceiving research participants; not obfuscating with editors and reviewers; not exaggerating or misleading journalist, policymakers, and other stakeholders; and demonstrating integrity in one's interpersonal relationships at all stages of the research life cycle.

9.3 Conclusion

There are many paths one could follow to become an ethical applied economist. And being an ethical applied economist requires renewal every day. Throughout this book, we have highlighted and discussed numerous ethical issues and ethical considerations that arise in the life cycle of a research idea. The myriad ethical challenges that can arise in conducting applied economic research can seem daunting. How does one know what the ethical choice is? How does one not become overwhelmed with the responsibility of guiding a research project from idea to published paper, let alone do it all while adhering to the highest ethical standards?

For us, the answer to these quandaries, and the way we work to stay, imperfectly, on track, is to focus on a set of virtues that can guide us both in our personal and professional lives. These virtues are fairness, respect, care, and honesty. While we find these virtues to be effective at motivating action and operating as guides, there are substitute and complement virtues that one may find are a better fit for their professional and/or personal life. Above all, these four virtues, and this entire book, are not a code or set of rules to be followed. Ethical conduct should always be the goal. Beware making a fetish of ethical compliance and rule following. Do not confuse the use value of virtues and ethical conduct with the exchange value of box checking in order to get a compliance officer or review board off one's back. We hope this book, and the concrete examples we have provided throughout, will guide and inspire researchers to ethical conduct.

ACKNOWLEDGMENTS

Though the writing process is often solitary, even when there were two of us writing in the same room, the final product is a group endeavor and we are grateful to all who contributed with their time, energy, and ideas to improve this book.

We are extremely grateful to Andy Humphries, our first editor at Routledge, who initially approached us with the idea for this book. We appreciate the patience and careful guidance Michelle Gallagher provided as the editor who saw this project to completion. Chloe Herbert and the others on the Routledge team always shared helpful and responsive answers to our questions and confusions in navigating the publishing process.

We owe a great debt to those who have mentored and guided us professionally and personally. These include Mary Arends-Kuenning, April Athnos, Joe Balagtas, Kathy Baylis, Will Masters, Maria Marshall, Jake Ricker-Gilbert, Gerald Shively, Brigitte Waldorf, and Steve Wu. Gary Thompson, our department head at the University of Arizona, has always been encouraging and embodies the virtues of fairness, respect, care, and honesty better than anyone we know in the profession.

Special thanks goes to Marc Bellemare for first soliciting our thoughts on research ethics and publishing them in *Food Policy*. He provided excellent advice as we began to develop and expand that initial article into a book. We also greatly appreciate Craig Gunderson for being willing to edit and publish our mini-special issue on research ethics in *Applied Economic Perspectives and Policy* and to those who contributed to that special issue: Steve Buccola, Sarah Janzen, Travis Lybbert, Will Masters, and Melinda Smale. Additionally, our views on research ethics have, to a great extent, been shaped by the work of and conversations with Ted Miguel, Aleksandar Bogdanoski, Katie Hoeberling, and others associated with the Berkeley Initiative for Transparency in the Social Sciences (BITSS). BITSS not only provided a forum for us to present and talk through some of these ideas at an early stage, but the Initiative has provided financial support and encouragement for this work and for our students working on issues of ethics, transparency, and reproducibility. We are proud to be BITSS Catalysts.

Much of our motivation in writing this book is to encourage our students to ensure their research is ethical. But the causal pathway is not unidirectional. Our students have been a great encouragement to us in thinking about what it means to do ethical research and to be an ethical applied economist. We have enjoyed sharing and discussing these ideas with our students who participate each year in our graduate research seminar on research ethics. We appreciate the feedback and insights from both the undergraduate and the graduate students who work with us in the Applied International Development Economics (AIDE) Lab. In particular, we are grateful to Lorin Rudin-Rush and Andrew Soderberg for proofreading and comments on structure; to Chandrakant Agme and Samantha Wetherell for proofreading and building the index; and to Ann Furbush for helping us find ways to relate what tend to be very academic topics to an audience outside the academy.

Acknowledgment hardly does justice to the love and support we have received from our families and friends over the last several years as we tried to write a book while having two kids and surviving a pandemic. We are especially grateful to those in our daily support network, including Dora Rodriguez and Tía Laura. And though our girls, Ingrid and Greta, and our cat Clementine, are sometimes more hindrance than help with respect to work, we are thankful for the light they are in our lives. We could never name everyone who has helped and supported us as we wrote and revised and revised again, but please know that we love all of you very much!

GLOSSARY

Access bias   A form of bias that gives preference to those who have gained access to elite universities, journals, funders, or other institutions, simply because they have gained access to these institutions. Access bias assumes that access is an accurate signal of quality and tends to ignore the fact that there are structural inequalities that limit access based on race, gender, socioeconomic status, and the like.

Anonymity   A component of the principle respect for persons and a key concept in data security. Anonymity refers to data acquired about an individual that contains no PII. The source of the data is anonymous and unknown to whoever collected the data and, by extension, anyone who analyzes the data. Examples include data on internet searches or ad clicks.

Asymmetric information   When parties to a transaction (buyers and sellers, principals and agents) have different sets of information, then the market is said to suffer from information asymmetries. These asymmetries typically result in suboptimal outcomes, relative to markets with perfect information.

Audience   The intended reader or listener of a piece of communication. Determining one's audience is the first step in fashioning effective communication. Identifying and understanding to whom the communication is addressed dictates both how (genre) and what (composition) is communicated.

Belmont Report   The final report written by the National Commission for the Protection of Human Subjects of Biomedical and Behavioral Research as part of its inquiry into the Tuskegee Syphilis Study and its abuse of human subjects. The report, published in 1979, sets out three principles for human subject research (respect for persons, beneficence, and justice) that form the basis for the Common Rule.

Bootstrapping   An approach to calculating confidence intervals and test statistics that uses numerical methods instead of relying on asymptotic theory, as is traditional in statistics. The bootstrap resamples from the existing data in such a way as to mimic the underlying data. By doing this over and over again, one can more precisely calculate certain statistics than using asymptotic theory, especially when key assumptions of asymptotic theory might not hold.

Categorical imperative   In Kantian ethics, the categorical imperative is a way for evaluating whether one's motivations are ethical. In its best known form, it states, "Act only according to that maxim whereby you can at the same time will that it should become a universal law."

Cognitive bias   A form of bias that gives preference to an individual's own subjective reality to form decisions as opposed to objective reality and rational judgment. Cognitive bias assumes that one's own personal experience and perceptions are an accurate reflection of reality, ignoring the fact that human cognition is limited and often operates through self-serving simplifications of complex situations.

Common Rule   The informal name for Title 45 of the Code of Federal Regulations Part 46 (45 CFR 46), the guiding principle of IRB in the U.S. The Common Rule effectively mandates that all federally funded work, involving human subjects, be reviewed and/or regulated by an IRB in order to ensure the research meets the principles set forth in the Belmont Report.

Communality   A Mertonian norm expressing the idea that scientific progress involves the entire community of researchers through a process of open exchange and discussion. Communality encompasses two principles: (1) science is inherently collaborative, and (2) scientific discoveries are claimed or "owned" by the entire scientific community, not an individual researcher.

Composition   The actual content of a piece of communication. Audience and genre help assist the author in making the difficult choices regarding what to include and what to exclude from a piece of communication. The actual composition of a piece is often the process of revising text for emphasis and clarity to ensure the audience is able to understand and correctly interpret the work.

Confidentiality   A component of the principle of respect for persons and a key concept in data security. Confidentiality refers to actions undertaken to preserve personal privacy by de-identify data when they contain PII. As such, confidentiality, like anonymity, is a property of data.

Conflicts of interest (COIs)   A situation in which an individual has a vested interest in a particular outcome. COIs can result in individuals making decisions or taking actions that benefit their personal interests at the cost of fulfilling their duty to a third party. COIs often involve financial interests, but can extend to allegiances, preferences, or opinions about a topic of study.

Consequentialist ethics   A form of ethics that maintains that what determines if an act is ethical or not is the consequences, outcomes, or end of an action. Outcome-based or teleological ethics are types of consequentialist ethics.

Cooperative Extension A pillar of the Land Grant University system, along with teaching and research. Cooperative Extension is the application of research to agricultural practices through farmer education and community outreach.

Coproduction One of four models of research–policy relations developed by Boswell and Smith (2017). The "coproduction" model not only sees research as being deeply influenced by politics but also allows for research to direct and shape policy. Thus, the model represents a more complex interrelationship between knowledge production and knowledge use.

Credibility Revolution A term coined by Joshua Angrist to describe the shift in economics from theory to empirics. Research since the start of the revolution has a particular focus on rigorous research design in order to establish causal relationships either through controlled experiments or through quasi-experimental methods.

CRediT Model An acronym for Contributor Roles Taxonomy, the model provides a set of terms and definitions to help demarcate the different contributions made to a paper by each author. The CRediT Model is discussed in more detail in Chapter 8.

Data embargo A way to encourage data sharing by providing the original researchers with a period of time under which the data are kept private. This provides the researcher with a time-limited "patent" to the data in which they have exclusive use of that data. However, this limits the ability of others to replicate recently published research until the embargo period ends.

Data extract Another way to encourage data sharing by providing only the portion of the complete data set that is required to produce the analysis in the published paper. This allows the researcher to keep the remainder of the data private until they have the time to analyze and publish out of it. Similar to data embargoes, publishing only a data extract limits the ability of others to replicate the research, since only the cleaned variables that make it into the final analysis are provided.

Data mining A somewhat dated term for a type of specification search that involves combing through data looking for significant relationships between variables that can then be presented as tests of *a priori* hypotheses. With the growth of machine learning, data mining has lost some of its derogatory meaning.

Database reconstruction theorem A theorem developed by Irit Dinur and Kobbi Nissim that establishes that publishing too many statistics too accurately from a confidential database exposes the entire database with near certainty. The implication of the theorem is that there is a hard trade-off between accuracy in data and confidentiality in data. The theorem has spurred on a number of new advancements in cryptography and database management.

Differential privacy (DP) An approach to data privacy developed in light of the database reconstruction theorem as a way to provide a precise measure of disclosure risk. Like many SDL methods, DP is essentially a process of noise infusion. However, the exact process of achieving DP means that database managers can provide a precise measure of disclosure risk and can also release the parameters of the noise infusion process without increasing the risk of disclosure.

Disinterestedness   A Mertonian norm expressing the idea that a researcher should only be interested in identifying the truth, and should thus be unconcerned with professional advancement, pecuniary motivation, or other elements of self-interest. Disinterestedness entails is that a research must report findings simply as they are, even if this goes against general wisdom, one's own beliefs, or self-interest in some other way.

Economist capture   Similar to regulatory capture, in which regulators fall under the influence of those firms they are meant to regulate, economist capture describes the tendency for economists to fall under the influence of funding agencies. Instead of pursuing research based on the Mertonian norm of disinterestedness, the captured economists pursues research for the self-serving interests of a specific funding agency, be it governmental, industrial, or philanthropic.

Equipoise   The balance of forces as is seen in an equilibrium. The term is often applied to the ethics of clinical and social science research. For a study to satisfy clinical equipoise requires that there is uncertainty about whether or not the treatment is effective. For a study to satisfy social science equipoise requires that there is uncertainty regarding the most cost-effective treatment.

Ethical pluralism   A pragmatic approach to ethics that recognizes that multiple ethical frameworks can help explain the behavior and choices of actors in the real world.

Ethics dumping   When research projects that may not be able to obtain informed consent in high-income countries move to low- and middle-income countries, where people may be more willing to consent to participate in research with risky procedures. Ethics dumping is more common in medical and pharmaceutical research than in social science research, although that does not mean it is unknown in the social sciences.

Fabrication   The making up of data and the recording or reporting of results based on that data as if the data had actually been collected.

Falsification   The manipulation of research materials, equipment, or processes, or the changing of or omission of data or results so that the results are not accurately represented in the research record.

File-drawer problem   A type of publication bias in which studies which do not produce significant results are less likely to be published than those which produce significant results. Papers with weak or nonsignificant results tend to get put into a "file drawer" instead of being published, which creates bias in the scientific record because only one type of result gets published.

Fisherian null hypothesis testing (NHT)   The primary approach in applied economics to hypothesis testing, developed by Ronald Fisher. Fisherian NHT assumes the researcher begins from a place of ignorance in which alternative hypotheses are unknown. This assumption allows for a clear statistical tests to reject the null hypothesis with a certain level of confidence. However, if one fails to reject the null, Fisherian NHT does not allow one to accept the null. The researcher is left in a place of ignorance.

Genre   The style or category of a piece of communication. Based on one's audience, the author can then select a genre that is know or common for that audience. Genre's are characterized by certain structure and syntax, which provides shortcuts or tropes that the author can use in communicating with their audience. Selecting the appropriate genre for one's audience then dictates what (composition) is communicated.

Global plagiarism   A form of plagiarism in which an author wholesale copies an existing work and passes it off as their own. In global plagiarism, the author not only reproduces verbatim pieces of text but also copies the entire original.

HARKing   An acronym for "hypothesizing after results are known." HARKing occurs when researchers determine their results and then add or remove hypotheses, without acknowledging this process. It inverts the process of the classic scientific method, which calls for researchers to first develop hypotheses and then empirically test them.

Impact factor   A measure of the importance or significance of a journal. Impact factors are calculated as the yearly mean number of citations of articles published in a journal in the last two years. So an impact factor of 4 means that the average article in the journal gets cited four times in a year.

Implicit bias   A form of bias that is unintentional or occurs automatically, without the individual necessarily being aware of it. Despite its unintentional nature, implicit bias still manifests as prejudice or stereotypes about individuals or groups and affects judgments, decisions, and behaviors.

Induced innovation   An economic theory that seeks to explain why different technologies develop along different paths with different characteristics. A classic example is the development of labor saving agricultural technology, like the mechanical thresher, in the labor-scarce but land-rich U.S. By contrast, labor-rich but land-scarce Japan developed land augmenting technologies such as chemical fertilizer and high yielding seed varieties.

Inferential disclosure   An approach to data privacy that evaluates disclosure risk as a probabilistic event. Inferential disclosure is concerned not with the perfect identification of an individual's identity or attributes, but with one's ability to infer an identity or attribute with high probability.

Informed consent   The practice of informing potential research participants about the requirements of participating in a research study, including any potential benefits and risks. After being informed, potential participants must consent to be enrolled in the study. The practice of informed consent is associated with the principle of respect for subjects in the Belmont Report.

Institutional Review Board (IRB)   Sometimes called ethical review boards (ERBs), these committees review research involving human subjects to ensure they comply with ethical rules and government regulations. Originally developed to review research in the medical sciences, IRBs now review all human subject research at U.S. universities that receive federal funds. At many economics journals, proof of IRB review is now a requirement for publishing research using experimental methods.

Instrumental good   Something that is good because it leads to a good outcome, regardless of the intent or its own inherent value. Instrumental goods fit within a consequentialist approach to ethics, where an action or thing is ethical because of it has good consequences not because it adheres to a duty or virtue.

Intellectual property (IP)   A type of property that includes intangibles, such as ideas, inventions, trademarks, designs, and artwork. Unlike tangibles, such as real estate, it can be difficult to assert ownership over IP, particularly in the context of developing a research idea.

Intrinsic good   Something that is good for its own sake, regardless of what it leads to. Intrinsic goods fit within a non-consequentialist approach to ethics, where an action or thing is ethical because of it adheres to a duty or virtue and not because it has good consequences.

Knowledge shapes policy   One of four models of research–policy relations developed by Boswell and Smith (2017). The "knowledge shapes policy" model takes an enlightenment perspective, in which policymakers will eventually be enlightened by the research, drawing the right conclusions from the research and implementing the correct policy.

Land Grant   The term refers to universities in the U.S. set up under the Morrill Acts of 1862, which provided grants of land on which to build universities. In exchange for the land, these universities focus on teaching and researching practical sciences, like agriculture and engineering. Land Grant Universities also typically engage in extension to disseminate new knowledge to those in the agricultural sector. The Three Pillars that guide Land Grants are teaching, research, and extension.

Mandated reporter   A person who is in regular contact with vulnerable populations and who has a legal mandate to ensure members of those populations are not abused and to report any observed abuses. In certain situations, a researcher conducting research among vulnerable populations may be considered a mandated reporter and be legally required to report any abuse observed in the study population.

Mertonian norms   A set of norms or values developed by Robert K. Merton to define the ethos, or characteristic spirit, of science. These norms are defined by the scientific community and individual scientists or researchers come to believe or adhere to these norms as scientifically, morally, and ethically right.

Moral hazard   A specific type of information asymmetry in which one party has an incentive to take on greater risk because they will not bear the full cost of any loss. Moral hazard results in suboptimal outcomes, relative to markets without moral hazard.

Multianalysis approach   An approach to robustness checks which the data are taken as given and the econometric specification is varied while holding the data constraint. The motivation for multianalysis comes from the fact that in empirical research there is a near infinite set of specifications that could be run and which specifications actually get selected from this larger set depends on the researcher. Multianalysis tests the sensitivity of the result to different choices of specification.

Multiverse approach   An approach to robustness checks which holds the specification constant and then varies the data used in the model. The motivation for multiverse comes from the fact that in empirical research one typically samples, at random, from a larger population and which individuals actually end up in the sample may influence the results. The multiverse approach tests the sensitivity of the result to different choices of data.

Negative assortative matching   A term borrowed from genetics, negative assortative matching refers to a process of matching in which people or species avoid matching or mating with others like themselves. Also known as dis-assortative matching, in research it refers to building a team made up of dissimilars, in terms of rank, experience, or expertise.

Noise infusion   The most common approach to SDL. Noise infusion adds random noise to the values of a variable so as to disguise the true value of the variable. Standard noise infusion methods preserve certain characteristics of the original distribution, such as the mean and the standard deviation of a variable or the correlation between variables, but are vulnerable if the exact parameters of the noise infusion process are made public.

Non-consequentialist ethics   A form of ethics that maintains that what determines if an act is ethical is whether it conforms to some proper characteristic. Duty- and rule-based or deontological ethics are types of non-consequentialist ethics.

Normative   A normative statement is one that puts forward a value judgment or makes a claim about what should be or ought to be the case, such as "the tax rate should be lowered." The term can be applied to fields of study to indicate the goal of targeting and improving certain outcomes, as in the case of normative economics and normative ethics.

Organized skepticism   A Mertonian norm expressing the idea that one must suspend judgment until all the facts are in and not leap to support or defend one's own preferred or "pet" theories. Organized skepticism involves not only questioning the work of others but also one's own work.

***p*-hacking**   Describes the conscious or subconscious manipulation of data so as to produce a desired *p*-value. While data mining searches for any significant relationship, and HARKing works backwards from a significant relationship to a hypothesis, *p*-hacking starts with a hypothesis and then manipulates the data or specification until one gets the desired result. *p*-hacking goes by many names, including data dredging, data snooping, data butchery, significance chasing, and selective inference.

Paradigm shift   A concept developed by Thomas Kuhn to describe fundamental shifts in scientific knowledge. In science, a paradigm is a framework for understanding the world. As time passes, adherence to the dominant paradigm can become dogmatic as those within the paradigm reject empirical evidence that does not fit into the paradigm. Eventually, enough evidence accrues that the dominant paradigm is no longer tenable and a shift or revolution occurs to a new paradigm that can make sense of the new evidence.

Paraphrasing   A form of plagiarism in which an author reworks the words or ideas of another but does not site the original source. While the author has not reproduced the original verbatim, they have still plagiarized by not giving credit to the original. Simply citing the original source would resolve the issue.

Patchwork plagiarism   A form of plagiarism similar to paraphrasing. In patchwork, sometimes called mosaic, plagiarism, the author copies and pastes pieces together from various texts, in order to create a new text from these pieces. The pieces might be reproduced verbatim or they may be paraphrased. If they are paraphrased, simply citing the original source would resolve the issue.

Personally identifiable information (PII)   Data that can be used to identify an individual in the population. The most commonly data considered to be PII are names, addresses, birth dates, and government ID number. However, increased data availability and the ability to combine various data sets have lead to the realization that many apparently innocuous data points can be used to identify an individual and thus must be considered PII. We discuss more about PII along with anonymity, privacy, and confidentiality in Chapter 5.

Policy shapes knowledge   One of four models of research–policy relations developed by Boswell and Smith (2017). The "policy shapes knowledge" model is inherently political, in that government entities are directing or driving research for both tactical and strategic purposes.

Positive   A positive statement is one that puts forward a verifiable or testable hypothesis, such as "an increase in the tax rate will increase revenue." The term *positive* can also be used to describe how one approaches a field of study, such as positive economics or positive ethics.

Positive assortative matching   Also borrowed from genetics, positive assortative matching refers to a process of matching in which people or species seek to match or mate with others like themselves. In research it refers building a team made up of similars, in terms of rank, experience, or expertise.

Pre-analysis plan (PAP)   A document that, prior to any analysis taking place, defines how the researcher plans to analyze a set of data while answering a hypothesis or several hypotheses. PAPs are designed to force the researcher to follow the classic scientific method of disinterestedly proposing and testing hypotheses by limiting the researcher's ability to engage in *p*-hacking or other forms of specification search. Often PAPs are filed in public repositories.

Predatory publication Predatory journals charge publication fees to authors without providing the review and editorial services associated with legitimate journals. Predatory conferences charge researchers registration fees without providing the scholarly interactions expected from legitimate conferences. They prioritize self-interest at the expense of scientific knowledge.

Pre-print Similar to a working paper, although a preprint is self-published by posting it to an internet archive or website in order to get comments and critiques prior to submission to a journal. A preprint lacks the credibility of a working paper, because it was not invited for inclusion in an ongoing series. However, like a working paper, a preprint has not undergone peer review.

Primary data Data that are collected by the researcher, meaning collecting it will most likely require ethical review and obtaining informed consent. Primary data can either be experimental or observational.

Privacy A component of the principle of respect for persons and a goal in data security. Privacy refers to a person's right or ability to control who has access to data about them and the extent to which data may reveal information about them. By definition, data that are anonymous protects an individual's privacy, though privacy can be protected even when data contain PII.

Publication bias A trend in publishing toward an overabundance of statistically significance results. The outcome of publication bias is that the published literature does not reflect the truth, as readers only see the true significant results plus many false positives. Left out of the published literature, in the file drawer, are the true nonsignificant results plus the false negatives.

Registered reports A unique track for submitting a paper to a journal in which the author submits the research idea and analysis plan and the editor and reviewers accept or reject the plan based on the merits of the research idea and not the results. If accepted, the authors then undertake the research and publish the paper, regardless of what the results end up showing.

Reidentification attack An attempt to use a data base or a combination of several data bases to reidentify the data of individuals that had previously been de-identified. Reidentification attacks frequently combine various public data sets with de-identified data in such a way that they can infer the identity of an individual in the original data set. Reidentification attacks have expanded the scope of what is considered personally identifiable information (PII).

Replicability An original result is considered replicable when one obtains consistent results across studies that are working to answer the same question but using new data or different methods. This procedure is often called a conceptual replication, an extension, or a verification test.

Replication package A digital package that includes data, code, and implementation details in a README file, such that others can replicate and reproduce the original work. Many journals in economics now require replication packages be posted with the published paper.

Repository   Any permanent, online, time-stamped archive that provides a DOI (digital object identifier) to the information placed in the repository. In economics, repositories are used to store PAPs and provide a way to combat the file-drawer problem by creating a record of all studies undertaken, regardless of whether the results are eventually published. Repositories are also used to store data and code for replication.

Reproducibility   The degree of similarity (or extent of differences) between an original result and the results of analysis carried out by others with the same data, using the same method. This procedure is often called direct replication or reanalysis.

Researcher degrees of freedom   The concept that in any research project, researchers have flexibility in designing the study as well as cleaning and analyzing the data. The more degrees of freedom the greater the flexibility and the greater the flexibility the more opportunities a researcher has to accidentally or surreptitiously make a choice that impacts the results. Larger degrees of freedom mean more opportunity for a researcher to engage in misconduct.

Risk–benefit assessment   The practice of comparing and judging the relative potential risks and benefits of a study on research participants. A common criteria for making risk–benefit assessments is the concept of equipoise. The practice of risk–benefit assessment is associated with the principle of beneficence in the Belmont Report.

Robustness checks   Any one of a variety of alternative econometric specifications or variations on the data designed to test the sensitivity of the main results. Also called sensitivity analysis, the goal of robustness checks is to examine the sturdiness of potentially critical assumptions to variations in the model and data.

Salami slicing   A type of self-plagiarism in which the author publishes slight variations on an idea in order to maximize the total number of publications from that single idea. Salami slicing wastes the time of editors and reviewers on papers that make little contribution. The practice distorts the state of knowledge because it cuts a single piece of evidence into many pieces and then presents them as if they were a set independent pieces of evidence.

Secondary data   Data that are collected by a third party instead of the research, meaning the research does not need to undergo ethical review to use the data. The third party that collected the data may have had to obtain informed consent or the data may be administrative data or passively collected data, such as clicks on an internet ad, and did not require IRB approval.

Self-plagiarism   A form of plagiarism in which an author reproduces their own ideas published elsewhere without citing those other publications. Self-plagiarism is an attempt by an author to get credit multiple times for the same idea by hiding or eliding the fact that they have previous published the idea.

Separate spheres   One of four models of research–policy relations developed by Boswell and Smith (2017). In the "separate spheres" model research and policy exist in autonomous realms, each operating with a different set of objectives, logic, and meanings. This is sometimes described the two communities thesis, in which a boundary or gap separates researchers and policymakers.

Source-based plagiarism   A form of plagiarism in which sources for facts or ideas are either invented or corrupted to a degree that it no longer reflects the idea in the original. Source-based plagiarism occurs when an author wants to give their own idea a semblance of credibility by citing a source in support of their own idea.

Specification search   A catchall term for any type of falsification of empirical results through a process of opportunistic searching for models or variables that yield the desired results. Examples include data mining, HARKing, and p-hacking.

Statistical disclosure limitation (SDL)   The primary way for ensuring confidentiality in publicly available data sets prior to the database reconstruction theorem. SDL is not one method but a suite of methods that can be used to reduce the likelihood that an individual could use the data for a reidentification attack.

Synthetic data   A variant of noise infusion that seeks to create an entirely new, noise infused data set, instead of just adding noise to a single variable. The synthetic data are drawn from the same data-generating process as the original data so as to preserve the same structure of the original data, although not all original relationships can be preserved.

Text recycling   A type of self-plagiarism in which the author reuses sentences or phrases from their own previously published works. Text recycling is a mild form of self-plagiarism, since it does not present an old idea as a new idea. Rather, it re-uses pieces of existing text as a shortcut to rewriting that text. In some cases, such as describing data that has been used in multiple papers, it can be difficult to completely avoid text recycling.

Type I error   Also known as a false positive, a Type I error is when one rejects a true null hypothesis. The classic example is when a jury votes to convict an innocent person.

Type II error   Also known as a false negative, a Type II error is when one fails to reject a false null hypothesis. The classic example is when a jury votes to acquit a guilty person.

Type M errors   An alternative to the classic Type I and II errors in Fisherian NHT. A Type M error, or magnitude error, is when the magnitude of the point estimate over or under estimates the true effect size.

Type S errors   An alternative to the classic Type I and II errors in Fisherian NHT. A Type S error, or sign error, is when the sign on the point estimate is in the opposite direction of the true effect.

Ulysses pact   A term from the medical and legal profession that refers to a freely made decision to bind oneself to a set of actions in the future. In social science, a PAP is a type of Ulysses pact that binds the researcher to a specific research design and plan of analysis.

Universalism   A Mertonian norm expressing the principle that the acceptance (or rejection) of claims does not depend on the attributes and traits of researchers or investigators themselves. Universalism is the idea that the process of research is inherently impersonal.

Working papers   A version of a paper that has been invited to to be published by an organization as part of an ongoing series of such publications. An important distinction between a working paper and a paper published in a journal is that working papers have not undergone peer review. The purpose of a working paper is to present a work in progress in order to get comments and critiques on it, as the author prepares the paper for submission to a journal.

BIBLIOGRAPHY

AAEA (2019). *AAEA Anti-Harassment and Code of Conduct Policy*. www.aaea.org/about-aaea.

Abadie, A. (2020). Statistical non-significance in empirical economics. *American Economic Review: Insights 2*(2), 193–208.

Abadie, A., S. Athey, G. W. Imbens, and J. M. Wooldridge (2020). Sampling-based versus design-based uncertainty in regression analysis. *Econometrica 88*(1), 265–96.

Abeler, J., D. Nosenzo, and C. Raymond (2019). Preferences for truth-telling. *Econometrica 87*(4), 1115–53.

Abowd, J. M. (2018). Staring down the database reconstruction theorem. *Presentation Made at the Joint Statistical Meetings*, Vancouver, BC, Canada.

Abowd, J. M. and I. M. Schmutte (2015). Economic analysis and statistical disclosure limitation. *Brookings Papers on Economic Activity 46*, 221–93.

Abowd, J. M. and I. M. Schmutte (2019). An economic analysis of privacy protection and statistical accuracy as social choice. *American Economic Review 109*(1), 171–202.

Abowd, J. M., I. M. Schmutte, W. N. Sexton, and L. Vilhuber (2019). Why the economics profession must actively participate in the privacy protection debate. *AEA Paers and Proceedings 109*, 397–402.

Abraham, K. G. (2019). Reconciling data access and privacy: Building a sustainable model for the future. *AEA Paers and Proceedings 109*, 409–13.

Abramowicz, M. and A. Szafarz (2020). Ethics of RCTs: Should economists care about equipoise? In F. Bédécarrats, I. Guérin, and F. Roubaud (Eds.), *Randomized Control Trials in the Field of Development: A Critical Perspective*, pp. 280–92. Oxford: Oxford University Press.

Acciai, F., A. J. Yellow Horse, S. Martinelli, A. Josephson, T. P. Evans, and P. Ohri-Vachaspati (2020)1. *Impacts of Covid-19 on Food Security in Arizona*. College of Health Solutions, Arizona State University.

Acemoglu, D., S. Johnson, and J. A. Robinson (2001). The colonial origins of comparative development: An empirical investigation. *American Economic Review 91*(5), 1369–401.

Adler, P. A. and P. Adler (2016). IRBan renewal. In W. C. Van Den Hoonaard and A. Hamilton (Eds.), *The Ethics Rupture: Exploring Alternatives to Formal Research Ethics Review*, pp. 73–90. Toronto: Toronto University Press.

AEA (2012). *AEA Disclosure Policy*. www.aeaweb.org/journals/policies/disclosure-policy.

AEA (2018). *AEA Code of Professional Conduct*. www.aeaweb.org/about-aea/code-of-conduct.

AEA (2019). *AEA Data and Code Availability Policy*. www.aeaweb.org/journals/policies/data-code.

AEA (2020). *AEA Data and Code Availability Policy*. www.aeaweb.org/journals/data/data-code-policy.

AEA (2021). *Preparing Your Files for Verification*. aeadataeditor.github.io/aea-de-guidance/preparing-for-data-deposit.html.

Agrawal, A. and A. Goldfarb (2008). Restructuring research: Communication costs and the democratization of university innovation. *American Economic Review 98*(4), 1578–90.

Ahamed, L. (2009). *Lords of Finance: The Bankers Who Broke the World*. New York: Penguin Press.

Ahmadpoor, M. and B. F. Jones (2019). Decoding team and individual impact in science and invention. *Proceedings of the National Academy of Sciences 116*(28), 13885–90.

AJAE (n.d.). *AJAE Policy on Data and Documentation*. onlinelibrary.wiley.com/page/journal/14678276/homepage/author-guidelines.

Akerlof, G. A. (1970). The market for "lemons": Quality uncertainty and the market mechanism. *Quarterly Journal of Economics 84*(3), 488–500.

Akerlof, G. A. (1991). Procrastination and obedience. *American Economic Review 81*(2), 1–19.

Al Rafi, D. A., A. Josephson, J.D. Michler, and V. Pede (2023). Impact of stress tolerant rice varieties adoption in flood prone regions of South Asia. *OSF Registries* doi.org/10.17605/OSF.IO/YE7PV.

Allen, L., A. O'Connell, and V. Kiermer (2019). How can we ensure visibility and diversity in research contributions? How the Contributor Role Taxonomy CRediT is helping the shift from authorship to contributorship. *Learned Publishing 32*, 71–74.

Allgood, S., L. Badgett, A. Bayer, M. Bertrand, S. E. Black, N. Bloom, and L. D. Cook (2019). AEA professional climate survey: Final report. *Technical Report*, AEA, Nashville.

AlShebli, B. K., T. Rahwan, and W. L. Woon (2018). The preeminence of ethnic diversity in scientific collaboration. *Nature Communications 9*, 5163.

Alston, J. M., M. A. Andersen, J. S. James, and P. G. Pardey (2011). The economic returns to U.S. public agricultural research. *The American Journal of Agricultural Economics 93*(5), 1257–77.

American Economic Review (n.d.). *Guidelines for Accepted Articles*. www.aeaweb.org/journals/aer/styleguide#IVH.

Anderson, J. R. and G. Feder (2007). Agricultural extension. In R. Everson and P. Pingali (Eds.), *The Handbook of Agricultural Economics*, pp. 2343–78. Amsterdam, Netherlands: North Holland Publishing Company.

Anderson, M. L. and J. Magruder (2017). Split-sample strategies for avoiding false discoveries. *Working Paper 23544*, National Bureau of Economic Research.

Anderson, M. S., B. C. Martinson, and R. De Vries (2007). Normative dissonance in science: Results from a national survey of U.S. scientists. *Journal of Empirical Research on Human Research Ethics 2*(4), 3–14.

Andrews, I. and M. Kasy (2019). Identification of and correction for publication bias. *American Economic Review 109*(8), 2766–94.

Angrist, J. D. and J.-S. Pischke (2009). *Mostly Harmless Econometrics: An Empiricist's Companion*. Princeton: Princeton University Press.

Anonymous (1893). Contributor's club: Self-plagiarism. *The Atlantic Monthly 72*(431), 429–32.

Arbel, Y., R. Bar-El, E. Siniver, and Y. Tobol (2014). Roll a die and tell a lie – What affects honesty? *Journal of Economic Behavior and Organization 107*(A), 153–72.

Arendt, H. (2018). *Thinking Without a Banister: Essays in Understanding, 1953–1975*. New York: Schocken Books.

Aristotle (2019). *Nicomachean Ethics* (3rd ed.). Indianapolis: Hackett.

Asiedu, E., D. Karlan, M. Lambon-Quayefio, and C. Udry (2021). A call for structured ethics appendices in social science papers. *Proceedings of the National Academy of Sciences 118*(29), e2024570118.

Autor, D. H. (2011). Correspondence: David H. Autor and Bruno S. Frey. *Journal of Economic Perspectives 25*(3), 239–40.

Babbie, E. R. (2009). *The Practices of Social Research*. Belmont, CA: Wadsworth Publishing.

Bailey, M., R. Cao, T. Kuchler, and J. Stroebel (2018). The economic effects of social networks: Evidence from the housing market. *Journal of Political Economy 126*(6), 2224–76.

Bailey, M., R. Cao, T. Kuchler, and J. Stroebel (2020). The determinants of social connectedness in Europe. In S. Aref, K. Bontcheva, M. Braghieri, F. Dignum, F. Giannotti, F. Grisolia, and D. Pedreschi (Eds.), *Social Informatics*, pp. 1–14. Cham: Springer International Publishing.

Bailey, M., A. Gupta, S. Hillenbrand, T. Kuchler, R. Richmond, and J. Stroebel (2021). International trade and social connectedness. *Journal of International Economics 129*, 103418.

Bailey, M., D. Johnston, M. Koenen, T. Kuchler, D. Russel, and J. Stroebel (2020)23. Social networks shape beliefs and behavior: Evidence from social distancing during the COVID-19 pandemic. *NBER Working Paper No. 28234*.

Bailey, M., D. Johnston, T. Kuchler, J. Stroebel, and A. Wong (2022). Peer effects in product adoption. *American Economic Journal: Applied Economics 14*(3), 488–526.

Banerjee, A. V. (2005). 'New development economics' and the challenge to theory. *Economic and Political Weekly 40*(40), 4340–4.

Barbaro, M. and T. Zeller (2006). A face is exposed for AOL searcher no. 4417749. *The New York Times*.

Bardhan, P. (2003). Journal publication in economics: A view from the periphery. *The Economic Journal 113*(June), F332–7.

Bardhan, P. (2005). Theory or empirics in development economics. *Economic and Political Weekly 40*(40), 4333–5.

Baron, N. (2010). *Escape from the Ivory Tower: A Guide to Making Your Science Matter*. Washington, DC: Island Press.

Barrett, C. B., A. Agrawal, O. T. Coomes, and J.-P. Platteau (2009). *Stripe Review of Social Sciences in the CGIAR*. Consultative Group on International Agricultural Research: CGIAR Science Council.

Barrett, C. B. and M. R. Carter (2010). The power and pitfalls of experiments in development economics: Some non-random reflections. *Applied Economics Perspectives and Policy 32*(4), 515–48.

Barrett, C. B., J. W. Cason, and E. Lentz (2020). *Overseas Research: A Practical Guide*. New York: Routledge.

Barry, P. J. (1993). Coordinating research, extension, and outreach in agricultural economics. *The American Journal of Agricultural Economics 75*(5), 1091–101.

Basken, P. (2017). Why Beall's list died – and what it left unresolved about open access. *The Chronicle of Higher Education: Opinion*. www.chronicle.com/article/why-bealls-list-died-and-what-it-left-unresolved-about-open-access/.

Basu, K. (2005). New empirical development economics: Remarks on its philosophical foundations. *Economic and Political Weekly 40*(40), 4336–9.

Baumann, A. and K. Wohlrabe (2020). Where have all the working papers gone? Evidence from four major economics working paper series. *Scientometrics 124*, 2433–41.

Beauchamp, T. L. (2005). On the origins and evolution of the *Belmont Report*. In J. F. Childress, E. M. Meslin, and H. T. Shapiro (Eds.), *Belmont Revisited*, pp. 12–25. Washington, DC: Georgetown University Press.

Becker, G. (1968). Crime and punishment: An economic approach. *Journal of Political Economy 76*(2), 169–217.

Becker, G. (1973). A theory of marriage: Part I. *Journal of Political Economy 81*(4), 813–46.

Beecher, H. K. (1966). Ethics and clinical research. *New England Journal of Medicine 274*(24), 1354–60.

Bellemare, M. F. (2022a). *Doing Economics: What You Should Have Learned in Grad School – But Didn't*. Cambridge, MA: MIT Press.

Bellemare, M. F. (2022b). *Top Journals in Agricultural Economics – 2022 Edition*. Marc Bellemare: Agricultural and Applied Economics – Without Apology.

Bellemare, M. F., L. Novak, and T. L. Steinmetz (2015). All in the family: Explaining the persistence of female genital cutting in West Africa. *Journal of Development Economics 116*, 252–65.

Belluz, J. (2015). Worm wars: The fight tearing apart the global health community, explained. *Vox*. www.vox.com/2015/7/24/9031909/worm-wars-explained.

Benford, F. (1938). The law of anomalous numbers. *Proceedings of the American Philosophical Society 78*(4), 551–72.

Benjamin, D. (1992). Household composition, labor markets, and labor demand: Testing for separation in agricultural household models. *Econometrica 60*, 287–322.

Bentham, J. (1780). An introduction to the principles of morals and legislation. In J. Burns and H. Hart (Eds.), *The Collected Works of Jeremy Bentham*, Volume 2. Oxford: Oxford University Press. Reprint (1996).

Berg, J. and H. Johnston (2019). Too good to be true? a comment on Hall and Krueger's analysis of the labor market for Uber's driver-partners. *ILR Review 72*(1), 39–68.

Bernanke, B. S. (2004). Editorial statement. *American Economic Review 94*(1), 404.

Berrett, D. (2012). Economists adopt new disclosure rules for authors of published research. *The Chronicle of Higher Education*. www.chronicle.com/article/economists-adopt-new-disclosure-rules-for-authors-of-published-research/.

Bertrand, M., S. Djankov, R. Hanna, and S. Mullainathan (2007). Obtaining a driver's license in India: An experimental approach to studying corruption. *Quarterly Journal of Economics 122*(4), 1639–76.

Blanco-Perez, C. and A. Brodeur (2020). Publication bias and editorial statement on negative findings. *The Economic Journal 130*(July), 1226–47.

Blankespoor, B., T. Croft, T. Dontamsetti, B. Mayala, and S. Murray (2021). Spatial anonymization: Guidance note prepared for the Inter-Secretariat working group on household surveys. *UN Inter-secretariat Working Group on Household Surveys Task Force on Spatial Anonymization in Public Use Household Survey Datasets*. unstats.un.org/iswghs/taskforces/documents/Spatial_Anonymization_Report_submit01272021_ISWGHS.pdf.

Blattman, C. (2015). Dear journalists and policy makers: What you need to know about the worm wars. *Chris Blattman Blog*. chrisblattman.com/blog/2015/07/23/dear-journalists-and-policymakers-what-you-need-to-know-about-the-worm-wars/.

Bloem, J. R. (2018). Are economics papers too long? *Jeffrey R. Bloem Blog*. jeffbloem. wordpress.com/2018/07/27/are-economics-papers-too-long/.

Bogdanoski, A., A. Foster, D. Karlan, and E. Miguel (201845). Registered reports: Piloting a pre-results review process at the journal of development economics. *MetaArix*. osf.io/preprints/metaarxiv/v7pxe/.

Boldrin, M. and D. K. Levin (2005). The economics of ideas and intellectual property. *Proceedings of the National Academy of Sciences 102*(4), 1252–6.

Boseley, S. (2015). New research debunks merits of global deworming programmes. *The Guardian*.

Bosilovich, M., R. Lucchesi, and M. Suarez (2016). MERRA2: File specification. *GMAO Office Note No. 9 (Version 1.1)*. gmao.gsfc.nasa.gov/pubs/office_notes.

Boswell, C. and K. Smith (2017). Rethinking policy "impact": Four models of research-policy relations. *Palgrave Communications 3*(1), 44.

Bottoms, S. (2014). Timeliness cruelty: Performing the Stanford prison experiment. *Performance research 19*(3), 162–75.

Brodeur, A., N. Cook, and A. Heyes (2020). Methods matter: P-hacking and publication bias in causal analysis in economics. *American Economic Review 110*(11), 3634–60.

Brodeur, A., N. Cook, and A. Heyes (2022). *Data and Code For: Methods Matter: P-hacking and Publication Bias in Causal Analysis in Economics*. Nashville, TN: American Economic Association [publisher]. Ann Arbor, MI: Inter-University Consortium for Political and Social Research [distributor], 2022–02–16. doi.org/10.3886/E120246V2.

Brodeur, A., M. Lé, M. Sangnier, and Y. Zylberberg (2016). Star Wars: The empirics strike back. *American Economic Journal: Applied Economics 8*(1), 1–32.

Broockman, D., J. Kalla, and P. Aronow (2015). *Irregularities in LeCour (2014)*. Mimeo, Stanford University.

Brown, J. P., D. M. Lambert, and T. R. Wojan (2019). The effect of the conservation reserve program on rural economics: Deriving a statistical result from a null finding. *American Journal of Agricultural Economics 101*(2), 528–40.

Bryan, G., J. J. Choi, and D. Karlan (2021). Randomizing religion: The impact of Protestant evangelism on economic outcomes. *Quarterly Journal of Economics 136*(1), 293–380.

Burke, M., A. Driscoll, D. B. Lobell, and S. Ermon (2021). Using satellite imagery to understand and promote sustainable development. *Science 371*(6536), eabe8628.

Burris, S. (2008). Regulatory innovation in the governance of human subjects research: A cautionary tale and some modest proposals. *Regulation and Governance 2*(1), 65–84.

Cai, Y. and T. S. Lontzek (2019). The social cost of carbon with economic and climate risks. *Journal of Political Economy 127*(6), 2684–734.

Calarco, J. M. (2020). *A Field Guide to Grad School*. Princeton: Princeton University Press.

Callahan, J. L. (2013). Creation of a moral panic? Self-plagiarism in the academy. *Human Resource Development Review 13*(1), 3–10.

Callon, M. (1998). Introduction: The embeddedness of economic markets in economics. *The Sociological Review 46*(1_suppl), 1–57.

Caplan, N. (1979). The two-communities theory and knowledge utilization. *American Behavioral Scientist 22*(3), 459–70.

Card, D. (1992a). Do minimum wages reduce employment? A case study of California, 1987–1989. *Industrial and Labor Relations Review 46*(1), 38–54.

Card, D. (1992b). Using regional variation in wages to measure the effects of the federal minimum wage. *Industrial and Labor Relations Review 46*(1), 22–37.

Card, D. and S. Della-Vigna (2013). Nine facts about top journals in economics. *Journal of Economic Literature 51*(1), 144–61.

Card, D. and S. Della-Vigna (2014). Page limits on economics articles: Evidence from two journals. *Journal of Economic Perspectives 28*(3), 149–68.

Card, D. and S. Della-Vigna (2020). What do editors maximize? Evidence from four economics journals. *Review of Economics and Statistics 102*(1), 195–217.

Card, D., L. F. Katz, and A. B. Krueger (1994). Comment on David Neumark and William Wascher, "employment effects of minimum and subminimum wages: Panel data on state minimum wage laws". *Industrial and Labor Relations Review 47*(3), 487–96.

Card, D. and A. B. Krueger (1994). Minimum wages and employment: A case study of the fast-food industry in New Jersey and Pennsylvania. *American Economic Review 84*(4), 772–93.

Carletto, C., S. Gourlay, S. Murray, and A. Zezza (2017). Cheaper, faster, and more than good enough: Is GPS the new gold standard in land area measurement. *Survey Research Methods 11*(3), 235–65.

Carreyrou, J. (2018). *Bad Blood: Secrets and Lies in a Silicon Valley Startup*. New York: Alfred A. Knopf.

Carrick-Hagenbarth, J. and G. A. Epstein (2012). Dangerous interconnectedness: Economists' conflicts of interest, ideology and financial crisis. *Cambridge Journal of Economics 36*(1), 43–63.

Cartwright, N. (2007). *Hunting Causes and Using Them: Approaches in Philosophy and Economics*. Cambridge: Cambridge University Press.

Casey, K., R. Glennerster, and E. Miguel (2012). Reshaping institutions: Evidence on aid impacts using a preanalysis plan. *Quarterly Journal of Economic 127*(4), 1755–812.

Cassidy, J. (2010). *How Markets Fail: The Rise and Fall of Free Market Economics*. New York: Picador.

CGIAR (n.d.). *Ethics Training, Advice, and Additional Resources*. cgiar.org/howwe-work/accountability/ethics/training-advice-and-additional-resources/.

Chambers, C. D. and L. Tzavella (2022). The past, present and future of registered reports. *Nature Human Behaviour 6*, 29–42.

Chang, A. C. (2018). A replication recipe: List your ingredients before you start cooking. *Economics: The Open-Access, Open-Assessment E-Journal 12*, 1–8.

Chang, A. C. (2020). Personal Communication, June 30.

Chang, A. C., L. R. Cohen, A. Glazer, and U. Paul (2020a). *Politicians Avoid Tax Increases Around Elections*. Mimeo.

Chang, A. C., L. R. Cohen, A. Glazer, and U. Paul (2020b). *Politics of Gasoline and Other Taxes*. osf.io/f2nr9.

Chang, A. C. and P. Li (2017). A preanalysis plan to replicate sixty economics research papers that worked half of the time. *American Economic Review 107*(5), 60–4.

Chang, A. C. and P. Li (2018). Measurement error in macroeconomic data and economics research: Data revisions, gross domestic product, and gross domestic income. *Economic Inquiry 56*(3), 1846–69.

Chang, A. C. and P. Li (2022). Is economics research replicable? Sixty published papers from thirteen journals say "often not". *Critical Finance Review 11*. doi.org/10.1561/104.00000053.

Chen, M., W. Shi, P. Xie, V. B. Silva, V. E. Kousky, R. W. Higgins, and J. E. Janowiak (2008). Assessing objective techniques for gauge-based analyses of global daily precipitation. *Journal of Geophysical Research 113*, D04110.

Chetty, R. and J. N. Friedman (2019a). A practical method to reduce privacy loss when disclosing statistics based on small cells. *Journal of Privacy and Confidentiality 9*(2). doi.org/10.29012/jpc.716.

Chetty, R. and J. N. Friedman (2019b). A practical method to reduce privacy loss when disclosing statistics based on small samples. *AEA Paers and Proceedings 109*, 414–20.

Chetty, R. and J. N. Friedman (2019c). *Replication Data For: A Practical Method to Reduce Privacy Loss When Disclosing Statistics Based on Small Samples*. Nashville, TN: American Economic Association [publisher]. Ann Arbor, MI: Inter-university Consortium for Political and Social Research [distributor], 2019–12–07. doi.org/10.3886/E116494V1.

Chetty, R., J. N. Friedman, N. Hendren, M. R. Jones, and S. R. Porter (2018)67. The opportunity atlas: Mapping the childhood roots of social mobility. *NBER Working Paper 25147*.

Chetty, R., E. Saez, and L. Sándor (2014). What policies increase prosocial behavior? An experiment with referees at the journal of public economics. *Journal of Economic Perspectives 28*(3), 169–88.

Chetty, R., E. Saez, and L. Sándor (2019). *Replication Data For: What Policies Increase Prosocial Behavior? An Experiment with Referees at the Journal of Public Economics*. Nashville, TN: American Economic Association [publisher]. Ann Arbor, MI: Inter-university Consortium for Political and Social Research [distributor], 2019–10–12. doi.org/10.3886/E113930V1.

Christensen, G. (2016). Figures on AEA registrations and AER proprietary data. *Harvard Dataverse V*(11). https://doi.org/10.7910/DVN/FUO7FC.

Christensen, G., J. Freese, and E. Miguel (2019). *Transparent and Reproducible Social Science Research: How to Do Open Science*. Oakland: University of California Press.

Christensen, G. and E. Miguel (2018). Transparency, reproducibility, and the credibility of economics research. *Journal of Economic Perspectives 56*(3), 920–80.

Clemens, M. A. (2017). The meaning of failed replications: A review and proposal. *Journal of Economic Surveys 31*(1), 326–42.

Coase, R. (1994). *Essays on Economics and Economists*. Chicago: Chicago University Press.

Coffman, L. C. and M. Niederle (2015). Pre-analysis plans have limited upside, especially where replications are feasible. *Journal of Economic Perspectives 29*(3), 81–98.

Coffman, L. C., M. Niederle, and A. J. Wilson (2017). A proposal to organize and promote replications. *American Economic Review 107*(5), 41–5.

Cohen, J. and P. Dupas (2010). Free distribution or cost-sharing? evidence from a randomized malaria prevention experiment. *Quarterly Journal of Economics 125*(1), 1–45.

Comstock, G. (2013). *Research Ethics: A Philosophical Guide to the Responsible Conduct of Research*. Cambridge: Cambridge University Press.

Corno, L., N. Hildebrandt, and A. Voena (2020). Age of marriage, weather shocks, and the direction of marriage payments. *Econometrica 88*(3), 879–915.

COS (n.d.). *Center for Open Science Mission*. www.cos.io/about/mission.

Coville, A., S. Galiani, P. Gertler, and S. Yoshida (2020)89. Financing municipal water and sanitation services in Nairobi's informal settlements. *NBER Working Paper No. 27569*.

Crew, B. (2019).1011 10 tips for tweeting research. *Nature Index*.

Croft, G. K. (2019). The U.S. land-grant university system: An overview. *Technical Report, Congressional Research Service (CRS)*, Washington, DC.

Cronin, B. (2013). Self-plagiarism: An odious oxymoron. *Journal of the American Society for Information Science and Technology 64*(5), 873.

CRS (2022). US research and development funding and performance: Fact sheet. *Congressional Research Service (CRS) Report R44307*, Washington, DC.

Currie, J. and B. Fallick (1996). The minimum wage and the employment of youth evidence from the NLSY. *Journal of Human Resources 31*(2), 404–28.

Dahringer, H. K. (2016). The Internet as a stage: Dramaturgy, research ethics boards, and privacy as "performance". In W. C. Van Den Hoonaard and A. Hamilton (Eds.), *The Ethics*

Rupture: Exploring Alternatives to Formal Research Ethics Review, pp. 135–52. Toronto: Toronto University Press.

Davey, C., A. M. Aiken, R. J. Hayes, and J. R. Hargreaves (2015). Re-analysis of health and educational impacts of a school-based deworming programme in western Kenya: A statistical replication of a cluster quasi-randomized stepped-wedge trial. *International Journal of Epidemiology 44*(5), 1581–92.

De Angelis, C., J. M. Drazen, F. A. Frizelle, C. Haug, J. Hoey, R. Horton, S. Kotzin, C. Laine, A. Marusic, A. J. P. Overbeke, T. V. Schroeder, H. C. Sox, and M. B. Van Der Weyden (2004). Clinical trial registration: A statement from the international committee of medical journal editors. *New England Journal of Medicine 351*(12), 1250–1.

Deaton, A. (2010). Instruments, randomization, and learning about development. *Journal of Economic Literature 48*(2), 424–55.

Deaton, A. (2020). Randomization in the tropics revisited, a theme and eleven variations. In F. Bédécarrats, I. Guérin, and F. Roubaud (Eds.), *Randomized Control Trials in the Field of Development: A Critical Perspective*, pp. 29–46. Oxford: Oxford University Press.

Deere, D., K. M. Murphy, and F. Welch (1995). Employment and the 1990–1991 minimum-wage hike. *American Economic Review Papers and Proceedings 85*(2), 232–7.

DeMartino, G. F. (2011). *The Economist's Oath: On the Need for and Content of Professional Economic Ethics*. Oxford: Oxford University Press.

DeMartino, G. F. and D. N. McCloskey (2016). Introduction, or why this handbook? In G. F. DeMartino and D. N. McCloskey (Eds.), *The Oxford Handbook of Professional Economic Ethics*, pp. 3–10. Oxford: Oxford University Press.

de Souza Leão, L. and G. Eyal (2020). Searching under the streetlight: A historical perspective on the rise of randomistas. *World Development 127*, 104781.

Dewald, W. G., J. G. Thursby, and R. G. Anderson (1986). Replication in empirical economics: The *Journal of Money, Credit, and Banking Project. American Economic Review 76*(4), 587–603.

Diaconis, P. and D. Freedman (1979). On rounding percentages. *Journal of the American Statistical Association 74*(366), 359–64.

Dillard, A. (1989). *The Writing Life*. New York: Harper & Row.

Dinur, I. and K. Nissim (20031213). Revealing information while preserving privacy. *Proceedings of ACM SIGMOD-SIGACT-SIGART Symposium on Principles of Database Systems 22*, 202–10.

Doherty, M. (2022). Scholars and journalists, stop fighting! These related endeavors deserve cooperation, not competition. *The Chronicle of Higher Education: Opinion.* www.chronicle.com/article/scholars-and-journalists-stop-fighting.

Doleac, J. L. and A. Mukherjee (2022). The effects of naloxone access laws on opioid abuse, mortality, and crime. *Journal of Law and Economics 65*(2), 211–38.

Dubner, S. (2010). Towards an ethical economics of food policy. *Blog Post at Freakonomics Blog.* freakonomics.com/2010/06/toward-an-ethical-economics-of-food-policy.

Duflo, E., A. Banerjee, A. Finkelstein, L. F. Katz, B. A. Olken, and A. Sautman (2020)1415. In praise of moderation: Suggestions for the scope and use of pre-analysis plans for RCTs in economics. *NBER Working Paper No. 26993*.

Duflo, E., R. Glennerster, and M. Kremmer (2007). Using randomization in development economics research: A toolkit. In T. P. Schultz and J. A. Strauss (Eds.), *Handbook of Development Economics*, pp. 3895–962. Amsterdam: North Holland.

Durlauf, S. N. and A. Seshardi (2003). Is assortative matching efficient? *Economic Theory 21*(2), 475–93.

Duvendack, M., R. Palmer-Jones, and W. R. Reed (2017). What is meant by "replication" and why does it encounter resistence in economics? *American Economic Review 107*(5), 46–51.

Dwork, C., F. McSherry, K. Nissim, and A. Smith (2006). Calibrating noise to sensitivity in private data analysis. In S. Halevi and T. Rabin (Eds.), *Theory of Cryptography*, pp. 265–84. Berlin and Heidelberg: Springer.

Econometrica (n.d.). *Instructions for Submitting Articles.* www.econometricsociety.org/publications/econometrica/information-authors/instructions-submitting-articles# supplementary.

Edwards, D. J. (2015). Dissemination of research results: On the path to practice change. *Canadian Journal of Hospital Pharmacy 68*(6), 465–9.

Elliott, C. (2017). Tuskegee truth teller. *The American Scholar.*

Ellis, L. M. (2022). The interpersonal consequences of stealing ideas: Worse character judgments and less co-worker support for an idea (vs. money) thief. *Organizational Behavior and Human Decision Processes 171*, 104165.

Ellison, G. (2002). The slowdown of the economics publishing process. *Journal of Political Economy 110*(5), 947–93.

Enders, W. and G. A. Hoover (2004). Whose line is it? Plagiarism in economics. *Journal of Economic Literature 42*, 487–93.

Enserink, M. (2021). When his suspicions went unanswered, this biologist decided to disavow his own study. *Scholar Insider.* www.science.org/content/article/when-his-suspicions-went-unanswered-biologist-decided-disavow-his-own-study.

Evans, D. (2015). *Worm Wars: The Anthology.* World Bank Development Impact Blog. blogs.worldbank.org/impactevaluations/worm-wars-anthology.

Everson, R. E. (2001). Economic impacts of agricultural research and extension. In B. L. Gardner and G. C. Rausser (Eds.), *The Handbook of Agricultural Economics*, pp. 573–628. Amsterdam, Netherlands: North Holland Publishing Company.

Faas, S., S. Makhija, E. Bryan, A. Go, and H. Malapit (2022). *Considering Gender in Research: An Ethics and Standards Toolkit.* Nairobi: CGIAR GENDER Impact Platform.

Fafchamps, M. and J. Labonne (2017). Using split samples to improve inference about causal effects. *Political Analysis 25*(4), 465–82.

Fama, E. F. (1970). Efficient capital markets: A review of theory and empirical work. *Journal of Finance 25*(2), 383–417.

Fanelli, D. (2009). How many scientists fabricate and falsify research? A systematic review and meta-analysis of survey data. *PLoS ONE 4*(5), e5738.

Farmer, P. (2013). Clinical trials and global health equity. *The Lancet Global Health Blog.* www.thelancet.com/journals/langlo/blog.

Ferguson, C. (2010a)1617. Inside job. *Sony Pictures Classic.*

Ferguson, C. (2010b). Larry summers and the subversion of economics. *The Chronicle of Higher Education.* www.chronicle.com/article/larry-summers-and-the-subversion-of-economics/.

Ferguson, L. (2014). How and why researchers share data (and why they don't). *The Wiley Network.*

Finkelstein, A., S. Taubman, B. Wright, M. Bernstein, J. Gruber, J. P. Newhouse, H. Allen, K. Baicker, and O. H. S. Group (2012). The Oregon health insurance experiment: Evidence from the first year. *Quarterly Journal of Economic 127*(3), 1057–106.

Fischbacher, U. and F. Föllmi-Heusi (2013). Lies in disguise – An experimental study on cheating. *Journal of the European Economic Association 11*(3), 525–47.

Fisher, R. (1956). *Statistical Methods and Scientific Inferences*. Oxford: Hafner.

Foot, P. (1973). *Virtues and Vices and Other Essays in Moral Philosophy*. Berkeley: University of California Press.

Franco, A., N. Malhorta, and G. Simonovits (2014). Publication bias in the social sciences: Unlocking the file drawer. *Science 345*, 1502–5.

Frankel, A. and M. Kasy (2022). Which findings should be published? *American Economic Journal: Microeconomics 14*(1), 1–38.

Freedman, B. (1987). Equipoise and the ethics of clinical research. *New England Journal of Medicine 317*(3), 141–5.

Freedman, D. H. (2010). *Wrong: Why Experts Keep Failing Us*. New York: Little Brown and Company.

Freeman, R. B., I. Ganguli, and R. Murciano-Goroff (2015). Why and wherefore of increased scientific collaboration. In A. B. Jaffe and B. F. Jones (Eds.), *The Changing Frontier: Rethinking Science and Innovation Policy*, pp. 17–48. Chicago: University of Chicago Press.

Frey, B. S., D. A. Savage, and B. Torgler (2011). Behavior under extreme conditions: The Titanic disaster. *Journal of Economic Perspectives 25*(1), 209–22.

Funk, C. (2020). About half of U.S. adults are wary of health effects of genetically modified foods, but many also see advantages. *Pew Research*. www.pewresearch.org/fact-tank/2020/03/18/about-half-of-u-s-adults-are-wary-of-health-effects-of-genetically-modified-foods-but-many-also-see-advantages/.

Furbush, A. M., A. Josephson, and J. D. Michler (2021)1819. Understanding Households' Resilience to and Recovery from COVID-19 in Sub-Saharan Africa. *OSF Registries*. doi.org/10.17605/osf.io/NU593.

Galiani, S. and U. Panizza (2020). *Publishing and Measuring Success in Economics*. London: CEPR Press.

Garg, T., M. Jagnani, and V. Taraz (2020). Temperature and human capital in India. *Journal of the Association of Environmental and Resource Economists 7*(6), 1113–50.

Gelman, A. (2004). Type 1, type 2, type S, and type M errors. *Statistical Modeling, Causal Inference, and Social Science Blog*. statmodeling.stat.columbia.edu/2004/12/29/type_1_type_2_t/.

Gelman, A. (2012). Ethics and statistics: Statistics for cigarette sellers. *Chance 25*(3), 43–6.

Gelman, A. (2013). Preregistration of studies and mock reports. *Political Analysis 21*, 40–1.

Gelman, A. (2022). How do things work at top econ journals, exactly? This is one weird-ass story. *Statistical Modeling, Causal Inference, and Social Science Blog*. statmodeling.stat.columbia.edu/2022/01/25/how-do-things-work-at-top-econ-journals-exactly-this-is-one-weird-ass-story/.

Gelman, A. and J. Carlin (2014). Beyond power calculations: Assesing Type S (sign) and Type M (magnitude) errors. *Perspectives on Psychological Science 96*(6), 641–51.

Gelman, A. and F. Tuerlinckx (2000). Type S error rates for classical and Bayesian single and multiple comparison procedures. *Computational Statistics 15*, 373–90.

Gentzkow, M. and J. M. Shapiro (2014). Code and data for social sciences: A practitioner's guide. *Matthew Gentzkow's Page at Stanford*. web.stanford.edu/gentzkow/research/CodeAndData.pdf.

Gershman, S. (2014). *The Exploitative Economics of Academic Publishing*. Also published in the Boston Globe. footnote.co/the-exploitative-economics-of-academic-publishing/.

Gibson, J. L. (1995). Cautious reflections on a data-archiving policy for political science. *PS: Political Science & Politics 28*(3), 473–6.

Glaeser, E. (2008). Researcher incentives and empirical methods. In A. Caplin and A. Schotter (Eds.), *The Foundations of Positive and Normative Economics*, pp. 300–19. Oxford: Oxford University Press.

Glennerster, R. (2017). The practicalities of running randomized evaluations: Partnerships, measurement, ethics, and transparency. In E. Duflo and A. Banerjee (Eds.), *Handbook of Field Experiments*, Volume 1, pp. 175–243. Amsterdam: North Holland.

Glewwe, P., A. Park, and M. Zhao (2016). A better vision for development: Eyeglasses and academic performance in rural primary schools in china. *Journal of Development Economics 122*, 170–82.

Goldacre, B. (2015). Scientists are hoarding data and it's ruining medical research. *BuzzFeed News*. www.buzzfeednews.com/article/bengoldacre/deworming-trials.

Goncalves, F. and S. Mello (2021a). A few bad apples? Racial bias in policing. *American Economic Review 111*(5), 1406–41.

Goncalves, F. and S. Mello (2021b).2021 A few bad apples? Racial bias in policing. *American Economic Association*. doi.org/10.3886/E123921V1.

Gould, S. and R. Lewontin (1979). The spandrels of San Marco and the Panglossian paradigm: A critique of the adaptationist programme. *Proceedings of the Royal Society of London. Series B 205*(1161), 581–98.

Granger, C. (1969). Investigating causal relationships by econometric models and cross-spectral methods. *Econometrica 37*(3), 424–38.

Greely, H. T. (2007). The uneasy ethical and legal underpinnings of large-scale genomic biobanks. *Annual Review of Genomics and Human Genetics 8*, 343–64.

Green, L. (2005). Reviewing the scourge of self-plagiarism. *M/C Journal 8*(5), 2426.

Greer, P. and C. Horst (2014). *Mission Drift: The Unspoken Crisis Facing Leaders, Charities, and Churches*. Bloomington: Bethany House Publishers.

Grove, J. (2017)2223. Predatory conferences "now outnumber official scholarly events". *Times Higher Education*. www.timeshighereducation.com/news/predatory-conferences-now-outnumber-official-scholarly-events.

Grundniewicz, A., D. Moher, K. Cobey, G. Bryson, S. Cukier, K. Allen, et al. (2019). Predatory journals: No definition, no defense. *Nature 576*, 201–12.

Hadavand, A., D. S. Hamermesh, and W. W. Wilson (2021)2425. Publishing economics: How slow? Why slow? Is slow productive? Fixing slow? *NBER Working Paper No. 29147*.

Hall, J. V. and A. B. Krueger (2018). An analysis of the labor market for Uber's driver-partners in the United States. *ILR Review 71*(3), 705–32.

Hamermesh, D. (2018). Citations in economics: Measurement, uses, and impacts. *Journal of Economic Literature 56*(1), 115–56.

Haney, C., W. Banks, and P. Zimbardo (1973). A study of prisoners and guards in a simulated prison. *Naval Research Review 30*, 4–17.

Hardy, G. H. (1940). *Ramanujan: Twelve Lectures on Subjects Suggested by His Life and Work*. Cambridge: Cambridge University Press.

Harris, G. (2009). Academic researchers' conflicts of interest go unreported. *The New York Times*26.

Hausman, D. (1998). *Causal Asymmetries*. Cambridge: Cambridge University Press.

Hayami, Y. and V. W. Ruttan (1985). *Agricultural Development: An International Perspective*. Baltimore: Johns Hopkins Press.

Heckman, J. J. and S. Moktan (2020). Publishing and promotion in economics: The tyranny of the top five. *Journal of Economic Literature 55*(2), 419–70.

Hedt-Gauthier, B. L., H. M. Jeufack, N. H. Neufeld, A. Alem, S. Sauer, J. Odhiambo, Y. Boum, M. Shuchman, and J. Volmink (2019). Stuck in the middle: A systematic review of authorship in collaborative health research in Africa, 2014–2016. *BMJ Global Health 9*, e001853.

Heffetz, O. and K. Ligett (2014). Privacy and data-based research. *Journal of Economic Perspectives 28*(2), 75–98.

Heller, J. (1972). Syphilis victims in U.S. study went untreated for 40 years. *The New York Times*.

Hennermann, K. and P. Berrisford (2020). *ERA5: Data Documentation*. Last modified November 18, 2020. confluence.ecmwf.int/display/CKB/ERA5%3A+data+documentation.

Herndon, T., M. Ash, and R. Pollin (2014). Does high public debt consistently stifle economic growth? A critique of Reinhart and Rogoff. *Cambridge Journal of Economics 38*, 257–79.

Hexham, I. (2013). The plague of plagiarism: Academic plagiarism defined. *Working Paper*. people.ucalgary.ca/hexham/content/articles/plague-of-plagiarism.html.

Hicks, J. R. (1932). *The Theory of Wages* (2nd ed.). London: Macmillan Press.

Hilsenroth, J., A. Josephson, K. A. Grogan, L. M. Walters, Z. T. Plakias, L. H. Palm-Forster, S. Banerjee, and T. Wade (2021). Past, present, and future: Status of women and minority faculty in agricultural and applied economics. *Applied Economic Perspectives and Policy 44*(1), 71–91.

Hirschman, D. and E. P. Berman (2014). Do economists make policies? On the political effects of economics. *Socio-Economic Review 12*(4), 779–811.

Hoffman, D. (2010). *The Dead Hand: The Untold Story of the Cold War Arms Race and Its Dangerous Legacy*. New York: Anchor Press.

Hoffmann, N. (2020). Involuntary experiments in former colonies: The case for a moratorium. *World Development 127*, 104805.

Holland, K. (2016). Enriching ethics review processes in the spirit of participatory dialogue. In W. C. Van Den Hoonaard and A. Hamilton (Eds.), *The Ethics Rupture: Exploring Alternatives to Formal Research Ethics Review*, pp. 353–75. Toronto: Toronto University Press.

Hollenbeck, J. R. and P. M. Wright (2016). Harking, sharking, and tharking: Making the case for post hoc analysis of scientific data. *Journal of Management 43*(1), 5–18.

Hotelling, H., W. Bartky, W. Deming, M. Friedman, and P. Hoel (1948). The teaching of statistics. *Annals of Mathematical Statistics 19*, 95–115.

Huff, D. (1954). *How to Lie with Statistics*. New York: W.W. Norton & Company.

Humphreys, L. (1970). *Tearoom Trade: Impersonal Sex in Public Places*. London: Duckworth.

Humphreys, M., R. Sanchez de la Sierra, and P. van der Windt (2013). Fishing, commitment, and communication: A proposal for comprehensive nonbinding research registration. *Political Analysis 21*, 1–20.

Hunter, T. W. (1998). *To 'Joy My Freedom: Southern Black Women's Lives and Labors After the Civil War*. Cambridge, MA: Harvard University Press.

Hunter, T. W. (2006). *African American Labor History: A Survey of the Scholarship from Jim Crow to the New Millennium*. Ann Arbor: ProQuest Information and Learning.

Huntington-Klein, N. (n.d.). Robustness tests: What, why, and how. *Nick Huntington-Klein Blog and Website*. www.nickchk.com/robustness.html.

Huntington-Klein, N., A. Arenas, E. Beam, M. Bertoni, J. R. Bloem, P. Burli, N. Chen, P. Grieco, G. Ekpe, T. Pugatch, M. Saavedra, and Y. Stopnitzky (2020). The influence of hidden researcher decisions in applied microeconomics. *Economic Inquiry 59*, 944–60.

Hutton, J. L., M. P. Eccles, and J. M. Grimshaw (2008). Ethical issues in implementation research: A discussion of the problems in achieving informed consent. *Implementation Science 3*, 52.

Imbens, G. W. (2021). Statistical significance, *p*-values, and the reporting of uncertainty. *Journal of Economic Perspectives 35*(3), 157–74.

Imbens, G. W., R. Spiegler, and C. Taber (n.d.). Statement from the editors of *Econometrica*, *Quantitative Economics*, and *Theoretical Economics*. www.econometricsociety.org/publications/statement-editors-econometrica-quantitative-economics-and-theoretical-economics.

Ioannidis, J. P. A. (2005). Why most published research findings are false. *PLoS Med* *2*(8), e124.

Ioannidis, J. P. A., T. D. Stanley, and H. Doucouliagos (2017). The power of bias in economics research. *The Economic Journal 127*(October), F236–65.

Ioannidis, J. P. A. and J. F. Trepanowski (2018). Disclosures in nutrition research: Why it is different. *JAMA 319*(6), 547–8.

Iphofen, R. (2016). Professional research ethics: Helping to balance individual and institutional integrity. In W. C. Van Den Hoonaard and A. Hamilton (Eds.), *The Ethics Rupture: Exploring Alternatives to Formal Research Ethics Review*, pp. 391–406. Toronto: Toronto University Press.

Israel, M. (2015). *Research Ethics and Integrity for Social Scientists: Beyond Regulatory Compliance* (2nd ed.). Los Angeles: SAGE Publications.

ISU (n.d.). *Predatory Journals and Conferences . . . Beware*. Idaho Center for Health Research at ISU, Idaho State University. www.isu.edu/ichr/resources/predatory-journals-conferences.

Jacoby, W. and R. Luption (2016). Guidelines for preparing replication files. *American Journal of Political Science*. ajps.org/wp-content/uploads/2018/05/ajpsreplicationguide-lines-2-1.pdf.

Janzen, S. and J. D. Michler (2021). Ulysses' pact or Ulysses' raft: Using pre-analysis plans in experimental and non-experimental research. *Applied Economic Perspectives and Policy 43*(4), 1286–304.

Jasanoff, S. (2004). The idiom of co-production. In S. Jasanoff (Ed.), *States of Knowledge: The Co-production of Science and the Social Order*. London: Routledge.

Johnson, S. (2005). Did blogging doom prof's shot at tenure? *The Chicago Tribune*.

Johnson, W. B. and J. M. Huwe (2002). Towards a typology of mentorship dysfunction in graduate school. *Psychotherapy 39*(1), 44–55.

Jones, B. F. (2008). The burden of knowledge and the "death of the renaissance man": Is innovation getting harder? *Review of Economic Studies 76*(1), 283–317.

Jones, B. F. (2021). The rise of research teams: Benefits and costs in economics. *Journal of Economic Perspectives 35*(2), 191–216.

Jones, B. F., S. Wuchty, and B. Uzzi (2008). Multi-university research teams: Shifting impact, geography, and stratification in science. *Science 322*(5905), 1259–62.

Jonsen, A. R. (2005). On the origins and future of the *Belmont Report*. In J. F. Childress, E. M. Meslin, and H. T. Shapiro (Eds.), *Belmont Revisited*, pp. 3–11. Washington, DC: Georgetown University Press.

Josephson, A. and J. D. Michler (2018). Beasts of the field? Ethics in agricultural and applied economics. *Food Policy 79*, 1–11.

Josephson, A. and J. D. Michler (n.d.). *Applied International Development Economics (AIDE) Lab Statement on Fostering an Inclusive Work Environment*. osf.io/3vtng/wiki/Inclusive%20Environment/.

Josephson, A. and M. Smale (2021). What do you mean by "informed consent"? Ethics in economic development research. *Applied Economic Perspectives and Policy 43*(4), 1305–29.

Judd, K. (n.d.). *Economics Versus Science*. sites.google.com/site/commentsoneconomics.

Just, D. R. (20172728). Successful communication strategies. *AAEA Early Career Professionals Workshop Presentation*.

Kamau, C. (2019). Five ways median training helped me to boost the impact of my research. *Nature 567*, 425–6.

Kanbur, R. (2005). Goldilocks development economics: Not too theoretical, not too empirical, but watch out for the bears! *Economic and Political Weekly 40*(40), 4344–6.

Kanigel, R. (1991). *The Man Who Knew Infinity: A Life of the Genius Ramanujan*. New York: Scribner.

Kant, I. (1785). *Groundwork of the Metaphysics of Morals* (3rd ed.). Indianapolis: Hackett. Reprint (1993).

Kaplan, S. (2015). University of Illinois censured after professor loses job over tweets critical of Israel. *The Washington Post*.

Kara, H. (2018). *Research Ethics in the Real World*. Bristol: Policy Press: University of Bristol.

Karlan, D. and J. Appel (2016). *Failing in the Field: What We Can Learn When Field Research Goes Wrong*. Princeton: Princeton University Press.

Kasy, M. (2021). Of forking paths and tied hands: Selective publication of findings, and what economists should do about it. *Journal of Economic Perspectives 35*(3), 175–92.

Katz, J. (1996). The Nuremberg Code and the Nuremberg Trial a reappraisal. *Journal of the American Medical Association 276*(20), 1662–6.

Katz, L. F. and A. B. Krueger (1992). The effect of the minimum wage on the fast-food industry. *Industrial and Labor Relations Review 46*(1), 6–21.

Kelly, K. (2022). *Fight Like Hell: The Untold History of American Labor*. New York: Atria/ One Signal Publishers.

Kelsky, K. (2014)29. Five top traits of the worst advisors. *The Professor is In*. theprofessorisin.com/2014/02/23/the-5-top-traits-of-the-worst-advisors/.

Kennedy, P. E. (2002). Sinning in the basement: What are the rules? The ten commandments of applied econometrics. *Journal of Economic Surveys 16*(4), 569–89.

Kerr, N. (1998). HARKing: Hypothesizing after the results are known. *Personality and Social Psychology Review 2*, 196–217.

Kim, T. and L. J. Taylor (1995). The employment effect in retail trade of California's 1988 minimum wage increase. *Journal of Business & Economic Statistics 13*(2), 175–82.

Kimball, M. (2018). Must all economics papers be doorstoppers? *Confessions of a Supply-Side Liberal Blog*. blog.supplyside-liberal.com/post/2018/7/25/must-all-economics-papers-be-doorstoppers.

King, S. (2000). *On Writing: A Memoir of the Craft*. New York: Scribner.

Kirigia, J. M., C. Wambebe, and A. Baba-Moussa (2005). Status of national research bioethical committees in the WHO African region. *BMC Medical Ethics 6*, E10.

Klar, S., Y. Krupnikov, J. B. Ryan, K. Searles, and Y. Shmargad (2020). Using social media to promote academic research: Identifying the benefits of twitter for sharing academic work. *PloS One 15*(4), e0229446.

Knight, F. (1947). *Freedom and Reform: Essays in Economics and Social Philosophy*. Carmel: Liberty Fund. Reprint (1982).

Konnikova, M. (2015). How a gay-marriage study went wrong. *The New Yorker*. www.newyorker.com/science/maria-konnikova/how-a-gay-marriage-study-went-wrong.

Kotlikoff, M. I. (2018). *Statement of Cornell University Provost Michael I. Kotlikoff*. statements.cornell.edu/2018/20180920-statement-provost-michael-kotlikoff.cfm.

Kristal, A. S., A. V. Whillans, M. H. Bazerman, F. Gino, L. L. Shu, N. Mazar, and D. Ariely (2020). Signing at the beginning versus at the end does not decrease dishonesty. *Proceedings of the National Academy of Sciences 117*(13), 7103–7.

Krugman, P. (2009). How did economists get it so wrong? *The New York Times Magazine*.

Kuhn, T. S. (1962). *The Structure of Scientific Revolutions*. Chicago: University of Chicago Press.

Kweik, M. (2020). Internationalists and locals: International research collaboration in a resource-poor system. *Scientometrics 124*, 57–105.

Kwon, D. (2022). The rise of citational justice: how scholars are making references fairer. *Nature: News Feature*.

LaCour, M. J. and D. P. Green (2014). When contact changes mind: An experiment on transmission of support for gay equality. *Science 346*, 1366–9. RETRACTED.

Ladeiras-Lopes, R., S. Clarke, R. Vidal-Perez, M. Alexander, T. F. Lüscher, and O. B. O. T. E. E. S. O. C. M. C. E. H. Journal (2020). Twitter promotion predicts citation rates of cardiovascular articles: A preliminary analysis from the *ESC Journals Randomized Study*. *European Heart Journal 41*(34), 3222–5.

LaFave, D. and D. Thomas (2016). Farms, families, and markets: New evidence on completeness of markets in agricultural settings. *Econometrica 84*, 1917–60.

Laffont, J.-J. and D. Martimort (2002). *The Theory of Incentives: The Principal-Agent Model*. Princeton: Princeton University Press.

Laitin, D. D. (2013). Fisheries management. *Political Analysis 21*, 42–7.

Lamont, J. (1994). Pareto efficiency, egalitarianism, and difference principles. *Social Theory and Practice 20*(3), 311–25.

Lamott, A. (1995). *Bird by Bird: Some Instructions on Writing and Life*. New York: Knopf.

Lasalandra, M. (1997). Panel told releases of med records hurt privacy. *Boston Herald*.

Lawrence, F. (2022). Uber paid academics six-figure sums for research to feed to the media. *The Guardian*.

Leamer, E. E. (1978). *Specification Searches: Ad Hoc Inference with Nonexperimental Data*. New York: Wiley.

Leamer, E. E. (1983). Let's take the con out of econometrics. *American Economic Review 73*(1), 31–43.

Leamer, E. E. (1996). Questions, theory and data. In S. Medema and W. Samuels (Eds.), *Foundations of Research in Economics: How Do Economists Do Economics?*, pp. 175–90. Aldershot: Edward Elgar Publishing.

Lederman, R. (2016). Fieldwork double-bound in human research ethics review: Disciplinary competence, or regulatory compliance and the muting of disciplinary values. In W. C. Van Den Hoonaard and A. Hamilton (Eds.), *The Ethics Rupture: Exploring Alternatives to Formal Research Ethics Review*, pp. 43–72. Toronto: Toronto University Press.

Lee, S. M. (2018). Sliced & diced. *BuzzFeed News*. www.buzzfeed.com/stephaniemlee/brian-wansink-cornell-p-hacking.

Leonard, M., S. Stapleton, P. Collins, T. K. Selfe, and T. Cataldo (2021). Ten simple rules for avoiding predatory publishing scams. *PLOS Computation Biology 17*(9), e1009377.

Lesné, S., M. T. Koh, L. Kotilinek, R. Kayed, C. G. Glabe, A. Yang, M. Gallagher, and K. H. Ashe (2006). A specific amyloid-β protein assembly in the brain impairs memory. *Nature 440*, 352–7.

Levine, D. I. (2001). Editor's introduction to "the employment effects of minimum wages: Evidence from a prespecified research design". *Industrial Relations 40*(2), 161–2.

Levitt, S. D. and S. J. Dubner (2005). *Freakonomics: A Rogue Economist Explores the Hidden Side of Everything*. New York: William Morrow.

Lindquist, E. (1990). The third community, policy inquiry, and social scientists. In S. Brooks and A. G. Gagnon (Eds.), *Social Scientists, Policy, and the State*, pp. 21–51. New York: Praeger.

List, J. A., C. D. Bailey, P. J. Euzent, and T. L. Martin (2001). Academic economists behaving badly? A survey on three areas of unethical behavior. *Economic Inquiry 39*(1), 162–70.

Lobell, D. B., G. Azzari, M. Burke, S. Gourlay, Z. Jin, T. Kilic, and S. Murray (2020). Eyes in the sky, boots on the ground: Assessing satellite- and ground-based approaches to crop yield measurement and analysis. *American Journal of Agricultural Economics 102*(1), 202–19.

Long, H. (2020). Economists increasingly say it's acceptable for the U.S. to take on more debt – for the right reasons. *The Washington Post*.

Longo, D. L. and J. M. Drazen (2016). Data sharing. *New England Journal of Medicine 374*, 276–7.

Luc, G. and C. Altare (2018). Social science research in a humanitarian emergency context. In D. Schroeder, J. Cook, F. Hirsch, S. Fenet, and V. Muthuswamy (Eds.), *Ethics Dumping: Case Studies from North-South Research Collaborations*, pp. 9–14. Cham: Springer.

Luc, J. G., M. A. Archer, R. C. Arora, E. M. Bender, A. Blitz, D. T. Cooke, T. Ni Hlci, B. Kidane, M. Ouzounian, T. K. Varghese Jr., and M. B. Antonoff (2020). Does tweeting improve citations? One-year results from the TSSMN prospective randomized trial. *Annals of Thoracic Surgery 111*(1), 296–300.

Lucas, R. E. (2003). Macroeconomic priorities. *American Economic Review 93*(1), 1–14.

Lucas, R. E. (2013). *Collected Papers on Monetary Theory*. Cambridge, MA: Harvard University Press.

Lybbert, T. J., T. K. Beatty, T. M. Hurley, and T. Richards (2018). American Journal of Agricultural Economics Volume 100: A century of publishing the frontiers of the profession. *American Journal of Agricultural Economics 100*(5), 1253–74.

Lybbert, T. J. and S. T. Buccola (2021). The evolving ethics of analysis, publication, and transparency in applied economics. *Applied Economic Perspectives and Policy 43*(4), 1330–51.

Macfarlane, B. (2009). *Researching with Integrity: The Ethics of Academic Enquiry*. New York: Routledge.

MacIntyre, A. (1984). *After Virtue*. South Bend: University of Notre Dame Press.

MacKenzie, D. (2008). *An Engine, Not a Camera: How Financial Models Shape Markets*. Cambridge, MA: MIT Press.

Mackie, J. (1977). *Ethics: Inventing Right and Wrong*. New York: Penguin.

Maddox, B. (2003). The double helix and the "wronged heroine". *Nature 421*(6921), 407–8.

Mandal, J., M. Parija, and S. C. Parija (2012). Ethics of funding of research. *Tropical Parasitol 2*(2), 89–90.

Marx, K. (1867). *Capital: A Critique of Political Economy*, Volume 1. New York: International Publishers. Reprint (1967).

Marzano, M. (2016). Unfomartable truths, ethics, and qualitative research: Escaping the dominance of informed consent. In W. C. Van Den Hoonaard and A. Hamilton (Eds.), *The Ethics Rupture: Exploring Alternatives to Formal Research Ethics Review*, pp. 106–18. Toronto: Toronto University Press.

Mastroianna, A., R. Faden, and D. Federman (1994). *Women and Health Research: Ethical and Legal Issues of Including Women in Clinical Studies*. Washington, DC: National Academies Press.

McAfee, R. P. (2010). Edifying editing. *American Economist 55*(1), 1–8.

McCann, L. M., J. D. Michler, N. Estrada Carmona, and J. Raneri (2021)3132. Food without fire: Environmental and nutritional impacts from a solar cook stove field experiment. *Paper Presented at the Agricultural & Applied Economics Association (AAEA) Annual Meeting*.

McCloskey, D. N. (2006). *The Bourgeois Virtues: Ethics for an Age of Commerce*. Chicago: University of Chicago Press.

McCloskey, D. N. (2019a). *Economical Writing*. Chicago: University of Chicago Press.

McCloskey, D. N. (2019b). The Nobel committee has lost touch with actual science. *The Washington Times*.33

McCloskey, D. N. and S. T. Ziliak (1996). The standard error of regressions. *Journal of Economic Literature 34*(1), 97–114.

McCullough, B. and H. Vinod (2003). Verifying the solution from a nonlinear solver: A case study. *American Economic Review 93*(3), 873–92.

McKenzie, D. (2013). How should we understand "clinical equipoise" when doing RCTs in development. *World Bank Development Impact Blog*. blogs.worldbank.org/impactevaluations/how-should-we-understand-clinical-equipoise-when-doing-rcts-development.

McKenzie, D. (2022). The state of development journals 2022: Quality, acceptance rates, review times, and what's new. *World Bank Development Impact Blog*. blogs.worldbank.org/impactevaluations/state-development-journals-2022-quality-acceptance-rates-review-times-and-whats.

McKenzie, D. and B. Özler (2014). Quantifying some of the impacts of economics blogs. *Economic Development and Cultural Change 63*(3), 567–97.

McLean, B. and J. Nocera (2010). *All the Devils Are Here: The Hidden History of the Financial Crisis*. New York: Penguin.

McPeek, M. A., D. L. DeAngelis, R. G. Shaw, A. J. Moore, M. D. Rausher, D. R. Strong, A. M. Ellison, L. Barrett, L. Rieseberg, M. D. Breed, J. Sullivan, C. W. Osenberg, M. Holyoak, and M. A. Elgar (2009). The golden rule of reviewing. *The American Naturalist 173*, E155–8.

Merton, R. K. (1947). A note on science and democracy. *Journal of Legal and Political Sociology 1*, 115–26.

Mervis, J. (2017). Data check: U.S. government share of basic research funding falls below 50 percent. *Science*. www.sciencemag.org/news/2017/03/data-check-us-government-share-basic-research-funding-falls-below-50.

Michler, J. D., K. Baylis, M. Arends-Kuenning, and K. Mazvimavi (2019). Conservation agriculture and climate resilience. *Journal of Environmental Economics and Management 93*, 148–69.

Michler, J. D. and A. Josephson (2022). Recent developments in inference: Practicalities for the applied economist. In J. Hobbs and J. Roosen (Eds.), *A Modern Guide to Food Economics*. Cheltenham: Edward Elgar Publishing.

Michler, J. D., A. Josephson, T. Kilic, and S. Murray (2019). Empirically estimating the impact of weather on agriculture. *OSF Registries*, July 1. doi.org/10.17605/osf.io/Z3SNH.

Michler, J. D., A. Josephson, T. Kilic, and S. Murray (2021)3435. Estimating the impact of weather on agriculture. *World Bank Policy Research Working Paper, No. 9867*.

Michler, J. D., A. Josephson, T. Kilic, and S. Murray (2022). Privacy protection, measurement error, and the integration of remote sensing and socioeconomic survey data. *Journal of Development Economics 158*, 102927.

Michler, J. D., W. A. Masters, and A. Josephson (2021). Research ethics beyond the IRB: Selection bias and the direction of innovation in applied economics. *Applied Economic Perspectives and Policy 43*(4), 1352–65.

Michler, J. D., E. Tjernström, S. Verkaart, and K. Mausch (2019). Money matters: The role of yields and profits in agricultural technology adoption. *American Journal of Agricultural Economics 103*(3), 710–31.

Miguel, E. (2021). Evidence on research transparency in economics. *Journal of Economic Perspectives 35*(3), 193–214.

Miguel, E. and M. Kremer (2004). Worms: Identifying impacts on education and health in the presence of treatment externalities. *Econometrica 72*(1), 159–217.

Mill, J. S. (1863). *Utilitarianism* (2nd ed.). Indianapolis: Hackett. Reprint (2002).

Monogan III, J. E. (2013). A case for registering studies of political outcomes: An application in the 2010 house elections. *Political Analysis 21*, 21–37.

Mookherjee, D. (2005). Is there too little theory in development economics today? *Economic and Political Weekly 40*(40), 4328–33.

Morris, E. (2019). *Edison*. New York: Random House.

Morten, M. (2019). Temporary migration and endogenous risk sharing in village India. *Journal of Political Economy 127*(1), 1–46.

Murnane, R. J. and J. B. Willett (2011). *Methods Matter: Improving Causal Inference in Educational and Social Science Research*. Oxford: Oxford University Press.

Murray, B. L. (2016). Research ethics boards: Are they ready for autoethnography. In W. C. Van Den Hoonaard and A. Hamilton (Eds.), *The Ethics Rupture: Exploring Alternatives to Formal Research Ethics Review*, pp. 153–66. Toronto: Toronto University Press.

Murray, D. M. (2012). *The Craft of Revision* (5th ed.). Boston: Cengage Learning.

Muth, J. F. (1961). Rational expectations and the theory of price movements. *Econometrica 29*(3), 315–35.

Narayanan, A. and V. Shmatikov (2008). Robust de-anonymization of large sparse datasets. *2008 IEEE Symposium on Security and Privacy*, 111–25.

Naritomi, J., S. Sequeira, J. Weigel, and D. Weinhold (2020). RCTs as an opportunity to promote interdisciplinary, inclusive, and diverse quantitative development research. *World Development 127*, 104832.

Nash, J. F. (1950). The bargaining problem. *Econometrica 18*(2), 155–62.

Nature (2005). The cost of salami slicing. *Nature Materials 4*(1), doi.org/10.1038/nmat1305.

Nature (2011). Online image. *Nature 473*(7346). doi.org/10.1038/473124a.

Necker, S. (2014). Scientific misbehavior in economics. *Research Policy 43*, 1747–59.

Nelson, R. H. (1987). The economics profession and the making of public policy. *Journal of Economic Literature 25*(1), 49–91.

Nelson, R. H. (2016). Confessions of a policy analyst. In G. F. DeMartino and D. N. McCloskey (Eds.), *The Oxford Handbook of Professional Economic Ethics*, pp. 587–617. Oxford: Oxford University Press.

Neumark, D. (2001). The employment effects of minimum wages: Evidence from a pre-specified research design. *Industrial Relations 40*(1), 121–44.

Neumark, D. and W. Wascher (1992). Employment effects of minimum and subminimum wages: Panel data on state minimum wage laws. *Industrial and Labor Relations Review 46*(1), 55–81.

Neumark, D. and W. Wascher (1994). Employment effects of minimum and subminimum wages: Reply to Card, Katz, and Krueger. *Industrial and Labor Relations Review 47*(3), 497–512.

Neumark, D. and W. Wascher (1998). Is the time-series evidence on minimum wage effects contaminated by publication bias? *Economic Inquiry 36*(3), 458–70.

Neville, C. W. (2005). Beware the consequences of citing self-plagiarism. *Communications of the ACM 48*(6), 3.

NIH (2020). Final NIH policy for data management and sharing. *National Institutes of Health, Bethesda.*grants.nih.gov/grants/guide/notice-files/NOT-OD-21-013.html.

Nosek, B. A., G. Alter, G. C. Banks, D. Borsboom, S. D. Bowman, S. J. Breckler, S. Buck, C. D. Chambers, G. Chin, G. Christensen, M. Contestabile, A. Dafoe, E. Eich, J. Freese, R. Glennerster, D. Goroff, D. P. Green, B. Hesse, M. Humphreys, J. Ishiyama, D. Karlan,

A. Kraut, A. Lupia, P. Mabry, T. Madon, N. Malhotra, E. Mayo-Wilson, M. McNutt, E. Miguel, E. L. Paluck, U. Simonsohn, C. Soderberg, B. A. Spellman, J. Turitto, G. VandenBos, S. Vazire, E. J. Wagenmakers, R. Wilson, and T. Yarkoni (2015). Promoting an open research culture. *Science 348*(6242), 1422–25.

Nosek, B. A., J. Spies, and M. Motyl (2012). Scientific utopia ii. Restructuring incentives and practices to promote truth over publishability. *Perspectives on Psychological Science 7*(6), 615–31.

Novella, N. S. and W. M. Thiaw (2013). African rainfall climatology version 2 for famine early warning systems. *Journal of Applied Meteorology and Climatology 52*(3), 588–606.

Nozick, R. (1974). *Anarchy, State, and Utopia*. New York: Basic Books.

NSF (2016). Universities report four years of declining federal funding. *The National Science Foundation*. www.nsf.gov/news/news_summ.jsp?cntn_%20id=190299. National Science Foundation News Release 16–142.

Nuzzo, R. (2014). Scientific method: Statistical errors. *Nature 506*, 150–2.

Oettl, A. (2012). Reconceptualizing stars: Scientist helpfulness and peer performance. *Management Science 58*(6), 1122–40.

Offutt, S. (2016). Ethics and the government economist. In G. F. DeMartino and D. N. McCloskey (Eds.), *The Oxford Handbook of Professional Economic Ethics*, pp. 618–34. Oxford: Oxford University Press.

O'Grady, C. (2021)3839. When is self-plagiarism OK: New guidelines offer researchers rules for recycling text. *Science*. https://www.science.org/content/article/when-self-plagiarism-ok-new-guidelines-offer-researchers-rules-recycling-text.

Oh, S. S., J. Galanter, N. Thakur, M. Pino-Yanes, N. E. Barcelo, M. J. White, D. M. de Bruin, R. M. Greenblatt, K. Bibbins-Domingo, A. H. Wu, L. N. Borrell, C. Gunter, N. R. Powe, and E. G. Burchard (2015). Diversity in clinical and biomedical research: A promise yet to be fufilled. *PLoS Medicine 12*(12), e1001918.

Ohm, P. (2010). Broken promises of privacy: Responding to the surprising failure of anonymization. *UCLA Law Review 57*(6), 1701–77.

Oliver, P. (2010). *The Students' Guide to Research Ethics* (2nd ed.). Maidenhead: Open University Press.

Olken, B. A. (2015). Promises and perils of pre-analysis plans. *Journal of Economic Perspectives 29*(3), 61–80.

Ouss, A. and M. Stevenson (Forthcoming). Does cash bail deter misconduct? *American Economic Journal: Applied Economics*.

Oxford (2015). *Tips From a Journal Editor: Being a Good Reviewer*. OUPblog: Oxford University Press's Academic Insights for the Thinking World.

Oxford (2021). *Six Common Types of Plagiarism in Academic Research*. OUPblog: Oxford University Press's Academic Insights for the Thinking World.

Özler, B. (2015). Worm wars: A review of the reanalysis of Miguel and Kremer's deworming study. *World Bank Development Impact Blog*. blogs.worldbank.org/impactevaluations/worm-wars-review-reanalysis-miguel-and-kremer-s-deworming-study.

Parfit, D. (2013). *On What Matters*. Oxford: Oxford University Press.

Parker, A. R., E. Coleman, J. Manyindo, E. Mukuru, and B. Schultz (2020). Bridging the academic-practitioner gap in RCTs. *World Development 127*, 104819.

Pearl, J. (2009). *Causality: Models, Reasoning and Inference* (2nd ed.). Cambridge: Cambridge University Press.

Pearl, J. and D. Mackenzie (2018). *The Book of Why: The New Science of Cause and Effect*. New York: Basic Books.

Peltzman, S. (1975). The effects of automobile safety regulation. *Journal of Political Economy 83*(4), 677–726.

Perez-Haydrich, C., J. L. Warren, C. R. Burgert, and M. E. Emch (2013).4041 Guidelines on the use of DHS GPS data. *DHS Spatial Analysis Reports No. 8*. dhsprogram.com/publications/publication-SAR8-Spatial-Analysis-Reports.cfm.

Peterson, E. W. F. and G. C. Davis (1999). Consequences, rights, and virtues: Ethical foundations for applied economics. *American Journal of Agricultural Economics 81*(5), 1173–80.

Piketty, T. and E. Saez (2003). Income inequality in the United States, 1913–1998. *Quarterly Journal of Economics 118*(1), 1–41.

Piller, C. (2022). Blots on a field? A neuroscience image sleuth finds signs of fabrication in scores of Alzheimer's articles, threatening a reigning theory of the disease. *Science 377*(6604), 358–63.

Pogge, T. (2006). Justice. In D. M. Borchert (Ed.), *Encyclopedia of Philosophy* (2nd ed.), Volume 4, pp. 862–71. Detroit: Macmillan Reference USA.

Porter, J. J. and K. Birdi (2018). 22 reasons why collaborations fail: Lessons from water innovation research. *Environmental Science and Policy 89*, 100–8.

Pressman, S. (2014). *Econ Agonistes*: Navigating and surviving the publishing process. In M. Szenberg and L. Ramrattan (Eds.), *Secrets of Economics Editors*, pp. 297–309. Cambridge, MA: MIT Press.

Priem, J., P. Taraborelli, C. Groth, and C. Neylon (2010). *Altmetrics: A Manifesto*. altmetrics.org/manifesto/.

Pritchett, L. (2020). Randomizing development: Method or madness? In F. Bédécarrats, I. Guérin, and F. Roubaud (Eds.), *Randomized Control Trials in the Field of Development: A Critical Perspective*, pp. 79–107. Oxford: Oxford University Press.

Puniewska, M. (2014). Scientists have a sharing problem. *The Atlantic*.

Ravallion, M. (2014). Taking ethical validity seriously. *World Bank Development Impact Blog*. blogs.worldbank.org/impactevaluations/taking-ethical-validity-seriously.

Ravallion, M. (2020). Should the randomistas (continue to) rule? In F. Bédécarrats, I. Guérin, and F. Roubaud (Eds.), *Randomized Control Trials in the Field of Development: A Critical Perspective*, pp. 47–78. Oxford: Oxford University Press.

Rawls, J. (1971). *A Theory of Justics*. Cambridge: Belknap Press.

Reinhart, A. (2014). Huff and puff. *Significance 11*(4), 28–33.

Reinhart, C. M. and K. S. Rogoff (2010). Growth in a time of debt. *American Economic Review 100*(2), 573–8.

Reverby, S. M. (2000). *Tuskegee's Truth: Rethinking the Tuskegee Syphilis Study*. Chapel Hill: University of North Carolina Press.

Rhodes, R. (1986). *The Making of the Atomic Bomb*. New York: Simon & Schuster.

Ritchie, S. (2022). The real lesson of that cash-for-babies study. *The Atlantic*. www.theatlantic.com/science/archive/2022/02/cash-transfer-babies-study-neuroscience-hype/621488.

Robinson-Garcia, N. (2017). The unbearable emptiness of tweeting – about journal articles. *PLoS ONE 12*(7), 1–19.

Rodrik, D. (2008). The new development economics: We shall experiment, but how shall we learn? *Working Paper RWP08–055*, Harvard Kennedy School.

Rodrik, D. (2015). *Economics Rules: The Rights and Wrongs of the Dismal Science*. New York: W.W. Norton & Company.

Roig, M. (2015). *Avoiding Plagiarism, Self-Plagiarism, and Other Questionable Writing Practices: A Guide to Ethical Writing*. www.inmed.us/wpcontent/uploads/Avoiding-Plagiarism-Self-Plagiarism-and-Other-Questionable-Writing-Practices-2015-71-Pages.pdf.

Romer, D. (2020). In praise of confidence intervals. *AEA Papers and Proceedings 110*, 55–60.

Rosenthal, R. (1979). The file drawer problem and tolerance for null results. *Psychological Bulletin 86*(3), 638–41.

Ross, M. B., B. M. Glennon, R. Murciano-Goroff, E. G. Berkes, B. A. Weinberg, and J. I. Lane (2022). Women are credited less in science than men. *Nature 608*, 135–45.

Rosser Jr., J. B. (2014). Tales from the editor's crypt: Dealing with true, uncertain, and false accusations of plagiarism. In M. Szenberg and L. Ramrattan (Eds.), *Secrets of Economics Editors*, pp. 311–28. Cambridge, MA: MIT Press.

Rubin, D. (1974). Estimating causal effects of treatments in randomized and nonrandomized studies. *Journal of Educational Psychology 66*(5), 688–701.

Rubin, M. (2017). When does HARKing hurt? Identifying when different types of undisclosed post hoc hypothesizing harm scientific progress. *Review of General Psychology 21*, 308–20.

Rubin, P. H. and A. W. Dnes (2014). Notes from a second-line journal: Suggestions for authors. In M. Szenberg and L. Ramrattan (Eds.), *Secrets of Economics Editors*, pp. 191–6. Cambridge, MA: MIT Press.

Ruggles, S., C. Fitch, D. Magnuson, and J. Schroeder (2019). Differential privacy and census data: Implications for social and economic research. *AEA Paers and Proceedings 109*, 403–8.

Said, E. W. (1979). *Orientalism*. New York: Vintage.

Salmon, F. (2022). $100k got Uber research published in prestigious outlet. *Axios*.

Sandmo, A. (1971). On the theory of the competitive firm under price uncertainty. *American Economic Review 61*(1), 65–73.

Sardanelli, F., M. Al'ı, M. G. Hunink, N. Houssami, L. M. Sconfienza, and G. Di Leo (2018). To share or not to share? Expected pros and cons of data sharing in radiological research. *European Radiology 28*, 2328–35.

Sarsons, H. (2015). Rainfall and conflict: A cautionary tale. *Journal of Development Economics 115*, 62–72.

Sarsons, H., K. Gërxhani, E. Reuben, and A. Schram (2021). Gender differences in recognition for group work. *Journal of Political Economy 129*(1), 101–47.

Scanlon, T. (2000). *What We Owe to Each Other*. Cambridge: Harvard University Press.

Schlesinger Jr., A. M. (1958). *The Age of Roosevelt: The Coming of the New Deal*. Boston: Houghton Mifflin.

Schneider, L. (2015). What if universities had to agree to refund grants whenever there was a retraction? *Retraction Watch*. retractionwatch.com/2015/01/19/universities-agree-refund-grants-whenever-retraction/.

Schrag, Z. M. (2010). *Ethical Imperialism: Institutional Review Boards and the Social Sciences, 1965–2009*. Baltimore: Johns Hopkins University Press.

Schroeder, D., K. Chatfield, M. Singh, R. Chennells, and P. Herissone-Kelly (2019). *Equitable Research Partnerships: A Global Code of Conduct to Counter Ethics Dumping*. Cham: Springer.

Schumpeter, J. A. (1939). *Business Cycles*. New York: McGraw-Hill Book Company.

Scott, J. C. (1998). *Seeing Like a State: How Certain Schemes to Improve the Human Condition Have Failed*. New Haven: Yale University Press.

Searing, E. A. and D. R. Searing (2016a). Appendix 1: Ethical analysis workbook. In E. A. Searing and D. R. Searing (Eds.), *Practicing Professional Ethics in Economics and Public Policy*, pp. 273–87. New York: Springer.

Searing, E. A. and D. R. Searing (2016b). Framing the problem. In E. A. Searing and D. R. Searing (Eds.), *Practicing Professional Ethics in Economics and Public Policy*, pp. 55–69. New York: Springer.

Searing, E. A. and D. R. Searing (2016c). Hypothesis testing. In E. A. Searing and D. R. Searing (Eds.), *Practicing Professional Ethics in Economics and Public Policy*, pp. 71–104. New York: Springer.

Sent, E.-M. and A. Klamer (2002). The economics of scientific publication: Introduction. *Journal of Economic Methodology 9*(3), 265–73.

Shea, C. (2011). Economist slammed for "concurrent publications". *Wall Street Journal*. www.wsj.com/articles/BL-IMB-2442.

Shu, L. L., N. Mazar, F. Gino, D. Ariely, and M. H. Bazerman (2012). Signing at the beginning makes ethics salient and decreases dishonest self-reports in comparison to signing at the end. *Proceedings of the National Academy of Sciences 109*(38), 15197–200. RETRACTED.

Sieber, J. E. (n.d.). *Laud Humphreys and the Tearoom Sex Study*. www.drjkoch.org/Intro/Readings/Humphreys.htm.

Sieber, J. E. and M. B. Tolich (2006). *Planning Ethically Responsible Research* (2nd ed.). Los Angeles: SAGE Publications.

Silver, A. (2017).4344 Controversial website that lists "predatory" publishers shuts down. *Nature*. doi.org/10.1038/nature.2017.21328.

Simonsohn, U. (2013). Just post it: The lesson from two cases of fabricated data detected by statistics alone. *Psychological Science 24*(10), 1875–83.

Simonsohn, U., J. P. Simmons, and L. D. Nelson (2020). Specification curve analysis descriptive and inferential statistics for all plausible specifications. *Nature Human Behaviour 4*, 1208–14.

Simonsohn, U., J. P. Simmons, and L. D. Nelson (2021). Evidence of fraud in an influential field experiment about dishonesty. *Data Colada*. datacolada.org/98.

Singh, S. (1997). *Fermat's Last Theorem*. London: Fourth Estate.

Skinner, C. (2009). Statistical disclosure control for survey data. In C. Rao (Ed.), *Handbook of Statistics*, Volume 29, pp. 381–96. Amsterdam: Elsevier.

Skloot, R. (2011). *The Immortal Life of Henrietta Lacks*. New York: Crown.

Slade, P., J. D. Michler, and A. Josephson (2019). Foreign geographical indications, consumer preferences, and the domestic market for cheese. *Applied Economic Perspectives and Policy 41*(3), 370–90.

Smil, V. (2000). *Enriching the Earth: Fritz Haber, Carl Bosch, and the Transformation of World Food Production*. Cambridge, MA: MIT University Press.

Smith, A. (1759). *The Theory of Moral Sentiments*. New York: Penguin Press. Reprint (2010).

Stanton, B. F. (2007). *George F. Warren: Farm Economist*. Ithaca: Cornell University Press.

Steegen, S., F. Tuerlinckx, A. Gelman, and W. Vanpaemel (2016). Increasing transparency through a multiverse analysis. *Perspectives on Psychological Science 11*(5), 702–12.

Sterling, R. L. (2011). Genetic research among the Havasupai: A cautionary tale. *AMA Journal of Ethics 13*(2), 113–17.

Stigler, G. (1971). The theory of economic regulation. *The Bell Journal of Economics and Management Science 2*(1), 3–21.

Stigler, S. (1987). Testing hypotheses or fitting models? Another look at mass extinctions. In M. Nitecki and A. Hoffman (Eds.), *Neural Models in Biology*, pp. 147–59. New York: Oxford University Press.

Stiller-Reeve, M. (2018). How to write a thorough peer review. *Nature: Career Column*. www.nature.com/articles/d41586-018-06991-0.

Stodden, V. (2014). 2014: What scientific idea is ready for retirement? *Edge*. www.edge.org/response-detail/25340.

Stodden, V., J. Seiler, and Z. Ma (2018). An empirical analysis of journal policy effectiveness for computational reproducibility. *Proceedings of the National Academy of Sciences 115*(11), 2584–9.

Strunk, W. and E. White (1999). *The Elements of Style* (4th ed.). London: Pearson.

Suri, T. (2011). Selection and comparative advantage in technology adoption. *Econometrica 79*(1), 159–209.

Sweeney, L. (2002). *k*-anonymity: A model for protecting privacy. *International Journal on Uncertainty Fuzziness and Knowledge-based Systems 10*(5), 557–70.

Sweeney, L. (2007). Weaving technology and policy together to maintain confidentiality. *Journal of Law, Medicine, and Ethics 25*(2–3), 98–110.

Szenberg, M. and L. Ramrattan (2014). *Secrets of Economics Editors*. Cambridge, MA: MIT Press.

Tankersley, J. (2020). How Washington learned to embrace the budget deficit. *The New York Times*.

Taylor, C. (1990). *Sources of the Self: The Making of the Modern Identity*. Harvard University Press.

Taylor, M. (2019). Theme overview: The future of farm management extension. *Choices 2*, 1–2.

Taylor, M. and W. Zhang (2019). Training the next generation of extension economists. *Choices 2*, 1–7.

Taylor, R. and A. Wiles (1995). Ring-theoretic properties of certain Hecke algebras. *Annals of Mathematics 141*(3), 553–72.

Tedersoo, L., R. Küngas, E. Oras, K. Köster, H. Eenmaa, Ali Leijen, M. Pedaste, M. Raju, A. Astapova, H. Lukner, K. Kogermann, and T. Sepp (2021). Data sharing practices and data availability upon request differ across scientific disciplines. *Scientific Data 8*(4), 192.

Tesfaye, W., G. Blalock, and N. Tirivayi (2021). Climate-smart innovations and rural poverty in Ethiopia: Exploring impacts and pathways. *American Journal of Agricultural Economics 103*(3), 878–99.

Texier, T. L. (2019). Debunking the Stanford prison experiment. *The American Psychologist 74*(7), 823–39.

Thompson, D. F. (1983). Ascribing responsibility to advisors in government. *Ethics 93*, 546–69.

Thompson, D. F. (2016). Professional disequilibrium: Conflict of interest in economics. In G. F. DeMartino and D. N. McCloskey (Eds.), *The Oxford Handbook of Professional Economic Ethics*, pp. 455–74. Oxford: Oxford University Press.

Thompson, G. D., S. V. Aradhyula, G. Frisvold, and R. Tronstad (2010). Does paying referees expedite reviews: Results of a natural experiment. *Southern Economic Journal 76*(3), 678–92.

Thompson, K. A. and S. G. Newmaster (2014). Molecular taxonomic tools provide more accurate estimates of species richness at less cost than traditional morphology-based taxonomic practices in a vegetation survey. *Biodiversity and Conservation 23*, 1411–24. RETRACTED.

Thompson, K. A. and S. G. Newmaster (2021). Retraction note to: Molecular taxonomic tools provide more accurate estimates of species richness at less cost than traditional morphology-based taxonomic practices in a vegetation survey. *Biodiversity and Conservation 30*, 4437–8.

Timm, T. R. (1949). An introduction to extension economics. *Journal of Farm Economics 31*(1), 682–6.

Tindana, P. O., N. Kass, and P. Akweongo (2006). The informed consent process in a rural African setting: A case study of the Kassena-Nakana District of Northern Ghana. *National Institute of Health: IRB 28*(3), 1–6.

Tolstoy, L. (1878). *Anna Karenina*. New York: Penguin Press. Trans. by Richard Pevear and Larissa Volokhonsky. Reprint (2004).

Trafimow, D., and M. Marks (2015). Editorial. *Basic and Applied Social Psychology 37*(1), 1–2.

Troller-Renfree, S., M. Costanzo, G. Duncan, K. Magnuson, L. Gennetian, H. Yoshikawa, S. Halpern-Meekin, N. Fox, and K. Noble (2022). The impact of a poverty reduction intervention on infant brain activity. *Proceedings of the National Academy of Sciences 119*(5), e2115649119.

Turner, E. H., A. Cipriani, T. A. Furukawa, G. Salanti, and Y. A. de Vries (2022). Selective publication of antidepressant trials and its influence on apparent efficacy: Updated comparisons and meta-analyses of newer versus older trials. *PLoS Medicine 19*(1), e1003886.

Turner, E. H., A. M. Matthews, E. Linardatos, R. A. Tell, and R. Rosenthal (2008). Selective publication of antidepressant trials and its influence on apparent efficacy. *New England Journal of Medicine 358*, 252–60.

Tuskegee (n.d.). *About the USPHS Syphilis Study*. Tuskegee University Bioethics Center – Centers of Excellence.

Tversky, A. and D. Kahneman (1981). The framing of decisions and the psychology of choice. *Science 211*(4481), 453–8.

UN (1949). *Universal Declaration of Human Rights*. www.un.org/en/about-us/universal-declaration-of-human-rights.

United States (1978). The Belmont Report: Ethical principles and guidelines for the protection of human subjects of research. *Technical Report*, The Commission, Bethesda.

U.S. Department of Justice (2018). University of Pittsburgh professor pays $132,000 and agrees to exclusion to resolve allegations of false claims for federal research grants. *The U.S. Attorney's Office*, Western District of Pennsylvania [Press Release]. www.comscore.com/press/release.asp?press=1928.

Uzzi, B., S. Mukherjee, M. Stringer, and B. Jones (2013). Atypical combinations and scientific impact. *Science 342*(6157), 468–72.

Van Den Hoonaard, W. C. and A. Hamilton (2016). *The Ethics Rupture: Exploring Alternatives to Formal Research Ethics Review*. Toronto: Toronto University Press.

Vermeulen, F. (2012). I am an academic fraud. *Forbes*.

Vilhuber, L. (2020)4647. Reproducibility potpourri. *Paper Presented at the 9th Berkeley Initiative for Transparency in the Social Sciences (BITSS) Annual Meeting*.

Vilhuber, L. (20224849). Improved computational reproducibility: The technological cutting edge. *Paper Presented at the 10th Berkeley Initiative for Transparency in the Social Sciences (BITSS) Annual Meeting*.

Vilhuber, L., H. H. Son, M. Welch, D. N. Wasser, and M. Darisse (2022). Teaching for largescale reproducibility verification. *Journal of Statistics and Data Science Education*, 1–9.

Vilhuber, L., D. Wasser, and J. Turitto (2020). *Code and Data for: Report for 2019 by the AEA Data Editor*. Nashville, TN: American Economic Association [publisher]. Ann Arbor, MI: Inter-university Consortium for Political and Social Research [distributor], 2020–08–04. doi.org/10.3886/E117884V1.

Vivalt, E. (2019). Specification searching and significance inflation across time, methods and disciplines. *Oxford Bulletin of Economics and Statistics 81*(4), 0305–9049.

Vivalt, E. (2020). How much can we generalize from impact evaluations? *Journal of the European Economic Association 18*(6), 3045–89.

Vogel, A. (2013). Great idea, thanks: intellectual property and theft. *The Conversation*. the-conversation.com/great-idea-thanks-intellectual-property-and-theft-12322.

Voltaire (1759). *Candide*. New York: Bantam Books. Trans. by Lowell Bair. Reprint (1981).

Wakefield, A., S. Murch, A. Anthony, J. Linnell, D. Casson, M. Malik, M. Berelowitz, A. Dhillon, M. Thomson, P. Harvey, A. Valentine, S. Davies, and J. Walker-Smith (1998). RETRACTED: Ileal-lymphoid-nodular hyperplasia, non-specific colitis, and pervasive developmental disorder in children. *The Lancet 351*(9103), 637–4150.

Wallace, J. (2019). How to be a good peer reviewer. *The Scholarly Kitchen: What's Hot and Cooking in Scholarly Publishing*. scholarlykitchen.sspnet. org/2019/09/17/how-to-be-a-good-peer-reviewer/.

Warren, G. F. and F. A. Pearson (1932). *Wholesale Prices for 213 Years: 1720–1932*. Ithaca: Cornell University Press.

Wasserstein, R. L. and N. A. Lazar (2016). The ASA statement on *p*-values: Context, process, and purpose. *The American Statistician 70*(2), 129–33.

Watson, J. D. and F. H. Crick (1953). Molecular structure of nucleic acids: A structure for deoxyribose nucleic acid. *Nature 171*, 737–8.

Weiss, C. H. (1979). The many meanings of research utilization. *Public Administration Review 39*(5), 426–31.

West, J. D. and C. T. Bergstrom (2021). Misinformation in and about science. *Proceedings of the National Academy of Sciences 118*(15), e1912444117.

White, R. F. (2007). Institutional Review Board mission creep: The Common Rule, social science, and the nanny state. *The Independent Review 11*(4), 547–64.

Whitt, C., J. E. Todd, and A. Keller (2022). Financial health indicators for family farms show a mixed picture during the 2020 coronavirus (covid-19) pandemic. *USDA ERS Amber Waves*. www.ers. usda.gov/amber-waves/2022/march/financial-health-indicators-for-family-farms-show-a-mixed-picture-during-the-2020-coronavirus-covid-19-pandemic/.

WHO (n.d.). *WHO List of National Ethics Committees*. World Health Organization.

Wible, J. R. (2016). Scientific misconduct and the responsible conduct of research in science and economics. *Review of Social Economy 74*(1), 7–32.

Wight, J. B. (20145152). Vertical and horizontal pluralism. *Economics and Ethics Blog*. https://www.economicsandethics.org/2014/07/vertical-and-horizontal-pluralism.html.

Wight, J. B. (2015). *Ethics in Economics: An Introduction to Moral Frameworks*. Stanford: Stanford University Press.

Wiles, A. (1995). Modular elliptic curves and Fermat's Last Theorem. *Annals of Mathematics 141*(3), 443–551.

Winckler, G., C. Pissarides, and R. Layard (2011). *Allegations of Publication Misconduct Against Brunos. Frey et al.: Report of the Ad-Hoc Comissions* (adopted on 21 October 2011). docs.google.com/file/d/1GeaNAFcKZAEPJp69FDc3Res6VwP5vtKyse3si

WMA (n.d.). *WMA Declariation of Helsinki – Ethical Principles for Medical Research Involving Human Subjects*. World Medical Association.

Wood, A., M. Altman, A. Bembenek, M. Bun, and M. Gaboardi (2018). Differential privacy: A primer for a non-technical audience. *Vanderbilt Journal of Entertainment & Technology Law 21*(1), 209–76.

Woolston, C. (2002). When a mentor becomes a thief. *The Chronicle of Higher Education*.

Wright, P. G. (1928). *The Tariff on Animal and Vegetable Oils*. New York: Macmillian Press.

Wu, A. (2020). Gender bias in rumors among professionals: An identity-based interpretation. *Review of Economics and Statistics 102*(5), 867–80.

Wuchty, S., B. F. Jones, and B. Uzzi (2007). The increasing dominance of teams in the production of knowledge. *Science 316*(5827), 1036–9.

Yeh, C., A. Perez, A. Driscoll, G. Azzari, Z. Tang, D. Lobell, S. Ermon, and M. Burke (2020). Using publicly available satellite imagery and deep learning to understand economic well-being in Africa. *Nature Communications 11*, 2583.

Young, D. (1994). Ramanujan's illness. *Notes and Records of the Royal Society of London 48*(1), 107–19.

Zaveri, S. (2020). Making evaluation matter: Capturing multiple realities and voices for sustainable development. *World Development 127*, 104827.

Zeller, T. (2006). AOL executive quits after posting of search data. *The New York Times*.

Zeng, W. and F. Dong (2022). 2020 U.S. agricultural trade multiplier for soybeans. *USDA ERS Amber Waves*. www.ers.usda.gov/amber-waves/2022/february/2020-us-agricultural-trade-multiplier-for-soybeans/.

Ziliak, S. T. and D. N. McCloskey (2004). Size matters: The standard error of regressions in the American Economic Review. *Journal of Socio Economics 33*, 527–46.

Ziliak, S. T. and D. N. McCloskey (2008). *The Cult of Statistical Significance: How the Standard Error Cost Us Jobs, Justice, and Lives*. Ann Arbor: University of Michigan Press.

Zimbardo, P. (2004). *Stanford Prison Experiment: Design and Analysis Papers of Philip Zimbardo*. Akron: Cummings Center for the History of Psychology: University of Akron.

Zingales, L. (2013). Preventing economist capture. In D. Carpenter and D. Moss (Eds.), *Preventing Regulatory Capture: Special Interest Influence and How to Limit It*, pp. 124–51. Cambridge: Cambridge University Press.

Zinsser, W. (2006). *On Writing Well*. New York: Harper Perennial.

AUTHOR INDEX

Page numbers for entries occurring in figures are followed by an f; those for entries in notes, by an n; those for entries in tables, by a t; and those for entries in glossary, by a g.

SUBJECT INDEX

Page numbers for entries occurring in figures are followed by an f; those for entries in notes, by an n; those for entries in tables, by a t; and those for entries in glossary, by a g.

Printed in the United States
by Baker & Taylor Publisher Services